QUAKERISM IN THE ATLANTIC WORLD,
1690–1830

THE NEW HISTORY OF QUAKERISM

The first historical series in Quaker studies in over a century, these volumes offer a fresh, comprehensive, up-to-date treatment of the history of Quakerism from its seventeenth-century origins to the twenty-first century. Using critical methodologies, this limited series emphasizes key events and movements, examines all branches of Quakerism, and explores its global reach.

Quakerism in the Atlantic World, 1690–1830

Edited by Robynne Rogers Healey

The Pennsylvania State University Press
University Park, Pennsylvania

Library of Congress Cataloging-in-Publication Data

Names: Healey, Robynne Rogers, 1964– editor.
Title: Quakerism in the Atlantic world, 1690–1830 / edited by Robynne Rogers Healey.
Other titles: New history of Quakerism.
Description: University Park, Pennsylvania : The Pennsylvania State University Press, [2021] | Series: The new history of Quakerism | Includes bibliographical references and index.
Summary: "A collection of essays examining transatlantic Quakerism in the eighteenth century, a period during which Quakers became increasingly sectarian even as they expanded their engagement with worldly affairs"—Provided by publisher.
Identifiers: LCCN 2021001994 | ISBN 9780271089409 (cloth)
Subjects: LCSH: Society of Friends—North America—History—18th century. | Society of Friends—North America—History—19th century. | Quakers—North America—History—18th century. | Quakers—North America—History—19th century. | Society of Friends—Great Britain—History—18th century. | Society of Friends—Great Britain—History—19th century. | Quakers—Great Britain—History—18th century. | Quakers—Great Britain—History—19th century.
Classification: LCC BX7633 .Q35 2021 | DDC 289.6/709033—dc23
LC record available at https://lccn.loc.gov/2021001994

Copyright © 2021 The Pennsylvania State University
All rights reserved
Printed in the United States of America
Published by The Pennsylvania State University Press,
University Park, PA 16802–1003

The Pennsylvania State University Press is a member of the Association of University Presses.

It is the policy of The Pennsylvania State University Press to use acid-free paper. Publications on uncoated stock satisfy the minimum requirements of American National Standard for Information Sciences—Permanence of Paper for Printed Library Material, ANSI Z39.48–1992.

CONTENTS

Acknowledgments   vii
List of Abbreviations   ix

Introduction   1
ROBYNNE ROGERS HEALEY

PART I: UNIQUE QUAKER TESTIMONIES AND PRACTICES

1   "Our Dear Friend Has Departed This Life": Memorial Testimony Writing in the Long Eighteenth Century   23
ERICA CANELA AND ROBYNNE ROGERS HEALEY

2   "Within the Bounds of Their Circumstances": The Testimony of Inequality Among Eighteenth-Century New England Friends   44
ELIZABETH CAZDEN

3   Friendly Advice: The Making and Shaping of Quaker Discipline   65
ANDREW FINCHAM

4   Three Methods of Worship in Eighteenth-Century Quakerism   89
JON MITCHELL

PART 2: TENSIONS BETWEEN QUAKERISM IN COMMUNITY AND QUAKERISM IN THE WORLD

5 "Mrs. Weaver Being a Quaker, Would Not Swear": Representations of Quakers and Crime in the Metropolis, ca. 1696–1815   113
ERIN BELL

6 Quakers and Marriage Legislation in England in the Long Eighteenth Century   133
ROSALIND JOHNSON

7 Family, Unity, and Identity Formation: Eighteenth-Century Quaker Community Building   152
EMMA LAPSANSKY-WERNER

PART 3: EXPRESSIONS OF QUAKERISM AROUND THE ATLANTIC WORLD

8 Quakers, Indigenous Americans, and the Landscape of Peace   179
GEOFFREY PLANK

9 A Complex Faith: Strategies of Marriage, Family, and Community Among Upper Canadian Quakers, 1784–1830   200
SYDNEY HARKER AND ROBYNNE ROGERS HEALEY

10 Industrial Development and Community Responsibility: The Harford Family and South Wales, ca. 1768–1842   224
RICHARD C. ALLEN

Conclusion   251
ROBYNNE ROGERS HEALEY

Selected Bibliography   261
List of Contributors   266
Index   271

ACKNOWLEDGMENTS

Any work of scholarship represents a great deal of work; an edited collection like this one represents a great deal of work by many people. Thanks, therefore, are due to those who made this book possible. My first thanks must go to the contributors. They patiently and diligently participated in a long process of writing, reviewing, and revising material. We learned a lot from one another in the process. The work of historians is impossible without the work of archivists. We are all grateful to the staff at many Quaker libraries: the Library of the Society of Friends at Friends House, London; Woodbrooke Quaker Study Centre, Birmingham; the Friends Historical Library at Swarthmore College, Swarthmore, Pennsylvania; Haverford College Libraries Quaker and Special Collections, Haverford, Pennsylvania; and the Canadian Yearly Meeting Archives at Pickering College, Newmarket, Ontario. Thanks also to archivists at the many other repositories that hold Quaker records around the Atlantic world. The Conference of Quaker Historians and Archivists, the Quaker Studies Research Association, the Friends Historical Society, and the Friends Historical Association have provided support in multiple ways. These organizations create space for the discussion of Quaker history; that space allows scholars at any stage of their career to question received interpretations and offer potential revisions to our understanding of the Quaker past. Many of the ideas presented in the pages that follow have benefited from presentation at annual or biennial conferences hosted by these organizations. The Friends Historical Society provided funding through the Hodgett Grants to support presentation of the complete volume at the 2019 Friends Historical Society AGM and Day Conference in Lancaster, UK.

I am grateful to Andrew Dick, who created one comprehensive bibliography from ten disparate ones. Carolee Pollock provided thoughtful and thorough feedback on each chapter, catching errors I had missed. The reviewers graciously helped sharpen arguments considerably. I am particularly thankful to Kathryn Yahner, acquisitions editor at Penn State Press. She answered questions quickly, provided helpful insights throughout the production process, and was exceptionally patient as deadlines were pushed back many times.

—ROBYNNE ROGERS HEALEY

ABBREVIATIONS

BoC	Book of Cases
BYM	Baltimore Yearly Meeting
CYMA	Canadian Yearly Meeting Archives, Pickering College, Newmarket, Ontario
FHLSC	Friends Historical Library, Swarthmore College, Swarthmore, Pennsylvania
GWA	Gwent Archives, Ebbw Vale, Wales
HCLQSC	Haverford College Libraries Quaker and Special Collections, Haverford, Pennsylvania
LSF	Library of the Society of Friends
LYM	London Yearly Meeting
MfS	Meeting for Sufferings
NA	National Archives of Wales
NEYM	New England Yearly Meeting
NEYMA	New England Yearly Meeting Archives, Special Collections, W. E. B. DuBois Library, University of Massachusetts, Amherst, Massachusetts
NLW	National Library of Wales
NYYM	New York Yearly Meeting
PYM	Philadelphia Yearly Meeting
YSMM	Yonge Street Monthly Meeting

Introduction

ROBYNNE ROGERS HEALEY

This is the third volume in Penn State University Press's New History of Quakerism series, a series that seeks to provide up-to-date analysis of Quaker history in volumes accessible to a broad readership. This book addresses the long eighteenth century, a period that has remained largely unexplored as a whole, despite the growth of Quaker history as a field in the past twenty-five years. Interpretations of this period have undergone some revision in recent years as scholars have questioned earlier representations of what has been termed "quietist Quakerism." Was this period marked only by increased sectarianism, declining religious enthusiasm, and stagnation, even regression?[1] Undoubtedly, this was an era of paradox. During the long eighteenth century, Quakers articulated many of the characteristics associated with Quakerism today. Worship became more silent and Quakers used distinct dress and speech to identify and separate themselves from mainstream society. During this period, they established increasingly rigid organizational structures and behaviors, codified in the queries, advices, and discipline. This is the period associated with Quaker withdrawal into sectarianism. At the same time, the dynamic political, social, and economic context of this long century resulted in notably expanded Quaker engagement in politics, trade, industry, and science. The chapters presented here address and interrogate some of these points of view and complicate a number of traditional interpretations of this period in Quaker history.

Readers familiar with Richard C. Allen and Rosemary Moore's *The Quakers, 1656–1723* will note that the present book does not begin where that book ended. Rather, it overlaps with Allen and Moore's volume. Periodization is not an exact science. Allen and Moore extended their work to 1723 to account for what they call the "long coda," or intermediate period, after 1690, which ended with the death of George Whitehead in 1723 and the British Parliament's passage of the Affirmation Act in 1722.[2] Instead of commencing after the long coda, the present book includes it, weaving itself into the end of Allen and Moore's volume but also standing alone as a collection of essays focused on the eighteenth century.

A number of events mark the 1690s as a time of transition and the beginning of a new period of Quaker history. The Act of Toleration (1689) signaled the beginning of conciliation between the state and Quakers after decades of persecution under the Restoration monarchy. The death of George Fox in 1691, shortly after that of Robert Barclay in 1690, removed Quakerism's most recognized leader and its most influential theologian. The transatlantic Keithian controversy of the 1690s damaged relationships within the Religious Society of Friends. Moreover, in the context of post-toleration British society, Keith's polemical publications threatened to destabilize the Society's delicate legal position and renew persecution. While the 1696 Affirmation Act provided some relief to Friends who refused to use oaths, its wording remained the source of considerable concern until Friends accepted the 1722 Affirmation Act. Finally, the remnants of the first, apocalyptic generation of Friends died in this decade. Besides Barclay and Fox, Stephen Crisp (1692), Mary Fisher (1698), and Margaret Fell (1702) died, leaving the pious and dull—but powerful—George Whitehead to lead Friends in the post-toleration period.

When did the long eighteenth century end? Was it in the 1790s, when the Irish Friend Abraham Shackleton and the American Friend Hannah Barnard began to challenge scripture, behavior for which both were disowned, in 1801 and 1802, respectively? Did the 1807 passage of the Abolition of the Slave Trade Act mark the conclusion of the quietist age? Certainly, the Hicksite-Orthodox Schism of 1827–28, which divided a number of North American meetings, marks a watershed religious moment in Quaker history. Even so, in those yearly meetings that did separate, the schism in

1827 or 1828 did not end theological conflict. Quarrels over doctrine became disputes over property in monthly meetings, as individuals and families aligned themselves with various positions. Who retained the meetinghouse and burial ground? If doctrine was the primary issue for the devout, how did the adherent decide whom to support? The division of Quaker communities lingered and unfolded long after the formal separation of the yearly meetings. What of the economic periodization for Quakers so deeply involved in industry and commerce at the heart of the Industrial Revolution? Period breaks in these cases are indistinct and dependent on location. As Richard C. Allen's chapter in this volume demonstrates, when considering industrialization, the long eighteenth century extended into the 1840s. While the end of the long eighteenth century is imprecise, this work adopts a generous periodization of 1690–1830, noting multiple factors beyond doctrine that closed this paradoxical period of Quaker history.

The growth of Quaker history within the past twenty-five years has produced much innovative scholarship. In examining a number of aspects unique to Quaker history during this period, researchers have complicated our understanding of Quakers and Quakerism in the eighteenth century. Consider the impact of women's or gender history. Women have played significant roles at every point in Quaker history. They have also produced a substantial number of written sources. This drew the attention of women's and gender studies scholars from the discipline's earliest years. They have produced notable multidisciplinary texts.[3] These works tend to focus on individual Friends or a small segment of the period covered in the chapters that follow. Very recently, two books have added considerably to the literature on eighteenth-century Quaker women. Michele Lise Tarter and Catie Gill's *New Critical Studies on Early Quaker Women, 1650–1800* gathered scholars in the fields of religion, history, and literature "to assess the dynamic impact of [Quaker] women within their society and throughout the transatlantic world."[4] It is an impressive volume. The authors carefully interrogate the principle of spiritual equality and complicate conclusions about the ways in which Quaker women worked within the privilege of Quaker membership, the ways in which they were excluded or silenced, and the ways in which they might have excluded or silenced others. Naomi Pullin's *Female Friends and the Making of Transatlantic Quakerism, 1650–1750* challenges conventional feminist scholarship by contending that "the process of institutionalisation enhanced rather than diminished women's roles within transatlantic Quakerism."[5] In this anthology we have not separated women into a separate essay or series of essays; rather, authors have integrated women and gendered analysis—beyond a focus solely on women—where appropriate.

The role of Quakers in the abolition of the transatlantic slave trade and their place in eighteenth-century industry and commerce have been two other areas of significant publishing. Building on Jean Soderlund's and Gary Nash's work on Quakers and abolition (1985 and 1988), the last few years have produced rich scholarship exploring the role of Quakers in antislavery and abolition movements around the Atlantic world. This work addresses the complex nature of the Quaker relationship with slavery and slaveholding and the long road to adopting an abolitionist position.[6] James Walvin examined the role of Quakers in eighteenth-century business and industry in his 1997 work *The Quakers: Money and Morals*. A number of scholars have advanced this theme, situating their work strongly in the field of Atlantic history. The results offer comprehensive interpretations of Quaker mercantile success in the eighteenth-century consumer revolution and its connections to Quaker history.[7] Most recently, Stephen Angell and Pink Dandelion's edited collection *Quakers, Business, and Industry* proposes a number of new interpretations about the reasons for Quaker success in these areas. Given the strength of these book-length studies, neither abolition nor commerce is addressed on its own in this volume. As with women, both topics are integrated into chapters as appropriate.

A number of regional studies of the history of Quaker communities and meetings in the Atlantic world have advanced unique perspectives on Quakerism outside London and Philadelphia, broadening our understanding of the Quaker Atlantic world beyond Quaker metropoles.[8] Transatlantic Quakerism has also become the focus of a number of books that investigate the similarities in Quakerism around the Atlantic basin.[9] All of these works enrich our understanding of Atlantic Quakerism, but none has considered the period as a whole. This volume aims to situate Quakers in the eighteenth-century British Atlantic world, both those on the margins and those at the center of that geographic and conceptual space; this allows for comparative views that include peripheral Quaker histories alongside those of London and Philadelphia Friends. Readers will see all three concepts of Atlantic history—transatlantic, "circumatlantic," and cisatlantic—represented here. David Armitage and Michael Braddick have defined these approaches. Transatlantic history is "the history of the Atlantic world told through comparisons."'"Circumatlantic" history considers "the history of the people who crossed the Atlantic, who lived on its shores and who participated in the communities it made possible." Cisatlantic history "studies particular places as unique locations within an Atlantic world and seeks to define that uniqueness as the result of the interaction between local particularity and a wider web of connections."[10]

The essays collected here are presented thematically rather than chronologically. The book is divided into three parts: "Unique Quaker Testimonies and Practices," "Tensions Between Quakerism in Community and Quakerism in the World," and "Expressions of Quakerism Around the Atlantic World." These themes address, interrogate, and deconstruct the paradox of long eighteenth-century Quakerism (the withdrawal into sectarianism, with more rigid adherence to Quaker discipline coupled with increased engagement with the world through social reform). At the same time, these themes expand geographic understandings of the Quaker Atlantic world to determine how local events shaped expressions of Quakerism. Authors often challenge traditional or oversimplified interpretations of Quaker practices outlined in the book of discipline (in American meetings) and book of extracts (in British meetings). They present the Quaker world as a complex one in which prescription and practice were more often negotiated than dictated, even after the mid-eighteenth-century "reformation" and tightening of the discipline on both sides of the Atlantic.

With the exception of Elizabeth Cazden's chapter, analysis of the eighteenth-century positions for which Quakers remain best known today—equality, abolition, and pacifism—is not isolated in individual chapters. This allows readers to see the complex ways in which Quaker testimonies emerged and evolved during the long eighteenth century. Given the time and space covered, this collection of essays is not without gaps. Examination of the role of Quakers in colonization and interaction with the Indigenous peoples of North America is just beginning. Geoffrey Plank's chapter helps move this conversation forward. Similarly, all the chapters focus on topics frequently unaddressed in the current literature. Given the thematic approach, many chapters cover the entire period; others focus on a portion of the century germane to the topic under consideration. We hope that these fresh perspectives will encourage readers to reevaluate what has often been viewed as the dull Quaker century. The following overview of the period establishes context for the essays that follow.

CONTEXTUAL OVERVIEW OF THE LONG EIGHTEENTH CENTURY

Space limitations prohibit an introduction to Quakers and Quakerism from its origins in mid-seventeenth-century England. Readers unfamiliar with Quakerism should consult the first two volumes in this series.[11] To situate eighteenth-century Quakerism, however, it is helpful to understand its seventeenth-century precedents. Quakerism emerged in the late 1640s during a turbulent period in English history. Against the backdrop of civil wars and the lifting of restrictions on speech, printing, and modes of worship, a number of political and religious factions appeared alongside the "separated" churches of Independents and Baptists. In 1647, George Fox, son of a Leicestershire weaver, had a transformative experience of the divine. He recalled this experience as a voice saying, "There is one, even Christ Jesus, that can speak to thy condition."[12] The experience changed his life and led to the founding of the Quaker movement. While Fox is often identified as the "founder" of Quakerism, most scholars consider him "the leading personality," one of a number of early Friends with strong messages.[13]

Divine revelation (the Inward Light) and the belief that freedom from sin (perfection) was possible were central to early Quaker theology. Together, revelation and perfection culminated in the "Lamb's War"—the defeat of evil in oneself and the battle against evil in the world. The Quaker message spread quickly through northern England in the 1650s. From there, Quakers traveled across England, Wales, Scotland, and Ireland, usually in pairs. These "First Publishers of Truth" also went to Europe and the Atlantic colonies. In their Lamb's War, Quakers were militant; this alarmed authorities and resulted in arrests and imprisonments throughout the Interregnum. Quakers shocked authorities, and even themselves, with spectacles such as James Nayler's 1656 procession into Bristol, re-creating Christ's entry into Jerusalem. Authorities responded with harsher persecution; Friends responded with stronger organization and behavioral regulations.

The religious toleration alluded to in the Declaration of Breda that accompanied the restoration of King Charles II to the throne in 1660 did not materialize. Anglican clergy retaliated against the sects, especially Quakers. With conservative Anglicans firmly entrenched in the Cavalier Parliament, what followed was a legislative program of religious intolerance and brutal suppression of sects. The Clarendon Code (1661–65) and the Quaker Act (1662) were punitive laws used to persecute dissenters between 1660 and 1689. Persecution occurred in many forms; Quakers recorded this persecution in the *Great Book of Sufferings*. During the Restoration, suffering became a central aspect of Quaker identity.[14] At the same time, Quakers learned the law and became proficient in using it to contest persecution. They actively lobbied Parliament and the courts for religious liberty.[15]

Between 1666 and 1668, Fox altered the meeting structure. In what he called "Gospel Order," different levels of meetings were placed into an ordered structure of governance. The smallest units of local congregations were known as particular meetings, or preparative meetings in North America. A number of these meetings reported to a monthly meeting. Monthly meetings played the most significant role in Friends' lives, as they had the authority to admit and discipline members and to approve marriages. Monthly meetings were organized regionally into quarterly meetings, and quarterly meetings into yearly meetings. In the 1670s, administrative meetings were added: the Second Day [Monday] Morning Meeting (1673) oversaw publishing and managed the itinerant ministry, and the Meeting for Sufferings (1676) recorded sufferings, lobbied government, and handled finances. Quakers outside the center occasionally challenged London's efforts to impose uniformity of practice, and there were minor separations. Even so, the Quaker world expanded despite efforts to suppress it. In the years leading up to the Act of Toleration (1689), Quakers established a successful transatlantic network of meetings in the British Atlantic colonies.

A number of factors around 1690 altered the political and religious climate for Quakers in the British Atlantic world. Under the 1689 Toleration Act, nonconformists such as Friends gained limited rights. They were permitted to worship without fear of arrest or persecution in registered places of worship. But they still could neither attend universities nor hold political office. Moreover, the Church of England remained the established church and the Crown demanded that Friends who were British subjects pay tithes for its support.

In this new reality, eighteenth-century Quakers fixed their sights on survival as a separated, peculiar people. This was not an altogether new development. Robert Barclay's introspective theology, outlined in his *Apology* (1678), had been formed in the context of persecution and debate.[16] What emerged was a "meantime," not an end-time theology.[17] Quaker interactions in their local communities and their well-developed lobbying efforts had moved Quakers toward a measure of accommodation with mainstream society.[18] Still, non-Quakers questioned the orthodoxy of Quakers' theology and their inclusion in toleration. It was in the midst of this uncertain period that a number of prominent Friends died. Fox's death in 1691 was a particular loss; his charismatic leadership was almost impossible to replace. Barclay's death in 1690 and Stephen Crisp's in 1692 also removed valuable leaders. At the same time, William Penn, Pennsylvania's founder, was embattled. His close relationship with James II meant that the Crown considered him a traitor. He lost his colony between 1691 and 1693 and lived in perilous uncertainty for a number of years.[19]

In these uncertain times, Quakers faced a threatening internal disagreement, the Keithian controversy, a theological dispute that became colored by politics.[20] At its center was George Keith, initially viewed as one of the Society's "best systematic theologians," now remembered as "the great apostate."[21] Originally from the Aberdeen Meeting, Keith had ministered alongside Robert Barclay, George Fox, William Penn, and George Whitehead before emigrating to East Jersey in 1684 as surveyor-general. When he relocated to Philadelphia in 1689, Keith encountered Quakers he considered to be both biblically illiterate and unorthodox in their commitment to the incarnation and the physical Christ. Post-toleration Friends did not feel that this piece of doctrine required a unified position. Keith disagreed. In "Gospel Order Improved," he called for a number of reforms, including the necessity of a written creed.[22] This raised the ire of noncreedal Friends who opposed any attempt to limit the power of the Light to a set of statements.

What followed was deeply acrimonious. Keith pointed to Quakers' rejection of his proposed reforms as evidence of their heretical beliefs. Keith's "high opinion of himself" and his "acerbic manner" made matters worse.[23] The Philadelphia Yearly Meeting (PYM) disowned him in 1692, "not for doctrinal matters but for his divisiveness."[24] The conflict was neither easily nor quickly resolved. It soon became public, and potentially embarrassing, when Keith published his version of events.[25] Philadelphia Friends attempted to silence him through a failed defamation trial.

In 1694, both parties traveled to London to seek satisfaction. Reprints of Keith's polemical works had already arrived in London in 1693, setting the stage for the arrival of colonial Friends the following year. The extent and significance of transatlantic networks is evident in the way this conflict reverberated throughout the Quaker Atlantic. Within the delicate political context of toleration, the dispute became grounds for a schism. The London Yearly Meeting (LYM) disowned Keith in 1695, again for his manner, not his beliefs, although the differences were theological.[26] For years afterward, Keith and other former Quakers like Francis Bugg continued to denounce Quaker "heresies" in writing or in public meetings. Friends found themselves in the difficult position of defending the Christian orthodoxy of their faith and their inclusion in the Toleration Act. One survival strategy was an increased reliance on meeting organization and discipline. Quakers' focus on order, expressed in plain dress and speech patterns or endogamy, was a reminder to others and themselves that they were a peculiar people. Another survival strategy was migration and settlement in areas where Friends believed they could live out their testimonies freely.

The Quaker Atlantic world expanded significantly in the eighteenth century. Although individual communities could be located at quite some distance from one another, they were connected to the transatlantic Quaker network though epistolary correspondence, Quaker publications, and the traveling ministry. As Quakerism became a transatlantic faith, it was changed. Despite the LYM's best efforts to control the periphery from the center, transatlantic Quakerism was increasingly shaped by a variety of local expressions. New yearly meetings were created in response to the spread of Friends across North America. The New England, Baltimore, Virginia, and Philadelphia Yearly Meetings all existed before 1690; the New York Yearly Meeting (NYYM) was created in 1695 and the North Carolina Yearly Meeting in 1698. As maps I.1 and I.2 show, transatlantic migration negatively affected some British meetings. Wales Yearly Meeting was a case in point. So many Quakers left Wales for the British North American colonies that in 1797 the yearly meeting was reduced to a half-yearly meeting, under the LYM. The maps also show the impact of westward migration in North America after the American Revolution, with Ohio and Indiana Yearly Meetings being added in 1813 and 1821, respectively. Map I.2 identifies the North American yearly meetings that divided in the Hicksite-Orthodox Schism of 1827–28. The Genesee Yearly Meeting was set off from the Hicksite branch of the NYYM in 1834. Although its location is shown in the state of New York, it was a transnational meeting and met alternately in New York and the Canadian province of Ontario. Because the maps show only yearly meetings, they do not show the Quaker population shifts in the Caribbean. At the beginning of the long eighteenth century, the islands of Jamaica and Barbados hosted sizeable Quaker populations; there were almost no Friends on either island by the middle of the century. Nor do the maps show the Quaker communities in the Netherlands. Throughout

INTRODUCTION

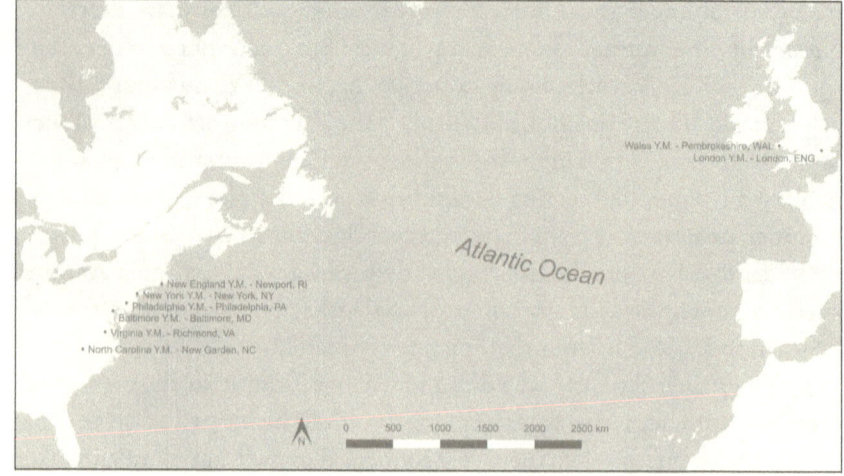

MAP I.1   Yearly Meetings of the Religious Society of Friends, 1690s. Map by John Grotenhuis.

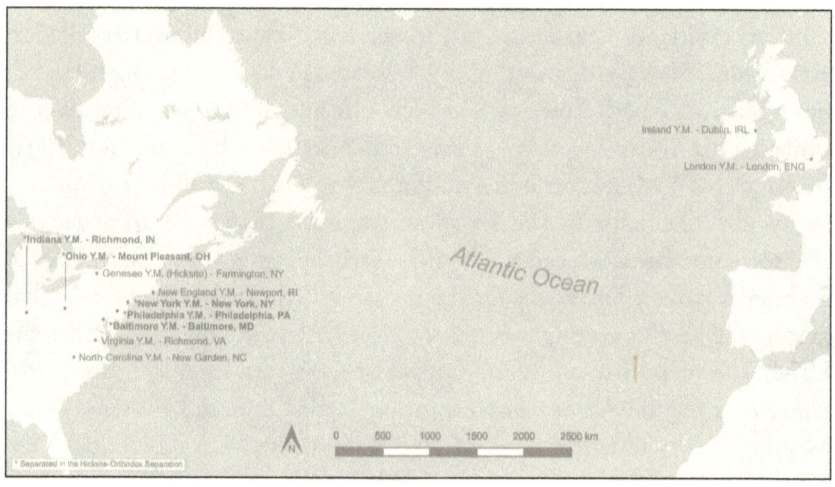

MAP I.2   Yearly Meetings of the Religious Society of Friends, 1830s. Map by John Grotenhuis.

the eighteenth century, many Dutch Friends emigrated to North America (largely Pennsylvania); by the end of the century, only a handful remained in the Netherlands. Quakers established communities in Norway in 1814, when Norwegian prisoners of war who had become convinced Friends while in English captivity returned to their country. Quakers were among the Norwegians who sought religious freedom in the United States in the

1820s. This reduced the number of Quakers in Norway but did not eliminate their presence there.

Partly out of a protectionist posture, Quakerism became more organized, bureaucratic, hierarchical, and sectarian over the course of the eighteenth century. Consider membership. Before significant transatlantic migration began in the late seventeenth century, local meetings recognized who belonged and who did not. Colonial meetings, swelling with newly arrived immigrants, could not be certain. After 1700 they requested that the LYM and its constituent meetings issue certificates to emigrating Friends, confirming that migrants were members in good standing, that they were free to marry or not, and that their financial status was sound.[27] Poor relief, a benefit of membership, was another concern in the migratory Atlantic world. The need to reliably identify members and determine the meeting responsible for poor relief or relocation costs compelled stricter classification. The LYM first defined membership, including birthright membership, in a 1737 minute on "removals and settlements." It dictated that children and wives of members were to be counted as members. While Quakers had conventionally identified children of members as members, they had not yet codified this practice. The change expanded the ranks of nominal Friends who were Quaker by birth, not by choice, and this affected spiritual vigor.[28]

The focus on uniformity of practice is apparent in the codification and collection of what Quakers called advices, queries, and rules of discipline. The New England Yearly Meeting replaced the advices of Fox and other visitors with a formal discipline in 1708. The Philadelphia Yearly Meeting approved its first discipline in 1704, then lengthened and more carefully arranged it in 1719. The London Yearly Meeting issued copies of Christian and brotherly advices, called *The Book of Extracts*, in 1738. *The Book of Extracts* became the first officially printed discipline in 1783; the American yearly meetings printed their disciplines shortly thereafter.[29] There was some consistency of testimonies across the Atlantic. Still, local contexts affected expressions of Quakerism, as is demonstrated in Andrew Fincham's comparison of the LYM and PYM disciplines in this volume.

Despite their commitment to separating themselves from the world, eighteenth-century Quakers were active in worldly affairs. They expanded their mercantile interests, and some accumulated great fortunes. Expansive Quaker networks and business practices such as restricting debt created an environment in which Quaker industry flourished.[30] The Navigation Acts favored Atlantic trade, and an expanding empire multiplied mercantile opportunities. But Quakers, shut out of universities, professions, and the civil service, were innovative and entrepreneurial. They participated actively in every area of imperial commerce, including the trade in African slaves and goods produced by slaves.[31]

Interaction with the market and commercial success challenged quietist ideals of a separated life, creating anxiety and internal conflict for many Quakers. They addressed this conflict in multiple ways. Some left their faith. Others remained in the faith but did not follow the discipline. By the end of the century, Quakers themselves distinguished between plain Friends (those who observed regulations) and gay Friends (those who did not). Some extremely devout Quakers, like John Woolman, walked away from business entirely.[32] More often, Friends developed ways of moving between separate spiritual and temporal domains. For instance, plainness acted as a protective barrier; it permitted Friends to operate in the commercial world while maintaining their distance from it. Philanthropy and benevolence helped Quakers navigate this tension. Profit was permissible as long as Friends gained it honestly and cared for those in distress.[33]

Quakers clarified their testimonies on slavery and war in this period, often reacting to political, social, and economic circumstances in the Atlantic world. Their position on slavery and abolition was complex. Despite popular portrayals of Quakers as proponents of racial equality and abolition from the start, this was not the case. Eighteenth-century Quaker commercial accomplishments depended in no small part on the products of slave labor and the trade in slaves. Pressure from the periphery on the center instigated action. Colonial attempts to limit the trade compelled the LYM to articulate the Society's position on slavery, although the yearly meeting originally refused to use its powerful parliamentary lobby to support the Pennsylvania anti-import campaign.[34] Moreover, while the LYM advised the PYM in 1727 that the traffic in slaves was inconsistent with Friends' principles, it did not circulate this advice to British meetings until 1750, when it was finally included in *The Book of Extracts*. An official shift occurred at midcentury. This coincided with the Seven Years' War and the Quaker reformation, when enforcement of the discipline became a priority.[35] In 1754 the PYM published John Woolman's pamphlet *Some Considerations on the Keeping of Negroes*, and in 1758 the LYM printed an epistle condemning the trade and any involvement in it. It was not until later in the century, however, that Quakers focused on abolishing the trade instead of distancing themselves from it. Yet antislavery sentiments increased on both sides of the

Atlantic owing to the distribution of abolitionists' messages and the formation of antislavery societies. In 1787 the LYM's antislavery committee joined forces with non-Quaker abolitionists like William Wilberforce and Thomas Clarkson. Their persistent, highly organized campaign of petitions, boycotts, and lobbying eventually resulted in the 1807 Act for the Abolition of the Slave Trade.

The peace testimony was also complicated.[36] Early Quakers had participated in the mid-seventeenth-century civil wars that affected the British Isles and colonies and, despite Friends' declaration of peaceable principles to Charles II in 1660, behavior did not always reflect stated beliefs. Friends' mercantile interests in the British Atlantic compelled a clear position. Armed conflict was commonplace in the long eighteenth century; more than half of the period was punctuated by wars of empire or revolution. Could Quakers arm ships defensively or protect their homes? It was not until 1744 that Friends clearly equated war with "injustice, barbarity, and bloodshed" and determined that those associated with it were to be disowned.[37] Quakers in the Pennsylvania Provincial Assembly were divided in the war crisis of 1755 between those who supported a defensive war tax and those who did not. Influenced by the Quaker reformation, most Quakers withdrew from the Assembly in 1756.[38] In the American Revolution, the American yearly meetings adopted a position of strict neutrality. The impact of this position and the extent to which Friends complied depended on a number of factors. Despite their strong connections to Britain, most American Quakers reconciled with their new government. A few true Loyalists returned to England; some became refugees, or later settlers, in what remained of Britain's North American colonies. By the end of the century, aversion to war, war-related activities, or even discussion of war was complete, and pacifism became a defining feature of Quakerism.[39]

Throughout much of the eighteenth century, the bounds of Quaker orthodoxy were generous even if the limits of behavior and practice were not. Three theological tendencies—quietism, rationalism, and evangelicalism—functioned side by side among Quakers throughout the eighteenth century.[40] Through much of this period, Quaker culture throughout the Atlantic world demonstrated a capacity to hold diversity in tension. Behavior (or orthopraxy) was increasingly controlled, but theology (or orthodoxy) remained flexible. This world began to fracture late in the century. Theological conflict first emerged in the late 1790s when Irish Friend Abraham Shackleton and American Friend Hannah Barnard questioned the accuracy of an Old Testament passage in which God commanded the ancient Israelites to exterminate their enemies. William Savery, a visiting PYM minister, was horrified at Shackleton's views. Savery branded Shackleton a deist and urged the Irish Yearly Meeting (IYM) to disown him.[41] When Shackleton and some others who shared his views refused to renounce their position, the IYM disowned them. During this time, Barnard, a minister and member of the Hudson Monthly Meeting in the NYYM, was traveling through Europe, including Ireland. When visiting the LYM, Barnard came into conflict with Friends who challenged her questioning of scripture.[42] The LYM refused to endorse any further travel in ministry and Barnard returned to the United States, where, in 1802, her monthly meeting disowned her for challenging the accuracy of scripture.

Evangelical doctrines such as the divinity of Christ, the infallibility of the Bible, and the necessity of accepting Christ's atoning sacrifice began to occupy greater, more formal space in Quakerism, as they had in British and American society generally in the late eighteenth century. They gained formal expression in the LYM's 1805 publication of Henry Tuke's *Principles of Religion, as Professed by the Society of Christians Usually Called Quakers*. Not every Quaker agreed with Tuke's thinking. A significant group of Friends in North America expressed grave concerns that this form of Quakerism was unlike that of the faith's founders.[43] At the center of the theological disputes in the American meetings was Elias Hicks, a Long Island minister. "An extreme Quietist who feared acting without the guidance of the Holy Spirit," Hicks sought "to be empty, to know nothing, to call for nothing, and to desire to do nothing." He believed that Quakers' ties with non-Quakers through social reform activities were corrupting Friends. Beyond the desire to remain a separate and peculiar people, Hicks and his supporters disapproved of increasing the evangelical influence on American society, with its "ordained man-made ministry."[44] In an 1819 address on slavery to the PYM, he criticized the "worldly spirit" that had crept into Quakerism and stressed the importance of behavior over belief. He then urged young Friends to follow their consciences, even if this required disobeying their elders. In a move designed to insult Hicks, offended and powerful male leaders (who supported what would become known as Orthodox Quakerism) adjourned while Hicks was addressing the women's meeting. Hicks chose to overlook the slight by ignoring the authority of the leadership.[45]

Hicks's attempts at reformation among Friends pressed both sides to crystalize their beliefs. Those who criticized the "Hicksites" became known as Orthodox Friends. Their theology was very similar to that of non-Quaker evangelicals in the Atlantic world. There was never a unified Hicksite party, nor did those labeled Hicksite spread the ideas of Elias Hicks. Rather, Hicks's name was applied to a disparate group that disagreed with and responded to the rise of evangelicalism within Quakerism. Hicksites were unified in their commitment to the ongoing revelation of the Inward Light instead of specific doctrine determined by an external source. Both sides claimed that their positions were closest to original Quakerism. The disagreements dividing Quakers were predominantly theological ones, complicated and colored by geography, economics, governance, and kinship.[46]

The nastiness of the disagreements was not confined to the yearly meetings. Both sides began a fierce campaign of traveling and pamphleteering that spread discord throughout the North American meetings, from the metropoles of Philadelphia and New York to the distant peripheral meetings. The LYM, which supported the Orthodox Friends, sent in reinforcements in the form of weighty English Friends who toured the North American meetings extensively in the 1820s. While this may have been the LYM's attempt to support uniformity of faith and practice throughout the Quaker world, its interference made things worse. As Larry Ingle puts it, with the arrival of these English Friends, "all hope for conciliation vanished."[47] Where American Friends might have worked through disagreements in doctrine and power, the meddling of English ministers deepened rifts. Their participation, whether knowingly or not, in what amounted to a Quaker "imperial" process, marked the end of the LYM's authority at the center of the Quaker world.[48]

The conflict came to a head in April 1827 at the PYM when Orthodox members refused to replace the staunchly Orthodox clerk with a Hicksite one. Those identifying as Hicksites withdrew and called for a reorganized yearly meeting. The division in Philadelphia spread to other yearly meetings. Baltimore, Indiana, Ohio, and New York Yearly Meetings divided in 1828. The schism was devastating to North American Quakers. Quakers throughout the Atlantic world had established and strengthened their local communities through the carefully woven ties of family and faith. The schism dismantled this world. In the yearly meetings that separated, every constituent meeting, down to the level of preparative meeting, was forced to decide which yearly meeting it would recognize. In local communities where Friends lived, worked, and worshipped in proximity to one another, quarrels over belief extended into fractious disputes over property. In some cases, property disputes had to be resolved by legal means, something Quakers had scrupulously avoided throughout their history.

The Hicksite-Orthodox separation was a watershed event. Hugh Barbour has called it "the most traumatic event in American Quaker history."[49] It forever changed the Quaker Atlantic world. Some Quakers became more isolationist; others sought further connection with mainstream society through greater involvement in social reform or mercantile interests. Quaker unity gave way to diversity. Division seemed to become the accepted way of dealing with theological disagreement. Both the Hicksites and the Orthodox fragmented further in the years after 1830, including a division in the LYM. In terms of the periodization we have employed in this volume, the separation stands at the end of the long eighteenth century. Using a different periodization, it fits into the first third of the long nineteenth century, as seen in Thomas D. Hamm's *Liberal Quakerism in America in the Long Nineteenth Century, 1790–1920*.[50] Either way, the Quaker world of 1830 was significantly different from that of 1690.

NOTES

1. A number of scholars, beginning with William C. Braithwaite in 1919, portrayed eighteenth-century Quakerism as an unremarkable stage between the enthusiastic Quakerism of the seventeenth and nineteenth centuries. See William C. Braithwaite, *The Second Period of Quakerism* (London: Macmillan, 1919; 2nd ed., Cambridge: Cambridge University Press, 1961); Rufus M. Jones, *The Later Periods of Quakerism*, 2 vols. (London: Macmillan, 1921); Walter R. Williams, *The Rich Heritage of Quakerism* (1962; repr., Newberg, OR: Barclay Press, 1987); D. Elton Trueblood, *The People Called Quakers* (New York: Harper and Row, 1966); and John Punshon, *Portrait in Grey: A Short History of the Quakers* (London: Quaker Home Service, 1984).

2. Richard C. Allen and Rosemary Moore, eds., introduction to *The Quakers, 1656–1723: The Evolution of an Alternative Community* (University Park: Penn State University Press, 2018), 2.

3. Notable book-length contributions that focus on the eighteenth century include Margaret Hope Bacon, ed., *Wilt Thou Go on My Errand? Three Eighteenth-Century Journals of Quaker Women Ministers: Susanna Morris, 1682–1755; Elizabeth Hudson, 1722–1783; Ann Moore, 1710–1783* (Wallingford, PA: Pendle Hill, 1994); Cristine Levenduski, *Peculiar Power: A Quaker Woman Preacher in Eighteenth-Century America* (Washington, DC: Smithsonian Institution Press, 1996); Rebecca Larson, *Daughters of Light: Quaker Women Preaching and Prophesying in the Colonies and Abroad, 1700–1775* (New York: Knopf, 1999); Judith Jennings, *Gender, Religion, and Radicalism in the Long Eighteenth Century: The "Ingenious Quaker" and Her Connections* (Aldershot, UK: Ashgate, 2006); and Amanda Herbert, *Female Alliances: Gender, Identity, and Friendship in Early Modern Britain* (New Haven: Yale University Press, 2014).

4. Michele Lise Tarter and Catie Gill, eds., introduction to *New Critical Studies on Early Quaker Women, 1650–1800* (Oxford: Oxford University Press, 2018), 1.

5. Naomi Pullin, *Female Friends and the Making of Transatlantic Quakerism, 1650–1750* (Cambridge: Cambridge University Press, 2018), 1.

6. Recent works include Brycchan Carey, *From Peace to Freedom: Quaker Rhetoric and the Birth of American Antislavery, 1657–1761* (New Haven: Yale University Press, 2012); Elizabeth Cazden, "Quakers, Slavery, Anti-Slavery, and Race," in *The Oxford Handbook of Quaker Studies*, ed. Stephen W. Angell and Pink Dandelion (Oxford: Oxford University Press, 2013), 347–62; Bryccan Carey and Geoffrey Plank, eds., *Quakers and Abolition* (Urbana: University of Illinois Press, 2014); Julie Holcomb, *Moral Commerce: Quakers and the Transatlantic Boycott of the Slave Labor Economy* (Ithaca: Cornell University Press, 2016); Marcus Rediker, *The Fearless Benjamin Lay: The Quaker Dwarf Who Became the First Revolutionary Abolitionist* (Boston: Beacon Press, 2017); and Katherine Gerbner, "Slavery in the Quaker World," *Friends Journal*, September 1, 2019, http://www.friendsjournal.org/slavery-in-the-quaker-world.

7. See, for example, Mike King, *Quakernomics: An Ethical Capitalism* (New York: Anthem Press, 2014); Esther Sahle, "A Faith of Merchants: Quakers and Institutional Change in the Early Modern Atlantic, c. 1660–1800" (PhD diss., London School of Economics, 2016); Holcomb, *Moral Commerce*.

8. Examples of these works include Nicholas J. Morgan, *Lancashire Quakers and the Establishment, 1660–1730* (Halifax, UK: Ryburn, 1993); Adrian Davies, *The Quakers in English Society, 1655–1725* (Oxford: Clarendon Press, 2000); Robynne Rogers Healey, *From Quaker to Upper Canadian: Faith and Community Among Yonge Street Friends, 1801–1850* (Montreal: McGill-Queen's University Press, 2006); and Richard C. Allen, *Quaker Communities in Early Modern Wales: From Resistance to Respectability* (Cardiff: University of Wales Press, 2007).

9. These include Carla Gerona, *Night Journeys: The Power of Dreams in Transatlantic Quaker Culture* (Charlottesville: University of Virginia Press, 2004); Sarah Crabtree, *Holy Nation: The Transatlantic Quaker Ministry in an Age of Revolution* (Chicago: University of Chicago Press, 2015); and Jordan Landes, *London Quakers in the Trans-Atlantic World: The Creation of an Early Modern Community* (London: Palgrave Macmillan, 2015).

10. David Armitage, "Three Concepts of Atlantic History," in *The British Atlantic World, 1500–1800*, ed. David Armitage and Michael J. Braddick (Basingstoke: Palgrave Macmillan, 2002), 16–21.

11. Other helpful overviews of early Quaker history are available in Angell and Dandelion, *Oxford Handbook of Quaker Studies*, and in Stephen W. Angell and Pink Dandelion, eds., *The Cambridge Companion to Quakerism* (Cambridge: Cambridge University Press, 2018.)

12. George Fox, *The Journal of George Fox*, ed. John L. Nickalls (Cambridge: Cambridge University Press, 1952), 11.

13. Rosemary A. Moore, *The Light in Their Consciences: Early Quakers in Britain, 1646–1666* (University Park: Penn State University Press, 2000), 15. Other respected early leaders include James Nayler, Margaret Fell, Edward Burrough, Francis Howgill, Richard Hubberthorne, Richard Farnsworth, and William Dewsbury.

14. Raymond Ayoub, "The Persecution of 'an Innocent People' in Seventeenth-Century England," *Quaker Studies* 10, no. 1 (2006): 48–49; John Miller, "'A Suffering People': English Quakers and Their Neighbours, c. 1650–c.1700," *Past and Present* 188, no. 1 (2005): 71.

15. Richard L. Greaves, "Seditious Sectaries or 'Sober and Useful Inhabitants'? Changing Conceptions of the Quakers in Early Modern Britain," *Albion: A Quarterly Journal Concerned with British Studies* 33, no. 1 (2001): 24–50.

16. Hugh S. Pyper, "Robert Barclay: The Art of Apologetics," in *Early Quakers and Their Theological Thought, 1647–1723*, ed. Stephen W. Angell and Pink Dandelion (Cambridge: Cambridge University Press, 2015), 207–23.

17. Pink Dandelion, "Guarded Domesticity and Engagement with 'the World': The Separate Spheres of Quaker Quietism," *Common Knowledge* 16, no. 1 (2010): 95–109; Robynne Rogers Healey, "From Apocalyptic Prophecy to Tolerable Faithfulness: George Whitehead and a Theology for the Eschaton Deferred," in Angell and Dandelion, *Early Quakers and Their Theological Thought*, 273–92.

18. Craig W. Horle, *The Quakers and the English Legal System, 1660–1688* (Philadelphia: University of Pennsylvania Press, 1988); Davies, *Quakers in English Society*; Miller, "'Suffering People,'" 71–103; Allen, *Quaker Communities in Early Modern Wales*.

19. Andrew R. Murphy, *William Penn: A Life* (New York: Oxford University Press, 2019), 201–26.

20. Michael Birkel, "Immediate Revelation, Kabbalah, and Magic: The Primacy of Experience in the Theology of George Keith," in Angell and Dandelion, *Early Quakers and Their Theological Thought*, 264.

21. Ibid., 256; Hugh Barbour and J. William Frost, *The Quakers* (New York: Greenwood Press, 1988), 79.

22. Jon Butler, "'Gospel Order Improved': The Keithian Schism and the Exercise of Quaker Ministerial Authority in Pennsylvania," *William and Mary Quarterly* 31, no. 3 (1974): 435–37.

23. Clare J. L. Martin, "Tradition Versus Innovation: The Hat, Wilkinson-Story, and Keithian Controversies," *Quaker Studies* 8, no. 1 (2003): 17; Birkel, "Immediate Revelation," 264.

24. Birkel, "Immediate Revelation," 265.

25. George Keith, *Some Reasons and Causes of the Late Seperation* [sic] (Philadelphia: William Bradford, 1692); George Keith and Thomas Budd, *A True Copy of Three Judgments Given Forth by a Party of Men, Called Quakers at Philadelphia, Against George Keith and His Friends. With Two Answers to the Said Judgments* (Philadelphia: William Bradford, 1692).

26. Martin, "Tradition Versus Innovation," 15–18.

27. Jon Butler, "Power, Authority, and the Origins of American Denominational Order: The English Churches in the Delaware Valley, 1680–1730," *Transactions of the American Philosophical Society* 68, no. 2 (1978): 28–29.

28. Jones, *Later Periods of Quakerism*, 1:108–10.

29. Ibid., 1:143; Barbour and Frost, *Quakers*, 108.

30. Frederick B. Tolles, *Meeting House and Counting House: The Quaker Merchants of Colonial Philadelphia, 1682–1763* (New York: W. W. Norton, 1948); Landes, *London Quakers*.

31. See Jean R. Soderlund, *Quakers and Slavery: A Divided Spirit* (Princeton: Princeton University Press, 1985).

32. See Geoffrey Plank, *John Woolman's Path to the Peaceable Kingdom: A Quaker in the British Empire* (Philadelphia: University of Pennsylvania Press, 2012).

33. Mark Freeman, "Quakers, Business, and Philanthropy," in Angell and Dandelion, *Oxford Handbook of Quaker Studies*, 423.

34. For an outline of events, see Cazden, "Quakers, Slavery, Anti-Slavery, and Race."

35. Jack D. Marietta, *The Reformation of American Quakerism, 1748–1783* (1984; repr., Philadelphia: University of Pennsylvania Press, 2007). The LYM followed a similar reform beginning in 1760, as outlined in Punshon, *Portrait in Grey*, 142–44.

36. Meredith Baldwin Weddle, *Walking in the Way of Peace: Quaker Pacifism in the Seventeenth Century* (Oxford: Oxford University Press, 2001), 245–53.

37. LYM, *Extracts from the Minutes and Advices of the Yearly Meeting of Friends Held in London* (London: J. Phillips, 1783), 254.

38. Thomas D. Hamm, *The Quakers in America* (New York: Columbia University Press, 2003), 32.

39. LYM, *A Collection of the Epistles from the Yearly Meeting of Friends in London to the Quarterly and Monthly Meetings in Great-Britain, Ireland, and Elsewhere from 1675 to 1805: Being from the First Establishment of That Meeting to the Present Time* (Baltimore: Cole and Hewes, 1806), 378.

40. Healey, "From Apocalyptic Prophecy to Tolerable Faithfulness"; Robynne Rogers Healey, "Into the Eighteenth Century," in Allen and Moore, *Quakers, 1656–1723*, 287–312.

41. Thomas D. Hamm, *Liberal Quakerism in America in the Long Nineteenth Century, 1790–1920* (Leiden: Brill, 2020).

42. David W. Maxey, "New Light on Hannah Barnard, a Quaker 'Heretic,'" *Quaker History* 78, no. 2 (1989): 62–65.

43. Robert W. Doherty, *The Hicksite Separation: A Sociological Analysis of Religious Schism in Early Nineteenth-Century America* (New Brunswick: Rutgers University Press, 1967); Larry H. Ingle, *Quakers in Conflict: The Hicksite Reformation* (Knoxville: University of Tennessee Press, 1986); Hamm, *Liberal Quakerism in America*.

44. Thomas D. Hamm, "Hicksite, Orthodox, and Evangelical Quakerism, 1805–1887," in Angell and Dandelion, *Oxford Handbook of Quaker Studies*, 64.

45. Doherty, *Hicksite Separation*, 28–29.

46. Doherty posits that Orthodox Friends in the PYM were both wealthier and more powerful (ibid., 16, 46–48). Ingle identifies an urban-rural divide, with urban Quakers generally identifying as Orthodox and rural Quakers as Hicksite. He also demonstrates that Orthodox Friends in the PYM and NYYM were more frequently weighty, or powerful, Quakers. Ingle, *Quakers in Conflict*, 16–60.

47. Ingle, *Quakers in Conflict*, 30.

48. Robynne Rogers Healey, "Elizabeth Robson, Transatlantic Women Ministers, and the Hicksite-Orthodox Schism," paper presented to the Quaker Studies Research Association, June 22, 2019.

49. Hugh Barbour, Christopher Densmore, Elizabeth H. Moger, Nancy C. Sorel, Larry H. Ingle, and Alson D. Van Wagner, "The Orthodox-Hicksite Separation," in *Quaker Crosscurrents: Three Hundred Years of Friends in the New York Yearly Meetings*, ed. Hugh Barbour, Christopher Densmore, Elizabeth H. Moger, Nancy C. Sorel, Alson D. Van Wagner, and Arthur J. Worrall (Syracuse: Syracuse University Press, 1995), 100.

50. See Hamm, *Liberal Quakerism in America*, 14–29. In the *Oxford Handbook of Quaker Studies*, Angell and Dandelion end the long eighteenth century (the quietist period) about 1805. In the *Cambridge Companion to Quakerism*, they set the beginning of the period of "conflict and transformation" in 1808.

PART I

Unique Quaker Testimonies and Practices

CHAPTER 1

"Our Dear Friend Has Departed This Life"
Memorial Testimony Writing in the Long Eighteenth Century

ERICA CANELA AND ROBYNNE ROGERS HEALEY

In the preface to *A Collection of Testimonies Concerning Several Ministers of the Gospel Amongst the People Called Quakers*, published in 1760, the London Yearly Meeting (LYM) admonished its members:

> Greatly regret[ting], frequently, to find the solid and weighty Expressions of our dying Friends omitted, under the Excuse of Brevity, when oftentimes they are the most important, and would be the most likely to be of Advantage to those to whom they are communicated ... Friends are desired not to be negligent at such Opportunities, but to make as full and authentic a Collection of the last Words, and Deathbed Expressions, of our worthy departing Friends, as they are capable; as these are generally the most lively and affecting, and have a stronger Tendency to stir up the pure mind in the considerate Readers, and make them to desire and endeavour so to walk, in the Counsel of God, as to obtain the like precious Experience.[1]

Memorial testimony writing in the long eighteenth century developed into a standard transatlantic Quaker practice with multiple purposes. For those within the Religious Society of Friends, it offered a way of honoring the departed while providing a body of prescriptive texts to guide Quaker youths into the highest ideals of their faith.[2] Changes in testimony writing over the period—specifically, the emergence of more obituary-style testimonies narrating the memorialized person's life in addition to their death—point to the importance of memorial testimonies as a form of Quaker literature. By the end of the long eighteenth century, testimonies had become spiritual biographies through which yearly meetings could highlight the lives of those they considered exemplars of the faith. Valuable as a mechanism of socialization, published testimonies were also a means by which the Religious Society of Friends presented themselves and their faith to outsiders. The yearly meetings' control of the Society's private and public narratives reflects the "'pair of dualisms'—worldly and non-worldly and natural and supernatural—[that] functioned in tandem during the Quietist era."[3]

As outlined in the introduction, the long eighteenth century was a paradoxical period in Quaker history. At the same time that the Quaker reformation, beginning in 1755 in the Philadelphia Yearly Meeting (PYM) and 1760 in the LYM, seemed to signal retreat from mainstream society, Friends increased their engagement in secular affairs.[4] Their involvement in transatlantic business, industry, and banking increased throughout the century, as did their philanthropic work.[5] They also clarified their positions on war and slavery in response to political, social, and economic circumstances in the Atlantic world.[6] It was in this context that the LYM released *A Collection of Testimonies*, the first printed collection of memorials of deceased public Friends.[7] British North American meetings also collected memorials. The PYM published its first collection in 1787; other yearly meetings published similar volumes in the nineteenth century.[8] As a group of prescriptive texts, these works give us insight into the social and cultural forces that shaped eighteenth-century Quakers' lives.

Deathbed narratives are not exclusive to Quakers. The Christian idea of a good death had its roots in the Middle Ages with *Ars moriendi* (*The Art of Dying*), a collection of fifteenth-century Latin texts and woodcuts offering advice on the protocols for a good Christian death.[9] Many features of this deathbed piety persisted, as is evident in the seventeenth-century English treatise *The Rule and Exercises of Holy Dying* (1651), which outlined the expectations of the good death. Inasmuch as "living a good life in preparation for eternity" had superseded the importance of the good death by the late seventeenth century, "the huge industry for handbooks on the good death continued." As Elizabeth Tingle and Jonathan Willis contend, the eighteenth-century deathbed remained "a powerful place, where abstract ideas, new doctrines, old habits and almost forgotten shreds of half-belief crystallised into a messy and imperfect expression of individual identity."[10] Records from the seventeenth and early eighteenth centuries identified the following requirements for a good death: "the importance of repentance and assurance of salvation (both for the dying person and those observing the death), the necessity of resisting temptation, the exercise of faith and patience and the imminence of and even longing for the next world."[11] This paradigm remained largely unchanged until the late eighteenth century, when romanticism introduced new influences.[12] Evangelical impulses also presented new elements, including the possibility of a deathbed conversion, something seventeenth- and eighteenth-century Protestants, including Quakers, viewed skeptically.[13]

Words uttered on the deathbed also held special meaning. As Scott Stephan has shown, "the faithful believed that death froze an individual's religious and moral status, serving as an indicator of the life led and the fate to come." Should a dying individual's faculties be clear to the end, their last words conveyed "their thoughts and feelings during this time of utmost clarity and piety."[14] Scholarship examining deathbed narratives in different periods and cultural contexts demonstrates how authors in various contexts constructed them to fit particular expectations or serve certain purposes.[15] The significance of deathbed narratives in nineteenth-century British and American culture is evident in their position at the heart of nineteenth-century literature.[16] The widespread circulation of memorials throughout eighteenth-century Quaker culture demonstrates that weighty Friends in the Atlantic world invested deathbed narratives with significant instructive value.

What purpose did the memorials and collections of deathbed expressions serve for Quakers? Our examination of Quaker memorials accords with Bruce Gordon and Peter Marshall's conclusion that "relations of the living with the dead were profoundly embedded in religious cultures."[17] While Quakers were not alone in using this genre, their memorials are uniquely Quaker in their rhetorical composition.[18] Quakers did not just read memorials but participated in a series of "processes of reading, writing [copying], and remembering over time," through which they engaged in both "communal remembrance and personal faith." As Rebecca M. Rosen asserts in her examination of the Quaker poet Hannah Griffitts, these interactive processes made the memorials inspirational and enduring "beyond the memories of the living."[19] Moreover, the relations of the living with the dead, navigated through memorials, "were not only shaped by, but themselves helped to shape, the process of religious change."[20] The changes in testimonies over the long eighteenth century, from their focus on the memorialized person's death to expanded attention on that person's life, reflects the increased significance of orthopraxy, or correct practice, among Friends.

At first glance, an examination of *A Collection of Testimonies* and the unpublished memorials of the yearly meetings of New York, Philadelphia, and Baltimore suggests a formulaic structure.[21] The testimonies tell a story, from childhood, through convincement for those who had not been birthright Friends, to achievements in ministry or contributions to the local meeting, to death. The structure remains the same regardless of age or gender. An examination of the most commonly used terms reveals the characteristics and conduct Friends considered most worthy of recollection during this period.

We examined the testimonies of 187 Friends—101 men and 86 women. The memorials focused extensively on the temperament of public Friends, with words like "humble" and "charitable" most often describing ministers and elders, as shown in figure 1.1. The importance of devotion in the lives of public Friends is evident in the frequently cited characteristics "serviceable," "faithful," and "worthy." It goes without saying that being a "diligent attender" was an important indication of faithfulness; figure 1.1 shows that 59 percent of the testimonies we examined noted Friends' committed attendance at meetings.

Thirty percent of the Friends whose memorials we studied were praised for their zealous behavior; interestingly, this term described men and women in almost equal measure (55 to 45 percent). "Zeal" is a quality often associated with the first and second generations of Friends, but we found that the term persisted as an important descriptor throughout the long eighteenth century. Significantly, however, its meaning evolved. Among Quakers of the first and second generations, zeal or zealousness referred to religious enthusiasm. In Samuel Fisher's 1678 testimony, for instance, Ellis Hookes wrote that "the Lord opened his Mouth to Preach to others that precious Truth ... in great Fervency, Zeal, and Constancy."[22] Loveday Hambly of Cornwall, England, was known as "a person accounted famous among God's People, for Sufferings, and Zealous of Good Works, ever since the Day that she was turned from Darkness to Light, and from the Power of Satan to God."[23] This enthusiasm for the early Quaker message and its

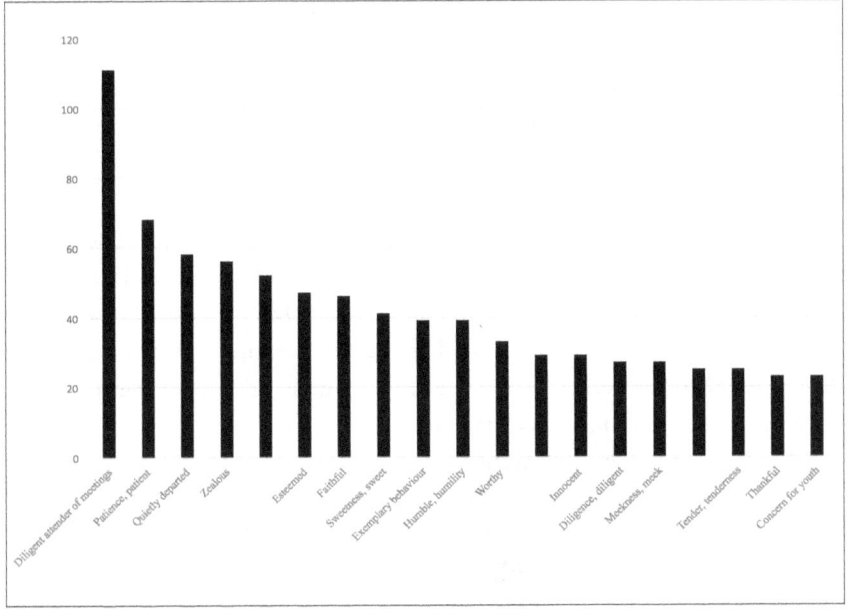

FIG. 1.1   Terms most commonly used in testimonies

propagation was critical to the success of the movement and, as such, a quality highly regarded in early Friends.

Throughout the eighteenth century, "zealousness" increasingly came to mean dedication to Quaker discipline and church order. In 1702, Hugh Roberts was remembered as "zealous for good order in the church, serviceable in the discipline, and skilful at accommodating differences."[24] In 1732, John Snashall of Brighthelmston, Sussex, was recalled as "zealous against the antichristian Yoke of tithes, for which . . . he was a faithful sufferer."[25] The Gwynedd Monthly Meeting in Pennsylvania said of Rowland Ellis in 1729 that "he was zealous for supporting our Christian discipline, and exemplary in conducting himself agreeable therewith, sometimes saying 'If the hedge of discipline was not kept up the labour of the husbandman would soon be laid waste.'"[26] Christopher Winn of Westmoreland, who died in 1732, was also zealous about church order, "being concerned in a particular manner that Discipline should be maintained, so that Judgment might be placed upon every Transgressor, and the Church be made clean."[27]

In 1733, the memorial testimony about Bridget Story noted that she was "zealous for promoting and maintaining good Order in the Church; and in

MEMORIAL TESTIMONY WRITING

particular, concerned for the inward Growth and Preservation of the rising Generation, that all Superfluity of Naughtiness might be avoided, and Decency and Plainness kept to." Irish Friend Elizabeth Balfour, who died in 1758, was also "zealous for preserving good Order," specifically concerned "that Christian plainness and moderation should be observed in all respects."[28] In 1779, the Purchase Monthly Meeting in Westchester County, New York, recollected Phebe Weeks as "zealous that Discipline might be maintained and friends Children kept in plainness of speech and apparel."[29] Similarly, Mary Mifflin of the Deer Creek Monthly Meeting in Baltimore was described in 1824 as "zealous for the maintenance of order and the discipline of the church."[30] The focus of religious zeal had shifted from the state of the soul to the state of the meeting.

Frequently invoked phrases describing the characteristics of the ideal Quaker man or woman reveal that socialization in the Society was gendered, in spite of the Quaker commitment to equality. Men and women were defined most often within the context of family. Men were often remembered as "loving" and "kind" husbands, "tender" fathers, and "prudent" masters. Women were frequently memorialized as "dutiful" and "affectionate" wives, "tender" mothers, and "faithful labourers." Figures 1.2 and 1.3 show the most common terms used to describe men and women. Terms used to describe men include "powerful," "gift of ministry," and "enlightening"—all words that demonstrate influence and aptitude. Women, by contrast, were described as "modest," "dutiful," and "reverent"—all traits typically desired of women of this time, regardless of faith. As ministers (some of whom traveled great distances), elders, and educators, Quaker women could create space for themselves as leaders within the Society. Despite the strength and authority inherent in these opportunities, eighteenth-century Quakers classified Quaker women using the gendered language of the era.[31]

Certainly, all of those memorialized accepted death and were reported to have died "well," despite the extreme pain and suffering some endured. The first generation of Friends established the tradition of the peaceful Quaker death. George Fox "quietly departed this life in peace, and sweetly fell asleep in the Lord."[32] The tradition of the peaceful Quaker death was important enough to Friends that memorials recorded instances of its occurrence. Thirty percent of the Friends we looked at "quietly departed." One, Evan Thomas, remarked toward the end of his life that he "felt no fears and saw no cloud in his way."[33] Thomas embodied the good Christian death that not only welcomed but even longed for the next world.

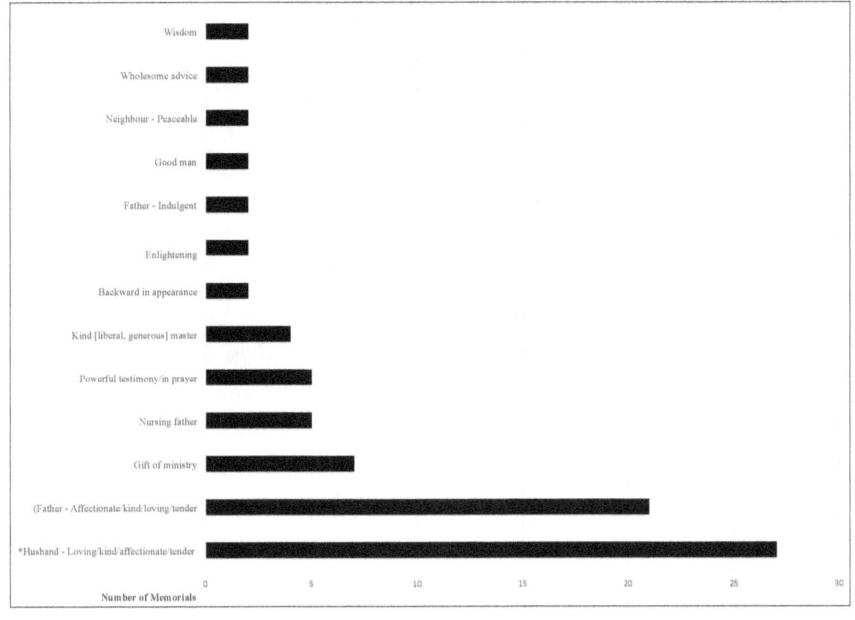

FIG. 1.2   Most common terms referring to men

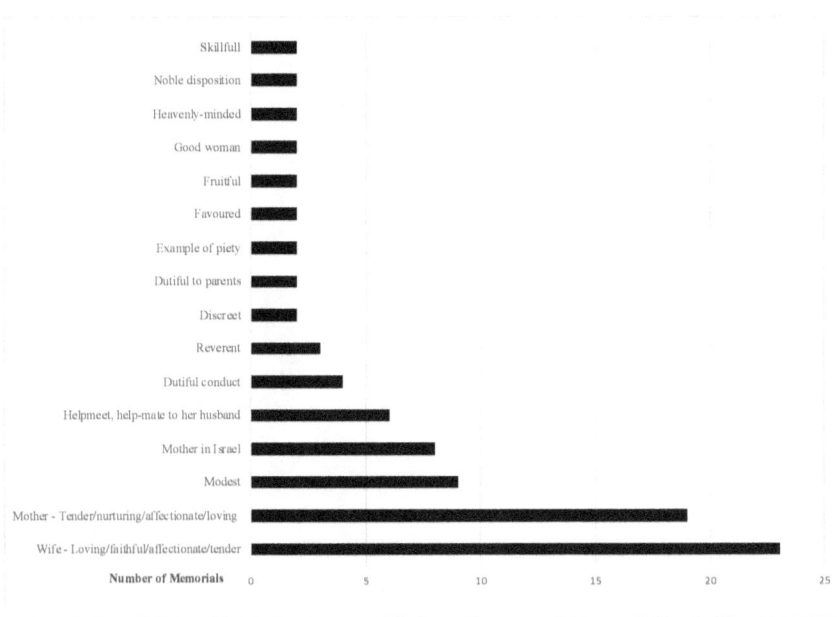

FIG. 1.3   Most common terms referring to women

MEMORIAL TESTIMONY WRITING

The faith journeys of public Friends, if not the specific details of their lives, provided models for Quaker youths, who had become a significant source of concern for older and weighty Friends.[34] The LYM's advice on youth and parenting demonstrates the Society's anxiety over the lack of piety displayed by its birthright youths. Consider the admonition to young people in 1739: "We earnestly beseech our friends, and especially the youth among us, to avoid all such conversation as may tend to draw out their minds into the foolish and wicked pastimes with which this age aboundeth (particularly balls, gaming-places, horse-races, and play-houses) those nurseries of debauchery and wickedness, the burthen and grief of the sober part of other societies, as well as of our own." Again, in 1751, the LYM "intreat[ed]" its young to "submit to its discipline," which "will preserve you from the deplorable effect of Satan's transformations."[35] And, in 1760, the same year that *A Collection of Testimonies* was published, the LYM "pressingly exhort[ed] all parents and heads of families" "to procure such useful learning for their children, as their abilities will admit; and to encourage them, as well by example as precept, to the frequent reading of the holy scriptures."

> It is requisite also that restraint be added to instruction, it being much easier, as well as more prudent, to be exercised upon the first appearances of an inclination to dangerous or hurtful liberties, than afterward; for where children, through the prevalence of fond affection, have been accustomed to improper indulgences, when they are grown to such a dangerous degree of ripeness, that the exertion of authority hath become absolutely necessary, the strength of their passions so habituated hath often proved unconquerable, or very difficult to overcome, to the great hurt of the unhappy youth, and the unspeakable grief of the imprudently indulgent parents.[36]

The tilt toward greater enforcement of the discipline was evident before formal reformation began in 1755 (PYM) and 1760 (LYM). As demonstrated in the discussion of zealousness, the increased importance of the discipline in this period is apparent in the lives of those lauded for their devotion in enforcing it.

As much as meetings applauded the disciplinary commitment of some Friends, they noted, on occasion, that faithfulness had a personal cost. Consider Thomas Chalkley's 1741 memorial: "he was often concerned zealously to incite and press Friends to the exercise of the good order and discipline established in the wisdom of truth, by admonishing, warning, and timely treating with such as fell short of their duty therein, and by testifying against those who, after loving and brotherly care and endeavours, could not be brought to the sense and practice of their duty; and thereby he sometimes shar'd the ill-will and resentment of such persons." Despite being the target of resentment, however, the Philadelphia Monthly Meeting ended Chalkley's testimony on a hopeful note: "we are fully persuaded the words with which he concluded his last public testimony on the island of Tortola, may be truly and properly applied to him, *that he had fought a good fight, and had kept the faith, and we doubt not, he now enjoys a crown of righteousness*."[37]

Viewed in the context of the reformation of the Religious Society of Friends, the publication of memorials, including specific deathbed expressions, served both internal and external purposes. For those within the Society, deathbed expressions pointed toward the promise of a heavenly reward, often concluding with that assurance, as Chalkley's did. Deborah Wardell's testimony concludes similarly: "She was even like a Shock of full ripe Corn, gathered in its due Season; and we doubt not but the Lord has received her Soul into the Mansions of Glory, where the Wicked cease from troubling, and the Faithful are at Rest."[38] The confidence of apocalyptic Quakerism was gone; the uncertainty, even anguish, of quietist Quakers included fear of death and the afterlife. Memorials reminded readers that eternal security could be gained by rigid adherence to the discipline. The certainty of salvation described in the testimonies—whether those memorialized possessed that certainty or not—alleviated spiritual crises for those left behind. Quakers were not alone in this; other faith traditions made similar assurances to the pious. Besides, the devotion to the discipline created its own problems for the Society. Membership declined as sectarianism increased. Nonetheless, belief in the promise of salvation through a life properly lived reflects most eighteenth-century Friends' commitment to the concept of gradual, not sudden, salvation.[39]

To the outside world, this purified Quakerism with its message of equality before God was potentially disturbing. If women had direct spiritual access to the divine, they had no need of men to guide them. Similarly, if slaves or Indigenous peoples were spiritually equal to whites, and if poverty was not the result of character flaws but of something else, the implications for the social order were dismal.[40] Readers of Elizabeth Ashbridge's autobiography learned that, even when threatened with physical harm, Ashbridge defied her second husband's demand that she not attend Quaker meetings.⁴¹ And at a time when women in public ministry generally faced strong opposition, a significant percentage of the public Friends represented in these memorials were women (34 percent in Britain and 47 percent in North America).⁴² Moreover, the decisions, between 1758 and 1784, to abolish slaveholding within the North American yearly meetings⁴³ and the efforts to assist in its abolition everywhere threatened social, political, and economic structures at the heart of the transatlantic world. Consider Quaker minister James Rigbie, who had been born into a slaveholding family of "planters in high rank." After becoming a Quaker, "his own example and labour was instrumental in helping forward our testimony against the practice of holding slaves for term of life."⁴⁴ Rigbie's position must have strained relations with family members who remained slave owners. Although the Quaker commitment to equality was complicated, and though there is little evidence that Quakers as a whole practiced true equality, the benign message presented in the testimonies of a disciplined, inoffensive life that focused on heaven's rewards allowed Friends to present themselves as harmless folk who were doing their best to live faithfully.

What stands out in this large collection of very similar testimonies are those that for one reason or another do not seem to conform to the norm. These include a few memorials for very young Friends who were not public Friends and a few for others whose devotion to Quakerism had wavered at some point. Also notable is a shift over time in the content of the testimonies, as noted above. Those written at the beginning of the period relate almost exclusively the deathbed experience, while those composed at the end of the era also include information about the memorialized person's life, demonstrating the evolution of memorials as a genre of Quaker literature.

Memorials for those who died young, before the age of twenty-five, were unusual, and it is not until the end of the period that they began to be included. A meeting's decision to include them at all merits attention, for it indicates that young people were an important audience for these memorials.⁴⁵ These young people lacked the ministerial experience of ministers and elders; nonetheless, their lives were devout enough, and their deaths sufficiently peaceful, that they were deemed worthy of memorializing. In some cases, these young Friends apparently showed greater maturity and religious clarity than some of their elders. Thomas Burling died in 1790 at the age of fourteen of what is depicted as an excruciatingly painful illness. Yet his memorial states that Burling accepted his fate and, in the midst of dying, expressed gratitude for "the many benefits and mercies he had received," concluding in his own words, "I cannot help acknowledging so many favours, the Lord hath bestowed on me." Despite his youth, Burling's death is presented as an example for young and old alike: "thus Died this Youth, exhibiting in his last moments such fortitude of Mind, and such a willingness and resignation to the Lord's Will, in hopes of a glorious Immortality, as may serve for an Example, not only to the Young and rising Generation, but also to those further advanced in Life, and is no doubt entered into that Rest, which he appeared to be Divinely favored to have a clear prospect of."[46]

Mary Wood, who died at age nineteen, had a similarly courageous yet peaceful end. Significantly, by 1819, the year Wood died, we see the value of social activism in a powerful memorial. Wood's testimony records that she was so concerned about the welfare of animals that "it often made her heart ache to see people so hardy as to abuse them." Wood also took a stand against slavery and refused to use "articles, the produce of their [slave] labour, saying if she should recover her health, she should endeavour to keep as clear as she could from contributing to the gain of oppression." As she was dying, she remarked, "when I reflect how many poor afflicted creatures there are in the world who have not the necessaries of life, how thankful I feel for having everything which I could desire."[47] Nearly all the people memorialized in the testimonies we examined were ministers or elders; the young Friends, in fact, are the only exceptions. Including these young Friends and highlighting their grace and gratitude in death served as a reminder to Quaker youths that their lives, too, could end at any time. The best preparation for an unexpected death was an ordered and faithful life.

Mary Wood's social awareness and activism suggest maturity beyond her nineteen years, which was also reflected in her deathbed counsel to her siblings, in which she cautioned them against the temptation of fashionable dress. Wood believed that fashionable clothing was a gateway to bad behavior. "Don't get one of the foolish fashionable coats made," she warned her brother. "Thou mayest think it is a small thing, but it will make way for greater." Likewise, she advised her youngest sister to "be careful not to let thy mind out after dress, it is a foolish thing." She was critical of peers who did not conduct themselves properly "at a place of worship" and "she did not know how friends could neglect meeting when in health that she had often sat meeting in so much pain." By all accounts, she was very close to her parents, God-fearing, unusually mature for her age, and graceful in death. Wood's testimony, written in 1819, eulogizes her life as well as her death. "In her more juvenile years," it reads, "she was strikingly noticed for quick sensibility of feeling for the animal & creation." She was "cheerful" and "participated freely in the innocent pleasures of a social life." None of this seems particularly remarkable, but what was exceptional was that "although she was thus some times thrown into the company of those not in membership with friends, yet she was not observed to depart from the simplicity of her profession."[48] Such remarkable piety was worthy of recognition. One need not be a minister or elder to lead by example.

Even the testimonies of "antient" Friends included references to the young. Mary Griffin, who died at age one hundred, "was frequently led in the flowings of Gospel love tenderly to invite the youth to forsake the vanities of this life clearly, boldly up to view the great advantage of an early dedication in choosing the Lord for their portion." Did young Friends view Griffin's tender invitation as scolding? Given the nature of the memorials, it is impossible to know. We read that "she continued lively and green in very advanced age, her mind appearing centered and settled on the living foundations," which allowed her to perform ministerial visits throughout her monthly and quarterly meetings at the advanced age of ninety-five. Nor did she stop then. As a centenarian, she felt called to make more ministerial visits, despite being "so weak in body as not to be well able to stand alone." In spite of her physical frailty, it was reported that she "communicate[d] suitable counsel in a very lively, and pertinent manner," proving that "those that be planted in the house of the Lord, shall flourish in the court of our God, they shall still bring fruit in old age, they shall be fat and flourishing." Raised a Presbyterian and convinced at age twenty, Griffin had been a faithful minister for sixty-five years. Her final prayer, which Friends "doubt[ed] not but she has obtained," was "that I may at last receive the reward of well done, and an entrance into the joy of my Lord." Unsurprisingly, Wood was described as "useful in management of the discipline of their church" and she counseled those at her deathbed at the end, "fear the Lord above all things and keep up your religious meetings."[49]

Undoubtedly, testimonies of devotion and constancy provided prescriptions for the ideal Quaker life. By contrast, the testimonies about Friends whose faith journeys were challenging were probably more representative of the experience of most young Friends, if the eighteenth-century decline in membership reflects a measure of piety.[50] Arguably, these testimonies provided a more powerful cautionary tale to the younger generation.

John Cope, who died in 1803 shortly before his twenty-fifth birthday, had "become more impressed with serious thoughts concerning death and a future state, which he confessed he had not been enough mindful of in time of health, saying he had been anxiously attended to his outward business with an eager desire to get forward in the world and to gain a portion of its treasure." He added that he had been "greatly deficient in his younger days, trifling away much time which he said ought to have been better spent or employed in attending religious meetings." He had dabbled in Methodism but questioned Methodists' confidence in their "sudden conversion," coming to believe in "pure religion and its gradual operation on the soul." Neither was he drawn to evangelizing, claiming, "I think it best for me to be modest and sparing if I speak of conversion. I believe I ought rather to be humbly thankful in secret for the favour received than to be too freely talking of it to my fellow creatures." Even so, in his last illness Cope expressed grave concern for those who "denied the dear Saviour." Having settled his own mind and soul, his testimony tells readers that he "made a happy conclusion."[51]

James Rigbie, the young man who rejected his family's slaveholding ways, presents another interesting case. Rigbie was convinced "in or near the year 1742" when he was about twenty-two; he became a minister seven years later. An attack of hubris, or the devil himself, caused Rigbie to stray from his ministry, however, and from Quakerism itself: "for want of more humble watchfulness, the enemy of souls was suffered to prevail over the weakness of his nature," says his testimony, "and to lead him out of that meek state of mind wherein stability and a growth in the pure unchangeable truth is witnessed." As much as Rigbie's crisis of faith "was to his own great loss, and to the great grief and exercise of many friends for a number of years," his faith was miraculously restored: "he being visited with Bodily affliction in the decline of life, was through a renewal of Divine favour again, enabled to submit under the refining power of the Lord, who is the merciful healer of Breaches to the great joy of those concerned for Zions prosperity." After this happy turn of events, the testimony concludes, "we have no doubt but that he entered into everlasting happiness."[52]

Why did Rigbie abandon his faith, and why did the Baltimore Yearly Meeting choose to include this particular testimony? Included in Rigbie's testimony is a supplemental testimony that Rigbie himself penned two years before his death. He wanted his testimony to serve as a warning to the youth, "feeling [himself] at this time, and for sometime past as a Brand plucked out of the fire; in a degree of deep thankfulness to the Lord for his adorable mercy." He wrote that he was led to give way to much weakness, to the subtle whispers of the enemy, and thereby to prefer my own Judgement in some respects, which gradually brought me into a light esteem and disregard of the seasonable advice and solid admonition of my friends.... My understanding became darkened, and my mind led away from the path of Innocent simplicity ... and my conduct towards others deviating from that brotherly love and patience which becomes the followers of Christ, to my own very great loss in the best things, and causing a long painful burthen of sorrow & distress to others who were constrained from time to time to seek my restoration to that state of unity with the living members, which through renewed mercy I am again favoured to see and feel.

Beyond regretting his behavior, Rigbie condemned his "deviating" as "a warning to others, to keep in a lowly watchful state, to prefer plain honest dealing to all flattering or unskilful pity; and to keep a heart and ear open to the wholesome council of their fellow members on all occasions."[53] The message that these memorial testimonies wanted to convey is clear: the path to mercy was faithfulness and submission to meeting discipline.

The shift to a more obituary-style testimony that recounted a person's life as well as his or her death points to the increasing importance of testimonies as a form of Quaker literature by the end of the long eighteenth century. In the absence of a journal, or spiritual autobiography, testimonies became spiritual biographies through which yearly meetings could highlight the lives of those they considered exemplars of the faith. Comparing the testimonies of Elizabeth Ashbridge, who died in 1755, and Evan Thomas, who died in 1826, is particularly illustrative.

Ashbridge was a well-known eighteenth-century Quaker minister. What we know of her life before her convincement comes from her autobiography, *Some Account of the Early Part of the Life of Elizabeth Ashbridge*, written sometime between the death of her second husband in 1741 and her marriage to Aaron Ashbridge in 1746. It was first published in 1774 as *Some Account of the Fore Part of the Life of Elizabeth Ashbridge* but had circulated in manuscript beforehand. It is a conversion narrative, the early portion of a spiritual autobiography.[54] Ashbridge takes readers from her childhood in Middlewich, Cheshire, through a tumultuous life of elopement at age fourteen and widowhood five months later, indenture shortly thereafter (today we might argue that she was trafficked) that brought her to North America, abuse by a non-Quaker husband, a number of deep spiritual crises, a visit to relatives in Pennsylvania, where she became a Quaker against her husband's wishes, appearance in ministry, and finally her husband's enlistment in the army, followed by his departure to fight in Cuba and his demise. All of this happened before Ashbridge was twenty-seven years old! In 1746, she married Aaron Ashbridge, an affluent Quaker farmer; he was also active in their meeting, serving as clerk of the men's monthly meeting, overseer, and representative to the quarterly meeting.[55]

In 1753, Ashbridge left Pennsylvania for an extended ministry tour of Britain, where she fell ill and died. Her testimony, included in the LYM's *Collection of Testimonies*, is a true deathbed narrative, barely touching on her arrival in Ireland and the onset of her illness before recounting the last nine—excruciatingly painful—days of her life. Friends who surrounded her in her exceedingly difficult final days dutifully recorded her last words. At one point, Ashbridge was said to have cried out, "Dearest Lord, though thou slay me, I will die at thy Feet, for I have loved thee more than Life." She was remembered in death as "clear in her Openings, plain and pertinent in her Expressions, solid and awful in her Deportment, and attended with that *baptizing Power*, which is the Evidence of a living Ministry." Her last public ministry, preached "in great bodily Weakness," was so affecting that those who wrote her testimony confidently declared that it "was as a Seal to the finishing of her Service in the Work of the Ministry; and, in which, being so owned to the last, we have no doubt but she now receives the Reward of the faithful Servant, and is entered into the Joy of her Lord."[56]

The testimony tells readers nothing of Ashbridge's life before her ministry, but her autobiography had circulated in manuscript form since its completion and would have been known among Friends.[57] It was, in fact, a powerful tool in the Quaker reformation, as more than one scholar has argued.[58] Ashbridge's ministry had been directed to Quaker youth. The "catalogue," Elisabeth Ceppi recounts, of "Ashbridge's own libertinism consisted of many acts that preoccupied the reformers: disobedience towards parents, singing and dancing, and marriage for other than spiritual reasons."[59] Her autobiography functions as an allegory of Quaker reform, a theme to which Ashbridge returned in a 1754 epistle she wrote from London to the Goshen Monthly Meeting (her home meeting).[60] Michele Lise Tarter maintains that this spiritual autobiography "sustained the significant, original, and radical tenets of early Friends. That is, while so much had changed within the religious society and its practices, literature remained a locus of

MEMORIAL TESTIMONY WRITING

spirit, a medium for moving others towards God."⁶¹ We see this quite clearly in Evan Thomas's memorial.

The memorial to Evan Thomas epitomizes deathbed testimony writing at the end of the long eighteenth century. Thomas was a minister when he died in 1826, but his memorial paints what appears to be a realistic picture of the difficulties he faced on his path to a life of faith. According to "documents left in the hand writing of this our beloved friend," Thomas was inspired in his youth by the sufferings of the earliest Friends. The testimony does not tell us whether he was descended from Friends, but his exposure to this literature suggests that his parents were Quakers. The importance of focusing the youthful mind on "divine impressions" was reinforced by the meeting's editorial commentary on the harms lurking in the world: "collision with a world lying in wickedness has a powerful tendency to stamp upon the soul its own harsh and unlovely features in place of the fair characters delineated by the Divine hand." By the time Thomas turned sixteen, he had succumbed to "the contaminating influence of evil communication, that powerful corrupter of good manners," which had "nearly obliterated all the traces of those tender impressions which had been made upon his mind." Thomas then became gravely ill with an unspecified illness, causing him to reject worldliness and promise renewed devotion to God if he recovered. Thomas did recover, but he backslid again as "he was led gradually into the vortex of a very corrupting and dangerous association in which he continued for several years." "Mercifully," his testimony tells readers, he was "preserved from the grosser vices," yet he was "plagued with nightmares when he spent time with 'unprofitable' company or in 'idle and profane' conversation." He married around the age of twenty-seven, and his "ambition for distinction in the world took possession of his mind."⁶²

At this point, Thomas became engaged actively in politics. He was a delegate at the first Maryland convention, but he felt that the convention's principles were inconsistent with those of Friends. Once he realized that the views he was promoting as a delegate were going to lead to war, he "immediately withdrew from any further active agency in public concerns," refusing to return as a delegate for the second convention. He appears to have found his way back to faithfully committed Quakerism. Again, the memorial testimony offers editorial commentary on the costs and rewards of Thomas's return to the true faith: "To give up the flattering prospects of worldly honour to one occupying a prominent station in Society and in the prime of life, during an eventful crisis in public affairs, was found to be a sacrifice which could only be made by a dedication to religious principle. The sacrifice, however[,] that was called for, it was made, and he has left it as his testimony, that in the reward of the peace which followed there was an abundant recompense." During the Revolutionary War, his goods were distrained because of his unwillingness to fight; he also refused to take an oath of allegiance or pay taxes that supported the war. Thomas's testimony never explains when or how he found his way back to Quakerism. While this is frustrating for the modern reader, the authors of the testimony apparently felt that this information was unnecessary. More important was the reminder to those who read Thomas's life story that "he walked with exemplary circumspection in much unity and nearness of affection during many of the last and best years of this life, . . . [and] he deported himself with what sweetness he manifested that he was in possession of that love, which is the essential characterstick of the Gospel, . . . [and] he adorned the doctrines of God our Saviour in all things, by a life & conversation becoming the Gospel."[63]

Testimony writing in the long eighteenth century advised Friends, particularly the young, on how to lead their lives, control their behavior, and demonstrate their collective piety to the outside world. The evolution of these memorials over this period, from deathbed expressions to spiritual biographies, demonstrates their importance to Quaker history and literature. The information contained in these collected memorials added value to the carefully controlled Quaker narrative of the long eighteenth century. The added focus on a life well lived, and not just on a good death, reveals the increased emphasis on the discipline and its enforcement that marked eighteenth-century Quakerism. This is underscored by the frequent inclusion of 2 Timothy 4:7–8 in a number of the testimonies. These verses remind readers of Paul's theme of passing the torch from one generation of church leadership to the next: "I have fought a good Fight. I have finished my Course. I have kept the Faith; henceforth there is laid up for me a Crown of Righteousness, which the Lord the Righteous Judge shall give me at that day, and not only to me but to them also that love his appearing." Friends used memorial testimony writing to remind themselves and others of the importance of faithfulness, especially faithful, disciplined living, in life and in death. Memorials connected eighteenth-century Friends to the heritage of their seventeenth-century spiritual ancestors. While eighteenth-century Quakers did not always share their ancestors' certainty about revelation and salvation, they increasingly located their confidence in the discipline, Gospel order, and orthopraxy. The testimonies reminded Friends that death need not be feared. A crown of righteousness awaited, if one's life had been suitably devout.

NOTES

1. LYM, *A Collection of Testimonies Concerning Several Ministers of the Gospel Amongst the People Called Quakers* (London: Luke Hinde, 1760), ii.

2. *Piety Promoted*, first published by Tace Sowle in 1701, contains such material, at times including a meeting's memorial testimony along with the account of the deceased's spiritual labors and dying words. Memorial testimony also served prescriptive purposes for Friends. This chapter's focus on memorial testimonies collected and then published by yearly meetings allows us to examine how this particular genre of Quaker writing changed within the context of the period. Many memorials circulated in manuscript form and were never published.

3. Robynne Rogers Healey, "Quietist Quakerism, 1692–c. 1805," in *The Oxford Handbook of Quaker Studies*, ed. Stephen W. Angell and Pink Dandelion (Oxford: Oxford University Press, 2013), 48. Pink Dandelion first suggested the idea of separate public and private narratives; the arguments are developed most completely in Pink Dandelion, "Guarded Domesticity and Engagement with 'the World': The Separate Spheres of Quaker Quietism," *Common Knowledge* 16, no. 1 (2010): 95–109.

4. Jack D. Marietta, *The Reformation of American Quakerism, 1748–1783* (Philadelphia: University of Pennsylvania Press, 1984), 54; John Punshon, *Portrait in Grey: A Short History of the Quakers* (London: Quaker Home Service, 1984), 142–44.

5. On commerce and industry, see, for instance, Frederick B. Tolles, *Meeting House and Counting House: The Quaker Merchants of Colonial Philadelphia, 1682–1763*, 2nd ed. (Chapel Hill: University of North Carolina Press, 2012); Helen Roberts, "Friends in Business: Researching the History of Quaker Involvement in Industry and Commerce," *Quaker Studies* 8, no. 2 (2003): 172–93; Margaret Ackrill and Leslie Hannah, *Barclays: The Business of Banking, 1690–1996* (Cambridge: Cambridge University Press, 2001); Ross E. Martinie Eiler, "Luxury, Capitalism, and the Quaker Reformation, 1737–1798," *Quaker History* 97, no. 1 (2008): 11–31; and Andrew Fincham, "Factors Supporting the Rise of Quaker Commerce," in *Quakers and the Disciplines*, vol. 4, *Quakers, Business, and Industry*, ed. Stephen W. Angell and Pink Dandelion (Philadelphia: Friends Association of Higher Education Press, 2017), 9–33.

6. On abolition efforts, see, for instance, Gary B. Nash and Jean R. Soderlund, *Freedom by Degrees: Emancipation in Pennsylvania and Its Aftermath* (New York: Oxford University Press, 1991); Brycchan Carey, *From Peace to Freedom: Quaker Rhetoric and the Birth of American Antislavery, 1657–1761* (New Haven: Yale University Press, 2012); J. William Frost, "Quaker Antislavery: From Dissidence to Sense of the Meeting," *Quaker History* 101, no. 1 (2012): 12–33; and Brycchan Carey and Geoffrey Plank, eds., *Quakers and Abolition* (Urbana: University of Illinois Press, 2014). On the position against war, see, for instance, Peter Brock, *The Quaker Peace Testimony, 1660 to 1914* (York, UK: Sessions Book Trust, 1990); Meredith Baldwin Weddle, *Walking in the Way of Peace: Quaker Pacifism in the Seventeenth Century* (Oxford: Oxford University Press, 2001).

7. Throughout the long eighteenth century, the meetings in North America and Great Britain used the terms "testimony" and "memorial" interchangeably.

8. PYM, *A Collection of Memorials Concerning Divers Deceased Ministers and Others of the People Called Quakers* [...] *to the Year 1787* (Philadelphia: Joseph Crukshank, 1787); PYM, *Memorials Concerning Deceased Friends* [...] *from the Year 1788 to 1819, Inclusive* (Philadelphia: Solomon W. Conrad, 1821); New York Yearly Meeting (NYYM), *Memorials Concerning Several Ministers, and Others, Deceased* (New York: Samuel Wood, 1814); NYYM, *Memorials Concerning Several Ministers, and Others, Deceased* [...] (New York: Mahlon Day, 1825).

9. Bruce Gordon and Peter Marshall, *The Place of the Dead in Late Medieval and Early Modern Europe* (Cambridge: Cambridge University Press, 2000); Kristy Owen, *Identity, Commemoration, and the Art of Dying Well* (Oxford: John and Erica Hedges, 2010); Mary Riso, *The Narrative of the Good Death: The Evangelical Deathbed in Victorian England* (Burlington, VT: Ashgate, 2015); Elizabeth C. Tingle and Jonathan Willis, *Dying, Death, Burial, and Commemoration in Reformation Europe* (London: Routledge, 2015).

10. Tingle and Willis, *Dying, Death, Burial*, 9, 10.

11. Riso, *Narrative of the Good Death*, 189.

12. Erik R. Seeman, "Reading Indians' Deathbed Scenes: Ethnohistorical and Representational Approaches," *Journal of American History* 88, no. 1 (2001): 23.

13. Ibid., 27; Riso, *Narrative of the Good Death*, 58–75. The majority of eighteenth-century Friends believed that the process of salvation was gradual, not sudden. See Nikki Coffey Tousley, "The Experience of Regeneration and Erosion of Certainty in the Theology of Second-Generation Quakers: No Place for Doubt?," *Quaker Studies* 13, no. 1 (2008): 46.

14. Scott Stephan, *Redeeming the Southern Family: Evangelical Women and Domestic Devotion in the Antebellum South* (Athens: University of Georgia Press, 2011), 183.

15. See, for instance, Ralph Houlbrooke, "Funeral Sermons and Assurance of Salvation: Conviction and Persuasion in the Case of William Lord Russell of Thornhaugh," *Reformation* 4, no. 1 (1999): 119–38; Seeman, "Reading Indians' Deathbed Scenes"; Scott Stephan, "Authoring the Good Death," in *Redeeming the Southern Family*, 183–220; and Bradley Kime, "Infidel Deathbeds: Irreligious Dying and Sincere Disbelief in Nineteenth-Century America," *Church History* 82, no. 2 (2017): 427–57.

16. For the British context, see Riso, *Narrative of the Good Death*. For the American context, see Elizabeth Dill and Sheri Weinstein, eds., *Death Becomes Her: Cultural Narratives of Femininity and Death in Nineteenth-Century America* (Newcastle: Cambridge Scholars, 2008).

17. Gordon and Marshall, *Place of the Dead*, 3.

18. As Elizabeth Bouldin has argued, "testimonies concerning deceased Friends often took on a hagiographic tone." Even so, they offer "insight into what Friends eulogized in others, as well as what testifiers assumed Quaker readers would find praiseworthy." Bouldin, "'The Days of Thy Youth': Eighteenth-Century Quaker Women and the Socialization of Children," in *New Critical Studies on Early Quaker Women, 1650–1800*, ed. Michele Lise Tarter and Catie Gill (Oxford: Oxford University Press, 2018), 203.

19. Rebecca M. Rosen, "Copying Hannah Griffitts: Poetic Circulation and the Quaker Community of Scribes," in Tarter and Gill, *New Critical Studies*, 178.

20. Gordon and Marshall, *Place of the Dead*, 3.

21. There are 126 testimonies in *Collection of Testimonies*, eighty-three by men and forty-three by women. In the unpublished collections of memorials, we examined those for Friends who died prior to the Hicksite-Orthodox Schism. This included thirty-four

(nineteen male and fifteen female) in the Baltimore Yearly Meeting (BYM) "Memorials" (bound), and thirteen (six male and seven female) in the BYM (loose) collections. All of the BYM memorials were written after *Collection of Testimonies* was published in 1760. In fact, the oldest memorial, for British minister Lydia Lancaster, was written in 1761. The NYYM "Memorials of Deceased Friends, 1707–1820" contains fifty-four memorials (twenty-nine male and twenty-five female), five of which were written prior to 1760. The PYM's Memorials and Testimonies miscellaneous papers contain eight memorials, evenly divided between male and female, the earliest of which was written in 1760. The more expansive collection of PYM memorials is in the PYM's published *Collection of Memorials Concerning Divers Deceased Ministers*. This collection does include early testimonies, the earliest written in 1683. All of the unpublished memorials are located at Friends Historical Library at Swarthmore College (FHLSC).

22. Ellis Hookes, "The Epistle to the Reader," in *The Testimony of Truth Exhalted: By the Collected Labours of that Worthy Man [. . .] Samuel Fisher* (London, 1679), B.

23. Thomas Salthouse et al., "A Copy of a Letter to M. D. [Margery Dyer]," in *A Relation of the Last Words and Departure of [. . .] Loveday Hambly* (London: John Gain, 1833), 4.

24. PYM, *Collection of Memorials*, 35.

25. LYM, *Collection of Testimonies*, 60.

26. PYM, *Collection of Memorials*, 92.

27. LYM, *Collection of Testimonies*, 50.

28. Ibid., 79 (Story), 363 (Balfour).

29. NYYM, "Memorials of Deceased Friends, 1707–1820," RG2/NYy/055 1.1, 16, FHLSC.

30. BYM, "Memorials," 1786–1889, RG2/By/1.23, 87, FHLSC.

31. Phyllis Mack, *Visionary Women: Ecstatic Prophecy in Seventeenth-Century England* (Berkeley: University of California Press, 1992), 234, 288–89; Sarah Crabtree, "In the Light and on the Road: Patience Brayton and the Quaker Itinerant Ministry," in Tarter and Gill, *New Critical Studies*, 128–45; Bouldin, "'Days of Thy Youth.'"

32. George Fox, *The Journal of George Fox*, ed. John L. Nickalls (Cambridge: Cambridge University Press, 1952), 760.

33. BYM, "Memorials," 1786–1889, RG2/By/1.23, 84, FHLSC.

34. Marietta, *Reformation of American Quakerism*, 32–72. This concern for young people continued to grow throughout the long eighteenth century, culminating in Thomas Evans, *Examples of Youthful Piety, Principally Intended for the Instruction of Young Persons* (Philadelphia: Thomas Kite, 1830). *Youthful Piety*, reprinted throughout the nineteenth century, consisted of excerpts from *Piety Promoted* and other memorial testimonies from children. Evans wrote that the volume was "compiled with a view of exhibiting to young persons the happy effects and peaceful termination of a religious life, in those of their own age" (3).

35. LYM, *Extracts from the Minutes and Advices of the Yearly Meeting of Friends Held in London* (London: J. Phillips, 1783), 275.

36. Ibid., 77–78.

37. PYM, *Collection of Memorials*, 107–8.

38. LYM, *Collection of Testimonies*, 63.

39. Tousley, "Experience of Regeneration."

40. Elizabeth Cazden's chapter in this volume demonstrates that this rhetorical commitment to equality was not always realized.

41. Elizabeth Ashbridge, *Some Account of the Early Part of the Life of Elizabeth Ashbridge* (Philadelphia: Benjamin and Thomas Kite, 1807), 42–44.

42. On the opposition women faced in ministry, see Rebecca Larson, *Daughters of Light: Quaker Women Preaching and Prophesying in the Colonies and Abroad, 1700–1775* (New York: Knopf, 1999).

43. Elizabeth Cazden, "Quakers, Slavery, Anti-Slavery, and Race," in Angell and Dandelion, *Oxford Handbook of Quaker Studies*, 352.

44. BYM, "Memorials," 1786–1889, RG2/By/1.23, 12, FHLSC.

45. For an expanded discussion on the role of informal education and socialization, especially women's role in that process, see chapter 4 in Robynne Rogers Healey, *From Quaker to Upper Canadian: Faith and Community Among Yonge Street Friends, 1801–1850* (Montreal: McGill-Queen's University Press, 2006), 74–92; Bouldin, "'Days of Thy Youth'"; and Rosen, "Copying Hannah Griffitts."

46. NYYM, "Memorials of Deceased Friends, 1707–1820," RG2/NYy/055 1.1, 37, FHLSC.

47. PYM, Memorials and Testimonies (Misc. MSS), Friends Historical Library Collection of Memorials, 1760–1920, MS 056, 1819, 7 mo 19, FHLSC.

48. Ibid.

49. NYYM, "Memorials of Deceased Friends, 1707–1820," RG2/NYy/055 1.1, 79, 81–82, FHLSC.

50. Marietta, *Reformation of American Quakerism*, 55–58.

51. BYM, "Memorials," 1761–1956, RG2/By/1.22, 31, FHLSC.

52. Ibid., 1786–1889, RG2/By/1.23, 14.

53. Ibid., 15.

54. Michele Lise Tarter, "Reading a Quaker's Book: Elizabeth Ashbridge's Testimony of Quaker Literary Theory," *Quaker Studies* 9, no. 2 (2005): 177, 176.

55. Larson, *Daughters of Light*, 306.

56. LYM, *Collection of Testimonies*, 295–300 (quotations on 299, 300).

57. Tarter, "Reading a Quaker's Book," 177.

58. In addition to Tarter's essay, see Cristine Levenduski, "'Remarkable Experiences in the Life of Elizabeth Ashbridge': Portraying the Public Woman in Spiritual Autobiography," *Women's Studies* 19 (1991): 271–81; D. Britton Gildersleeve, "'I Had a Religious Mother': Maternal Ancestry, Female Spaces, and Spiritual Synthesis in Elizabeth Ashbridge's Account," *Early American Literature* 36, no. 3 (2001): 371–94; Julie Sievers, "Awakening the Inner Light: Elizabeth Ashbridge and the Transformation of Quaker Community," *Early American Literature* 36, no. 2 (2001): 235–62; and Elisabeth Ceppi, "In the Apostle's Words: Elizabeth Ashbridge's Epistle to the Goshen Monthly Meeting," *Legacy* 21, no. 2 (2004): 141–55.

59. Ceppi, "In the Apostle's Words," 146–47.

60. Ibid., 142; Sievers, "Awakening the Inner Light," 236.

61. Tarter, "Reading a Quaker's Book," 183.

62. BYM, "Memorials," 1786–1889, RG2/By/1.23, 79, FHLSC.

63. Ibid., 83.

CHAPTER 2

"Within the Bounds of Their Circumstances"
The Testimony of Inequality Among Eighteenth-Century New England Friends

ELIZABETH CAZDEN

In twenty-first-century Quaker discourse, especially of the liberal or modernist variety, the "testimony of equality" is often listed as one of the core tenets of Quakerism. For example, a recent publication by the American Friends Service Committee links Friends' early affirmation that all had access to the "Inward Teacher" to present-day Quakers' rejection of "all forms of discrimination, whether based on race, ethnicity, nationality, religion, immigration status, class, gender, age, ability, or sexual orientation."[1] This linkage is not entirely new; one can find it from at least 1775, when the French philosopher Abbé Raynal wrote admiringly, though inaccurately, that Quakers of his day believed in both community of goods and equality of rank.[2] A historian at the end of the nineteenth century similarly extolled the complete lack of social hierarchy or ranking among her eighteenth-century Rhode Island Quaker forebears.[3]

Eighteenth-century Quaker sources and practices, however, do not depict social or political equality as a core value of Friends. Early Quakers did accept spiritual equality, at least in theory, periodically reaffirming Fox and Barclay's insistence that God "is no *Respecter* of *Persons*," that all humans are created of one blood and one family, that grace is available to all, that God is at liberty to call whomever God chooses to serve in ministry, and that we are commanded to love all men (and women) just as Christ did.[4] Decades later, in the 1740s, evangelical preachers in the First Great Awakening preached a similar spiritual equality, which transcended racial categories as well as gender and social standing. That spiritual equality did not, however, necessarily challenge the legal or social subordinate role imposed on women, people of color, and landless workers.

Instead, at least from the 1670s and throughout the long eighteenth century, Friends, like their non-Quaker contemporaries, viewed as both desirable and divinely ordained a hierarchically structured and static social, economic, and political order. This acceptance of hierarchies and inequality can be seen in a number of areas: Quaker attitudes toward civil governing authorities in the British Empire, the relationship between subordinate and superior meetings under the authority of the London Yearly Meeting (LYM), the dominance of social and economic elites within the Society of Friends, household and gender roles, and attitudes and practices toward servants and slaves.

QUAKERISM IN THE EXPANDING BRITISH EMPIRE

Quaker structures and practices developed in the late seventeenth century in response to the expanding British Empire, under the restored monarchy. That empire itself evolved significantly through the eighteenth century, from informal and largely ad hoc arrangements into an extensive bureaucracy of accountability and oversight.[5] The central authorities—the Lords of Trade and Plantations (1675), Board of Trade (1696), and Privy Council, along with the armed forces—struggled to know what was happening throughout the colonies, and to issue regulations that would be effectively communicated to and followed by those on the peripheries, in order to effectively administer a far-flung empire.[6] The Lords of Trade and Plantations demanded information from colonial governments about population and economic activities; by the 1690s these requests were called "queries."[7] The Crown also sent envoys or commissioners to visit the colonies and impart instructions from the central authorities and report on colonial conditions. In 1665, for example, the Crown sent "his Majestys Commissioners" to adjudicate a boundary dispute between Plymouth and Rhode Island colonies, with orders that those colonies bear the cost of hosting them. The commissioners then wrote a lengthy report on their visit, describing what they found, from the suitability of the harbors to the religious affiliation of the residents.[8]

This secular governance structure reflected deeply embedded assumptions of subordination: the colonies were dependent entities ("children" of a "mother"), their primary purpose was the well-being of the "parent," and their political systems must remain subordinate and accountable to the central government.[9] The Board of Trade was reluctant to concede power to local colonial legislatures and repeatedly tried to impose tighter regulations, with mixed success. Debates and power struggles over how much autonomy each colony had, and to what extent Parliament had the authority to legislate for the colonies if it so chose, were major irritants throughout the century, leading to the American War of Independence.

The secular preoccupation with order and structure can also be seen in cultural trends. In the new city of Philadelphia, in sharp contrast to the chaotic older streets of Boston and London, William Penn laid out an orderly grid of numbered and named streets and diagonal boulevards. Haphazard vernacular building styles gave way to symmetrical, balanced Palladian and Georgian architecture that used mathematical ratios to set room shapes and window dimensions. Botanists painstakingly classified every bit of the natural world into a ranked hierarchy of kingdoms, classes, genera, and species. Sir William Blackstone compiled and systematized the English common law into analytical categories that are still used by twenty-first-century law students. It is hardly surprising, then, that Quakers in the British Atlantic adopted similarly hierarchical modes of thought.

QUAKER STRUCTURES AND GOSPEL ORDER

Throughout the long eighteenth century, the Quaker movement primarily inhabited and adapted to a space within the British Atlantic, with only occasional ventures into non-British areas such as the Netherlands and Norway. The Quaker expansion explicitly adopted the language of conquest, albeit armed only with spiritual weapons. One 1660 epistle urged ministers to go forth boldly, "for England is as a family of prophets, which must spread over all the nations; . . . and out of which nation and dominion must go the spiritually-weaponed and armed men to fight and conquer all nations, and bring them to the nation of God."[10] Penn's charter praised his "commendable desire to enlarge the English Empire, and promote such usefull commodities as may bee a benefit to us [that is, the king] and our Dominions."[11] In the Quaker world, as in the secular empire, the population balance shifted over time in favor of the colonies.[12] At least for New England, however, the power balance remained heavily centered in London well into the nineteenth century.[13]

The development of Quaker governance structures addressed two overlapping needs: the need to ensure sufficient uniformity in Quaker practice across an expanding geographical area, and the need for effective negotiation between the Religious Society of Friends and the secular authorities on issues that affected Friends. What emerged bore a noticeable resemblance to the secular structure, with similar tensions between metropole and periphery, similar mechanisms for collecting information and disseminating advice or instructions, and similar debates about lines of authority.[14]

The Quaker structure, which Fox called "Gospel Order," was systematized in the 1670s to keep the scattered local meetings connected in an orderly fashion. Promoting this new structure was a key purpose of Fox's 1672 visit to the American colonies. Unlike Congregationalists or Baptists, who retained virtually complete autonomy for local congregations, the Quaker movement adopted—not without dissension—a hierarchical structure of accountability more akin to the Presbyterian one.[15] Although each local meeting exercised autonomy with respect to membership and pastoral care, it was also directly accountable to the superior bodies, the quarterly and yearly meetings.

Twentieth-century historians often described the Quaker Atlantic as an essentially egalitarian network of autonomous yearly meetings.[16] But eighteenth-century sources demonstrate that throughout the century, all other yearly meetings were accountable to the LYM and its executive committee, the London Meeting for Sufferings (MfS). Fox's final general epistle, read out after his death, directed "all Friends in all the world" who had previously written to him for advice to write instead to the "Second-day's Meeting in London."[17] In practice, it was the MfS, whose membership included the "public Friends" of the Second Day Morning Meeting, that corresponded with meetings throughout the world.[18] Through annual epistles to the other meetings containing "advices" and instructions, "queries" that each meeting was expected to answer by way of report to its superior body, and visits to other meetings by recognized English ministers, the London-based leadership sought to ensure that Friends everywhere would adhere to Quaker practices and procedures that it considered essential to the well-being and even the survival of the small sect.

In their pragmatic focus on sustaining the Quaker movement, London Friends after 1670 carefully negotiated and regulated the relationship between the secular government and Quakers throughout the empire.[19] In the 1660s, Friends in London had lobbied King Charles to stop Puritan persecution of Quakers in Massachusetts, and had lobbied the Lords of Trade against a Barbados law that prevented Quakers from holding religious meetings for enslaved Africans.[20] These events established the model for how colonial Quakers were to deal with persecution or other local difficulties: send detailed reports to London Friends, who would use their influence with the Crown, Parliament, Privy Council, or appointed governors. The London Meeting for Sufferings, established in 1675 to institutionalize these lobbying efforts, became, by one account, "one of the most sophisticated of the metropolitan-provincial lobbies."[21] It periodically reminded Friends that it was to be the exclusive Quaker body interacting with the government, so that Friends would speak with a single voice.[22] Over time, the London MfS assumed broad responsibility for communication throughout the world, including attempts to control publications and public pronouncements by Friends anywhere.[23] It also controlled expenditures from the yearly meeting stock, principally for lobbying and the clerk's office, a fund to which colonial meetings were expected to contribute generously.[24]

Officially and structurally an organ of the LYM, the Meeting for Sufferings viewed itself as representing all Friends everywhere, much as Parliament represented the entire empire.[25] Like Parliament, it functioned in practice with radically unequal voices. Meeting weekly in London, it officially included representatives of "the counties" within Britain.[26] Because they were unlikely to be able to attend, however, the MfS also named London-based "correspondents" for each county. The colonial meetings, unlike "the counties," had only "correspondents," named in London in consultation with the colonial meeting. The correspondents were men with substantial knowledge of the colonies, mostly wealthy merchants with business interests in North America or the Caribbean. The political and spiritual advice that the correspondents and the MfS supplied to Friends in the colonies was shaped by the worldview of these mercantile leaders.[27]

The LYM itself had essentially the same structure, with representation from counties and urban centers. It was established, at least in theory, to give advice about the public affairs of Friends to meetings "in any of the Countys or Places in England."[28] Frequently, however, it, like the MfS, also tried to assert supervisory authority over meetings outside Britain. In 1700, for example, it advised Friends in New England how to challenge enforced levies to support a town minister.[29]

In the 1670s, the newly imposed disciplinary structures provoked some protests—and some disownments—from those accustomed to the more chaotic individualistic and charismatic tenor of the earlier years of the Quaker movement.[30] By 1700, however, the new order was well established and embedded throughout the British Atlantic. It consisted of rules set by advices from the LYM and the local yearly meeting, together with developing "case law," as individual situations were adjudicated by local meetings, with occasional appeals up to the quarterly and even the yearly meeting.

Reinforcing the inequality of the Atlantic relationship, English Friends repeatedly spoke of meetings in the American colonies as less-developed "daughters" of the original English rootstock of Quakerism. In hindsight (and from the American perspective), one can just as easily see many American meetings as founded, as meetings in Britain were (and at the same time), by itinerant ministers who gathered clusters of already sympathetic seekers. Given Quaker confidence that Truth was single, and that the gathered meeting could discern it, it is curious that the discernment of colonial meetings was treated as less legitimate or authoritative than that which took place in London or even in the British counties.

At the time, most New England Friends readily accepted London's dominance. The New England Yearly Meeting's minutes and epistles repeatedly refer to the LYM as "our friends & Elder Brethren" or "Our Fathers and Elders in the Church," and thank London for its "Fatherly & Christian concern."[31] In one debate about paying taxes to build fortifications, a leading New England Friend asked a visiting English minister what English Friends would do, because, he said, "they in that country looked upon themselves but as the daughter, and Friends . . . in Old England as their mother."[32]

A key way in which London Friends sought to exert their authority over the colonial meetings was through epistles. Some, notably the printed general epistle of the LYM, were intended for widespread distribution; others were directed to particular meetings. Frederick B. Tolles writes of the exchange of epistles as if it were a circulation of letters among equals.[33] While the colonial meetings sometimes exchanged epistles among themselves, their primary correspondence—at least until the 1760s—was with

London. The exchange was hardly one of equality; London sent queries requesting information and provided advice, while the English counties and colonial meetings provided that information and requested advice. At first, the queries requested statistical information on deaths, convincements, imprisonments, and distraints on property, which would shape lobbying priorities.[34] Later, questions were added on behavioral standards such as the education of Friends' children, care for poor Friends, and tithes. After 1700, London added queries on spiritual condition and Friends' adherence to specific testimonies and practices, less a request for information than a measuring rod for what London considered best practice among Friends and what behavior should be grounds for disownment.[35]

London's supervisory role was promoted by traveling ministers, who provided counsel (and printed material) to local groups and brought news back, first to Swarthmoor Hall and later to the London bodies.[36] They communicated the beliefs and behaviors that English Friends considered essential, from plainness, to oaths, to prompt payment of debts.[37] They gave full oral reports to the sessions of the LYM on the spiritual and political condition of Friends in the colonies, which enabled the LYM to exercise better oversight over the subordinate bodies.[38] Through these reports, the perceptions of London-based Friends of the condition and needs of the peripheral meetings were shaped as much by the observations of English visitors as by direct reports from the colonial meetings.

The relationship between center and peripheries was far from even; about 150 Friends traveled from Britain to the colonies in the half century after 1652, while few ministers from the colonies traveled to the British Isles.[39] English ministers showed a parental concern for the presumably weaker and less advanced meetings in the colonies. It is not clear that they recognized that the colonial meetings, too, could produce spiritual leadership, much less that the Quaker communities on the periphery of empire might have valuable insights to impart to those in the metropolis. Like the envoys dispatched to the colonies by the Board of Trade, the visitors frequently lamented that the colonials refused or failed to take the good "advice" sent to them by the London hierarchy. After midcentury, more American ministers traveled to the British Isles, but the numbers seem to have remained lopsided through and beyond the American War of Independence.

The question of how much autonomy each yearly meeting had—which issues could be resolved locally, without waiting for London's "advice"—remained unresolved, much like the authority of the American colonies within the British Empire. In the normal course of things, each yearly meeting resolved its own disputes, raised funds as needed for meetinghouses, poor relief, and the support of traveling ministers, and set up new meetings and realigned meeting boundaries as needed. At the same time, all Friends were accountable to London, which occasionally intervened directly on some issue in the colonial meeting, either one raised in the meeting's epistle or one noticed by a visiting English minister. For example, after a report from a visiting minister, the MfS issued a directive on what Friends on the Massachusetts island of Nantucket were to do about a local dispute over payment of a tax said by some to be in lieu of militia service, with a request to report back promptly.[40] Just as many Englishmen assumed that Parliament had the right to legislate for the colonies if it chose, London Friends seem to have assumed that they had the right to send "advice" to one of the colonial meetings directing it to take a particular action, even on local disputes that do not seem to have implicated broader Quaker policy.[41] As Andrew Fincham's chapter in this volume points out, local practices, embodied in yearly meeting minutes and compilations of advices, could diverge quite significantly from the uniformity that the LYM envisioned. That divergence seems to have been more pronounced in the Philadelphia Yearly Meeting than it was in New England, an example of the local particularity that, as Robynne Rogers Healey notes in her introduction to this volume, enriches our understanding of the eighteenth-century Quaker world.

One topic on which London Friends sent clear directives was the Society's attitude toward and relationship with the English government. Early Friends had often railed against the governing authorities as corrupt Babylon, part of the worldly order to which Friends should resist conforming. After 1688, however, the official Quaker position was that the governing powers were God's representatives, instituted and appointed by God, to be obeyed not merely on pragmatic grounds but as a matter of conscience. As Paul and others admonished the early Christian communities, Friends were to "accept the authority of every human institution," including kings and governors, as God's envoys.

The official Quaker attitude toward the government in the long eighteenth century was set in 1689, immediately after the Toleration Act. The LYM advised Friends throughout the empire to "submit all to that Divine power and wisdom which rules over the kingdoms of men."[42] Thereafter, yearly meeting epistles repeatedly stressed the duty of faithful subjection to government, and obedience to all laws and royal decrees that did not directly impinge on Quaker practice.[43] Just as the members of a household should honor and respect its male head, all members of the community must—as a matter of religious doctrine and discipline—"be subject to the governing authorities," whose sovereignty carries the weight of divine imprimatur. Even on the question of participating in government-required armed slave patrols—which struck some Friends as contrary to the Quaker testimony against outward weapons—Fox and London Friends consistently advised that while Friends should not carry arms, participating in the patrols was not only permitted but an affirmative obligation. The magistrates, Fox reminded Friends, were put there by God "for the punishment of the evil doers" and to maintain good order, and it was Friends' duty to cooperate with them unless conscience (heavily guided by the "advice" from the London Quaker bodies) dictated otherwise.[44]

The advice to respect and uphold the secular government became particularly important during periods of political unrest. After the military defeat of the Jacobite uprising of 1715, the LYM sent a formal address to King George I, strongly implying that God had been on the side of the Whig-led government.[45] At the end of the Seven Years' War, the yearly meeting again attributed England's military victory to divine favor, and in its general epistle exhorted Friends everywhere that "although the Favour of Princes hath never been the Rule of our dutiful Submission and Fidelity to them," both a sense of religious duty and gratitude for religious liberty should provoke "an humble Thankfulness" to God and "the just Returns of Loyalty and Obedience" to the king.[46]

During the American War of Independence, the LYM and MfS repeatedly instructed Friends everywhere to avoid being implicated in any challenges to the Crown and Parliament. Some heeded the caution; six weeks after the 1775 Battle of Lexington and Concord, the New England Yearly Meeting recorded in its minutes that "we cannot consistently [with our principles] join with such as form combinations of a hostile nature . . . in opposition to those placed in sovereign or subordinate authority; . . . for it is written, 'thou shalt not speak evil of the ruler of thy people.' Acts 23:5."[47] The maintenance of order, and submission to those in authority except on specific matters of conscience, was paramount.

RESPECTABILITY AND ELITES

Another way in which Quaker practice reflected the social hierarchies of the surrounding culture was in its quest for respectability and elite status. The early Quaker movement had freely welcomed Levelers and Diggers among its adherents and dismissed hat honor, fancy titles, and other marks of status or privilege. After the 1660s, ensuring the survival of the Quaker movement depended, in part, on the forbearance of local judges and magistrates and was aided by the participation of respected community leaders. Friends on both sides of the Atlantic actively courted "the better sort" of people, muting in the process the otherwise characteristic Quaker disdain for rank and status.[48] In his *Journal*, for example, Fox comments frequently—and favorably—on the number of "considerable people of the world" who attended their meetings, or at whose homes he stayed or dined.[49]

In New England, this tendency was accentuated. New England Quakers, unlike those in Pennsylvania, were predominantly dissenters (or children of dissenters) who had left England in the 1620s and 1630s, well before the Civil War ferment.[50] While they disagreed with their Puritan neighbors about theology, tax-supported ministers, worship style, and militia duty, they do not seem to have challenged Puritan views about social hierarchies. On the island of Nantucket, for example, Quaker evangelists like Thomas Chalkley and John Richardson focused their efforts on community leaders Nathaniel and Mary (Coffin) Starbuck, holding meetings in their home, known as "Parliament House."[51]

In Rhode Island, as in Pennsylvania, through most of the century, there was a substantial overlap between the colonial government and the leadership of the yearly meeting. The clerk of the New England Yearly Meeting from 1729 to 1760 was also the treasurer of the Colony of Rhode Island, while carrying on extensive mercantile activities, and many other prominent and wealthy Friends served as colonial governors and members of the Rhode Island legislature. Similarly, in England, many members of the MfS were bankers, merchants, financial underwriters, and ship captains (including more than a few members of the Bristol Society of Merchant Venturers to Africa).[52] That strategy had obvious implications for the group's social and political outlook. Any group led by people of wealth, political power, and high social rank is not likely to espouse social or political views that directly challenge wealth, political power, or existing social hierarchies. For example, there is no evidence that New England Friends objected to laws that limited the franchise to white Protestant adult male property owners, excluding blacks, Catholics, Jews, landless workers, and women.

A few Friends openly criticized the acceptance of luxurious living and elite status, although John Woolman's most complete critique, *A Plea for the Poor*, was not published until 1793, long after his death. Some Friends, especially in the Philadelphia Yearly Meeting, saw the Seven Years' War as a warning to Friends not to allow wealth and property to interfere with faithful living. As the reform pressure was codified in the second half of the century, however, it largely avoided criticisms of wealth, luxury, or status, instead focusing on behaviors that posed little threat to the established social order, such as more diligent attendance at worship, stricter adherence to the marriage rules and peculiarities of speech and dress, and more rigorous policing of young people's participation in worldly entertainments. Fancy ornamentation on furnishings or dress was to be avoided, but fine imported mahogany or silks (of a suitably drab hue) were quite acceptable.

The meetings' dominance by social and economic elites was reflected in the concerns addressed in queries and advices, and in how meetings dealt with members in financial distress. The advice sent out from London, and duly repeated throughout the Quaker Atlantic, regularly included exhortations to make a legal will (a concern only for those with assets to bequeath) and queries such as, "Are Friends carefull to live within the bounds of their Circumstances, and to avoid launching into Trade & Business beyond their Ability to manage and thereby break their promises & neglect the payment of their just Debts?"[53] Notably, many of the debts owed by colonial Quaker merchants were owed to Quaker firms in Britain, whose members sat on the MfS.

When a Friend struggled financially, meetings could be helpful, but the help often came with a dose of harsh judgment. In Rhode Island, the non-Quaker system of poor relief was administered by towns, not the parish church, and some Friends served as town officials.[54] New England Quakers nevertheless followed the English discipline that required Friends to establish a parallel structure of poor relief and removal certificates.

The secular system of poor relief became increasingly judgmental and restrictive throughout the period. Poverty was assumed to mark a person who was either not working hard enough or was in some other way violating the rules of decorum and behavior. "Reformers" insisted that poor people had the power to change their own lives and that therefore the chronically poor bore the blame for their own suffering. Increasingly restrictive rules forced parents to indenture their children, sacrificing family for the sake of "rehabilitation."[55]

For Friends in need, the Quaker system seems to have been as punitive as the public system. A poor aging widow would be taken care of, generally by paying to board her in some wealthier Friend's home. But a younger Friend would be counseled to work harder and live more austerely. A Friend with debts would be instructed or "advised" how to pay them off, and could be disciplined for failing to comply. In one Rhode Island case, a man in financial difficulties, seeking to move his family, presumably in order to seek work, was told that he could not have a removal certificate until he paid off his debts, which he was unable to do. The meeting directed him to bind out his wife and children (separately) among Friends and hire himself out as a farm laborer, all his earnings going to his creditors. He apparently refused to break up his family, as he was disowned more than a year later "for neglecting to take friends advice."[56]

The meeting also discouraged anyone from changing occupations, apparently on the basis of Paul's admonitions that people should remain in the social status and conditions that were considered as assigned by God, and not seek to change their status, even from enslavement into freedom. Even after the American War of Independence had disrupted many Friends' livelihoods and created new opportunities, the New England (Men's) Yearly Meeting minuted that if Friends wished to "move in any business or calling different from what they had been brought up in, or accustomed to, that they endeavour to find the liberty of the Truth and the Unity of Friends before they engage therein."[57] Although this advice seems to have stemmed from concerns that Friends might move into areas inconsistent with Truth, it nevertheless embedded in the discipline a resistance to social mobility.

GOSPEL FAMILY ORDER AND THE ROLE OF WOMEN

The hierarchical and paternalistic attitudes of eighteenth-century Friends can also be seen in the roles of women within the family and within the meeting. Contrary to twenty-first-century imaginings, signs of a Quaker commitment to gender equality in the modern sense are noticeably absent. Quaker women lived within a deeply gendered society; within their households and daily lives, Quaker women's roles do not seem to have differed significantly from those of their Puritan, Anglican, or Baptist neighbors. Both Puritan and Anglican theorists on both sides of the Atlantic insisted that a paternalistic household was an essential adjunct to maintaining good order and divinely ordained authority in civil government and in society as a whole.[58] In the aftermath of the English Civil War, New England Puritans were especially keen to reinforce the demands that household heads enforce discipline on their subordinate wives, children, and servants.[59] Law, custom, and scripture required that women obey their husbands and deprived them of the legal capacity to own property, contract independently, or vote. They were entitled, in theory, to kindness and respect, but within an unequal relationship. Fathers, not mothers, were considered the primary governors of their children's well-being and spiritual development.[60] Enlightenment thinkers such as Jean-Jacques Rousseau viewed women as less intelligent than men, best suited to limited roles within the home, raising their children and serving and pleasing their husbands.[61]

George Fox's writings, echoed in numerous epistles and advices throughout the eighteenth century, reflected this paternalistic view. In a 1671 sermon published as "Gospel Family Order," Fox outlined the ideal Christian household, in which the male head is responsible (and accountable before God) for the physical well-being and spiritual instruction of the entire household—women, children, servants, apprentices—and they in turn have a duty to obey him.[62]

This advice directly affected how local meetings disciplined Friends according to family role expectations. For example, when a young person was caught playing cards, or attending corn-husking parties or weddings, or marrying a non-Friend, the meeting often disciplined the young person's parents for failing to exercise sufficient control. One prominent Rhode Island Friend was criticized for allowing his servant—a free white woman—to attend revival meetings during the midcentury Great Awakening.[63]

Interestingly, the Rhode Island colony, which had no established church, differed from its neighbors—and Fox's conception—by recognizing the right of women and servants to choose their religious path independent of their husbands or masters. In one early case, a husband who opposed all religious services beat his wife for attending church but was punished by the town for interfering with her religious liberty.[64] Many wives held different religious affiliations or attendance from their husbands, even among Friends. For example, when Sarah Smith Brown, wife of wealthy Providence merchant John Brown, chose to attend Quaker meeting or even yearly meeting, her Baptist-leaning husband did not object or try to coerce her to follow his religious preference. But Friends clung to a household model of religious affiliation, at least in theory, although actual practice clearly diverged.

Quaker women differed from their neighbors in two notable ways: the free gospel ministry and separate meetings for business or discipline. Unlike other Christian denominations, Quakers continued to accept the possibility that women could be called by God to public ministry, and if so called should respond obediently, just as men would, with the full support of their meetings and families. Such a call to ministerial service took precedence over family responsibilities, giving Quaker women ministers some independence and status apart from their husbands.[65]

The acceptable practice of women in ministry was well known in New England. The first "Publishers of Truth" to visit the region in the 1650s included servant Mary Fisher and matrons Ann Austin and Elizabeth Hooton. Rhode Islander Mary Dyer, a friend and follower of the antinomian preacher Anne Hutchinson, converted to Quakerism on a journey to England and repeatedly preached in Boston after being banished, an offense for which she was hanged in 1660. Dyer's descendants and Hutchinson's sister's family remained active Friends. Through the long eighteenth century, the lists of itinerant ministers and meeting minutes requesting permission to travel include many women from both sides of the Atlantic.[66] For example, Patience (Greene) Brayton, from Somerset, Massachusetts, traveled widely within New England and other colonies and visited England in 1784, promoting the abolition of slavery and, in conjunction with several other visiting women ministers, successfully urging the LYM to establish a women's yearly meeting. Even women like Brayton, however, agonized about the conflict between their call to ministry and their traditional "natural" bonds and duties as wives and mothers.[67]

The second Quaker innovation gave women the opportunity, and indeed the obligation, to participate in the meeting's decision making through separate women's business meetings. In directing that these be set up, Fox noted that "in the restoration by Christ, they are helpsmeet, man and woman, as they were in before the Fall." He encouraged the women's meetings to work jointly with the men's meeting if either faced an issue they could not resolve, or that seemed to need both points of view.[68]

But in many places the women's business meeting did not have the same authority or responsibility as the men's meeting. The central bodies in

London, notably the powerful Meeting for Sufferings, did not include women, and the LYM did not have a women's yearly meeting until 1784.[69] Even where they existed, the jurisdiction of the women's meetings seems to have been circumscribed by customary views of women's limited roles. Such meetings considered whether women who asked to be married under the meeting's care were clear of other engagements, and undertook discipline of women and girls, often for sexual misconduct, such as a child born too soon after the wedding. In some places they collected and administered funds just as the men did; in others, their financial duties seem to have been limited to hiring a poor woman to sweep the meetinghouse, and providing small sums to widows and other needy women, not for building a meetinghouse or augmenting the LYM stock. This undoubtedly reflects the small sums that women in most households had at their disposal. On major policy questions such as slavery, the women's minutes are often limited to answering queries on whether "servants" were taken to meeting and given religious instruction, while the men debated the morality of buying, selling, and holding people in slavery. The men's meeting in New England seems to have set the queries to be answered by both men and women, and the men alone adopted the 1760 Discipline (copied with only minor changes from a 1756 LYM manuscript volume) that governed all Friends' behavior and practice.

This paternalistic household structure was weakened by social trends, including urbanization and industrialization, during the late eighteenth century.[70] But in the Quaker community, the weight of tradition, embodied in generations of advices and epistles, seems to have maintained it well into the nineteenth and even the twentieth century.[71]

HOUSEHOLD STRUCTURE AND SLAVERY

Quaker discourse about the enslavement of Africans (and Indigenous people) was also shaped by this essentially hierarchical view of household structures, as well as by the desire to protect the reputation of Friends in the eyes of elites in both England and the colonies. In George Fox's crucial first encounter with the reality of slavery in Barbados, in 1671, he determined that it was more important to establish Friends as respectable law-abiding citizens—with submissive law-abiding slaves—than to challenge the system of chattel slavery. Fox, recovering from illness at the Barbados sugar plantation of his kinsman Thomas Rous, viewed plantation slavery as simply a larger manor house, subject to the normal Pauline rules of male-dominant household management. In a sermon to planters, printed and reprinted in London, Fox stressed the mutual responsibilities of masters and "servants" (including enslaved Africans) within a hierarchical household.[72] This model, deeply rooted in Roman practice as well as in Old and New Testament texts, has long served apologists for plantation slavery, although it is not clear whether Fox understood that.[73] In any event, Fox's "Letter to the Governor of Barbados" reassured the authorities that far from inciting slaves to rebel, Friends were teaching them "to be sober and to fear God . . . and to be faithful and diligent in their masters' service and business."[74] Advices issued in subsequent decades echoed this message; one 1703 entry, explicitly grounded in Paul's epistles, counseled servants to "behave themselves in due subjection, humility and plainness, as becomes their profession and places."[75] Fox's views, reinforced by Paul's epistles, were reflected in periodic exhortations throughout the eighteenth century that Quaker slave masters should "treat them with humanity, and in a Christian manner."[76]

Even when Quaker meetings declared that buying, selling, and holding people as slaves was contrary to discipline, they frequently did not endorse or demonstrate full social, economic, or political equality for free people of color.[77] The grandson of a man freed by Rhode Island Quaker Moses Brown, for example, complained bitterly that Brown and his wife treated his family poorly, and a dispute over a gift or loan of land persisted for decades.[78] While some Friends aided free people of color, and a few even invited them into their homes, there are also numerous indications that at least some Quaker meetinghouses, like churches of other denominations, required people of color to sit either in the gallery or on a rear bench well into the nineteenth century.[79]

CONCLUSION

For eighteenth-century Friends, living a faithful life meant living within an ordered and hierarchical household and social fabric. God loved all but intended that people fulfill different roles. A devout Christian woman would be subordinate to her husband; a devout Christian servant or slave would honor and respect his or her master's authority; a devout citizen would submit to the Crown; a well-ordered local meeting would submit to its superior bodies and ultimately to the "advice" sent out by London Friends. With the singular exception of allowing women in public ministry, little in Quaker rhetoric or a century of Quaker practice challenged that assumption.

NOTES

1. AFSC Working Group on Quaker Testimonies, *An Introduction to the Quaker Testimonies* (Philadelphia: AFSC, 2011), 8, available online in PDF format at http://www.afsc.org/testimonies/introduction. See also Fiona Reid and Sharif Gemie, "The Friends Relief Service and Displaced People in Europe After the Second World War, 1945–48," *Quaker Studies* 17 (2013): 227–29. Similar assumptions of "equality" as a core Quaker belief are found in many histories of the movement to abolish slavery. See, for example, Roger Amstey, *The Atlantic Slave Trade and British Abolition, 1760–1810* (Atlantic Highlands, NJ: Humanities Press, 1975), 203; Donna McDaniel and Vanessa Julye, *Fit for Freedom, Not for Friendship: Quakers, African Americans, and the Myth of Racial Justice* (Philadelphia: Quaker Press of Friends General Conference, 2009), 3.

2. Guillaume Thomas François Raynal, *A Philosophical and Political History of the British Settlements and Trade in North America* (Edinburgh: C. Denovan, 1779), 92.

3. Caroline Hazard, *Thomas Hazard, Son of Robt Call'd College Tom: A Study of Life in Narragansett in the Eighteenth Century* (Boston: Houghton Mifflin, 1893), 96.

4. Robert Barclay, *An Apology for the True Christian Divinity: Being an Explanation and Vindication of the Doctrines of the People Called the Quakers* (1678; repr., Glenside, PA: Quaker Heritage Press, 2002), 115; see also George Fox, "Gospel Family Order," in *The Quaker Origins of Antislavery*, ed. J. William Frost (Norwood, PA: Norwood Editions, 1980), 47, 51–52; George Fox, Epistle 153, "To Friends beyond Sea, that have Blacks and Indian Slaves" (1657), in *A collection of many select and Christian epistles, letters and testimonies, written on sundry occasions, by that ancient, eminent, faithful Friend and minister of Christ Jesus, George Fox* (London, 1698), 117.

5. Jack P. Greene, "Britain's Overseas Empire Before 1780: Overwhelmingly Successful and Bureaucratically Challenged," in *Creating the British Atlantic: Essays on Transplantation, Adaptation, and Continuity*, ed. Jack P. Greene (Charlottesville: University of Virginia Press, 2013), 113–39. Strictly speaking, "Britain" refers only to the period following the 1707 Acts of Union.

6. Ibid., 116n5.

7. Jack P. Greene, *Peripheries and Center: Constitutional Development in the Extended Polities of the British Empire and the United States, 1607–1788* (New York: W. W. Norton, 1990), 13–14. In 1698, for example, Rhode Island's Quaker governor, Walter Clarke, received "particular queries" asking, "Did you grant any commissions during the late war, to any privateers? To whom did you grant any such commissions?" See John Russell Bartlett, ed., *Records of the Colony of Rhode Island and Providence Plantations, in New England*, 10 vols. (1856–65; repr., New York: AMS Press, 1968), 3:363–64.

8. Bartlett, *Records of the Colony*, 2:90–93, 127–29.

9. Greene, *Peripheries and Center*, 18.

10. Epistle from Skipton General Meeting, April 25, 1660, quoted in William C. Braithwaite, *The Second Period of Quakerism*, 2nd ed. (Cambridge: Cambridge University Press, 1961), 351 (all citations of this source are to the second edition).

11. "Pennsylvania Charter to William Penn—March 4, 1681," http://www.phmc.state.pa.us/portal/communities/documents/1681-1776/pennsylvania-charter.html.

12. Frederick B. Tolles estimated that in 1700 there were about fifty thousand Quakers in the British Isles and at least forty thousand in British America. Over the ensuing century, the number in the American colonies grew rapidly. See Tolles, *Quakers and the Atlantic Culture* (New York: Macmillan, 1960), 5, 24.

13. The New England Yearly Meeting as a body remained resolutely Orthodox in the 1827–28 splits, although a number of individual Friends who sympathized with the Hicksite separation left the Society of Friends, and a few meetings divided briefly.

14. These parallels suggest both that London Friends intentionally borrowed from the secular governmental structures that they worked within and that some practices, such as the issuance of "queries" and "advices," considered to be "Quaker peculiarities," may instead be the fossil remains of secular empire building.

15. For a fuller discussion of the "Congregational" and "Presbyterian" models in Quaker polity, see Elizabeth Cazden, "Fellowships, Conferences, and Associations: The Limits of the Liberal Quaker Reinvention of Meeting Polity," in *The Bible, the Church, and the Future of Friends*, ed. Chuck Fager (Wallingford, PA: Pendle Hill, 1996), 6–40.

16. See, for example, Tolles, *Quakers and the Atlantic Culture*; Edwin B. Bronner, "Quaker Discipline and Order, 1680–1720: Philadelphia Yearly Meeting and London Yearly Meeting," in *The World of William Penn*, ed. Richard S. Dunn and Mary Maples Dunn (Philadelphia: University of Pennsylvania Press, 1986), 323–35.

17. Quoted in Henry J. Cadbury, "George Fox's Later Years," in George Fox, *The Journal of George Fox*, ed. John L. Nickalls (Philadelphia: Religious Society of Friends, 1985), 756.

18. Isaac Sharp Jr., "The Meeting for Sufferings: Its Origin and Constitution," *Friend* 36, no. 42 (10 Mo. 1896): 678–79.

19. William Beck and T. Frederick Ball, *The London Friends' Meetings* (London: F. Bowyer Kitto, 1869; repr., London: Pronoun Press, 2009); John Punshon, *Portrait in Grey: A Short History of the Quakers* (London: Quaker Home Service, 1984), 90–92.

20. George A. Selleck, *Quakers in Boston, 1656–1964* (Cambridge, MA: Friends Meeting at Cambridge, 1976), 13–17; Tolles, *Quakers and the Atlantic Culture*, 30.

21. Alison Gilbert Olson, *Making the Empire Work: London and American Interest Groups, 1690–1790* (Cambridge: Harvard University Press, 1992), 70.

22. See, for example, LYM, Meeting for Sufferings (July 1753), 270–71, LSF, noting (with approval) the apology from one quarterly meeting within Britain for having "deviated from good Order" in addressing the issue of the jurisdiction of ecclesiastical courts, with an assurance that they did not intend "to Obstruct or oppose the orders of the Yearly Meeting" in so doing.

23. A. T. Gary, "The Political and Economic Relations of English and American Quakers (1750–1785)" (DPhil thesis, St. Hugh's College, University of Oxford, 1935), 31–32. The Philadelphia Yearly Meeting developed a separate Publications Committee; the New England Yearly Meeting did not, with publications (of which there were few) being authorized on an ad hoc basis.

24. Braithwaite, *Second Period of Quakerism*, 280–86; Sharp, "Meeting for Sufferings."

25. Greene, *Peripheries and Center*, 58–59.

26. Braithwaite, *Second Period of Quakerism*, 275–76.

27. Gary, "Political and Economic Relations," 5, 16, 226–27.

28. Braithwaite, *Second Period of Quakerism*, 276; LYM, Epistles Sent, 1699, 1:337, LSF.

29. LYM, Epistles Sent, 1700, 1:367–69, LSF.

30. James Walvin, *The Quakers: Money and Morals* (London: John Murray, 1997), 19.

31. New England Yearly Meeting (NEYM) minutes (men's), 28 (June 1705), NEYMA; LYM, Epistles Received, NEYM, 1754, 3:356, LSF; LYM, Epistles Received, NEYM, 1739, 3:20, LSF.

32. *An Account of the Life of that Ancient Servant of Jesus Christ John Richardson*, 5th ed. (Philadelphia: T. W. Stuckey, 1867), 107. The visiting minister encouraged them to use their own discernment.

33. Tolles, *Quakers and the Atlantic Culture*, 32–33.

34. Punshon, *Portrait in Grey*, 136; Braithwaite, *Second Period of Quakerism*, 427; Beck and Ball, *London Friends' Meetings*, 54.

35. Braithwaite, *Second Period of Quakerism*, 617–18; Beck and Ball, *London Friends' Meetings*, 54–56, 187–88. Andrew Fincham, in chapter 3 in this volume, explores the extent to which local meetings adopted or adapted the queries sent out from London, or developed their own in response to local issues and conditions.

36. Jordan Landes, *London Quakers in the Trans-Atlantic World: The Creation of an Early Modern Community* (London: Palgrave Macmillan, 2015), 37–46; Tolles, *Quakers and the Atlantic Culture*, 14–18, 24–29.

37. Tolles, *Quakers and the Atlantic Culture*, 85.

38. Ibid., 28; Landes, *London Quakers*, 46.

39. Tolles, *Quakers and the Atlantic Culture*, 14, 18, 28–29. Tolles gives few examples of American ministers crossing the Atlantic before 1770. One of the earliest seems to have been Moses Aldrich of Smithfield, Rhode Island, in 1739. [Second Day] Morning Meeting minute book, 5:103, LSF.

40. Epistle from London Meeting for Sufferings to NEYM, MfS minutes, 14th of the 7 mo 1758, 30:197, and LYM, Epistles Sent, 1758, 4:60, LSF. The nature of the dispute is clarified by the NEYM response. LYM, Epistles Received, 1759, 4:30–31, LSF.

41. Greene, *Peripheries and Center*, 59–60, 68.

42. LYM, Epistles Sent, 1689, 1:44–45, LSF. Portions of this epistle and a similar one from 1690 were included in London's books of extracts through the 1911 edition. See Braithwaite, *Second Period of Quakerism*, 160.

43. Braithwaite, *Second Period of Quakerism*, 599–602.

44. Fox, Epistle 319, "To Friends in Nevis and the Caribee Islands," 1675, in T. Canby Jones, ed., *The Power of the Lord Is Over All* (Richmond, IN: Friends United Press, 1989), 323–26.

45. Braithwaite, *Second Period of Quakerism*, 615.

46. LYM minutes, 1763, 12:508, LSF.

47. NEYM minutes (men's), 1775, NEYMA. At least in Rhode Island, most Friends seem to have remained firmly Loyalist, not merely pacifist nonparticipants.

48. Walvin, *Quakers: Money and Morals*, 15–18.

49. *Journal of George Fox*, 609, 611, 616.

50. The Puritan migration to New England and the Quaker migration to Pennsylvania are two of the distinct cultural strands described in David Hackett Fischer, *Albion's Seed: Four British Folkways in America* (New York: Oxford University Press, 1989).

51. Robert J. Leach and Peter Gow, *Quaker Nantucket: The Religious Community Behind the Whaling Empire* (Nantucket: Mill Hill Press, 1997), 13, 21–23.

52. Gary, "Political and Economic Relations"; Landes, *London Quakers*, 26.

53. NEYM minutes (men's), 1760, NEYMA. The discipline and queries adopted at this session were largely copied from the 1756 Discipline sent from London.

54. See, generally, Ruth Wallis Herndon, *Unwelcome Americans: Living on the Margin in Early New England* (Philadelphia: University of Pennsylvania Press, 2001); Lynne Withey, *Urban Growth in Colonial Rhode Island: Newport and Providence in the Eighteenth Century* (Albany: State University of New York Press, 1984).

55. Catherine A. Brekus, *Sarah Osborn's World: The Rise of Evangelical Christianity in Early America* (New Haven: Yale University Press, 2013), 214–16.

56. South Kingstown [Rhode Island], Monthly Meeting minutes, June 1762–May 1765, in various places, NEYMA.

57. NEYM minutes (men's), 1784, NEYMA. One wonders how this advice sounded to the growing numbers of free people of color, some of them formerly claimed as slaves by Quaker masters, who were eager to move out of that condition into farming, shopkeeping, or artisanship that would better support their families. Not surprisingly, although some attended meetings, few chose to become members of the Society subject to its discipline.

58. Mary Beth Norton, *Founding Mothers and Fathers: Gendered Power and the Forming of American Society* (New York: Knopf, 1996), 4. Norton labels this view "Filmerian," after key proponent Sir Robert Filmer, also a noted apologist for Stuart claims to absolute power.

59. Thomas N. Ingersoll, "'Riches and Honour Were Rejected by Them as Loathsome Vomit': The Fear of Leveling in New England," in *Inequality in Early America*, ed. Carla Gardina Pestana and Sharon V. Salinger (Hanover: University Press of New England, 1999), 46–66.

60. Rebecca Larson, *Daughters of Light: Quaker Women Preaching and Prophesying in the Colonies and Abroad, 1700–1775* (New York: Knopf, 1999), 165.

61. Brekus, *Sarah Osborn's World*, 183.

62. George Fox, "Gospel Family Order," 36–39. See also Stephen W. Angell, "Gospel Family-Order: George Fox's Ministry in Barbados and the Development of a Quaker Testimony of Family," in *Keeping Us Honest, Stirring the Pot: A Festschrift in Honor of H. Larry Ingle*, ed. Chuck Fager (Fayetteville, NC: Kimo Press, 2011), 17–34.

63. Hazard, *Thomas Hazard, Son of Robt*, 129–30.

64. Catherine Osborne DeCesare, "Courting Justice: Rhode Island Women and the General Court of Trials, 1671–1729" (PhD diss., Providence College, 2000), 88. Mary Beth Norton reads this same case as imposing only "symbolic" punishment, a sign to her that obedience to one's husband took precedence over the wife's religious liberty even in Rhode Island. See Norton, "'Either Married or to Bee Married': Women's Legal Inequality in Early America," in Pestana and Salinger, *Inequality in Early America*, 39–40.

65. Larson, *Daughters of Light*, 133–71.

66. Ibid., appendix 2, 320–33, contains a partial list of colonial American Quaker women ministers, with their meetings and dates of activity.

67. Sarah Crabtree, "In the Light and on the Road: Patience Brayton and the Quaker Itinerant Ministry," in *New Critical Studies on Early Quaker Women, 1650–1800*, ed. Michele Lise Tarter and Catie Gill (Oxford: Oxford University Press, 2018), 128–45.

68. George Fox, Epistle 291, "To All Women's Meetings, That Are Believers in the Truth," in Jones, *Power of the Lord*, 286–87.

69. Punshon, *Portrait in Grey*, 85.

70. Elizabeth Fox-Genovese and Eugene D. Genovese, *Fruits of Merchant Capital: Slavery and Bourgeois Property in the Rise and Expansion of Capitalism* (Oxford: Oxford University Press, 1983), 35; Norton, *Founding Mothers*, 404–5.

71. Chapter 1 in this volume highlights the gendered language used to describe public Friends in memorial testimonies.

72. George Fox, "Gospel Family Order" (1676), in *Quaker Testimony Against Slavery and Racial Discrimination*, ed. Stella Alexander (London: Friends Home Service Committee, n.d.), 9. See also Angell, "Gospel Family-Order."

73. David Brion Davis, *Slavery and Human Progress* (New York: Oxford University Press, 1984), 13.

74. *Journal of George Fox*, 609.

75. LYM, Epistles Sent, 1703, LSF.

76. PYM, 1719, quoted in Frost, *Quaker Origins of Antislavery*, 131; NEYM minutes (men's), 1760, NEYMA.

77. Nathaniel Philbrick, *Away Off Shore: Nantucket Island and Its People, 1602–1890* (New York: Penguin Books, 1994; repr., New York: Penguin Books, 2011), 209–10; Elizabeth Cazden, "Quakers, Slavery, Anti-Slavery, and Race," in *The Oxford Handbook of Quaker Studies*, ed. Stephen W. Angell and Pink Dandelion (Oxford: Oxford University Press, 2013), 347–62; McDaniel and Julye, *Fit for Freedom*.

78. William J. Brown, *The Life of William J. Brown of Providence, R.I.* (1883; repr., Durham: University of New Hampshire Press, 2006), 4–5, 9, 14–16.

79. Margaret Hope Bacon, "New Light on Sarah Mapps Douglass and Her Reconciliation with Friends," *Quaker History* 90, no. 1 (2001): 30–31.

CHAPTER 3

Friendly Advice
The Making and Shaping of Quaker Discipline

ANDREW FINCHAM

The collected rules and advices, which combined to form "Quaker discipline," provided guidance that both reflected and reinforced the corporate values of the Religious Society of Friends, and the books of discipline played a significant role in shaping the Society during the long eighteenth century.[1] Yet the nature of that role, and what was shaped, may have been misunderstood by early scholars, with the result that more recent work has tended to misinterpret, or at worst misrepresent, both the impact and the importance of discipline in determining the course of Quaker development on both sides of the Atlantic.

The historiography of the Religious Society of Friends accepts a hierarchical view of an organization that was established by the last quarter of the seventeenth century; similarly, the academic consensus holds that members subscribed to a uniform code of discipline, which largely originated with, and was later maintained by, the London Yearly Meeting (LYM).[2] This consensus places the LYM squarely at the center of Quakerism for the duration of the long eighteenth century, while the treatment of discipline as both homogenous and consistent has promoted a similar view of the organization and its membership across the transatlantic world.[3] Yet the first "central" discipline produced by the LYM was not agreed upon until 1737 (almost eighty years after Fox began the movement), and local variations persisted for another half century before a revised collection was first printed in London in 1783.[4] Across the Atlantic, some local Quaker communities had printed collections as early as 1704, while other yearly meetings produced disciplines periodically throughout the eighteenth century. Local differences in content are therefore to be expected in any comparison of early eighteenth-century manuscript versions of the discipline—whether in or outside London or across the Atlantic—and these differences indicate the local emphasis on certain values.[5] This suggests a picture of early Friends coexisting with differing priorities, occasionally manifested in alternative directions evident in events such as the Perrot affair, which concerned men wearing hats during prayer, or the factionalism headed by William Rogers, Thomas Curtis, John Wilkinson, John Story, and, later, George Keith (and, even later, by Sarah Dixon and Joseph Nichols, which occurred well into the eighteenth century).[6]

As the century progressed, a tighter, more central management of discipline from yearly meetings across the Society is evident, while analysis of the timing and quantity of revised advices indicates a change in emphasis toward more rigorous church government. Taken together, this development suggests that, rather than experiencing common administration of monolithic, central rules, for much of the period transatlantic Friends enjoyed differing degrees of enforcement of localized advices. These changed according to geography and over time in a practice that continued long after the first centralized advices were promulgated, and they endured in places until the latter part of the eighteenth century. This scenario prompts an analogy with the apostolic church on which Quakerism had originally modeled itself. In this model, ever more widely dispersed groups of adherents proselytized their versions of the good news, guided by the local gospels of Thomas, Mary, or Judas before the church fathers erased them in creating the canon. From the late eighteenth century, Quaker disciplines display a homogeneity that masks the extent of the different traditions within the Society, reflecting a shift in priorities: the initial toleration of diversity that was needed to preserve unity gradually eroded over the eighteenth century and was replaced by an emphasis on discipline in pursuit of purity.[7]

This chapter takes a chronological approach. First, it establishes the origins of advices for the early Friends of England and Wales, illustrated by contemporary examples from Balby Meeting (in Yorkshire Quarterly Meeting). Next, it examines examples of the contrasting nature of transatlantic disciplines, and the process by which extracts came to be controlled, developed, and reproduced. Finally, it explores patterns in the selection of extracts in order to examine the evidence that suggests a shift in emphasis from "advices for unity" toward a later conception of a "discipline of purity."

ORIGINS OF DISCIPLINE

William Braithwaite's classic two-part history of the early Religious Society of Friends identifies the first attempt to describe the general principles by which Quakerism would govern itself as the "Epistle from the meeting of Elders at Balby." Written in November 1656, the epistle was "both quickly and widely emulated."[8] The elders who assembled this guidance had lost confidence in established forms of religion following the English Civil War; they were a "serious minded people ... widely scattered around England at the time of the commonwealth," who were products of the religious travail of the age.[9] A belief that the day of the Lord was at hand "united them the more closely both to primitive Christianity and to prophetic religion."[10] In this unity, early Quakers assembled a membership group prepared to subscribe to the communitarian advices agreed to at Balby—broadly characterized by a sharing of responsibility, of suffering, and of resources (not the least of which were financial). Beyond this, as Christopher Hill noted, nascent Quakerism was "a highly individualistic religion which grew up in a millenary atmosphere and was at first organizationally influenced mainly by a desire to hinder hindrances to spiritual freedom."[11] At this formative stage, the advices were not even to be considered as binding on future Friends. Braithwaite notes a "fine warning against the invasion of tradition" in a letter from Durham Friends to the General Meeting in Kendal. Similar sets of advices appeared in the four counties meetings of 1659 (Kent, Sussex, Surrey, and Hampshire). By 1660, the practice appears to have been established where representatives from all parts of the country gathered periodically to discuss matters of church business; after 1661, London became the primary meeting place of the Religious Society of Friends.[12]

A letter from Edward Burroughs describes the "proper work and service of the Meeting" as "the well-ordering of the affairs of Truth in outward things, among the body of Friends, and that a general concord and assent may be among the ancients of them."[13] By 1669, George Fox had circulated an expanded set of advices, which appeared under the title *Canons and institutions*, probably printed by Quaker opponents, judging from the preface that condemns the "ridiculous and infamous" regime.[14] These advices avoided contentious articles of faith, emphasized unity, and concluded with a plea that Friends not "leave a hoof in Egypt" by redeeming disorderly persons who had "gone from the Truth." Quaker meetings could disown members for a multitude of errors: procedural faults, such as marrying before a priest; theological transgressions, such as following "the old rotten principles of the Ranters"; or ideological offenses, as with Perrot's preference for wearing a hat during prayer. The advices were grouped under headings: marriage; remarriage (including finances); slander; railing; cheating by borrowing; poor relief; arbitration; tithes; sufferings; children; burying grounds; and registering births, marriages, and burials. Significantly, many of these headings survived into the LYM's first formal collection of advices and continued into the revisions of 1783, 1802, and 1822.[15] Braithwaite contends that the main challenge of Fox's canons arose from "a mass of wholesome though tedious advice," to be administered by Friends who were (potentially and relatively) spiritually unenlightened.[16]

The precise form and nature of this administration were not specified in the last quarter of the seventeenth century, resulting in the delegation of judgment to the discretion of the local monthly or quarterly meetings themselves. By the 1670s, the convention had arisen that the LYM would both record the deliberations of the representatives in its minutes and issue an annual epistle to each of its quarterly and monthly meetings.[17] These epistles often provided additional advices on specific concerns of the meeting, helping identify trends in the nature of Quaker corporate thought. While the early transmission mechanisms for these epistles has not been the subject of much research, some evidence suggests that timeliness was important, with local representatives copying the epistle in situ; some even used early postal services rather than carry epistles back to their home meetings themselves.

Archive records of the "Clerk of Doncaster" contain epistles, advices, letters, and other papers from Balby Monthly Meetings for the period 1675–1760, from which some aspects of the process of formation of early discipline may be reconstructed.[18] Among the surviving documents are copies of LYM minutes, including those of 1695, which first set out the discipline in twelve numbered sections:

1. Concerning Marriages of Kindred;
2. Concerning Contracts in and to Marriage;

3. Concerning men and women Meetings;
4. ... sighing groaning & singing in ye Church;
5. Concerning our Testimony agt Tythes;
6. Concerning our open Testimony or Publick Meeting in Times of Suffering;
7. Concerning ... Testimony & Condemnation agt Disorderly Walkers;
8. Our Judgement agt Contemptible Names given agt us;
9. Concerning expounding marriages;
10. Concerning Disputes;
11. Concerning Trading;
12. Of Friends Ancient Testimony agt ye Corrupt Fashions and ye Language of the World.

Comparison of the Balby papers with those recorded in the manuscript LYM minute book shows this to be a fair copy, including signatories.

Some marginalia suggest the use of a postal service. The Balby copy of the 1697 yearly meeting advices made by Thomas Hammond is addressed on the reverse to "Thomas Aldam att Warnsworth" with the request that "the Postmaster at Doncaster is Desired to send this as above Directed, Post Paid 2d." Marginalia also suggest a desire for prompt receipt of news about what had been discussed in London: "7th of ye 5th Month 1697: Dr ffriend; I here send a coppy of ye Yearly Meeting Paper of Advices in haiste I rest thy ffriend Thos: Hammond."[19] Such haste may have arisen from extreme motives, perhaps a wish to ensure rapid conformity with new London thinking. Alternatively, and equally possible, it may represent a desire to ensure that the LYM did not encroach upon established local practices.

Further meeting records preserve evidence that diversity in discipline between monthly meetings not only persisted but was deliberately preserved. The fonds contains copies of advices created by the York Quarterly Meeting, which are not replicated in other quarterly meeting advices or in minutes from the LYM. One such local advice contains exceptionally detailed advice condemning, among other things, excessive pewter, wig wearing, hair cutting, and "the setting of fringes upon curtains, or weaving of frogg poppets, or great buttons." One might conclude that some local Friends were poor at judging which of the worldly fashions they should avoid despite the existence of a testimony of plainness.[20] This manuscript advice from the York Quarterly Meeting is specifically addressed to the

Balby Monthly Meeting, which may indicate that a "copy and send" principle was echoed down the hierarchy, with quarterly meetings seeking to impose their own discipline on subordinate meetings. Other evidence of unique quarterly meeting preoccupations appears in a note warning against a "Young Woman . . . found and proved . . . to be a very great cheat," and described as "thick shouldered, round faced, red cheeks, thick lip'd, short chin'd, eyes a darke grey, about eighteen years." This warning was to be copied to "all ye several Monthly meetings in the County."[21]

The local Balby advices were collected along with the copies of yearly meeting minutes and epistles; the papers were sewn loosely together into a book. In his short history of *The Book of Extracts*, David Hall notes that in 1680 and in 1691, the yearly meeting encouraged quarterly meeting clerks to keep yearly meeting records. The practice of keeping abstracts of such advices is indicated in regional meeting minutes with a book purchased expressly in 1701 for that purpose. As Hall concludes in his survey of early discipline, such collections must have "varied very much in content." These unwieldy lexicons of discipline contributed to a general lack of clarity, eventually prompting the yearly meeting minutes of 1727 instructing quarterly meetings to transcribe their collected advices into a "fair book."[22] Even then, the contents of these local books of advices would have been dependent not only on the efficient communication of the epistles and the industriousness of the clerk, but also on the extent of local advices. Some indication of the extent of the diversity is evident in a list of advices to be transcribed, made by the Balby clerk around 1727.[23] This list begins with George Fox's 1668 epistle 263, "Exhortation to keep to ye Ancient Principles of Truth,"[24] before itemizing a collection of nineteen advices dating from 1680 to 1724. Of these nineteen advices, nine are stated as being from the yearly meeting, nine are identified as quarterly meeting advices, and one is attributed to G. W., presumably George Whitehead. While this proportion might have differed in other meetings, such a high proportion of advices that did not originate from the yearly meeting indicates that, by the end of the first quarter of the eighteenth century (almost seventy-five years from the inception of the Religious Society of Friends), there was great potential for a wide spectrum of discipline among Quakers.

It was probably in recognition of this continued variation that the LYM resolved to create and circulate a "central" volume in manuscript form. In 1735, the LYM commissioned an "Abstract of the Written Minutes and Advices of the Yearly Meeting; from the beginning." The title provides some indication of the importance given to previous advices. The following year, the Meeting for Sufferings (MfS) did "maturely Consider and Digest and Abridge and Connect" before the final compilation was approved in 1737.[25] It is important to note that, for early Quaker historians, the act of compilation itself represented evidence that the Society was "at one." Braithwaite treats the matter briefly, believing that the use of extracts from epistles demonstrated the "united judgment of the Church." Rufus Jones, in turn, cites Braithwaite, while making the mysterious claim that eighteenth-century Quaker elders and overseers "had no absolute rules to guide them, but there slowly accumulated . . . a body of Advices and Queries."[26] His statement that the book of discipline was "a thing of almost unconscious growth" and that "no individual or even committee 'made' it" was refuted by David Hall's history, as noted above.

This first centralized selection provided almost five hundred entries under fifty-two headings.[27] These headings bear a strong similarity to those in Fox's "Ancient Principles,"[28] including plainness, vanity, marriage, oaths, defamation, arbitration, children, servants, poor relief, tithes, and love and unity. Such continuity probably arises from the wide circulation of the "Principles" and suggests that the committee perceived Fox's document to be of continued importance in representing a core set of values across quarterly meetings. The actual extracts selected by the committee, and ultimately approved by the central Meeting for Sufferings, have been somewhat neglected. It is worth noting that, while keeping Fox's headings, very few extracts were from his lifetime, or even his century. Once approved by the MfS, the advices were laboriously copied and dispatched to all quarterly meetings at a cost of fifty shillings.[29] The decision to circulate the advices in manuscript form, instead of in print form, certainly restricted circulation; perhaps this decision sought to reduce the risk of attack from those opposed to the Society, as had happened with the "Canons." While this seems possible, other Friends' rules (such as those on removals and settlements) were printed in the same year as the manuscript discipline. It seems likely that these removal "Rules" (as they were titled) required wide circulation across the Society, whereas access to the discipline itself was restricted. Some evidence for this position can be found in a 1747 letter from William Cookworthy to an elder requesting confirmation on the length of time allowed for appeals. Cookworthy indicated that, despite being a minister, he had no direct access to the discipline. His grandson and biographer records how, some decades later, his father surreptitiously contrived access to a book of

FRIENDLY ADVICE

advices and spent many hours transcribing items of importance. "Copies having been multiplied from my father's copy," Cookworthy's grandson concluded, "Dr. Fothergill and other rulers of the day deemed it most prudent to issue an authentic print of such Minutes of the Yearly Meeting, as were fittest for general use. Such was the origin of The Book of Extracts."[30]

Even allowing for an element of veracity in this family legend, limiting copies of the first centralized discipline to one per quarterly meeting ensured that both the advices and their interpretation remained strictly the province of those weighty Friends selected for regional administration.[31] However, other copies certainly were made; a manuscript copy exists of this 1738 book of extracts, lacking the name of a quarterly meeting on the title page; it contains manuscript additions of advices until 1771.[32] Considering the cost of transcribing such a volume, it is interesting to speculate on who might have done so. Moreover, one wonders when and how this was accomplished. Perhaps its purpose was private access, presumably for one of the wealthier Quaker families. There is no doubt that quarterly meetings expected to supplement their volumes with both new and revised advice as they received it in annual LYM epistles. Examination of several surviving hand-copied volumes shows that all retain blank pages between sections, providing room for expansion; other sections contain insertions of subsequent advices. This confirms that quarterly meetings did not perceive the discipline as static, while they accepted centrally coordinated updates to minimize divergence. Contrast this position with the printed 1737 regulations on removals and settlements, which remained unchanged until 1761.[33]

TRANSATLANTIC ADVICES

As early as 1689, a simple "Paper of Discipline" was printed in Philadelphia, in order that Friends might "continue in practice those useful Instructions and that good Order established among us in our Native Land."[34] This ambition for continuity needs to be considered in light of the diversity of local discipline discussed above; once we allow for a tradition of regionalized discipline across the LYM, it may be less surprising to find similar variations prevailing across the Atlantic. In 1935, Rayner Kelsey outlined the development of Philadelphia disciplines; more recently, Edwin Bronner has produced a review of the relationship between the early disciplines of transatlantic Friends, helpfully charting the various routes toward a multiplicity of yearly meetings. Yet his approach remains founded on the Braithwaite-Jones assumption that all Friends' experiences of discipline would have been the same, regardless of their origin. For instance, consider Bronner's statement that Friends "took it for granted that a new member of the community would live by the strict puritanical code of the day."[35] Setting aside the "puritan" label,[36] consider both the wide spectrum of values represented within such codes and the motivations of immigrants who had crossed the Atlantic largely to escape external proscription. Rather, it appears that Friends took it for granted that new members would adapt to abide by the code of *their particular* community—particularly reinforced in the case of Quakers owing to their habit of group collocation.[37]

Transatlantic Quakers rapidly established multiple local mechanisms for administration: Salem, Massachusetts (1676), Burlington, Vermont (around 1677), Chester, Pennsylvania (1681), and more, as well as collective "General" meetings.[38] Fourteen monthly meetings are recorded in the colonies by 1685, when the first Yearly Meeting of Ministers and Elders was created; by 1720 this had increased to twenty monthly meetings that oversaw some sixty-five local preparative meetings. Thus by the turn of the eighteenth century, the potential for divergence already noted within the membership of the LYM was also present in North America. The separatist threat posed by the Keithian controversy of the 1690s may have hastened some Friends' desire to establish a definitive local discipline. In 1703, Delaware Friends presented a manuscript compilation of minutes that was adopted as a book of discipline for "All Quarterly and Monthly Meetings in East-Jersy, West-Jersy and Pensilvania" by the Yearly Meeting at Burlington in 1704,[39] with the aim that "all may walk by the same rule and mind the same thing."[40] Kelsey noted that some 80 percent of this discipline's content addressed testimonies on behavior, describing the administration of order, regulation of meetings, supervision, and dealing with disorderly walkers. Weighty Friends were "patiently & Meekly to Instruct and advise" transgressors; if their instruction or advice were rejected, they would "acquaint the next MM ... that farther Care may be taken ... with such according to the Established Rule amongst Friends."[41]

This manuscript compilation of the discipline endured for a decade and a half until local quarterly meetings pushed for a revision, resulting in the Pennsylvania Discipline of 1719, which made many changes. The 1719 document introduced sections on arbitration and slavery (against *trading* Indigenous slaves and against *importing*—but not *owning*—black slaves).

Simultaneously, overseers got a new heading to "Advise, Admonish or Deal," and a section was added on "dealing with offenders, including the steps leading to disownment." Indications such as these point to the origins of trends that mark the transition from a controlled (not to say Foxian) unity toward a more disciplined, quietist purity. The 1719 Discipline remained in force for members of the Philadelphia Yearly Meeting (PYM) until the edition of 1762, although there were regular (mostly annual) additions.

LONDON AND PENNSYLVANIA DISCIPLINES: A COMPARISON

Pending a detailed examination of the extant original advices of all transatlantic yearly meetings, it is unclear to what extent the impression of homogeneity arising from the later nineteenth-century texts gives an accurate or entirely false impression of earlier discipline.[42] However, it is possible to compare in detail the contents of two contemporary manuscript disciplines: one issued under the LYM and another described on the title page as Pennsylvania and New Jersey (PYM), both of which were updated with new advices for a large part of the eighteenth century.[43] Is it possible that the absence of such a comparison by historians thus far is evidence of the assumption of the homogeneity of disciplines? Superficial comparisons of the content pages suggest a more or less uniform approach to the structure, with headings similar in scope, if not always wording. However, a more detailed comparison of these books of discipline demonstrates that there was wide deviation in both the structure and the content of advices. A summary comparison is shown in table 3.1.

The headings of the 1738 LYM volume remained substantially unchanged in the printed revision that followed half a century later, suggesting that the scope of the concerns of that meeting remained fairly static. It is immediately clear that while many headings are shared, many are also unique to one discipline or the other. Numerically, the number of London advices is significantly larger (485 against 378). Of much greater significance is the diversity of content found on more detailed comparison. The 1771 copy of the PYM discipline reviewed here has almost no advices in common with the volume from LYM for the same period: to adapt an axiom of Anglo-American communication, here are two disciplines separated by an apparently common structure. The LYM selection rigorously removes earlier, overlapping advices so as to avoid duplication, with a view to producing

TABLE 3.1 Comparison of books of discipline, London and Pennsylvania and New Jersey

London	Heading	PA & NJ	London	Heading	PA & NJ
6	**Appeals**	3	23	**Meetings for Worship**	19
	Acknowledgements for Offences	4	8	**Ministers and Elders, and their Meetings**	16
	Affirmation	1	3	**Mourning Habits**	1
12	**Arbitration**	2	7	**National Stock**	4
19	**Books**	3	2	**Oaths**	10
	Burials	6	2	**Overseers**	4
	Charity and Unity	5	1	**Parents, Guardians, and Education**	
7	**Certificates**	10	16	**Plainness**	14
27	**Children**	19	17	**Poor**	13
13	**Conversation**	25		*Priests Wages*	2
18	**Correspondents**	1	16	**Preparative Meetings**	
6	Covetousness		12	**Quarterly Meetings**	
6	**Days and Times**	2	14	**Queries**	5
2	Defamation (and detraction)		15	Records	
25	**Discipline, and Meetings for Discipline**	30	1	**Removals and Settlements**	1
3	Disputes		4	**Schools**	7
	Diversions	4	15	**Scriptures**	5
10	Epistles			*Sorcery*	1
8	**Families**	23	1	**Slave-Trade and Slavery**	21
	Gaming	1	14	**Sufferings**	6
	Gravestones	10		*Talebearing and Backbiting*	5
	Government	11		*Taverns*	3
	Indians	4		*Tax*	1
8	Fighting		5	Tithes	
21	Kings and Governours		24	**Trade**	14
3	**Law**	4	20	**War**	9
6	Love		10	**Wills, Executors, and Administrators**	2
27	**Marriage**	31	25	**Yearly Meeting**	16
3	*Masters, Mistresses, and Servants*				
			485	TOTAL	378

Note: Nonitalic headings are unique to LYM; italic headings are unique to PYM; bold headings are common to both disciplines. Number of advices is given for each heading.

FRIENDLY ADVICE

a codified set of rules that are both detailed and unambiguous. New advices are often couched in legalistic terms. The importance of this historical approach is borne out by a sample of the distribution of dates of the advices: 25 percent originated before 1700, 33 percent originated between 1700 and 1725, with another 33 percent between 1725 and 1750, and the remaining 9 percent appeared between 1750 and 1772.[44] The PYM, by contrast, took only 6 percent of advices from before 1700; 38 percent originated between 1700 and 1725, 33 percent appeared between 1725 and 1750, and 23 percent were added between 1750 and the last addition of 1771. This clearly weights the PYM discipline toward contemporary concerns, despite the PYM's having yearly meeting records to draw upon from 1681.[45]

The single most surprising finding is that these headings have no advices in common; the contents are unique to each volume, presumably as a result of local autonomy, along with emphasis of concern in each location. A few examples are illustrative. First, consider the core Friends' testimony of "peace." A Friend seeking advice from the LYM might be guided by any of the five pages on fighting, with minutes cited from 1693 onward against bearing arms, ships carrying guns, serving in the militia, privateering, letters of marque, hiring substitutes in the militia, the confutation of poor tax and militia tax, the consequences of evading the same, and what should be done to those who had not followed these advices.[46] A colonial Friend might be offered one of the nine advices on war, or perhaps "Indians," with guidance from a 1759 note concerning the piety of living in peace, or a second gently worded 1761 advice on "the way to peace being through peace," the latter making one of very few direct references to London's Meeting for Sufferings.[47] Such divergence under a common testimony shows the powerful and persistent nature of the differences between disciplines among Atlantic Friends throughout the seventeenth and eighteenth centuries. Sarah Crabtree's work illustrates the confusion that the subject causes some historians. She states that "the Society's position of nonviolence was unambiguous," and that there was "no explicit doctrine or discipline to guide Friends."[48] On the contrary, there was an abundance of local advice, which, while potentially ambiguous for the Society, allowed local guidance to shape local practice.

The sections on government also offer an interesting comparison. One might suppose that the two sections would address similar issues. Not so. Instead, the LYM largely emphasizes the need to walk humbly while not defrauding state dues and taxes; the PYM, by contrast, addresses issues of magistracy, the need to suppress swearing and drunkenness and to avoid compelling Friends to behave contrary to testimonies. Similarly, under the heading "Conversation," London reaches back to the "Testimony of Truth begat in the beginning" to avoid, among other things, "concupiscence [lust]," pastimes, sports, vain company, fashions, and "declension." Colonial Friends used twice as many advices to proscribe pastimes and places, warning against engaging in drams, tippling, and sipping strong drink, whether in families or at funerals, inns, or "vendues."[49] London had a single advice on avoiding oaths, while their colonial counterparts mustered a dozen; the critical LYM testimony against tithes does not require mention on the western side of the Atlantic.[50]

Beyond this absence of direct correlation, the advices themselves are generally of a different character. The PYM advices appear somewhat parochial in style and content: many are, even by the standards of the day, trivial, referring to requests from quarterly meetings for the resolution of queries; some simply record local advices, as in the 1735 Chester Meeting ban on lotteries.[51] Among the thirty-one advices on marriage, almost half are concerned with a decade-long exchange of views on the merits of a man's marrying a deceased wife's first cousin. Many of the remaining advices are heavily repetitious. The virtues of visiting make up almost a dozen advices in the section on families. The avoidance of tippling, drams, or other spirituous liquors was clearly a significant concern, appearing dozens of times, under headings as diverse as marriage, mourning, trading, and conduct. A good many advices are simply duplicated as "the advice of [XXXX] year repeated."

Interestingly, the content of both disciplines expanded substantially over the second half of the century, with advices more than doubling the size of the PYM volume, while the LYM's increased by slightly less. This may prompt further reflection among historians who have tended to regard the publication dates of subsequent editions of the *Book of Extracts* as points of change in an otherwise static regime. The mechanisms for such aggregation were ultimately similar on both sides of the Atlantic. Annual epistles from yearly meetings to quarterly meetings provided a source from which extracts were used by "Weighty Friends" to augment their more or less closely guarded local disciplines. With respect to the LYM volume, the nature of the changes during the period from 1738 until the revision of the first printed *Book of Discipline* in London in 1783 is suggestive. Headings with a substantial increase in advices include appeals (50 percent), certificates (75 percent), discipline (79 percent), marriage (59 percent), and meetings for discipline (52 percent). The last three alone amassed thirty-eight new advices during the period. In contrast, books, children, conversation, correspondents, covetousness, days and times, defamation, disputes, epistles, families, law, love, kings and governors, and meetinghouses together totaled less than twenty new extracts.[52] The extent and focus of additions seem to provide evidence of the changing priorities of the LYM, with its steady emphasis on recording and administering the mechanisms of discipline.

In this context it should be observed that yearly meetings employed a secondary mechanism—the queries—to monitor the health of the Society. The queries served an important administrative function for yearly meetings across the century. Their exact nature (and evolution) is beyond the scope of this chapter, but a useful, if brief, chronology of LYM queries and advices by Richard Stagg illustrates, chronologically, how the yearly meeting sought to obtain ever wider written evidence that subsidiary meetings were indeed acting in accordance with key "advices."[53] In 1694, six queries were established. Three asked about prisoners (how many, how many discharged, and how many died). Three other queries asked if any public Friends (ministers or elders) had died, how many meetinghouses were built, and how "Truth" and "Unity" prospered. This last query was extended in 1700 to inquire about the raising of godly children.[54] Crucially, a seventh query was added in 1703 that required information on the implementation of yearly meeting advices.[55] In 1753, the LYM revised this query to demand: "How are the Several Advices of this Yearly Meeting made known and put in Practice?" And by 1755, the yearly meeting increased the burden of reporting by adding eight quarterly meeting queries to be asked of monthly meetings on a quarterly basis.[56]

The queries and their development indicate a desire by yearly meetings to achieve uniform administration of both their Society and its subordinate meetings. Meanwhile, in 1774, Cookworthy's "rulers" at Durham Monthly Meeting insisted that postal and copying errors had once again resulted in some divergence from the desired uniformity of disciplines and suggested that a new edition be created.[57] Perhaps they were responding to the appearance in print of John Fry's private publication *Alphabetical Extract of All the Annual Printed Epistles*, which appeared in 1762.[58] A wide circulation of a volume like Fry's would have run contrary to the imposition of central authority in the yearly meeting,[59] and the LYM responded with a new selection of extracts, the final discipline under examination here.

TOWARD AN ORTHODOXY: THE LYM REVISION OF 1783

With the printed selection of 1783, the LYM at last produced a discipline that was widely available, being offered for sale not only to monthly meetings but possibly also to individuals.[60] Significantly, this first edition not only contained blank sheets between advice headings, but the printed "Advertisement" expressly states that "no other additions are to be made"—a proscription suggesting a divergence from established practice.[61] Hall states that, at the request of the yearly meeting, two Friends selected the extracts that were included. The LYM and the MfS approved the final selection. Hall believed that, despite approximately one hundred deletions and one hundred additions, "in substance the revision was not [as] important as this may suggest."

A more detailed breakdown challenges that view, suggesting that the 1783 revisions can be seen as a further shift in the center of gravity of the Society of Friends toward an ever more centralized, inflexible set of rules designed to promote uniformity in practice under the guise of purity. The evidence comes from an analysis of the continuity of advices across editions (see fig. 3.1, "Origin and distribution of LYM Advices, 1737–1802"). Two main trends may be discerned: first, there are numerically more additions and changes in those headings that involve organization, suggesting an ever increasing focus on administration. The six headings, which cover more than fifteen advices—following revision, removal of duplicate advices, and rationalization—are Ministers and Elders, and Their Meetings; Tithes; Discipline, and Meetings for Discipline; Yearly Meeting; Meetings for Worship; and Marriage. One might assume that this complex regulation would be unnecessary in a sect with a testimony on simplicity. Tithe advice could have been expressed as "never pay under any circumstances." Yet it seems that Friends had established various methods of getting around this simple rule, necessitating twenty-two advices. Half of these were issued after the previous discipline, which suggests that Friends were not following the rules as they had been set out. Similarly, marriage advice did not appear as a simple ban on exogamy but was outlined in an elaborate set of regulations,

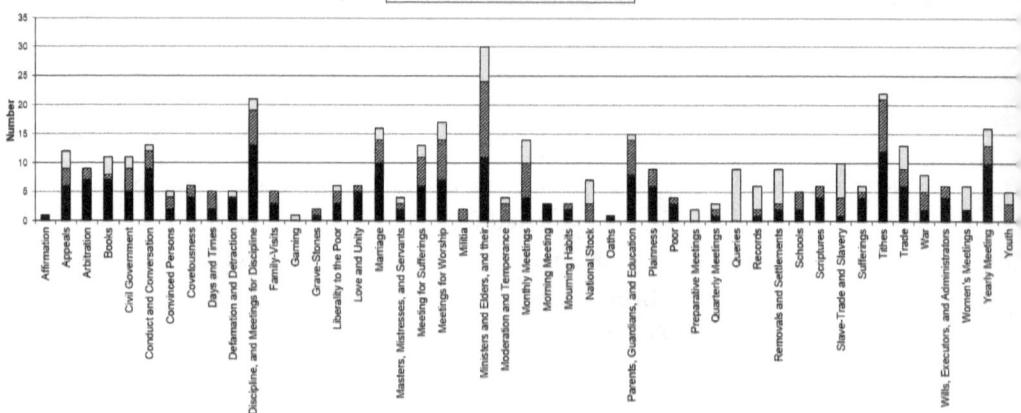

FIG. 3.1 Origin and distribution of London Yearly Meeting Advices, 1737–1802

including closeness of kin on remarriage, proper periods of mourning, widows' provision, education, and a dozen other administrative issues. It is important to note that in all of these major areas of concern, more than one-third of the advices were changed in the new edition. This seems to confirm that the leadership in the MfS saw a need to adapt as well as to update and increase the weight of advice.

The pace of change in the pursuit of a "purer" discipline appears also to have increased toward the end of the century, as new regulations that appeared in the decade following printing rapidly rendered the *Extracts* imperfect. This prompted the LYM and MfS to collect material for an appendix that was printed in 1792. Further rules and advices followed, and in 1800 the LYM recommended that all quarterly meetings send deputies to an extended MfS, where, for three weeks, November 7–29, 1800, extracts were reordered for sense, removed for duplication, replaced when "superior pertinency" was found, and subjected to "considerable abridgement." All of this was to reflect "full and free conference respecting the general operation of existing regulations." The MfS added "a set of pretty copious marginal, and other references" to aid comprehension and interpretation.[62] In between these formal revisions, key themes were emphasized by the yearly advices. The printed *Extracts* were subsequently revised three times in the first decades of the nineteenth century (in 1801, 1822, and 1833, the last published under the title *Rules of Discipline*). The trajectory of the London discipline landed the Society in the nineteenth century with an ever more perfect set of rules for administration. While outside the scope of this chapter, it is worth noting that the revision of 1822 contained an entirely new section on removals that runs to fifteen pages and completely superseded the earlier advices 1–7. In contrast, "Slavery" gained two pages and "Tithes" no more than a modest paragraph.[63]

FROM UNITY TO PURITY

Having surveyed the case for the prevalence and persistence of multiple disciplines within transatlantic Quakerism, what can be concluded? Any conclusions must account for the beliefs of the members themselves. It seems safe to say that seventeenth-century Friends believed they shared a common discipline, and that they passed this belief on to their descendants. These beliefs developed locally from shared values. They were shaped by communitarian advices from yearly meetings, by weighty Friends in the traveling ministry, and by the hierarchy of local supervisory meetings. It seems that the last may have had the most influence in forming the advices. Even so, regional differences do not appear to have dominated the lives of Friends. Indeed, it seems likely that these literally loosely bound rules were not commonly accessed by the majority of Friends in any local meeting. Moreover, the imposition of discipline would be expressed in a visit from experienced Friends eager to offer reformatory advice, rather than through the waving of any rulebook. The common goal of the original disciplines was to preserve unity, keeping the flock within the fold in order to increase the spread of George Fox's "Gospel Order." Differences of interpretation, or of regulation, were largely irrelevant in a movement that wished to see the world converted to Truth.

Fox and others in the earliest period saw the Religious Society of Friends as an institution in which Quakers were united. Certainly, at the heart of all early advices created by the Quakers is the common desire for the preservation of "Unity." This was key to the initial millenarian perspective of Friends who saw in their worship the path to a new world in which all would be convinced. During this earlier time, advices centered on drawing the disorderly back into the fold, "carried on their backs" if need be.[64] Disownment was neither desired nor necessarily permanent, as long as the transgressor showed appropriate contrition.[65]

Local traditions of autonomy in rule making accompanied Friends who migrated across the Atlantic. These Friends created volumes of local discipline without reference to the LYM. Regional differences in discipline persisted from the first days of the Quakers until at least the middle of the eighteenth century, a period of more than seventy-five years. Differences in discipline mattered little, as long as the administrative locus for resolving such differences remained local. Early advice on procedure defines a multistage process aimed at reconciliation: the errant Friend was first spoken with, then exhorted, then admonished, and finally testified against, before being disowned as a last resort. The transgressor remained part of the local meeting and the Society until all steps in the process were exhausted.[66] Local authority was evidently prized, as is indicated by the disputes process over which the MfS later sought control. Differences in local disciplines are illustrated by the central advices offered on controversial issues. These included matters as important as paying (or not paying) tithes, the levy for traveling ministers, trading or not in prize goods or contraband, and, not least, oaths versus affirmations. Equally, the yearly meetings determined that they would manage the minutiae, creating rules to prevent marrying the cousin of a dead spouse, or women's attending funerals dressed in mourning clothes, or serving funeral drink after set times, or cheese ever.[67]

It appears that members of the Society, enjoying local regulation in the natural way, were no less prone to error than nonmembers. Yet the imposition of centralized rule appears to have been a somewhat surreptitious process. As a contemporary foreigner observed in 1748, "Their Rules and Church Ordinances, according to which they are regulated, ... they hold as a *chose sainte*, that only the principal among them have in manuscript, but which are never allowed, with their knowledge, to be seen by anyone else."[68] Reformer Anthony Benezet is noted as possessing the 1719 Discipline of the PYM in his library, but not the subsequent edition, which was in force for the last thirty years of his life.[69] The small number of manuscript copies made in 1738 for quarterly meetings, and the guarded nature of those copies, as suggested by Cookworthy's biography, suggests a nervousness in seeking Society-wide approbation.[70] No such qualms existed by the end of the century. An advice of 1798 admonishes the monthly meetings for "remissness in dealing, and weakness ... in accepting superficial and insincere acknowledgements," citing laxity of discipline as the cause of declining standards "inconsistent with our religious profession."[71] The printed "Discipline" from Philadelphia in 1797 includes similar advices against "lukewarmness," urging visitation if there is "occasion to suspect" that Friends are so declining as to bring reproach (advice of 1724, repeated in 1734 and 1746).[72] Significantly, the "Advertisement" for this edition explains that the origin of each advice is indicated: those from London (marked "E.D." for English discipline) are all but absent.[73]

Bronner makes an interesting observation with respect to the establishment of the yearly meetings discussed above: the Philadelphia Yearly Meeting, which included Pennsylvania and New Jersey, was from its origins an annual meeting for worship. The LYM, by contrast, was the permanent hub of a centralized, self-funded administration.[74] London's control of the hierarchical meetings was fundamentally an extension of the work originally performed by the MfS in coordinating assistance for imprisoned Friends. As a single, London-based body interacting with regional meetings throughout the year, the MfS first centralized, and later extended, the central role from the provision of advice into disciplinary procedures.[75] This offers an intriguing explanation of some of the differences that grew between the London discipline and that of the colonies: the national sufferings of the seventeenth-century Quakers under the LYM were made the concern of a specific meeting of the Society. This seems to have acted as a spur toward central administration; it may be that without this catalyst, the centralization process among colonial Friends would not only have taken longer but would have been less intensive and less effective.

This is not to say that all Quaker disciplines were always different, or that local interpretations were never the same. Rather, this chapter suggests that transatlantic disciplines could—and did—vary to a sufficient degree, to the extent that, during the second half of the eighteenth century, and certainly before the century's final quarter, the transatlantic leadership concluded that the interests of the Society demanded the imposition of a more homogenous ("purer") set of central rules.[76] These leaders approved a collection of advices selected by a small and tightly controlled subcommittee; these were then distributed with an increasing focus on the adherence of membership, as exemplified by new advices and queries. All of this was an attempt to concentrate authority in the hands of that leadership. This purification process came to dominate the Society, which had previously tolerated a much wider spectrum of behaviors in pursuit of expanding the number of faithful. Only after the visions of King Jesus had completely faded did subsequent generations of Friends begin to regard their discipline as an important mechanism for maintaining the "hedge" that preserved the peculiar people from worldliness. In so doing, Quakers began a quest for centrally imposed purity that was a hallmark of the period known as quietism.[77] This quest endured to the end of the long eighteenth century, before new leadership sought to return the Society once more "from the disciplinary to the devotional."[78]

NOTES

1. The names by which the Society of Friends referred to its books of collected advice varied by time and place. Titles include books of extracts, books of advices, and books of discipline. This diversity is significant, as is the use here of the plural "books" of discipline: it refers equally to the diverse nature of local meeting books and to the evolving central disciplines that would present successive editions of collected advices from various yearly meetings during the period. The concept of a "book of discipline" continues within the Society of Friends: the 1994 rulebook of the Britain Yearly Meeting is titled *Quaker Faith and Practice*, but it carries the subtitle *The Book of Christian Discipline of the Yearly Meeting of the Society of Friends (Quakers) in Britain*.

2. Superficial comparisons of disciplines reveal similar structures, and even common tables of contents, which could lead a hasty observer to overestimate homogeneity.

3. For recent examples of this view, see Jordan Landes, *London Quakers in the Trans-Atlantic World: The Creation of an Early Modern Community* (London: Palgrave Macmillan, 2015); Frederick B. Tolles, *Meeting House and Counting House: The Quaker Merchants of Colonial Philadelphia, 1682–1763*, 2nd ed. (Chapel Hill: University of North Carolina Press, 2012); and James Walvin, *The Quakers: Money and Morals* (London: John Murray, 1997).

4. LYM, *Extracts from the Minutes and Advices of the Yearly Meeting of Friends Held in London from Its First Institution*, 2nd ed. (London: W. Phillips, 1802). Unless otherwise noted, all references to the *Extracts* are to this edition. David Hall's conclusion—that the changes for the printed edition were "in substance" not important although one-quarter of the advices were deleted and more than a quarter added—is questioned below.

5. Further evidence for local emphasis is found in records of local sufferings: the treatment of, for example, the tithe testimony or customs and excise, as recorded in the *Books of Sufferings*.

6. For information on the controversies of the second period, see Rosemary Moore, "Gospel Order: The Development of Quaker Organization," in *The Quakers, 1656–1723: The Evolution of an Alternative Community*, ed. Richard C. Allen and Rosemary Moore (University Park: Penn State University Press, 2018), 54–75. William C. Braithwaite, in *The Second Period of Quakerism* (London: Macmillan, 1919), notes the Frenchay separation of Dixon and her "disciples and accomplices" as late as 1718 (480). For Nichols, see Kenneth L. Carroll, "The Nicholites Become Quakers: An Example of Unity in Disunion," *Bulletin of Friends Historical Association* 47, no. 1 (1958): 3–19.

7. The discipline of the LYM was first aligned in 1737, before it again diverged, to be restated in the printed edition; other yearly meetings followed a similar course. A printed PYM edition is noted from 1797, while as late as 1835 an unauthorized edition of the

Philadelphia Discipline was also printed. See *The Old Discipline: Nineteenth-Century Friends' Disciplines in America* (Glenside, PA: Quaker Heritage Press, 1999), 1.

8. William C. Braithwaite, *The Beginnings of Quakerism* (London: Macmillan, 1912), 329 (attributed to Anthony Pearson). See also Braithwaite, *Second Period of Quakerism*; Thomas D. Hamm, ed., *Quaker Writings: An Anthology, 1650–1920* (New York: Penguin, 2010), 64–68.

9. Rufus M. Jones, introduction to *The Journal of George Fox*, ed. Rufus M. Jones (London: J. M. Dent and Sons, 1924), 8.

10. Braithwaite, *Second Period of Quakerism*, 249.

11. Christopher Hill, *The World Turned Upside Down* (London: Penguin Books, 1991), 116. Hill neglects the powerful financial motivation behind the strong anticlerical levy and, equally important, anti-tithe sentiment among early Friends.

12. Braithwaite, *Beginnings of Quakerism*, 314–16, 333, 337.

13. Ibid., 340. The role of these "ancients" is discussed below.

14. George Fox, *Canons and institutions drawn up and agreed upon by the General Assembly or Meeting of the heads of the Quakers from all parts of the kingdom at their New-Theatre in Grace-church-street in or about January 1668/9; George Fox being their president* (London, 1669).

15. Similarities to the headings later used in the disciplines of transatlantic Friends are more limited.

16. Braithwaite, *Second Period of Quakerism*, 259.

17. The epistles are designated in the *Extracts* as written or printed. Both appear throughout the period. The earliest advice extracted from a printed epistle noted is marriage (1690), the latest 1799 (convinced persons). Written epistles date from 1675 (conduct and conversation) to 1799 (meeting for discipline).

18. TMP MSS 298 (1693–1760), folders 2/1, 2/2, 2/3, LSF.

19. Copy of yearly meeting advices, 1697, TMP MSS 298, LSF.

20. See advice on plainness (6 and 7 Second Month 1698), ibid.

21. Undated loose single manuscript sheet, folder 2/2, ibid.

22. David J. Hall, "Christian and Brotherly Advices," *Friends' Quarterly* (July 1981): 506–7. Requests for a "fair book" came from Leeds (1711) and Yorkshire Quarterly (1723).

23. TMP MSS 298, LSF, undated folio (but after 1724); this list may be in response to the yearly meeting minutes of 1727 (above) regarding "fair" copies.

24. George Fox, *A collection of many select and Christian epistles, letters and testimonies, written on sundry occasions, by that ancient, eminent, faithful Friend and minister of Christ Jesus, George Fox*, ed. Marcus T. C. Gould, vol. 1 (Philadelphia: Marcus T. C. Gould, 1831), 328.

25. LYM Minutes (1736), 8:187, LSF; Hall, "Christian and Brotherly Advices," 507.

26. Braithwaite, *Second Period of Quakerism*, 377; Rufus M. Jones, *The Later Periods of Quakerism*, 2 vols. (London: Macmillan, 1921), 1:142, 132.

27. Based on a review of the Peel Quarterly Meeting Manuscript Book of Discipline (1737), MGR11b5/MISC3, LSF.

28. Fox, Epistle 263, LSF.

29. LYM Minutes (1738), 8:396, LSF; Hall, "Christian and Brotherly Advices," 514. The price reflects approximately two or three weeks' effort for a copyist, with materials.

30. George Harrison, *Memoir of William Cookworthy* (London: William and Frederick Cash, 1854), 38–40.

31. The epithet "ruler" evidences a perceived hierarchy, albeit retrospectively.

32. MS copy of the 1738 book of extracts, presented by J. H. Lloyd to Woodbrooke, Quaker Cupboard 2, no. 13282, WQSCL. It is not known who copied this or when (it was donated in 1938), but the donor suggests a possible connection with the Birmingham Quaker family.

33. Blank pages could have been included in a printed edition, as they were in the James Phillips edition of 1783; of course, it may be that the advices on removals remained static *precisely because* they had been widely circulated.

34. This single-sheet printed paper of advices is reproduced in Rayner W. Kelsey, "Early Books of Discipline of Philadelphia Meeting," *Bulletin of Friends Historical Association* 24, no. 1 (1935): 16–17.

35. Edwin B. Bronner, "Quaker Discipline and Order, 1680–1720: Philadelphia Yearly Meeting and London Yearly Meeting," in *The World of William Penn*, ed. Richard S. Dunn and Mary Maples Dunn (Philadelphia: University of Pennsylvania Press, 1986), 323–35 (quotation on 324).

36. Melvin B. Endy, "Puritanism, Spiritualism, and Quakerism: An Historiographical Essay," in Dunn and Dunn, *World of William Penn*, 281–301. Endy rejects the "Puritan" Quaker, concluding bluntly, "If Quakers were Puritan in the proper sense, then I'm a monkey's uncle" (297).

37. A trait emulated solely by the Moravians, according to J. Hector St. John de Crèvecoeur, *Letters from an American Farmer* (London: Thomas Davis, 1782).

38. Bronner, "Quaker Discipline and Order," 334. Bronner refers to "Advices from the General [i.e., not Yearly] Meeting" at Burlington from September 1682 (325).

39. Kelsey, "Early Books of Discipline," 12–13. Keith had by this time led away most of his separatists. See Ned Landsman, "William Penn's Scottish Counterparts: The Quakers of 'North Britain' and the Colonization of East New Jersey," in Dunn and Dunn, *World of William Penn*, 241–57.

40. Bronner, "Quaker Discipline and Order," 329.

41. Tim Hayburn, "Words to Live by: Society of Friends Books of Discipline, 1704–1747," *Pennsylvania History: A Journal of Mid-Atlantic Studies* 72, no. 3 (2005): 369–85. Extracted from the 1719 Book of Discipline, Magill Library, HCLQSC; compare with Luke 6:31.

42. See *Old Discipline*.

43. These are the "Peel" Discipline, MGR11b5/MISC3, from the LYM, and the Pennsylvania Discipline, MS vol. 50 (PYM), LSF. Both were in use from 1738 to 1771, the latter from 1719.

44. Sample of the first 260 advices in LYM; sample of the first 187 advices in PYM.

45. Bronner notes that the PYM claimed its foundation from this date. "Quaker Discipline and Order," 325.

46. LYM, MGR11b5/MISC3, "Peel," 24–28, LSF.

47. PYM, Discipline, 85–86; note that this is *not* a reference to LYM advices or discipline; such detailed awareness of the views of the Meeting for Sufferings might imply that the PYM was similarly aware of LYM advices, thus raising the question as to why the PYM was familiar with them.

48. Sarah Crabtree, *Holy Nation: The Transatlantic Quaker Ministry in an Age of Revolution* (Chicago: University of Chicago Press, 2015), 114.

49. LYM, MGR11b5/MISC3, 59–66, LSF. Interestingly, the LYM contains only one advice on "strong liquour": that those who deal therein observe the laws of the land (1738).

50. The later LYM *Extracts* (1783) refer to the New England Quakers' victory over "Steeplehouse rates" (1733).

51. PYM, Discipline, 75; see also 95 for advice against Chester's going to law in 1751.

52. All numbers are from analysis of LYM, MGR11b5/MISC3, LSF. The numbers do not always agree with those given by David Hall. Unfortunately, Hall does not identify which book of extracts he consulted, beyond its location in the Library of the Society of Friends.

53. Richard E. Stagg, "Friends Queries and General Advices," *Journal of the Friends' Historical Society* 49 (1959): 209–35.

54. A query regarding the "signal judgment that had fallen upon persecutors" was also used between 1696 and 1707. See Hall, "Christian and Brotherly Advices," 511.

55. Later queries monitored poor relief (1720), tithes (1721), taxes (1723), education (1735), and prosecutions (1737).

56. See Stagg, "Friends Queries and General Advices," 213–17.

57. Hall, "Christian and Brotherly Advices," 512.

58. John Fry, *An Alphabetical Extract of all the Annual Printed Epistles Which Have been Sent to the Several Quarterly-Meetings of the People call'd Quakers, in England and elsewhere, from their Yearly-Meeting held in London [...] from the Year 1682 to 1762 [...]* (London, 1762).

59. I have seen a copy with the inscription "John Elliott, Philadelphia 1765" on the flyleaf, which indicates international distribution.

60. Stagg, "Friends Queries and General Advices," 219. See also Jones, *Later Periods of Quakerism*, 1:143. This 1783 edition, titled *Extracts from the Minutes and Advices of the Yearly Meeting of Friends Held in London from Its First Institution* (London: J. Phillips, 1783), is better known as the *Book of Extracts*. It is not clear whether nonmembers could also purchase the book.

61. LYM, *Extracts from the Minutes and Advices*. A copy at Woodbrooke contains no such additions (uncatalogued, QC2 collection).

62. Ibid., introduction.

63. LYM, *Extracts from the Minutes and Advices of the Yearly Meeting of Friends Held in London, Supplement to the Second Edition* (London: W. Phillips, 1822).

64. The "Canons" conclude with a plea from Fox not to "leave a hoof in Egypt," a reference to the biblical Exodus.

65. See William Beck and T. Frederick Ball, *The London Friends' Meetings* (London: F. Bowyer Kitto, 1869; repr., London: Pronoun Press, 2009), 85–109. Friends disowned, or under threat of disownment, could expect to return to unity after issuing a self-condemning paper of contrition. This practice continued throughout the eighteenth century.

66. LYM, *Extracts from the Minutes and Advices* (1783), arbitration advice no. 5, 1697, 7–8.

67. These advices all appear in the PYM manuscript Book of Discipline.

68. Pehr Kalm, *Kalm's Account of His Visit to England*, trans. Joseph Lucas (London: Macmillan, 1892), 71.

69. Henry J. Cadbury, "Anthony Benezet's Library," *Bulletin of Friends Historical Association* 23, no. 2 (1934), n. 64. This volume, unfortunately, is missing; if found, its annotations will be highly informative.

70. Cookworthy himself is a splendid example of the trivialities of "patchwork" Quaker discipline. In a letter dated December 24–25 (rather than Twelfth Month), signed "thy affectionate friend," he omits any reference to Christmas!

71. LYM, *Extracts from the Minutes and Advices* [. . .] *Supplement* (1822), 72, advice no. 16 (of 1798).

72. PYM, *Rules of Discipline and Advices of the Yearly Meeting of Friends for Pennsylvania and New Jersey* (Philadelphia: Samuel Samson Jr., 1797), 127.

73. There is some evidence that advices might pass eastward: a copy of the 1806 Philadelphia Discipline (printed by Conrad Kimber) was kept and annotated by the Upper Dublin Women's Meeting. This may be yet further evidence of the continued scarcity of disciplines. A facsimile was printed by Herbert S. Haigh in 1990.

74. Bronner, "Quaker Discipline and Order," 331–33.

75. See Arnold Lloyd, *Quaker Social History, 1669–1738* (London: Longmans, Green, 1950).

76. For a colonial perspective, see Jack D. Marietta, *The Reformation of American Quakerism, 1748–1783* (Philadelphia: University of Pennsylvania Press, 1984).

77. Robynne Rogers Healey, "Quietist Quakerism, 1692–c. 1805," in *The Oxford Handbook of Quaker Studies*, ed. Stephen W. Angell and Pink Dandelion (Oxford: Oxford University Press, 2013), 47–62.

78. Hall, "Christian and Brotherly Advices," 511.

CHAPTER 4

Three Methods of Worship in Eighteenth-Century Quakerism

JON MITCHELL

Worship was an integral part of Quaker life in the eighteenth century. Writing in 1757, Quaker elder John Rutty indicated that Quakers were expected to attend various meetings for worship for up to eight hours a week.[1] Itinerant ministers held meetings almost daily, often calling extra meetings upon their arrival, or holding several small meetings a day during visits to Quaker families. Some Quakers also practiced privately "in the closet";[2] the ministers Mary Waring and Jane Pearson worshipped alone "almost daily."[3]

This chapter examines three methods of eighteenth-century Quaker worship, focusing on the Georgian period (1714–1830), with an emphasis on the theological context in which these practices took place. Quakers assert that intuitive insight or divine guidance drives their movement, a claim that is sometimes taken at face value by Quaker historians. For example, Carole Dale Spencer takes Quaker religious experience to be the unique preserve of an insider's perspective; "perhaps Quaker mysticism will always be in part an enigma to outside interpreters unless they have taken that step into the transcendent themselves."[4] Yet it would be irresponsible for historians to assume that Quakers were led by the Holy Spirit or by intuition operating in a vacuum, divorced from the religious frames of reference of the time, hence the contextual emphasis of this chapter. It is presumed here that Quaker religious practice was imbued with the theology of Georgian Quakerism, which itself addressed soteriological issues in seventeenth- and eighteenth-century Protestantism.

This approach need not invalidate the experiences described by Quakers during worship. Louis Komjathy points out that one risks "becoming a dogmatist oneself . . . under the implied hegemony of secular materialism and scientific reductionism" if the claims of religious adherents are not given due weight alongside historical, cultural, theological, and linguistic factors. Balancing contextual approaches to mystical literature with the experiential claims of practitioners, this chapter takes Quaker religious experience seriously while examining it critically.[5]

PREVIOUS SCHOLARSHIP—QUIETIST AND APOPHATIC QUAKERISM

Since the work of Rufus Jones almost a century ago, eighteenth-century Quaker worship has been associated with the Catholic quietist mysticism of Madame Guyon (1648–1717), François Fénelon (1651–1715), and Miguel de Molinos (1628–1696). While many aspects of Jones's writing are problematic,[6] the argument that Catholic quietist literature was largely responsible for the supposed spiritual passivity and uncertainty of eighteenth-century Quakerism is still influential.[7] This chapter challenges that interpretation.

Recent authors have delved more deeply into Catholic mysticism in search of similarities between Quakerism and the late medieval apophatic movement. Michael Birkel compares quietist Quakerism to the fourteenth-century Dominicans Johannes Tauler and Meister Eckhart, the quintessential mystical theologians of medieval apophasis.[8] Likewise, Spencer finds the roots of Quaker worship in the desert fathers, Greek fathers, Spanish Carmelites, and Eckhart's Rhineland school.[9] The defining characteristic of apophasis is stressed by the eminent scholars of Christian mystical theology Denys Turner and Bernard McGinn as "the importance it attaches to the experience of the *absence* of God."[10] Apophatic mysticism involved negation heaped upon negation: not only negation of "self" but a decisive not-finding of God. Through these negations, the ultimate "consciousness of the ground" upon which God and the soul coexist is said to be unveiled, as a "presence" that defies conceptualization.[11] Despite Spencer's and Birkel's assertions, Quakerism is clearly not apophatic in this sense of the term. Quakers across the ages affirm the presence of a discernible spirit, the "Inward Light." Rather than find an ineffable existential truth in all-encompassing negation, Quakers aim to discern and follow this knowable divine guidance.

Nevertheless, the Quaker historians cited above unequivocally trace Quakerism back to medieval apophasis. They do so on the grounds that apophasis, Catholic quietism, and Georgian Quakerism are all said to be passive or negative practices, in which agency in prayer is suspended or surrendered. For example, Birkel defines quietist Quakerism as "a practice of apophatic prayer, that is, prayer that is without content as much as is humanly possible.... When one empties the mind of all distracting thoughts and feelings, God will fill the vacuum."[12] Likewise, despite a complete lack of documentary evidence, Spencer sees the Catholic quietist movement as the conduit for the "direct transference of ideas" from Christian apophatic mystics to Quakers.[13]

This chapter finds such generalizations about the heritage of Quaker worship unhelpful. To begin with, the waters have been muddied by a false equivalency between Catholic quietism and medieval apophasis. It is not the case that Catholic quietists advocated a wholly passive, or apophatic, spiritual path. Catholic quietism was a democratized, simplified, but essentially orthodox approach to Catholic contemplative prayer, as will become evident. Furthermore, negativity regarding human agency toward God, and the language of passive absorption in God, was widespread in the reformed spirituality of the seventeenth and eighteenth centuries in the context of the passive reception of grace. This negativity and passivity made their way into Quaker worship but are not evidence of apophasis.

While this chapter finds little reason to place Quakerism in a quietist or apophatic lineage of Christian mysticism, it invites further research. A modest yet textually grounded similarity between three distinct methods of Quaker worship is evident in the concept of "recollection," a widespread practice in Christian contemplative traditions. Those who wish to place Quaker worship in the context of Christian contemplation may find this fruitful.

SOURCES

Birkel's article on William Backhouse's 1813 tract *A Guide to True Peace, or A Method of Attaining to Inward and Spiritual Prayer* was the first academic study of a Quaker devotional text from this period.¹⁴ This chapter builds upon and challenges Birkel's article and examines several similar Quaker texts. The first method of worship, which I call silent waiting, is examined by way of Robert Barclay's *Apology for the True Christian Divinity* (1678) and Mary Brook's *Reasons for the Necessity of Silent Waiting* (1775).[15] A search of the Friends Historical Library at Swarthmore College reveals that Brook's pamphlet had been reprinted twenty-five times by 1877, and had been translated into French and German. The second method discussed in this chapter, quietist prayer, was most fully articulated in Backhouse's *Guide to True Peace* and was the subject of Birkel's analysis, as mentioned above. The tract consists of paraphrased or directly quoted passages from the leading writers of the Catholic quietist movement, and was the most influential articulation of the quietist Quaker position.[16] This tract was also published throughout the nineteenth century, twelve times by 1877.[17] Finally, I examine the third method, watchfulness, as outlined in pamphlets by John Bellers (1702, reprinted in 1760 and 1802), Joseph Phipps (1781), and Richard Phillips (1815).[18]

MYSTICS AND PURITANS

To see God's providence in everyday events, to reflect on the progress of grace in the soul, and to seek out and claim an unmediated relationship with the divine through practical divinity or experiential Christianity were all common in seventeenth- and eighteenth-century Protestantism. Quakerism arose in a hotbed of popular spirituality, in which claims of a personal inward relationship with the divine were controversial but not unusual.[19] Yet Quakers also alluded to the extraordinary mystical union described in Catholic traditions. As a result of this tension, a "Mystics vs. Puritans debate" has arisen[20] over how similar Quakerism was to Catholic mysticism, or how much it was the product of "puritan attitudes pushed to severe conclusions."[21] Puritans certainly translated and read Catholic tracts, and they engaged in spiritual exercises based in part on this inheritance.[22] But Quaker historians have not considered the possibility that Catholic mystical language took on different meanings in a post-Reformation context, dominated by unprecedented emphasis on predestination and grace.

Catholic mystical literature was a notable element of radical Protestantism all over Europe until the mid-eighteenth century.[23] The condemnation of Molinos and Guyon by the Catholic Church greatly aided the wide dissemination of their writings among Protestants, while the authors themselves had little involvement in the interpretation and assimilation of their ideas.[24] The use of Catholic quietist texts by Methodists such as John Wesley and William Cowper (who of course rejected many of the practical and theoretical tenets of quietism and Quakerism) attests to the diverse interpretations that mystical language can accommodate.[25] Dennis Tamburello suggests that reformed theologians found the language of medieval mysticism, particularly apophatic mysticism, amenable to their sense of the passive reception of justifying grace. Passive reception of grace occurs toward the beginning of Protestant spiritual life, but it was discussed using the language of passive mystical absorption, which occurred at the culmination of the Catholic contemplative ascent to God.[26] Likewise, William Ward summarizes this dynamic in Puritanism: "The Puritans scored an advantage over the Catholics by moving mystical union, conversion, into the first stage of their doctrinally framed scheme of justification, sanctification and glorification." This difference did not prevent Pietist and Puritan groups from appropriating Catholic mystical language, as Ward notes: "Mystical union, in the Catholic schemes the ultimate reward for the spiritual elite, was now available to all the faithful, and available where it was most needed, at the beginning of the saints' pilgrimage, as encouragement for everything ahead."[27]

Given the free flow and appropriation of mystical literature throughout Protestantism in this period, it is problematic to conclude that Quakers preserved Catholic contemplative traditions simply because they (along with many other radical Protestant movements) read and republished these texts. All forms of religious practice, including those that claim intuitive insight through interior silence, should be considered in the context of the belief systems in which they are found.[28] Scholars and practitioners from modern liberal Protestant backgrounds and those who wish to promote perennial mysticism or holiness narratives are wont to turn a blind eye to the fundamentally divergent sacramental, confessional, syllogistic, liturgical, and soteriological frameworks in which Catholicism and radical Protestantism operated,[29] leading to the conflation of apophatic theology, quietism, and Quakerism.

Nevertheless, in an era in which theology could be unabashedly related to experience, the value of these practices of interior silence is clearly evident. Accounts of divinely infused interior silence are found throughout the

Pietist movement, notably and beautifully in the eighteenth-century writing of Gerhard Tersteegen.[30] Even Jacob Boehme, one of the most idiosyncratic mystics of the period, started his esoteric alchemical panentheism with inward silence, a "Gelassenheit" of silent surrender to God.[31] The issue of "stillness" in prayer caused John Wesley to split from the Moravian advocates of this practice in 1740,[32] and silent worship can be found among the radical movements that preceded Quakerism, among them the Family of Love, the Seekers, and the Waiters.[33] The experiential value of such practice may also be demonstrated by the unlikely allegiances to which it gave rise. The iconoclastic Barclay cited an orthodox Benedictine prayer manual titled *Holy Wisdom* (1657) in support of Quaker worship,[34] Scottish Episcopalians tended to Madame Guyon on her deathbed,[35] and quietism was "common talk of the coffeehouses of Bath" in the mid-eighteenth century thanks to Dr. George Cheyne's holistic approach to aristocratic nervous afflictions.[36] Therefore, while the experiential claims in the texts under study must be taken seriously, it is clearly evident from Ward's and Tamburello's work that the Reformation significantly altered the context in which these experiences were described.

RECOLLECTION

A central feature of these contemplative practices that spread across Europe in Catholic literature was the prayer of "recollection."[37] This practice, known in Molinos's *Spiritual Guide* as "internal recollection," involved repeatedly re-collecting the mind to an affective response to the idea (or, to the faithful, the truth) of God's immanent presence or omnipresence (usually experienced as pure love), thereby gradually excluding all external and mental distractions. The 1688 English translation of Molinos's *Spiritual Guide* explained, "Internal Recollection is Faith and Silence in the Presence of God. Hence thou oughtest to be accustomed to recollect thy self in his Presence, with an affectionate attention, as one that is given up to God, and united unto him, with Reverence, Humility and Submission."[38] Guyon's *Short and Easy Method of Prayer* described how the active exercise of recollection gradually became passive, as recollection became "infused" with divine presence. The 1775 translation by the Quaker Thomas Digby Brooke, for example, instructs readers that "our direct and principal exercise should consist in the contemplation of the Divine Presence; we should be also exceedingly watchful and diligent in recalling our dissipated senses.... Though recollection is difficult in the beginning, from the habit the soul has acquired of always being away from home ... it soon will be rendered perfectly easy."[39]

Birkel briefly describes the essence of this practice, which he correctly identifies as the "heart of the message" of the "quietist" Quaker text *A Guide to True Peace*. It "might be considered as the method for this prayer," says Birkel; one should "imagine" oneself in God's presence. Yet it is not clear how this active and imaginative method is squared with Birkel's assessment of Quaker worship as wholly "without conscious effort and use of images" and therefore, by Birkel's definition, "apophatic."[40] There is a tension in Birkel's article between the overarching insistence that quietist "apophatic" practice involved "self-emptying" until "God filled the vacuum," and the text itself, which as Birkel briefly states described an effortful turning of the mind to the idea of God's presence.

Catholic quietism was not unorthodox in its passivity. Catholic mystical itineraries chart how practitioners might progress from effortful recollection to "infused" or "passive" contemplation by way of subtly graduated steps.[41] While these stages of contemplation were debated in Catholic mystical theology, the writings of Miguel de Molinos, which underpinned the Catholic quietist movement, featured only a slight variation on this orthodox formulation. Molinos insisted unequivocally that the practice of recollection in silent prayer was not passive: "I'll conclude this Chapter by undeceiving thee of the vulgar errour of those who say, that in this internal Recollection, or Prayer of Rest, the faculties operate not, and that the Soul is idle and wholly unactive.... This is a manifest fallacy of those who have little experience."[42] Although passive contemplation was emphasized in relatively imprecise and democratized quietist spiritual literature, so-called quietism was an essentially orthodox articulation of Catholic practice. Accusations of unorthodox passivity and antinomianism against Catholic quietists were largely motivated by ecclesiastical politics and a growing ambivalence toward mystical contemplation in the Roman Church, and had no basis in Molinos's published work.[43] Furthermore, there is little practical difference between Molinos and Guyon.[44]

This is a vital point. The incorrect assumption that Catholic quietists advocated a wholly passive and unorthodox practice has been assimilated into Quaker histories since Rufus Jones's account of the quietist Quakers. It is still to be found in recent treatments of the subject—thus the tension in Birkel's analysis noted above. The proposition that quietist prayer was wholly passive appeals to the reformed preference for freely given grace rather than methodical praxis. But Catholic "quietist" practice was based on "recollection": attentional training upon an affective response to considering oneself in God's presence. Like the Catholic "quietists," eighteenth-century Quakers practiced recollection in a similar way, as will be shown after a further word on passivity in Quaker practical theology.

QUAKER PASSIVITY

The source of eighteenth-century Quaker passivity may well be found within the Quaker movement itself. Hugh Pyper comments that "in light of the modern Quaker reputation of humanism and 'that of God' in every human being, it comes as a surprise to realize that Barclay's view on human nature outdoes the pessimism of Calvinism."[45] Barclay affirmed the totally depraved and sinful human condition, with the small caveat that children are not born into a state of sin.[46] Regarding adults, Barclay affirmed the imputation of original sin as usually conceived, in keeping with most contemporaneous Protestant theologies.[47] Barclay insisted that any religious act in this fallen state was ineffectual or counterproductive, "altogether useless and ineffectual to him in the things of God."[48]

In this framework, Barclay insisted that agency to lift the soul out of its fallen state always and only came from the divine rather than from the "creature." It is like "Diverse men lying in a dark pit together, where all their senses are so stupefied, that they are scarce sensible of their own misery. To this I compare man in his natural, corrupt, fallen condition." One cannot "deliver" oneself or entice the "one able to deliver" down into the pit; thus Barclay dismissed the effortful prayer of Jesuit spiritual exercises, or the Arminian view of co-agency with grace. Finally, Barclay stated the Quaker position: "the deliverer comes at certain times, and fully discovers and informs them of the great misery and hazard they are in, if they continue in that noisome and pestiferous place; yea, forces them to a certain sense of their misery . . . lays hold upon them, and gives them a pull, in order to lift them out of their misery; which if they resist not will save them; only they may resist it."[49]

The despair that attends becoming fully aware of one's fallen state was of the same nature as saving grace; when the "deliverer" descends into

Barclay's pit, he "forces them to a certain sense of their misery" and "gives them a pull." This conviction of sin ("convincement," in Quaker terminology)[50] was catalyzed by a visitation of the Inward Light, which was held to be synonymous with the redeeming aspect of the Christ of John's Gospel (the "light of the world"), the Holy Spirit, or the will of God.[51] Scholars agree that Inward Light in this period was "not a testimony to innate goodness, but rather an illumination of sin."[52] In contrast, the importance of realizing one's own sinful nature was stressed from the early Puritan divines to John Wesley and George Whitefield's Methodism,[53] yet justifying divine inspiration via the Holy Spirit was different in kind from the former conviction of sin.[54] This was not the case in Quakerism. The language of mystical contact thus became applicable to all stages of convincement, justification, and sanctification,[55] and left a spiritual itinerary in which everything depended upon the Holy Spirit and in which co-agency was impossible: "only they may resist it."

To sum up, Ward and Tamburello show that Puritans brought the language of mystical contact to the beginning of the spiritual path. Drawing on historians of Quakerism and Puritanism, I have outlined how Puritan models of spiritual progression were further "compressed" in Quakerism, making Quakers dependent on the Holy Spirit for everything, with little agency of their own.[56] With these contextual points in mind, let us turn to practice.

SILENT WAITING

The practice of silent waiting was said to engender readiness, to create a state of passivity in which the Inward Light could become manifest. As Barclay put it, "denying self, both inwardly and outwardly, in a still and mere dependence upon God, in abstracting from all the workings, imaginations, and speculations of his own mind, that being emptied as it were of himself, and so thoroughly crucified to the natural products thereof, he may be fit to receive the Lord, who will have no co-partner nor co-rival of his glory and power."[57] Quakers "waited upon" God in silent prayer, with the "self brought to nothingness" in an "attentive, submissive" "inward watchfulness and retiredness of mind."[58]

However, it was not the case that all "human emotions and impulses" were to be shunned in an apophatic silence and vacuous "nothingness," as often suggested.⁵⁹ On the contrary, this attitude of waiting and watching was imbued with fear, humility, "self-abasement," awe, and reverence, which were encouraged as appropriate responses to the omnipresence of God and the awesome power of God alone to bring about salvation. Like the practices advocated by Molinos and Guyon, Brook's practice was built on recollecting the mind to an affective response to considering oneself in God's presence. Rather than recollecting what Molinos held to be the theological truth of God's "pure love," Brook's approach demanded that God be approached in an attitude of self-abnegation and fear: "Is not a humble, conscientious, silent Waiting in Submission, to be influenced and led by him, abundantly more preferable in his sight? Then how much more the sighs and expressions that proceed from a real heart-affecting sense of his Greatness and Omnipresence, and the Lowness and Unworthyness of the Creature that considers itself as Dust and Ashes before him!" This theme runs throughout *Necessity of Silent Waiting*; Quakers should be "deeply humbled into a Feeling of our Inability and Nothingness."⁶⁰ Illustrating "powerful convictions of the Holy Spirit" by way of Isaiah 6:5, Brook explained, "What a deep reverence of his maker and just abhorrence of self filled his humbled Mind, when he was favoured with this awful sight of the Supreme Glory." Likewise, Barclay advised, "fear the Lord, to stand in awe before him," and worship "in the pure fear of the Lord."⁶¹

Brook advised that practitioners must "shut out everything that would amuse or divert attention from the Reverence due to the great Object of our Adoration," and that the mind should be "uninterruptedly stayed upon him [God]" with a "solid attention to hear what he shall reveal." Obstacles to this attention, which "scatter and divert his [the practitioner's] attention from the right object," were "thoughts, imaginations and propensities of an earthly or sensual nature" that should be abandoned in favor of the "attention . . . fixed upon and stayed in true watchfulness towards the Lord."⁶²

The affectively rich inner silence that was said to arise from such practice was held to be an apt expression of humility before God; "what more becoming a humble dependent creature, sensible of the depravity of its nature," asked Brook, "than a deeply expressive solemn silence before him?"⁶³ Quakers were advised to silence their "roving imaginations"⁶⁴ and to recollect their minds upon God, in a "nothingness" that was not a vacuous absence of phenomenal or emotive content but an affective response to the power and sovereignty of God.

The practice contained ambiguities, which became characteristic of Quaker spirituality in the eighteenth century. It was not clear where the action of the "creaturely" agent ended, whether the practitioner should exert effort in maintaining concentration upon the idea of God's presence, or whether this concentration upon God was itself a sign of "natural man" becoming subject to God's power. It was theologically problematic to credit an improvement in "staying" the mind to depraved human agency. Therefore, progress in this practice was always and only ascribed to the divine, and Quaker literature dispensed with the gradations of effort and co-agency found in Catholic mystical theology. Regarding people with ill-disciplined concentration, Brook reckoned that it was "the necessity of the Holy Spirit to disengage them from roving thoughts and concerns of a temporal nature." Brook was clear that "nothing less than the Holy Spirit can chain down and subdue the carnal mind."[65]

An articulation of this ambiguity between divine and human agency is found in the Quaker minister Mary Waring's journal, published in 1809, in which Waring writes, "I did not eat the bread of idleness this morning at meeting; though have no doubt but my labour was increased by my unwatchfulness at first sitting down, suffering my mind to wander, hither and thither; so that I could not easily get it centred; yet the Lord was not unmindful of me."[66] Despite Waring's effort to re-collect her wandering mind upon God, the desired mental attitude was only achieved with divine intervention.

If one became fixed upon the divine, distracting thoughts and imaginings were now seen to originate from "the enemy" or the "carnal mind," which was now identified as that which drew attention away from being stayed on God. For Brook, some could not wait correctly because "the enemy is too strong for such worshippers, and carries their thoughts and imaginations after strange objects."[67] For Barclay, "the devil" could appear in meetings, exciting the mind from being stayed upon God or causing laxity, dulling the mind from attending fully in worship: "He [the devil] can well enter and work in a meeting, that is silent only as to words, either by keeping the minds in various thoughts and imaginations, or by stupefying them, so as to overwhelm them with a spirit of heaviness and slothfulness: but when we retire out of all, and are turned in, both by being diligent and watchful upon the one hand, and also silent and retired out of all our thoughts upon the other, as we abide in this sure place, we feel ourselves out of his reach."[68]

The appropriate response to these obstacles was not effortful concentration but more humility, until the mind became stayed once more, as illustrated by an 1816 Quaker pamphlet titled *Christian Instruction: In a Discourse Between a Mother and Her Daughter*. A sudden inability to stay the mind in prayer led the daughter to exclaim, "I am afraid he has cast me off; my thoughts ramble so, I cannot get my mind stayed, when I wish to wait on the Lord." In response, the mother did not advocate effortful recollection of the mind but advised more humility and awe: "That my dear is the one thing that gives thee a clear sense of thy weakness and how little thou canst do for thyself; and by which thou mayst be instructed to depend on the Lord for everything."[69] Thus a Quaker formulation of recollection was established, which circumvented effortful prayer by the use of humility, in keeping with the assumptions of Quaker theology.

AN EXCURSUS INTO QUAKER APOPHASIS

Carole Spencer, Michael Birkel, Pink Dandelion, and Yasuharu Nakano have recently applied apophasis to Quaker spirituality, thereby locating Quakerism within the rich history of Christian mysticism. Spencer's argument makes a case study of the "true apophatic mystic" and Quaker minister Anthony Benezet, through Benezet's 1780 edition of William Law's devotional treatise, *Spirit of Prayer*, which, according to Spencer, advocated "an apophatic approach to mystical union." Spencer finds Benezet's apophatic credentials in "one of his favourite phrases 'it is in nothingness that God is found,'" a phrase from Law's *Spirit of Prayer*.[70] Likewise, Nakano draws parallels between Meister Eckhart and Robert Barclay over their use of the term "nothingness."[71] Dandelion cites an epistle from the 1738 London Yearly Meeting: "we exhort Friends to feel their minds abstracted from visible objects into a true nothingness of self."[72] Yet Quakers' use of "nothingness" or "emptiness" of "self" in worship was not used to denote experiential vacuity or metaphysical negation; it was an attitude of humble and "awful" supplication that was used interchangeably to denote inner silence or a reverent fear of God, with the latter used to bring about the former.

Numinous self-abasement and subjection before God is to be found in Luther and Calvin,[73] and throughout Puritan literature. According to Dewey Wallace, "Awe, terror, fear of the 'sacred' or the 'numinous'" was a widespread element of Puritan religiosity.[74] Similarly, as Marinus van Beek observes, "self-emptiness" was in common usage among Puritans, to denote "the utter dependence on God in all one's actions," given their unprecedented emphasis upon predestination and providence.[75] Nigel Smith has shown that "self-annihilation" was advocated by the early Puritan Richard Rogers and throughout Puritan practical theology.[76] Passive self-surrender before God as a reaction to human depravity was a staple of Puritanism and had a long half-life in Georgian Quakerism. It is not evidence of apophasis in the tradition of the medieval mystics.

QUIETIST PRAYER

A notably different practice drew on Catholic quietist methods and was articulated in William Backhouse's *Guide to True Peace, or A Method of Attaining to Inward and Spiritual Prayer* (1813). Backhouse paraphrased Guyon's *Short and Easy Method of Prayer* to describe the "heart" of the practice as identified by Birkel, discussed above: "You should consider yourself in the Presence of God, looking with a single eye to him, resigning yourself entirely into his hands, to receive from Him whatsoever he may be pleased to dispense ... fix your mind in peace and silence; quitting your own reasonings, and not willingly thinking on anything, how good and how profitable soever it may be." Like Brook's method of silent waiting, *A Guide to True Peace* advocated placing attention upon God's immanent presence or omnipresence, and staying the mind in that attitude. This method used a loving and trusting concentration on God, rather than the fearful awe so evident in methods inspired by the Puritan mindset: "Giving ourselves up to Him fixing our eyes continually on Him, placing all our confidence in His Grace, and turning with all the strength of our soul to His pure love ... as a child casts itself into the safe bosom of its mother."[77]

Birkel shows that Backhouse emphasized passages from Catholic quietist literature relating to passivity and humility in *A Guide to True Peace*. The effortful stage of "interior recollection" is still noticeably evident in this Quaker appropriation of Catholic quietism, exhibiting a notable departure from the passivity advocated by Barclay and Brook. In a passage taken from Guyon's *Short and Easy Method* that illustrates this difference,

Backhouse likens spiritual progression to a vessel setting out to sea. We have seen in Barclay's *Apology* how the Holy Spirit descends into the pit of human corruption, to inform the depraved soul of its condition and wrench it from the shackles of sin. But in *A Guide to True Peace*, a strong, concerted effort is required from the practitioner upon the commencement of the spiritual journey: "At first we should labour with diligence and toil ... when the vessel is in port, the mariners are obliged to exert all their strength that they may clear her thence, and put to sea ... in a like manner, while the soul remains in sin, and creaturely entanglements, very frequent and strenuous endeavours are requisite to effect its freedom; the cords which hold it must be loosed; and then by strong and vigorous efforts, it pushes gradually off from its old port." When at sea, the vessel continues under oar until "at length she begins to get sweetly under sail." The analogy for this stage of co-agency with the divine is "to spread the sails, to lay the mind open before God that it may be acted upon by his Spirit." Even after the sail is set, the captain must exert gentle direction: "to hold the rudder is to restrain the mind from wandering from the true course, recalling it gently, and guiding it steadily to the dictates of the blessed spirit, which gradually gains possession and dominion of it; just as the wind by degrees fills the sails and impels the vessel."[78]

This passage from Guyon that Backhouse paraphrased in *A Guide to True Peace* shows a subtly active method with a gradual shift to passivity, in keeping with the orthodoxies of Catholic contemplative prayer. It is thus difficult to see how such practice can be described as imageless and effortless, as Birkel and Spencer suggest. What was required was not an attitude of passivity whereby God "filled the vacuum," as Birkel suggests.[79] The practitioner deliberately filled her awareness with the idea of divine presence, using subtle effort to recollect the mind to this idea and the affective state of "pure love" that consequently arose. Furthermore, the methods Backhouse advocates in *A Guide to True Peace* contrast sharply with the approach found in Brook's *Necessity of Silent Waiting* and demonstrate that quietist influence cannot be blamed for introducing a passive element into Quaker worship. If anything, quietist-influenced methods were more active than Brook's method in *Necessity of Silent Waiting*. Unlike most early modern reformed theologies, Catholicism did not assert the total corruption of the fallen human will and was therefore more forthright in asserting will toward God.

WATCHFULNESS

I have called a third method of worship watchfulness. The importance of maintaining a vigilant, alert watchfulness was stressed in all Quaker methods of worship. Yet watchfulness had a further meaning; it described a method of prayer. The method was to watch the mind without getting caught up in the mind, and to re-collect the mind to that watchfulness. No image or thought was to be created by the practitioner, as the naturally occurring contents of the mind became the object upon which attention should be placed, but without becoming carried away by the referents of those thoughts.

In *Concise Remarks on Watchfulness and Silence*, Richard Phillips explained the method: "If a man, in communing with his own heart, becomes still, he will greatly profit. For this purpose he must abstain from any vocal expression and keep a watch over his own thoughts, as to prevent his attention from being carried away by them, and not attempt to obstruct the prevalence of such thoughts by exciting other thoughts of his own." Watchfulness required disengagement from thoughts, watching without "being carried away," or exerting effort to stop thoughts. On this point Phillips restated that, unlike the other two methods, practitioners should not "attempt to prevent the occurrence of their own thoughts, by exciting other thoughts of whatsoever description." The practitioner should not actively try to achieve mental silence by bringing God to mind. But, Phillips explained, when attention was not "carried away" and remained in "watchfulness," a greater ability to "watch over" thoughts would lead to an "inward spiritual and profitable silence." Similarly, as with becoming "stayed" on God, a qualitative improvement in mental calmness and self-awareness was associated with divine agency. It was "the evident work of the Redeemer, bringing into subjection the thoughts cogitations and imaginations of man."[80]

Watchfulness was an attitude to be cultivated with a gentle touch, with little of the abasement found in *Reasons for the Necessity of Silent Waiting*. For example, Phillips cited the Catholic mystic François Fénelon on how to recollect the mind to this watchful attitude: "If your Will never concur your straying, you will never stray"; however, "each time you perceive yourself straying, let it fall, without combatting it; and return gently to the side of God without any struggle of mind."[81] In the original context of the 1750 translation of Fénelon's *Advice and Consolation for a Person in Distress and*

Dejection, such instruction advised how the mind should be recollected to the attitude of "pure love" of quietist prayer. "If by any straying of the mind we lose sight of him," Fénelon continued, "without stopping at this, we turn again from whom we had wandered. If we commit faults, the penitence we have for them is all of love."[82] That Phillips appropriated Fénelon's remark ("return gently to the side of God") to the context of watchfulness is key to reading this method. The attitude of watchfulness was a facsimile of the self-awareness that the Inward Light was said to bring about. As Bellers put it in the context of watchfulness practice, "he that watches in the light (to bring his thoughts into captivity to the obedience of Christ) it will lead him to the New Jerusalem (from whence it shines)."[83] Like the other two practices, the method of watchfulness similarly involved placing and recollecting the mind on the idea of the divine, in this instance the distinctive Quaker idea of God's presence through Inward Light.

As Bellers's remark shows, in this method of worship there is again an ambiguity between natural and supernatural agency, and uncertainty over the point at which recollection of the mind became prayer infused with the spirit. Watchfulness was of the nature of divine influence in the mind; nevertheless, it was also an exercise that made the practitioner fit to receive the spirit. In this regard, Habakkuk 2:1 played an important role in Quaker discussions of this method. "I will stand upon my watch, and set me upon the tower" was a prerequisite to prayer being infused with the spirit: "and will watch to see what he will say unto me, and what I shall answer when I am reproved."[84] Watchfulness was, therefore, framed as an attitude of passivity and was permissible despite the Quaker reticence to admit agency from the side of the "creature." Echoing Barclay's view of the impossibility of cooperative grace given the human condition ("only they may resist it"), practitioners must "maintain the watch" to ensure that they are not "retarding, adulterating, or preventing the work and frustrating the design of the visitation." Phillips continued: "When this Divine operation, or exercise, is not adulterated, or interrupted, by meddling, active man but the watch is faithfully maintained and the mind kept passive and dependent to the conclusion of the work ... its effects will occasionally proclaim it to be the gracious operation of Him who is the root and offspring of David, the bright and morning star."[85]

Phillips drew on an ecumenical range of writers when presenting this practice in his *Concise Remarks on Watchfulness and Silence*, appending footnotes and quotations throughout from Puritans John Hales and Robert

Gell, the Anglican mystic William Law, Catholic quietists Fénelon, Guyon, and Molinos, the Quaker William Penn, and a now obscure early eighteenth-century Irish vicar named George Munro. The term "watchfulness" was also in widespread use in Puritan devotional literature on self-examination.[86] Nevertheless, the method of watchfulness in Quaker literature can be read as distinctly Quaker, a method of recollection using the Quaker idea of the divine as Inward Light.

CONCLUSION

Quakers wrote of becoming aware of the "carnal mind" by maintaining watchfulness over it without engaging with it, or of experiencing a "stayed" mental attitude toward God, whereby pulls on the attention from the carnal mind decreased. This stayed mind was central to Quaker practice, be it stayed upon an attitude of watchfulness, an awful fear of God, or the love of God. According to Phipps, devout Quakers found their thoughts "gradually diminished (sometimes attended by a calming humbling, yet gratifying influence) until they are entirely subdued, and the mind completely relieved therefrom."[87] As John Woolman put it, "through an inward approaching to God, the mind is strengthened in obedience."[88] Or, according to Backhouse (paraphrasing Guyon), "at length, to have a mind turned toward God, becomes, as it were, habitual."[89]

I have offered brief accounts of these three methods of worship, two of which (silent waiting and watchfulness) have previously eluded scholarly attention. These practices have not been set alongside one another before, and doing so raises a number of questions. Did particular Quakers choose one method over the others, or did they switch between all three? Did Quakers comprehend a theological and practical dissonance between *Reasons for the Necessity of Silent Waiting* and *A Guide to True Peace*, or was this dissonance of little importance in the experiential and geographically dispersed Quaker movement? Only a more detailed investigation can establish how Quakers integrated Catholic quietist literature into their worship, despite its incongruities with Barclayan theology. It may be that Quakers valued the relatively proactive Catholic perspective, the emphasis on God's love, and the copious consolatory advice found in Catholic literature. Far from being the cause of passivity, it may be that so-called Catholic quietism ameliorated the severity of Quakerism's puritanical heritage.

To place Quaker worship in the context of Christian praxis, I suggest that apophasis be dropped completely from discussions of eighteenth-century Quakerism, and that the term "quietism" should be used with caution and precision. It is highly problematic that recent authors have attempted to trace Quaker worship back to medieval apophatic mysticism via Catholic quietism. In so doing, Catholic quietism and monastic apophasis have been uncritically homogenized to fit into ill-defined histories of Quaker mysticism. This does little to aid our understanding of these practices, and does not entice non-Quaker religious historians to engage with Quaker studies. Following Ward and others, I suggest here that mystical literature was appropriated by Quakers as well as Puritans; the "nothingness" and "emptiness" of "self-abasement" were more Puritan than mystical.

Quaker worship may be understood within the rich history of Christian contemplative prayer by way of the concept of recollection, noting the ambiguities of Quaker theological bias against spiritual agency and preference for freely given grace. The nuanced stages found in Catholic mystical literature, such as purgation, illumination, recollection (which can be subdivided into several stages of decreasing effort), passivity, and union, are not evident in Quaker texts, as Quakers practiced within the reformed binary of salvation or reprobation.

NOTES

1. John Rutty, *Extracts from the Spiritual Diary of John Rutty, M.D.* (Falmouth, UK: J. Trathan, 1840), 29.

2. Joseph John Gurney, *Observations on the Distinguished Views and Practices of the Society of Friends* (Norwich, UK: Fletcher, 1842), 334.

3. Mary Waring, *A Diary of the Religious Experience of Mary Waring, Daughter of Elijah and Sarah Waring; Late of Godalming* (London: William Phillips, 1809), 1; Thomas Wilkinson, ed., *Sketches of Piety: In the Life and Religious Experiences of Jane Pearson* (York, UK: W. Alexander, 1817), viii.

4. Carole Dale Spencer, *Holiness: The Soul of Quakerism; An Historical Analysis of the Theology of Holiness in the Quaker Tradition* (Milton Keynes: Paternoster, 2007), 43, 92.

5. Louis Komjathy, "Approaching Contemplative Practice," in *Contemplative Literature: A Comparative Sourcebook on Meditation and Contemplative Prayer*, ed. Louis Komjathy (Albany: State University of New York Press, 2015), 11, 38–39. This chapter uses eighteenth-century devotional or prescriptive texts on Quaker worship to examine methods of worship among Friends. Scholars have overlooked these texts, perhaps because of current and past reticence about discussing spiritual agency. While experiences described in journals have been studied since Howard Brinton and Rufus Jones,

this chapter focuses on "method" in the broadest sense: on what Quakers did during worship, including the assumptions they brought with them. Journals do not unpack the theological assumptions that framed their authors' experiences. And the raw data of Quaker religious experience in published journals have already been examined by several historians. This chapter offers tools that may help decode journal accounts.

6. See esp. vol. 1 of Rufus M. Jones, *The Later Periods of Quakerism*, 2 vols. (London: Macmillan, 1921). On the problematic nature of Jones's work, see Carole Dale Spencer, "Holiness: The Quaker Way of Perfection," in *The Creation of Quaker Theory*, ed. Pink Dandelion (Farnham, UK: Ashgate, 2004), 149–71, 196; Spencer, *Holiness*, 91–92; Elaine Pryce, "Negative to a Marked Degree or an Intense and Glowing Faith? Rufus Jones and Quaker Quietism," *Common Knowledge* 16, no. 3 (2010): 518–31.

7. Helen Plant, "Subjective Testimonies: Women Quaker Ministers and Spiritual Biography in England, c. 1750–1825," *Gender and History* 15, no. 2 (2003): 298; Robynne Rogers Healey, "Quietist Quakerism, 1692–c. 1805," in *The Oxford Handbook of Quaker Studies*, ed. Stephen W. Angell and Pink Dandelion (Oxford: Oxford University Press, 2013), 49.

8. Michael Birkel, "Quaker Silent Prayer: A Guide to True Peace," in Komjathy, *Contemplative Literature*, 152; Michael Birkel, *Silence and Witness: The Quaker Tradition* (New York: Orbis Books, 2004), 32.

9. Spencer, *Holiness*, 92.

10. Denys Turner, *The Darkness of God: Negativity in Christian Mysticism* (Cambridge: Cambridge University Press, 1995), 262 (emphasis in original).

11. Ibid., 252–73; Bernard McGinn, *The Mystical Thought of Meister Eckhart: The Man from Whom God Hid Nothing* (New York: Crossroad, 2001), 39.

12. Birkel, "Quaker Silent Prayer," 152.

13. Spencer, *Holiness*, 92, 270; Spencer, "Holiness," 158. See also Pink Dandelion, "Guarded Domesticity and Engagement with 'the World': The Separate Spheres of Quaker Quietism," *Common Knowledge* 16, no. 1 (2010): 95–109; Birkel, *Silence and Witness*; Birkel, "Quaker Silent Prayer"; Pryce, "Negative to a Marked Degree."

14. Birkel, "Quaker Silent Prayer"; William Backhouse, *A Guide to True Peace, or A Method of Attaining to Inward and Spiritual Prayer* (York, UK: W. Alexander and Son, 1813).

15. Robert Barclay, *An Apology for the True Christian Divinity: Being an Explanation and Vindication of the Doctrines of the People Called the Quakers* (1678; New York: Samuel Wood and Sons, 1827)—the 1827 edition is cited throughout; Mary Brook, *Reasons for the Necessity of Silent Waiting, in Order to the Solemn Worship of God: To Which Are Added, Several Quotations from Robert Barclay's Apology* (London: Mary Hinde, 1775).

16. Jones, *Later Periods of Quakerism*, 1:58; Spencer, *Holiness*, 145; Birkel, "Quaker Silent Prayer."

17. Birkel, "Quaker Silent Prayer," 162.

18. John Bellers, *Watch unto Prayer, or Considerations for All Who Profess They Believe in The Light* (London, 1760); Joseph Phipps, *Dissertations on the Nature and Effect of Christian Baptism, Christian Communion, and Religious Waiting upon God* (London: James Phillips, 1781); Richard Phillips, *Concise Remarks on Watchfulness and Silence* (London: W. Phillips, 1815).

19. Nigel Smith, *Perfection Proclaimed: Language and Literature in English Radical Religion* (New York: Oxford University Press, 1989), 33–34; Owen C. Watkins, *The Puritan Experience: Studies in Spiritual Autobiography* (London: Routledge, 1972), 226–38; Geoffrey Fillingham Nuttall, *The Holy Spirit in Puritan Faith and Experience* (Oxford:

Basil Blackwell, 1946), 150–67; D. Bruce Hindmarsh, *The Evangelical Conversion Narrative: Spiritual Biography in Early Modern England* (New York: Oxford University Press, 2005), 33–61.

20. Spencer, *Holiness*, 40–43.

21. Hugh Barbour, *The Quakers in Puritan England* (New Haven: Yale University Press, 1964), 2, 32; Hugh Barbour and J. William Frost, *The Quakers* (New York: Greenwood Press, 1988), 5.

22. Spencer, *Holiness*, 59–63; Hugh Barbour, "Sixty Years in Early Quaker History," in Dandelion, *Creation of Quaker Theory*, 24.

23. William R. Ward, "Anglicanism and Assimilation, or Mysticism and Mayhem in the Eighteenth Century," in *Crown and Mitre: Religion and Society in Northern Europe*, ed. W. M. Jacob and Nigel Yates (London: Boydell Press, 1993), 81–91.

24. Bernard McGinn, "Miguel de Molinos and the Spiritual Guide: A Theological Reappraisal," in *Miguel de Molinos: The Spiritual Guide*, trans. Robert P. Baird (Mahwah, NJ: Paulist Press, 2010), 22; William R. Ward, *Early Evangelicalism: A Global Intellectual History, 1670–1789* (Cambridge, Cambridge University Press, 2006), 61–66.

25. Patricia A. Ward, *Experimental Theology in America: Madame Guyon, Fénelon, and Their Readers* (Waco: Baylor University Press, 2009), 94–97.

26. Dennis E. Tamburello, "The Protestant Reformers on Mysticism," in *The Wiley-Blackwell Companion to Christian Mysticism*, ed. Julie A. Lamm (Oxford: Blackwell, 2013), 414–20.

27. Ward, *Early Evangelicalism*, 87.

28. Komjathy, "Approaching Contemplative Practice," 38–39.

29. Leigh Eric Schmidt, "The Making of 'Mysticism' in the Anglo-American World," in Lamm, *Companion to Christian Mysticism*, 463–68.

30. William R. Ward, "Mysticism and Revival: The Case of Gerhard Tersteegen," in *Revival and Religion Since 1700: Essays for John Walsh*, ed. Jane Garnett and Colin Matthew (London: Hambledon Press, 1993), 41–58; Ward, *Experimental Theology in America*, 72–79.

31. William R. Ward, *Christianity Under the Ancien Régime, 1648–1789* (Cambridge: Cambridge University Press, 1999), 20–29.

32. Hindmarsh, *Evangelical Conversion Narrative*, 66, 162–69.

33. William C. Braithwaite, *The Beginnings of Quakerism* (London: Macmillan, 1912), 25–26; Barbour, *Quakers in Puritan England*, 31–32.

34. Barclay, *Apology for the True Christian Divinity*, 277–78.

35. Ward, "Anglicanism and Assimilation," 87.

36. Ward, *Early Evangelicalism*, 120.

37. McGinn, "Miguel de Molinos," 29.

38. Miguel de Molinos, *The Spiritual Guide Which Disentangles the Soul and Brings It by the Inward Way to the Getting of Perfect Contemplation and the Rich Treasure of Internal Peace* (London: Printed for Thomas Fabian at the Bible in St. Paul's Churchyard, 1688), 30.

39. Jeanne Guyon, *A Short and Easy Method of Prayer*, trans. Thomas Digby Brooke (London: T. J. Carnegy, 1775), 9–10.

40. Birkel, "Quaker Silent Prayer," 159, 147–52.

41. Catholic University of America, *New Catholic Encyclopedia* (New York: McGraw-Hill, 1967), 4:259; 12:128–29.

42. Molinos, *Spiritual Guide*, 37.
43. McGinn, "Miguel de Molinos," 24–39; Bernard McGinn, ed., *The Essential Writings of Christian Mysticism* (New York: Random House, 2006), 144, 502.
44. Ward, *Christianity Under the Ancien Régime*, 22–23.
45. Hugh S. Pyper, "Robert Barclay: The Art of Apologetics," in *Early Quakers and Their Theological Thought, 1647–1723*, ed. Stephen W. Angell and Pink Dandelion (Cambridge: Cambridge University Press, 2015), 214.
46. Barclay, *Apology for the True Christian Divinity*, 94.
47. Pyper, "Robert Barclay," 216.
48. Barclay, *Apology for the True Christian Divinity*, 88.
49. Ibid., 124–25.
50. "Convincement" was used synonymously with "conversion" in this period of Quakerism. In seventeenth-century England, "convincement" meant "1. The proving a person guilty; 2. to produce conviction of sinfulness; or, 3. Mental convincement." See Marinus van Beek, *An Enquiry into Puritan Vocabulary* (Groningen: Wolters-Noordhoff, 1969), 93. It is likely that Quakers used the term because it embraced all of these meanings.
51. Hugh S. Pyper, "Resisting the Inevitable: Universal and Particular Salvation in the Thought of Robert Barclay," *Quaker Religious Thought* 29, no. 1 (1998): 5–18.
52. Thomas D. Hamm, "George Fox and the Politics of Late Nineteenth-Century Quaker Historiography," in Dandelion, *Creation of Quaker Theory*, 14.
53. Watkins, *Puritan Experience*, 5, 7; Jean Delumeau, *Sin and Fear: The Emergence of the Western Guilt Culture, Thirteenth–Eighteenth Centuries* (New York: Palgrave Macmillan, 1990), 523–44.
54. Delumeau, *Sin and Fear*, 491–97.
55. Justification and sanctification, before the influence of evangelicalism in the nineteenth century, were of a piece. See Thomas D. Hamm, *The Transformation of American Quakerism: Orthodox Friends, 1800–1907* (Bloomington: Indiana University Press, 1988), 6; Stephen W. Angell, "God, Christ, and the Light," in Angell and Dandelion, *Oxford Handbook of Quaker Studies*, 149.
56. Watkins, *Puritan Experience*, 215, 238; Nuttall, *Holy Spirit in Puritan Faith*, vii; Barbour, *Quakers in Puritan England*, 2.
57. Barclay, *Apology for the True Christian Divinity*, 270.
58. Brook, *Necessity of Silent Waiting*, 12.
59. Birkel, "Quaker Silent Prayer," 147, 152; Plant, "Subjective Testimonies," 298; Dandelion, "Guarded Domesticity."
60. Brook, *Necessity of Silent Waiting*, 8, 7.
61. Barclay, *Apology for the True Christian Divinity*, 261, 387.
62. Brook, *Necessity of Silent Waiting*, 13, 5–6, 12.
63. Ibid., 12.
64. Barclay, *Apology for the True Christian Divinity*, 264.
65. Brook, *Necessity of Silent Waiting*, 17, 22, 9.
66. Waring, *Religious Experience*, 86.
67. Brook, *Necessity of Silent Waiting*, 15.
68. Barclay, *Apology for the True Christian Divinity*, 273.
69. John Wigham, *Christian Instruction: In a Discourse Between a Mother and Her Daughter* (Burlington, NJ: David Allinson, 1816), 34.

70. Spencer, *Holiness*, 95.

71. Yasuharu Nakano, "Self and Other in the Theology of Robert Barclay" (PhD diss., University of Birmingham, 2011), 51–54.

72. Dandelion, "Guarded Domesticity," 96.

73. Tamburello, "Protestant Reformers on Mysticism."

74. Dewey D. Wallace, *Puritans and Predestination: Grace in English Protestant Theology, 1525–1695* (Chapel Hill: University of North Carolina Press, 1982), 194–95.

75. Beek, *Puritan Vocabulary*, 69.

76. Smith, *Perfection Proclaimed*, 39, 66.

77. Backhouse, *Guide to True Peace*, 23, 25.

78. Ibid., 78–79.

79. Birkel, "Quaker Silent Prayer," 152.

80. Phillips, *Watchfulness and Silence*, 6, 12, 9.

81. Ibid., 6n1.

82. François Fénelon, *Advice and Consolation for a Person in Distress and Dejection of Mind, with Some Thoughts on the Remedys of Dissipation* (Glasgow: R. and A. Foulis Fox, 1750), 20.

83. Bellers, *Watch unto Prayer*, 3–7.

84. Phipps, *Nature and Effect of Christian Baptism*, 62; Henry Tuke, *The Duties of Religion and Morality, as Inculcated in the Holy Scriptures: With Preliminary and Occasional Observations* (York, UK: William Alexander, 1808), 54–55.

85. Phillips, *Watchfulness and Silence*, 12.

86. Beek, *Puritan Vocabulary*, 127.

87. Phipps, *Nature and Effect of Christian Baptism*, 68.

88. John Woolman, *Selections from the Writings of John Woolman*, No. 21 (London: William and Samuel Graves, 1816), 25.

89. Backhouse, *Guide to True Peace*, 62.

PART 2

Tensions Between Quakerism in Community and Quakerism in the World

CHAPTER 5

"Mrs. Weaver Being a Quaker, Would Not Swear"
Representations of Quakers and Crime in the Metropolis, ca. 1696–1815

ERIN BELL

Quaker suffering is well known: at the hands of Anglican legal and ecclesiastical authorities who sought to maintain hegemonic ideals beyond a dichotomy of legal and illegal, Friends were "othered," depicted as lesser, both as individuals and as a denomination.[1] In this respect, their experiences were similar to those of other religious minorities, most notably Jews, to whom Friends were likened by critics from the mid-seventeenth century[2] and with whom they shared business, philanthropic, and intellectual interests.[3] Comparing Quakers and Jews, therefore, offers an opportunity to consider how and why Quakers were represented in accounts of London crime, primarily in *The Proceedings of the Old Bailey* and *The Ordinary of Newgate's Accounts* (or *Ordinary's Accounts*, for short). It also offers an opportunity to analyze the use of othering to conflate two distinct communities.

In response to efforts to denigrate them, Friends were proactive in representing themselves as respectable and law-abiding unless conscience dictated otherwise. From the Restoration of the monarchy in 1660 until the early nineteenth century, they used their experiences of oppression to position themselves as godly sufferers undeserving of the ill treatment they received, while depicting oppressors as ungodly, violent, and unmanly.[4]

Quakers were prosecuted for a range of crimes in both ecclesiastical and civil courts, from nonattendance at church to holding meetings for worship and, rarely, blasphemy. However, they were also, as a denomination, well educated, relatively wealthy, and well informed of their need to seek legal advice and represent themselves in an appropriate manner to authorities, to whom appeals were frequently made. By Quakerism's second generation, this recourse to law lay at its administrative core: the Meeting for Sufferings originated in the mid-1670s and offered legal advice to those burdened by anti-Quaker laws.[5] Such activities were intended to rouse sympathy in non-Quaker readers, or at least recognition of the dubious uses to which existing laws were put, as William C. Braithwaite notes.[6] However, Friends' appeals, which continued beyond the 1689 Toleration Act owing to, for example, Quaker refusal to pay tithes, also encouraged non-Quakers' resentment. This is particularly apparent in Old Bailey publications that, especially before 1778, offered a selective, largely unsympathetic representation of Friends, in part by conflating them with other minorities perceived as undesirable, particularly Jews.

While there are no surviving Old Bailey publications that make direct links between Jews and Quakers, such publications often depicted the two groups similarly. Therefore, comparison of the groups' representation is useful, in part because Jewish experience, in particular in the years following the unique Jewish "resettlement" in England in the mid-seventeenth century, may be archetypal of persecution (although Salo Baron's work argues that European Jews more broadly were not "the subject of special unfavorable discrimination"),[7] but more specifically because seventeenth- to nineteenth-century commentators identified supposed likenesses. In the 1660s, links were made between Jewish messianism and the Quaker James Nayler,[8] and later commentators drew parallels between the two groups. The Anglican priest Thomas Lewis, in his periodical *The Scourge in Vindication of the Church of England*, noted in 1717 supposed similarities of religious practice, language, and dress,[9] while the essayist Charles Lamb asserted in 1821 that "a moderate Jew is a more confounding piece of anomaly than a wet Quaker."[10] This comparison implies, as Aaron Kaiserman notes of Lamb's representation of Jews, the "essentially separative" nature of both.[11] This alleged separatism will be considered in more detail, with reference to the idea of "othering"; it is sufficient here to note that Lamb, a respected author, albeit a dissenter, asserted that both groups were keen to withdraw from wider society, perhaps in order to blame them for their oppression by the majority and to encourage their depiction as outsiders. Consideration of Jews alongside Quakers offers, then, an opportunity to better understand aspects of Friends' history, and to raise broader questions regarding minorities in the long eighteenth century, when resentment informed the authorities' depiction of both groups.

One clear difference in the groups' representation relates to the far longer history of anti-Semitism, which was apparent in the *Ordinary's Accounts*, a publication based on Old Bailey cases published between 1676 and 1772 and written by Anglican clergymen—or "ordinaries" (officers of the church who by reason of office had ordinary power to execute law)—who ministered to the prisoners held at the Old Bailey in London, England's central criminal court, adjoining Newgate Prison. The *Ordinary's Accounts* offered biographies of condemned criminals that sometimes included assertions that the convicted had acted, "like the Jews, in [his] own Willfulness and Stubbornness,"[12] and often reported that the condemned had been reminded of his similarity to the "Incorrigibleness and Impenitence of the Jews."[13] References were made to biblical Jews' failure to convert to Christianity in a third of the biographies published in the *Ordinary's Accounts* in the 1730s and 1740s, the publication's most intense period of anti-Semitism.[14] This may be a result of the increased numbers of poor Ashkenazi migrants in England circa 1720–50, which probably met with increased anxiety on the part of authorities, who drew upon anti-Semitism in encouraging fears of Jewish criminality.[15] While Jews were clearly linked with criminals, the conflation of Jews and Quakers in seventeenth- to nineteenth-century culture may have perpetuated the positioning of both groups as criminal: Jews were marginalized for their rejection of Christianity and Quakers were likened to Jews explicitly elsewhere. Anti-Quaker accounts also criticized Friends for rejecting the established church and tithes,[16] which, given their historical criminality as dissenters, was enough to mark them as similarly "othered."

Othering functions by creating in-groups and out-groups; the latter may be subjected to discrimination and considered "lacking" in some respect. Many scholars have noted that otherness, a concept that originated in Simone de Beauvoir's analysis of the position of women, is less about real than about perceived difference, which helps a dominant group maintain superiority and oppress other groups or individuals.[17] Therefore, Åsa Boholm concludes that during early modern Rome's Carnival, Jews were othered and positioned as barely human in order to vindicate Christian supremacy.[18] In England in the same period, othering led to the merging of very different groups: Bernard Glassman notes that Jews and Catholics were linked as "part of the general 'Menace' of that age."[19] We will return to this kind of conflation after considering the Old Bailey proceedings and laws applied to Quakers, Jews, and other minorities.

Analysis of another publication, *The Proceedings of the Old Bailey*, reveals that Friends appeared with relative frequency as witnesses, victims, and occasionally even perpetrators of crime: extant records of the Old Bailey proceedings begin in 1674, and the first reference to a Friend appears in 1676. The period considered in this chapter is circa 1688–1815; the first case I examine occurred in 1696. In the 127 years analyzed, 163 accounts included a reference to Quakers, including those who would not swear and so did not appear. Given a broader tendency to depict minorities negatively in works intended for a wider readership,[20] it is hardly surprising that Quakers were often depicted disparagingly, especially for refusing to swear oaths, which often resulted in the court's rejection of evidence. But there has been a paucity of research into Friends' appearances in the court; even the leading historians of crime, Tim Hitchcock and Robert Shoemaker, offer little information on the subject.[21] The *Ordinary's Accounts*, available for purchase shortly after cases were heard, were mediated, shaped to reflect the interests of an urban readership, and the characterizations used in them are similar at times to those in other literature of the period. In addition, the selection of particular trials for publication led to an overemphasis on types of crimes, victims, and perpetrators likely to entertain readers, until the City of London began to exercise more control in 1778, when the revolt in the American colonies and the fear of social upheaval at home led to a desire to represent the court, and by extension the legal system, as protecting citizens' rights.[22]

Such issues must be borne in mind when using these rich resources. Despite Shoemaker's assertion that "no ulterior motives"[23] can be identified behind the selection of trials made by publishers prior to 1778, analysis of those referring to Friends, along with consideration of trials not included, suggests that accounts were selected and edited to meet readers' expectations of how religious minorities behaved in certain circumstances, in implicit contrast to respectable middling members of the established church, who epitomized hegemonic behavioral norms. These accounts may be viewed as a means of circulating stereotypical representations of groups such as Quakers by London authorities in the long eighteenth century.

The accounts offer insights into continuity and change in legal and cultural attitudes toward Friends, including the limited influence of the 1689

Toleration Act. After the passage of that act, authorities continued to fear a distinctive minority that refused to conform fully to the social mores followed by others of middling status. Fears of social disorder abounded during the Revolutionary War in the American colonies. Given the City of London's desire that the *Ordinary's Accounts* should offer a "fair" narrative of trials,[24] the authorities' various and changing fears can be considered through the lens of a significant publication and its assumed readership of urban Anglicans of middling status.

It is useful, then, to outline key laws affecting Friends in the long eighteenth century. Many of these laws applied to other minorities, including Jews (to whom only the Poll Act and Militia Act did not notionally apply),[25] and comparison of how the two groups were depicted is therefore fruitful in identifying whether Friends' experience, including their representation in the accounts, was distinctive. The oldest piece of legislation used after 1688 was the 1581 Recusancy Law, originally a penalty for Roman Catholics. Refusal to attend Anglican church services was an indictable offense punishable by fines and forfeiture of estates; after the Toleration Act, refusal to pay church rates still led to prosecution, usually via magistrates rather than higher courts.[26]

Other laws originated from fear of nonconformity: the 1650 Blasphemy Act, used to prosecute the early Quaker leader James Nayler, stemmed from a desire to "return to an older era of church government" in which an established church, a licensed press, and the Blasphemy Act would sustain social and moral order.[27] Nayler's activities were problematic; he entered Bristol on Palm Sunday 1656 in apparent imitation of Christ entering Jerusalem.[28] His trial was unusual, though: Friends were more often accused of blasphemy in theological debates, as criminal blasphemy was a "complex and obscure crime," and few cases met legal requirements for prosecution. Many zealous Protestants saw Friends as blasphemous both before and after the 1689 Toleration Act,[29] but the difficulty of proving it may explain the absence of blasphemy cases, which would probably have piqued readers' interest.

After the Restoration of the monarchy in 1660, an increasing range of anti-nonconformist legislation was passed, including the 1661 Corporation Act. Not specifically anti-Quaker, it excluded those who refused to take the Anglican sacrament, or to swear oaths of supremacy and allegiance, from town, county, and national government until the law's repeal in 1828. This limited Friends' potential to represent their regional communities, although it did not lead to prosecutions. Quakers' persecution also continued with the Five Mile Act (1665), also repealed in 1828, which sought specifically to limit Friends' preaching by prohibiting those who refused to swear oaths of loyalty from coming within five miles of any borough sending burgesses to Parliament. Under this act, William Penn and William Mead were tried at the Old Bailey in September 1670.[30] Similarly, the 1673 Test Act required officeholders to swear an oath to the king and Church of England and to deny the Catholic doctrine of transubstantiation. Predominantly aimed at Catholics, it continued sanctions against dissenters and prevented attendance at English universities or the holding of public office until 1828, although as Mark Freeman notes, some male Friends may have sworn oaths to maintain public roles.[31] It was unlikely, though, to lead to trial.

Although William of Orange and his wife, Mary, were crowned in 1689, and the Toleration Act later that year enabled Protestant dissenters to worship without hindrance, the following quarter century saw additional laws oppress Friends. A significant example that led to the distrainment of Quakers like Robert Wardell of Durham was the 1691 Poll Act, which required all non-Anglican preachers and teachers, among others, to contribute twenty shillings per quarter, for a year, for William's war with France.[32] Similarly, the 1690 Militia Act revisited the 1661 act and affected Friends wealthy enough to be taxed, who were distrained after refusing to contribute.[33] The 1711 Occasional Conformity Act then outlawed the practice by which dissenters took Anglican Communion occasionally in order to avoid the limitations of the Test Acts. This affected Quakers insofar as "church reforms" supported by Queen Anne positioned nonconformists negatively, with the 1714 Schism Act inspired by the University of Oxford preacher Henry Sacheverell's sermon attacking dissenters' schools for alleged "irreligion and disunity."[34] Anne's death, on August 1, 1714, the day the legislation was intended to be implemented, prevented this.

When George, Anne's distant German cousin, ascended to the throne shortly thereafter, he did not seek to implement the act, and both the Occasional Conformity and Schism Acts were repealed in 1718. John Seed interprets this as a reward for "dissenting loyalty" to the Hanoverian succession during the 1715 crisis, which witnessed violence against dissenters.[35] Quakers continued, though, to be persecuted, not least owing to their refusal to swear oaths. As analysis of Old Bailey publications reveals, this proved a stumbling block for many Quaker victims, emphasizing their apparent refusal to engage with civil society. Although the Affirmation Act was made perpetual in June 1715, with the affirmation simplified in 1722 to acknowledge some Friends' disquiet at the earlier reference to "the presence of Almighty God,"[36] it did not apply to criminal cases, hence, as the *Proceedings* relate, the relatively high number of Quakers who could not testify.

Furthermore, although all trials for serious crimes committed in Middlesex and the City of London, excepting south of the River Thames, took place at the court, no trials relating to tithes, the tenth of earnings parishioners were expected to donate to the church, which were occasionally dealt with at the Old Bailey,[37] appear in the *Proceedings*. This is the case even though Friends continued to be prosecuted for their refusal to pay until the 1836 Tithe Commutation Act. Joseph Besse's *Sufferings* refers to Newgate Prison, often used to hold prisoners after Old Bailey trials; references in Friends' accounts to imprisonment there may relate to trials at the Old Bailey. For example, Jeremiah Waring was accused of "riot" in 1684[38] and possibly was tried in the Old Bailey since riot was occasionally tried in criminal courts.[39] This suggests that some cases involving Quakers were excluded from published accounts; perhaps their refusal to pay tithes was viewed as problematic by authors seeking to minimize sympathy for nonconformists who denied the clergy a controversial tax. On the other hand, Friends were often depicted as hypocritical. Although some later eighteenth- and early nineteenth-century representations were more sympathetic, possibly owing to changes from 1778, when the City of London authorities were "concerned to demonstrate to the public the fairness and impartiality of judicial procedures,"[40] even this was colored by stereotyping.

Of the cases referring to Quakers that appear in the Old Bailey *Proceedings* for the period 1696–1815, the majority did not, however, relate directly to the laws outlined above. Readers of the accounts were probably aware, though, that aspects of Friends' religious practice were illegal, and, as this involved refusal to pay the established church, it is hardly surprising that accounts of Quakers in court were rarely sympathetic. Indeed, they often provided depictions of Friends in ways that, although changing over time, offered a stereotype to a largely non-Quaker readership, possibly because Friends were sometimes viewed with sympathy, as evidenced by Besse's accounts of non-Quaker neighbors' or family members' paying fines and buying distrained goods; Anglican clerics may have found this dangerously subversive. It is useful, therefore, to consider this legal and cultural landscape, and its reliance on the othering of Friends and other minorities that affected how Quakers were depicted, irrespective of their status as victim, perpetrator, or witness.

MAKING VICTIMS INTO VILLAINS

In the few murder trials that included a Quaker victim, the description of the deceased reveals ongoing resentment of Friends and, probably, other minority groups. While the first such example, an account of the execution of Thomas Randal in 1696, referred to his victim, Roger Levens, as "the Quaker" on all but one occasion,[41] emphasizing the murdered man's inferior status, other accounts of murder trials were even less sympathetic. In the same year, Edward Holland and Peter Robinson were tried for the murder of "William Iles a Quaker."[42] According to the account, Iles defended himself initially and "broke [Holland's] head" with Holland's stick. Holland then "gave him the aforesaid [sword] Wound," killing Iles and leading to Holland's execution. Despite the verdict, the account's emphasis on Iles's self-defense represents Quakers as selective in their peace testimony, which by 1696 was relatively well known among non-Quakers.

It is revealing that there is a lack of comparable published cases involving Jewish murder victims until almost a century later. This may reflect a lack of interest among the readership of the Old Bailey publications, possibly stemming from the fact that at the time of Holland's trial, Quakers were a larger minority and were therefore perceived as more problematic by the Anglican hierarchy, especially given their refusal to pay tithes, their rejection of clergy, and their pacifism. Even as murder victims, then, Friends might be positioned as hypocritical if attempting self-defense. That is not to suggest that anti-Semitism did not flavor accounts; rather, only after the city's intervention in 1778 were accounts of Jewish victims published. Previously, such cases were presumably viewed as not of interest to most readers, suggesting different, though equally problematic, prejudice. Todd Endelman notes how the late eighteenth-century stereotype of the criminal Jew was influential even among higher-status members of the Jewish community[43] who may have read Old Bailey accounts positioning lower-status Jews, possibly recent immigrants, as criminals. This was the case in the account of the trial of Porter Ridout.

In October 1784 a young Jewish boy, Moses Lazarus, died in St. James's Parish after Ridout, a coffeehouse keeper, fired shots at a reportedly rowdy crowd of local people celebrating Simchat Torah; this led to Ridout's trial for murder.[44] The apparent rowdiness mirrors Endelman's remarks on the later Georgian stereotype of criminal Jews. This may be why Ridout was found not guilty after a trial involving a number of character witnesses and a detailed account of the events; it suggests a desire to persuade Jewish as well as other readers of the court's fairness. Of additional interest is the account's reference to Daniel Dias, the apothecary who testified to Lazarus's injuries. The defense counsel, implicitly questioning Dias's capacity to assess injuries, asked him, "you are only an apothecary?" Although the question was intended to belittle him, J. Burnby notes that the terms *surgeon* and *apothecary* were used interchangeably. In Dias we see a Jewish figure of authority whose account was viewed as less significant than that of the non-Jewish surgeon Mr. Sheppard, who described the injuries in more detail (or his account was granted more space).[45] Nevertheless, Lazarus is referred to by name or as "the deceased"; he was not depersonalized, in contrast to Roger Levens. As the account of Lazarus's death was written decades after Levens's, the differences may reflect stylistic changes. Or they may reflect the City of London's desire for fairness as much as they do a difference between the representation of Quakers and Jews, a point I shall return to shortly.

Other cases include Quakers *accused* of murder, which offer insights into changes in the representation of Friends but also into the ongoing fascination with the conundrum of Quakers engaged in violence, albeit in self-defense. In September 1744, Thomas James was tried for the murder of William Corryndon.[46] James had struck Corryndon "with a stick on the nose" in early May 1744, after which Corryndon "languished" for almost three weeks before dying. The trial revealed that a quarrel had taken place, although the court determined that the death resulted from self-defense. A witness, John Smart, asserted that Corryndon struck first, possibly because of drunkenness, and was better armed, having "the biggest stick," although the violence was soon mutual. James had reportedly "laid hold of the deceased and threw him down with his face upon the ground; his face was very bloody and the blood run down very sadly between his Eyes. After he was down [James] beat him with his stick several times, and broke his stick upon him.... [James] went to strike at him again, though I don't know that he struck him any more, but the deceased lay in a dismal condition; for I believe he was in liquor, and what between that and the blows he could not stir himself." A surgeon, Sparham, who treated Corryndon referred to "Mr. James the Quaker," before outlining the fatal injuries. Based on Sparham's testimony, it was concluded that Corryndon would probably have survived had he received prompt medical attention. Certainly, the degree of detail seems intended for those interested in morbid details of murder cases, and designed to position Friends as inherently hypocritical given their peace testimony. Striking a man initially may have been viewed by many readers as understandable, but to continue to beat Corryndon when his drunkenness meant that he could not defend himself was likely to be viewed as both cowardly and unmanly. Although such terms were not used, the image of James "[breaking] his stick" underlines the account's salacious nature. Edwina Newman concludes that such reports may have been intended to sully Friends' good name by positioning them as acting unlawfully and hypocritically. She therefore rightly asks whether James was a Quaker.[47] Certainly, Friends' self-defense seems rarely to have been viewed sympathetically in the publications, perpetuating preconceived ideas of Quakers.

More commonly, Quakers were victims of theft. Yet in many cases, particularly before 1778, accounts of crimes aimed to titillate a non-Quaker readership by listing how Quakers had been robbed, and of what. Although other accounts of robbery also sought to entertain readers greedy for details of items taken, the inclusion of Friends made such accounts additionally satisfying for Anglican authors aware of plain testimony; anything smacking of hypocrisy offered an opportunity to ridicule. Grand larceny was the most common offense in the *Proceedings* and related to the theft of goods worth one shilling or more,[48] suggesting that accounts often served to emphasize stereotypes of wealthy Friends. An illustrative case is that of Sarah Tonge, accused of shoplifting from Quaker haberdasher Joseph Green in early 1773.[49] Green's stock reportedly included French silk laces and gauze, underlining the apparent limitations of Friends' plain testimony. Another is William Hurt and William Kenton's trial for highway robbery of a Quaker family in January 1785, which relied upon the evidence of their coachman, John Acksin, the only non-Quaker present. Acksin confirmed the items stolen, including Mrs. Walker's purse, "a kind of sky blue ... [with] trinkets of gold about it, or it was gilded a little"; Master Walker's was green.[50] As for Joseph Green, apparent hypocrisy was highlighted with the description of items contrasting with Friends' aesthetics, also disseminated in the *Proceedings*: terms such as "Quaker brown" were reported to describe colors worn by those seeking to dress according to plain testimony.[51] It is useful, then, to compare this case to accounts of wealthy Jews in the same decade: David Levy was assaulted and robbed by a distant cousin in 1782 and had valuable belongings stolen, in this instance a gold medal, silver cups, gold rings, and a quantity of money.[52] However, while "othering" was attempted in both accounts, that of Levy probably confirmed non-Jewish expectations of Jewish wealth, rather than the charge of hypocrisy implicitly levied at Friends.

Although the ultimate verdict was out of the hands of Quaker victims, punishment of the guilty could be represented as Friends' responsibility. In no grand larceny cases with a Quaker victim was the guilty party executed. This may reflect the court's noting of Friends' sensibilities, or perhaps it reveals a view that Quaker victims such as Marmaduke Westwood, a cabinetmaker who in 1802 refused to be sworn in a case involving a stolen knife case, did not deserve full recognition of the crime.[53] This treatment stands in contrast to the representation of Jewish victims, who, in part owing to their willingness to swear and then testify, were not often represented as problematic: the 1716 trial of serial robber James Bullock enabled his victim, Nathan Samuel, to testify, resulting in Bullock's execution.[54] That is not to say that Jews were always depicted as good citizens; the Ridout trial suggests otherwise.

It should also be noted that in half of the twelve cases of grand larceny in which Quakers were witnesses, they were granted generic titles such as "an old quaker," as in the account of Charles Simpson's trial in 1782.[55] As noted elsewhere, the stock character of the Quaker originated in the seventeenth century and continued well into the nineteenth.[56] Seymour Chatman's 1978 work on flat characterization, *Story and Discourse*, may, if applied to depictions of Friends by non-Quakers, suggest that it was not always necessary for them to be described in detail. Readers were aware of stereotyped behavior associated with Quakers and brought their preconceptions to bear when consuming accounts that were not, seemingly, viewed as less accurate despite the use of stereotypes. Therefore, "an old quaker" may have signified a range of qualities, depending on the author and text as much as on the individual represented. Similarly, albeit less frequently, the phrase "several Jews" appears, for example, in accounts of the 1719 trial of Gothard Davis and 1724 trial of Moses Ouseman.[57] If the term held a range of well-known and distinctive connotations, this may explain an unwillingness to discard it, especially if the process of othering Friends or Jews served to confirm, to the Anglican authorities, what the majority were *not*.

CONDEMNATION BY ASSOCIATION

Ongoing suspicion of religious nonconformists based on decades-old stereotypes probably also led to condemnation by association, either through reference to sites of criminal activity that were current or former areas of Quaker activity or through Friends' refusal to swear. The latter, especially, could be extremely problematic in criminal trials where Quakers were called as witnesses. Accounts that noted how refusal to swear led to the acquittal of possibly guilty parties implicitly condemned such behavior, hinting, perhaps, at Quaker sympathy for criminals. On several occasions, the accounts include references to non-Quakers who represented themselves as Friends in order to commit crimes. Thus in accounts selected to appeal to a readership already aware of Quaker stereotypes, Friends became associated with criminal activities in which they had not participated.

Othering experienced by Quakers and Jews in eighteenth-century England may certainly have been tied to location; there are references in the *Proceedings* to areas historically linked to one group or the other, meaning that they continued to be linked to criminality. For example, Quakers were implicitly associated with Quaker Street in London's East End, which was notorious for crime in the later eighteenth century, and near Wheeler Street meetinghouse, which Friends sold in the same period.[58] Friends founded a "soup society" to alleviate poverty locally,[59] although their philanthropy did not prevent the publication of accounts of fourteen crimes, mainly theft, occurring on or around the street between 1768 and 1815. Three were published before the City of London took over the *Proceedings* in 1778 and eleven in the following thirty-eight years. Therefore, the London authorities' desire that the *Proceedings* represent trials more reliably did not deter ongoing and possibly deliberate reference to areas nominally affiliated with Friends. A less significant geographical relationship between Jews and crime is apparent; Poor Jewry Lane was referred to six times in the years 1739–77, suggesting an aim to other both groups, though with different motives, a point to which I return in the conclusion.

Friends' refusal to swear was not treated as equally problematic in all accounts; rather, it must be considered in relation to other factors: gender, status, and the caliber of other witnesses. However, authors probably welcomed the opportunity to depict Quakers as problematic, albeit in a more restrained manner by the mid-eighteenth century. Mary Bland, a midwife whose actions led to the servant Hannah Perfect's acquittal after a trial for infanticide in January 1747, is a useful example. Bland was the only witness, other than another servant, but, as a Friend, Bland refused to swear and so could not testify.[60] Although Perfect was the accused, Bland's refusal was likely to be viewed as a failure to act as an expert witness, thereby aiding the alleged perpetrator of infanticide and failing in her duty to uphold social norms.[61] A similar example appears in early 1772: Francis Talbot was ultimately acquitted of the charge of breaking and entering because "the constable who apprehended him being a Quaker, and refusing to take an oath," could not testify.[62] However, the Friend's refusal prevented the prosecution of a suspected thief, not a suspected murderer, which may explain the rather shorter account, intended still, it seems, to identify the Quaker's failings as a representative of the local legal system.

On other occasions, as for Bland, the refusal of a Quaker witness to swear continued to be a potent means of critiquing Friends for a perceived failure to fulfill their societal duties, as analysis of the account of the 1788 trial of William Mason, found guilty of stealing from the Duke of Devonshire, suggests. Mason's defense called several character witnesses, including one Mrs. Sparrow, identified only as "a Quaker," who attested to his "unblemished character," although she would not be sworn in; she reportedly responded, "I will affirm to any thing."[63] If the published accounts are representative, the later eighteenth century (ca. 1788–1801) saw the highest number of Friends as witnesses, averaging one a year. This did not mean that Quakers were depicted as trustworthy citizens by the authors of the *Proceedings*. The generic term "anything" that Mrs. Sparrow allegedly used seems intended to suggest her, and by extension Friends', unreliability: instead of taking an oath, she affirms without reflection. Certainly, a female Quaker of presumably low status linked to a thief would not endear herself to the authorities.

An alternative example, differing perhaps because of the Friend's gender, is offered in the account of the trial of twenty-three-year-old James Smith in 1801, at which John Kent refused to swear and therefore did not give evidence. He did assist the victim, Mrs. Weston, a sailor's wife, by accompanying her to court when her husband's silver watch was stolen.[64] That the account included details of Kent's support of Mrs. Weston may suggest that, in part thanks to the intervention of the authorities, lower-status male Friends began to be viewed with less suspicion, and their refusal to swear with less derision. Indeed, two further cases involving Quakers who witnessed violent crimes suggest that male Friends, especially those of higher status, were less likely to be condemned, even before 1778. Certainly, their role as surgeons rather than midwives meant that they enjoyed a growing level of status and recognition for their apparently higher level of medical skill. In addition, several witnesses were available, such as when Datleft

[Detlef] Christopher Krause, Lord Harrington's cook, was fatally attacked in 1753 by two highwaymen. He was initially taken to the Quaker surgeon Mr. West, although the prosecution counsel noted that West "is a quaker, and we cannot call him in."[65] Owing to the large number of other witnesses, however, including another surgeon, William Cleator, West's failure to testify was less significant, and those accused of Krause's murder were found guilty. In a second case, in 1771, the poacher Richard Mortis was prosecuted for shooting Thomas Parkinson, who was then treated by the Quaker surgeon Mr. Baker; Baker, in Parkinson's words, "won't take an oath."[66] However, there were other witnesses, including Parkinson's father, and Mortis was found guilty. Although in both cases Friends' refusal to swear and hence to testify was noted, the reliability of the men as professionals was unquestioned. On the other hand, the account of Perfect's trial positioned it as hinging on a midwife's withheld testimony, suggesting a desire to identify Quaker women as inherently unreliable, in contrast to the male surgeons, who remained respected citizens.

Guilt by association can also be identified in cases in which non-Quakers claimed to be Quakers in order to dupe others. An early eighteenth-century gang of criminals included one "like a Quaker."[67] Decades earlier, a "lusty young wench" pretended to be a Quaker so that she could become a servant and rob a household of plate and clothes worth more than £50.[68] Such accounts warned unwitting citizens that Friends might not be what they seemed: they could be robbers or they might be Quakers, but either way they would not live up to societal expectations. Inability to prosecute Friends for nonattendance after 1689 was replaced by an ability to condemn their symbolic, professional, or historical proximity to crime and criminals.

CHANGE OVER TIME

The crimes considered in this chapter range across the long eighteenth century, making it useful, in conclusion, to determine whether representations of Friends changed over time, especially after 1778. There was a move to acknowledge respectable male Friends, although reference to individuals such as Mr. Baker and Mr. West did not prevent continued reference to places associated with Friends as sites of crime. This was even more the case with Quakers than with places linked to Jews. Published reports of crime in Quaker Street probably related to growing impoverishment in the area but may also signal the desire of the *Proceedings*' authors to continue to imply a link between a formerly illegal religious group and current crimes, regardless of Friends' growing respectability in the community. Similarly, the ongoing use of flat characterization is apparent when Quakers are referred to as refusing to swear. Although possibly an accurate account of the trials, when offered alongside stereotypes of Friends as difficult, such references position Quakers, even in their absence, as disruptive individuals acting outside law-abiding society and thus wielding a disproportionate amount of influence. Their actions, or lack thereof, might lead to the acquittal of a guilty party.

Furthermore, while Endelman notes that witnesses and criminals were not officially identified as Jewish in Georgian Old Bailey records,[69] the absence of Quakers from criminal trials, largely because they could not affirm,[70] was officially represented as a function of moral failing rather than limited legislation. Nevertheless, Endelman concludes that non-Jews thought that crimes perpetrated by Jews were common,[71] which might be linked to references to biblical Jews in the *Ordinary's Accounts*. Before 1778, the *Proceedings*' authors sought to position Friends as similarly criminal, with little recognition of crimes against Quakers. Kaiserman's assertions regarding the literary and cultural underpinnings of stereotypes of Jews may, then, also be applied to Friends: "establishmentarian thinkers ... work[ed] with inherited prejudices supported by literary convention,"[72] which marked them as incompatible with mainstream English values.[73] To suggest this via accounts of criminal activity was particularly damning. It drew upon centuries of depictions of such groups as divisive at best and actively nefarious at worst. However, while many trial records reveal authorities' suspicion of Quakers and a desire to select cases depicting them in an unflattering light, their good standing in society is also apparent. Perhaps, as Ursula Henriques notes, groups faced stigma until they had full legal emancipation.[74] That the *Proceedings* emphasized Quaker failings to a greater degree than it did those of a group stigmatized for much longer suggests that *partial* legal acceptance did little to remove suspicion stemming from an apparent failure in court as citizens. Moreover, Friends' economic success had developed alongside their refusal to integrate themselves fully into the larger society. Perhaps because of this refusal, Quakers do not seem to have been positioned much closer to hegemonic ideals than their Jewish counterparts.[75] It is difficult to know what impact this had on London's Quakers and Jews; as readers' criticisms suggest, published accounts of cases did not necessarily influence readers.[76]

By way of conclusion, underlining how contradictory representations of a minority might exist simultaneously, aspects of Friends' growing respectability are also apparent: the middling male Quaker was, by the mid-eighteenth century, implicitly associated with honesty and reliability. Esther Sahle's work on Friends in business reveals that Quakers actively sought such associations after being criticized in the 1750s for their perceived failure, allegedly originating from greed rather than pacifism, to protect Pennsylvania's inhabitants from French soldiers during the Seven Years' War.[77] Conflicting depictions in the second half of the long eighteenth century may, then, reflect confusion about a group that was trying to maintain a reputation for honesty in business while also being criticized for excessive interest in profit and lack of wider social engagement. This was a stereotype perpetuated by those seeking to keep Friends othered. Trial accounts might, therefore, have been read as—and might even have been written to depict—an Anglican majority helping Quakers despite their refusal to integrate.

When the tailor Deborah Weaver was robbed by a former journeyman in 1758, and "being a quaker, would not swear," her servant Anne Peirce and lodger John Fosset testified.[78] A sympathetic reader might have viewed this as reflecting the esteem in which she was held; a cynic might have seen it as nonconformist women's worrying influence. Although mid-eighteenth-century courts were no longer keen to prosecute Friends for refusing to swear, in other ways their publications continued to position Quakers as problematic. Even after 1778, the reiteration of Quaker Street as a site of crime and the inclusion of Friends in apparently close communion with criminals, alongside the tithe testimony, meant that Quakers remained linked to crime in the eyes of those influenced by decades of inherited prejudice. The persecution that Friends experienced originated in their history as a distinctive, criminalized minority, but it was perpetuated owing to their perceived affiliation with other groups, such as Jews, to whom they were linked in reality, and especially in the minds of critics.

NOTES

1. Jean-François Staszak, "Other/Otherness," in *International Encyclopedia of Human Geography*, ed. Rob Kitchin and Nigel Thrift (Amsterdam: Elsevier, 2008), 43–47.

2. Gary K. Waite, *Jews and Muslims in Seventeenth-Century Discourse: From Religious Enemies to Allies and Friends* (New York: Routledge, 2019), 7.

3. Geoffrey Cantor, *Quakers, Jews, and Science: Religious Responses to Modernity and the Sciences in Britain, 1650–1900* (Oxford: Oxford University Press, 2005), 111.

4. Erin Bell, "The Early Quakers, the Peace Testimony, and Masculinity in England, 1660–1720," *Gender and History* 23, no. 2 (2011): 283.

5. Erin Bell, "Quakers and the Law," in *The Quakers, 1656–1723: The Evolution of an Alternative Community*, ed. Richard C. Allen and Rosemary Moore (University Park: Penn State University Press, 2018), 263–72.

6. William C. Braithwaite, *The Beginnings of Quakerism* (London: Macmillan, 1912), 261.

7. Salo W. Baron, "Ghetto and Emancipation," in *The Menorah Treasury: Harvest of Half a Century*, ed. Leo W. Schwartz (Philadelphia: Jewish Publication Society of America, 1964), 51. Baron does not acknowledge opposition to resettlement in 1650s England—see, for example, William Prynne, *A short demurer to the Jewes* (London, 1656).

8. Matt Goldish, *The Sabbatean Prophets* (Cambridge: Harvard University Press, 2004), 111; Brandon Marriott, *Transnational Networks and Cross-Religious Exchange in the Seventeenth-Century Mediterranean and Atlantic Worlds* (London: Routledge, 2015), 55.

9. Thomas Lewis, *The Scourge in Vindication of the Church of England* (London, June 17, 1717), 162.

10. Charles Lamb, "Imperfect Sympathies," *London Magazine* 20, no. 4 (1821): 154.

11. Aaron Kaiserman, *Evolutions of Jewish Character in British Fiction* (London: Routledge, 2018), 18.

12. *Old Bailey Proceedings Online* (now available as a searchable online database covering the years 1674–1913, at http://www.oldbaileyonline.org, version 8.0, March 4, 2019), *Ordinary of Newgate's Account*, July 1684 (OA16840710).

13. Ibid., July 1716 (OA17160713).

14. Of Ordinary's accounts published in 1730–32 and 1743–44, nine (30 percent) referred to the immorality of biblical Jews. Roughly 5 percent of all Ordinary's accounts (25 of 495), and roughly 6 percent of those published from 1695 to 1772 (25 of 448) contained anti-Semitic slurs.

15. See Frank Felsenstein, *Anti-Semitic Stereotypes: A Paradigm of Otherness in English Popular Culture, 1660–1830* (Baltimore: Johns Hopkins University Press, 1995), 51.

16. See, for example, Charles Leslie, *The Snake in the Grass, or Satan Transform'd to an Angel of Light* (London: Charles Brome, 1696).

17. Lajos Brons, "Othering, an Analysis," *Transcience* 6, no. 1 (2015): 69–70.

18. Åsa Boholm, "Christian Construction of the Other: The Role of Jews in the Early Modern Carnival of Rome," *Journal of Mediterranean Studies* 24, no. 2 (2015): 37–52.

19. Bernard Glassman, *Antisemitic Stereotypes Without Jews: Images of the Jews in England, 1290–1700* (Detroit: Wayne State University Press, 2017), 53.

20. See Erin Bell, "Stock Characters with Stiff-Brimmed Bonnets: Depictions of Quaker Women by Outsiders, c. 1650–1800," in *New Critical Studies on Early Quaker Women, 1650–1800*, ed. Michele Lise Tarter and Catie Gill (Oxford: Oxford University Press, 2018), 91–109; Kaiserman, *Evolutions of Jewish Character*.

21. In *Tales from the Hanging Court* (London: Hodder Arnold, 2006; repr., London: Bloomsbury Academic, 2010), 47–50, Tim Hitchcock and Robert Shoemaker consider anti-Semitism but not the similar stereotyping of other religious minorities.

22. Clive Emsley, Tim Hitchcock, and Robert Shoemaker, "The Proceedings—Publishing History of the Proceedings," *Old Bailey Proceedings Online* (https://www.oldbaileyonline.org/, version 7.0, July 27, 2018); Robert Shoemaker, "The Old Bailey Proceedings and the Representation of Crime and Criminal Justice in Eighteenth-Century London," *Journal of British Studies* 47, no. 3 (2008): 562.

23. Shoemaker, "Old Bailey Proceedings," 580.

24. Emsley, Hitchcock, and Shoemaker, "Publishing History of the Proceedings."

25. Seven of the nine post-toleration laws were also applicable to Jews. See H. S. Q. Henriques, *The Jews and the English Law* (Oxford: Oxford University Press, 1908); David Katz, *The Jews in the History of England, 1485–1850* (Oxford: Clarendon Press, 1994), 170.

26. Nicholas J. Morgan, "Lancashire Quakers and the Tithe, 1660–1730," *Bulletin of the John Rylands Library* 70, no. 3 (1988): 65.

27. Randy Robertson, *Censorship and Conflict in Early Modern England* (University Park: Penn State University Press, 2009), 126.

28. Erin Bell, "Eighteenth-Century Quakerism and the Rehabilitation of James Nayler, Seventeenth-Century Radical," *Journal of Ecclesiastical History* 59, no. 3 (2008): 426–29.

29. David Manning, "Accusations of Blasphemy in English Anti-Quaker Polemic, c. 1660–1701," *Quaker Studies* 14, no. 1 (2009): 28, 27.

30. Bonnelyn Young Kunze, *Margaret Fell and the Rise of Quakerism* (Stanford: Stanford University Press, 1994), 140; Jane Calvert, *Quaker Constitutionalism and the Political Thought of John Dickinson* (Cambridge: Cambridge University Press, 2009), 58; Nancy Black Sagafi-Nejad, *Friends at the Bar: A Quaker View of Law, Conflict Resolution, and Legal Reform* (Albany: State University of New York Press, 2011), 31.

31. Mark Freeman, "Quakers, Business, and Philanthropy," in *The Oxford Handbook of Quaker Studies*, ed. Stephen W. Angell and Pink Dandelion (Oxford: Oxford University Press, 2013), 421.

32. Joseph Besse, *A Collection of the Sufferings of the People Called Quakers*, 2 vols. (London: Luke Hinde, 1753), 1:190; "William and Mary, 1691: An Act for Raiseing Money by a Poll [. . .] for the carrying on a vigorous War against France" (1691), in *Statutes of the Realm*, vol. 6, 1685–94, ed. John Raithby (London: Great Britain Record Commission, 1819), 302–10, http://www.british-history.ac.uk/report.aspx?compid=46360.

33. Bell, "Quakers and the Law," 277.

34. William Gibson, *The Church of England, 1688–1832* (London: Routledge, 2001), 83.

35. John Seed, *Dissenting Histories: Religious Division and the Politics of Memory in Eighteenth-Century England* (Edinburgh: Edinburgh University Press, 2008), 29.

36. R. K. Webb, "From Toleration to Religious Liberty," in *Liberty Secured? Britain Before and After 1688*, ed. J. R. Jones (Stanford: Stanford University Press, 1992), 175.

37. See, for example, John Rayner, *Cases at Large Concerning Tithes [. . .]*, vol. 1 (London: W. Strahan and W. Woodfall, 1783), cv–cvi.

38. Besse, *Collection of the Sufferings*, 1:473.

39. London Lives, 1690 to 1800: Crime, Policy, and Social Policy in the Metropolis, "The Courts," https://www.londonlives.org/static/CriminalCourts.jsp (version 2.0, March 2018).

40. Emsley, Hitchcock, and Shoemaker, "Publishing History of the Proceedings."

41. *Old Bailey Proceedings Online*, January 1696 (OA16960129).

42. Ibid., September 1696, trial of Edward Holland and Peter Robinson (t16960909-46).

43. Todd M. Endelman, *The Jews of Georgian England, 1714–1830* (Philadelphia: Jewish Publication Society, 1979; repr., Ann Arbor: University of Michigan Press, 1999), 298–300.
44. *Old Bailey Proceedings Online*, October 1784, trial of Porter Ridout (t17841020-1).
45. J. Burnby, "Jewish Apothecaries and Surgeons in Eighteenth-Century London," *Pharmaceutical Historian* 21, no. 4 (1991): 9–10.
46. *Old Bailey Proceedings Online*, September 1744, trial of Thomas James (t17440912-37).
47. Edwina Newman, "Children of Light and Sons of Darkness: Quakers, Oaths, and the Old Bailey Proceedings in the Eighteenth Century," *Quaker Studies* 12, no. 1 (2008): 81.
48. Clive Emsley, Tim Hitchcock, and Robert Shoemaker, "Crime and Justice—Crimes Tried at the Old Bailey," *Old Bailey Proceedings Online*, https://www.oldbaileyonline.org/static/Crime.jsp (version 7.0, July 27, 2018).
49. *Old Bailey Proceedings Online*, April 1773, trial of Sarah, the wife of Stancey Tonge, otherwise Thomas Tonge (t17730421-2).
50. Ibid., January 1785, trial of William Hurt and William Kenton (t17850112-51).
51. See a reference to stolen thread, ibid., January 1788, trial of John Langford, William Annand (t17880109-40).
52. Ibid., July 1782, trial of Henry Jacobs (t17820703-55).
53. Ibid., July 1802, trial of James Sheppard (t18020714-23).
54. Ibid., January 1716, trial of James Bullock (t17160113-27).
55. Ibid., October 1782, trial of Charles Simpson (t17821016-15).
56. Bell, "Stock Characters."
57. *Old Bailey Proceedings Online*, May 1719, trial of Gothard Davis (t17190514-3), and October 1724, trial of Moses Ouseman, alias Souseman (t17241014-6).
58. Simon Dixon, "Quakers and the London Parish, 1670–1720," *London Journal* 32, no. 3 (2007): 230.
59. Dan Cruickshank, *Spitalfields: A History of a Nation in a Handful of Streets* (London: Windmill, 2016), xii.
60. *Old Bailey Proceedings Online*, February 1747, trial of Hannah Perfect (t17470225-1).
61. Denise Ryan, "Playing the Midwife's Part in the English Nativity Plays," *Review of English Studies* 54, no. 216 (2003): 438.
62. *Old Bailey Proceedings Online*, January 1772, trial of Francis Talbot (t17720109-57).
63. Ibid., September 1788, trial of William Mason (t17880910-62).
64. Ibid., October 1801, trial of James Smith (t18011028-82).
65. Ibid., December 1753, trial of John Hambleton (t17531205-47).
66. Ibid., February 1771, trial of Richard Mortis (t17710220-12).
67. Ibid., February 1719, trial of William Wilson (t17190225-27).
68. Ibid., December 1677, trial of young wench (t16771212-9).
69. Endelman, *Jews of Georgian England*, 298.
70. Newman, "Children of Light," 73.
71. Endelman, *Jews of Georgian England*, 300.
72. Kaiserman, *Evolutions of Jewish Character*, 18.
73. Bell, "Stock Characters," 93.
74. U. R. Q. Henriques, "The Jewish Emancipation Controversy in Nineteenth-Century Britain," *Past and Present* 40, no. 1 (1968): 126.

75. John Barrell offers a division between "that," the culturally similar, and "the other," the very different. Friends and Jews occupy "the other" in this analysis. See Barrell, *The Infection of Thomas de Quincey: A Psychopathology of Imperialism* (New Haven: Yale University Press, 1991).

76. Shoemaker, "Old Bailey Proceedings," 577.

77. See Esther Sahle, "A Faith of Merchants: Quakers and Institutional Change in the Early Modern Atlantic, c. 1660–1800" (PhD diss., London School of Economics, 2016).

78. *Old Bailey Proceedings Online*, April 1758, trial of George Smith (t17580405-2).

CHAPTER 6

Quakers and Marriage Legislation in England in the Long Eighteenth Century

ROSALIND JOHNSON

Quakers developed their own marriage practices from the very earliest days of their movement. A couple would announce their intention to the Quaker meeting, following which enquiries would be made regarding their clearness from engagements to others. All being satisfactory, the couple would marry in an open meeting before Friends, and a certificate signed by all present would formally record the marriage.[1] But marrying within their own faith challenged accepted marriage procedures. As early as 1654, a man was tried at Newcastle Assizes after he married in the manner of Quakers.[2] Following the Restoration of Charles II in 1660, Quakers were prosecuted for marrying outside the Church of England and for failing to pay marriage fees to the parish priest.[3] Friends were also forced to defend their marriages against suits brought by potential heirs challenging the validity of a marriage, and Quaker widows were at risk from landlords who would deny a widow's right to remain in possession of a property by claiming that she had not been lawfully married to her husband.

QUAKERS AND MARRIAGE LEGISLATION IN ENGLAND

The Act of Toleration of 1689 allowed Quakers in England and Wales the right to worship in their own meeting places, but that did not extend to the right to marry in those meeting places. The only way to ensure a legal marriage was to marry before an ordained Church of England clergyman. Quaker marriages, not being contracted before such a minister, were still vulnerable to claims of invalidity after 1689.[4] They posed a threat to the established church's authority, and claims that they were irregular also reflected concerns relating to the wider issue of clandestine marriages and the threat such marriages represented to the control of inheritance.[5]

The subject of marriage law as it affected English Friends in the long eighteenth century has received limited attention from historians. Studies of marriage in the period vary in the extent of their treatment of Quaker marriages, but usually mention Quakers briefly in the context of a broader analysis of society, or only in the context of the exemption granted to Quakers in the 1753 Clandestine Marriage Act.[6] Quakers may have formed just 0.73 percent of the total population of England in the early eighteenth century, which could account for their limited consideration in the secondary literature.[7] An exception is a study by Rebecca Probert, which is a work of legal rather than social or family history, and considers the legal aspect of Quaker marriages in some detail.[8]

In studies of Quaker history in the period, when the issue of Quaker marriage has been discussed, it has invariably focused on marriage procedure within meetings and disciplinary cases directed at those who failed to conform to the accepted protocol.[9] It is not surprising, however, that historians of Quakerism have focused on Quaker marriage discipline rather than on legal issues. It is issues concerning marriage discipline that are most commonly found in monthly and quarterly meeting minute books, rather than challenges from non-Friends regarding the validity of such unions. Given the number of marriages known to have been contracted between Quakers, claims that such marriages were invalid are uncommon. William Braithwaite estimated the number of Quaker marriages in England and Wales between 1690 and 1699 as 2,193, between 1700 and 1709 as 2,221, and between 1710 and 1719 as 1,930.[10] The evidence of both Meeting for Sufferings minutes and the minutes of monthly and quarterly meetings reveals that the overwhelming majority of these couples would not have been pursued for a marriage fee by the parish priest, nor would their marriage have been called into question in a lawsuit over inheritance or a widow's rights. But the threat was there; if a newly married couple escaped attention from the parish priest over their marriage fees, they could not be secure that a suit would not threaten the legitimacy of their children, or the right of a widow to remain in her home or in possession of land or property that might provide her with an income.

Mindful of these threats, Quaker marriages were governed by an established procedure by 1689. George Fox may have taken steps as early as 1653 to regulate the marriage procedure of Friends, and in 1668 he further strengthened procedure to ensure that marriages were properly conducted and recorded.[11] Quakers took pains to emphasize that their weddings were not clandestine ceremonies. By the eighteenth century, couples were subject to an investigation before marriage by the monthly meetings of both parties, and the consent of parents was sought if applicable. The wedding itself was a public meeting conducted before Friends, during which the couple made a simple vow of commitment to each other. The couple and those present would sign a certificate recording that the marriage had taken place.[12]

Despite these precautions, Quaker marriages were still subject to challenge after 1689. Friends were still prosecuted for not paying marriage fees to parish priests, and Quakers still had to defend their marriages against claims regarding inheritance and the rights of widows. Friends experiencing such challenges often wrote to the Meeting for Sufferings in London, which advised and in some cases provided legal support on behalf of Friends.

THE ROLE OF THE MEETING FOR SUFFERINGS

The Meeting for Sufferings (MfS) had been established by 1675 to collect details of the suffering of Friends on account of their faith and to make representations to the authorities on their behalf. It monitored bills coming before each session of Parliament and appointed Friends to put forward the Quaker case as necessary.[13] By the early eighteenth century, it functioned as the central business meeting for Friends. It recorded in its minutes accounts of Quaker suffering and legal cases concerning Friends. Selected cases were recorded in the Books of Cases, a series of volumes of precedents and legal opinions. The Books of Cases were concerned with many issues other than marriage, but the importance of marriage law to the MfS is shown by the fact that selected cases concerning marriage were compiled into a separate manuscript sometime around or after 1700.[14]

A number of the cases and opinions collected by the MfS predated the 1689 Toleration Act. In a Nottinghamshire case from 1661, an attempt was made to eject a child from a copyhold property after the death of her father on the grounds that she was illegitimate, as her Quaker parents had not been lawfully married.[15] In that case the judge found in favor of the heir, asserting that her parents' marriage had been lawful.[16] The case has been claimed to have established Friends' marriages as valid in law and to have established a precedent for future legal challenges.[17] But the fact that similar cases continued to appear in the Books of Cases and in the minutes of the MfS indicates that contemporaries did not regard this case as decisive. Furthermore, as Probert has observed, the only surviving contemporary account of the case is in the Quaker records. The case was decided at Nottingham Assizes, a low-level court for making such decisions. The marriage in question had taken place in 1658, a time when marriages were required to be celebrated before a justice of the peace but when the law did not invalidate marriages that were not so conducted. Probert goes on to note that if the judge had, as alleged, referred to the marriage of Adam and Eve in asserting that the marriage was valid, it may have been because he had no more recent examples to which he could refer.[18]

From its beginnings, the Meeting for Sufferings sought advice from legal counsel and recorded these "advices" in the Books of Cases. In 1679, the MfS made a statement that if a man and a woman declare that they take the other to be their wife or husband as long as they both live, that should be lawful.[19] It was further the opinion of legal counsel Thomas Corbett in the same year that statute law did not make a marriage void if it was contracted other than according to the rites of the Book of Common Prayer.[20]

The case studies collected by the MfS, both before and after the 1689 Act of Toleration, were almost entirely English case studies. Marriage law in other jurisdictions was not routinely cited as a precedent, even when those laws were more accommodating to Quaker marriage. The law in Scotland throughout the long eighteenth century recognized marriage by consent as legal, if irregular.[21] The legal situation in Ireland was complex, and the history of the family in the long eighteenth century has received limited attention from scholars.[22] On the other side of the ocean, the American colonies and, after independence from British rule, the individual states of the United States of America developed their own marriage laws.[23] Much remains to be written about Quakers and marriage law on both sides of the Atlantic.

ABUSE OF QUAKER MARRIAGE PROCEDURE

The precedents and opinions recorded by the Meeting for Sufferings related to challenges to Quaker marriages from outside the community of Friends. But Quaker marriages and the Quaker marriage procedure, not being regulated by statute law, were at risk of abuse even among Friends. In 1695, the Alton Monthly Meeting in Hampshire refused to clear a couple for marriage after the prospective groom was found to have had a liaison with his grandfather's serving maid, but the couple nonetheless came to a meeting in the town of Basingstoke and declared that they took each other as husband and wife.[24] Despite its condemnation in the monthly meeting minutes, in 1697 the Alton Monthly Meeting was obliged to record a similar incident in its minutes. Without any of the usual preliminaries, a couple, the man not being a Friend, entered a meeting in the village of Baughurst and declared that they took each other in marriage. The woman was admonished for her actions by the women's meeting but refused to condemn herself.[25] Such occurrences were uncommon, but they were by no means confined to Alton.[26]

The lack of statute law regulating Friends' marriages could lead to a situation where one spouse rejected responsibility for the other, claiming that the Quaker marriage was not good in law. In one reputed case prior to 1689, a man claimed that he was not liable for his wife's debts because their Quaker wedding had not been solemnized according to the rites of the Church of England. But the judge was said to have repudiated the man's argument and found him liable for the debts.[27]

Furthermore, if a Quaker marriage was not recognized in law, then it would be possible to take a second spouse in a Church of England ceremony on the assumption, or in the hope, that the courts would not recognize the Quaker marriage. But despite the lack of statute recognition of marriages outside the Anglican Church, such an action could potentially lead to prosecution for bigamy. Lawrence Stone records a bigamy case from 1706 in which a man's first marriage had been performed by a Jesuit priest and the second by an Anglican minister. Despite the irregularity of the first marriage, the court found it to be valid, and the bigamist narrowly escaped execution for felony.[28] Quaker cases are almost unheard of, though in 1704 a case was reported to the MfS of a man tried for felony after he married a second wife in an Anglican ceremony and deserted his first wife, whom he had married among Friends. The details were unclear, and the MfS was unable to find anything more about it.²⁹ An instance of a second marriage when a first (Quaker) spouse was still living was recorded by Wiltshire Quakers. In 1721, Edward Jones abandoned his children and his wife of twelve years, Ann, for which offense he was disowned. He was reported as having married another woman, though this second marriage was mentioned only once in the monthly meeting minutes. A lawsuit between Jones and John Clark, Ann's father, dragged on for more than three years, but if it related to Jones's alleged second marriage rather than to his desertion of Ann, this was not stated in the minutes of either the monthly or the quarterly meeting.³⁰

QUAKERS AND MARRIAGE LEGISLATION, 1689–1753

The situation after the Toleration Act of 1689 was, therefore, one in which Quakers could worship in their own manner, but the position on marriage was still unclear. Although various lawsuits during the Restoration period had upheld Quaker marriages, and legal opinions sought by the MfS had expressed confidence in their validity, they were still not recognized by any statute law passed by Parliament, nor were they accepted as valid by the ecclesiastical courts. Lawsuits were still decided on a case-by-case basis, with all the expense and effort this involved for the parties concerned. Despite their rigorous marriage procedure, Quakers were still vulnerable to changes in the law affecting marriage. Parliament's ongoing concern regarding clandestine marriage in the first half of the long eighteenth century, until the Clandestine Marriage Act of 1753, was therefore a matter on which the MfS kept a close watch.

Parliament had made attempts after 1660 to prevent clandestine marriages, and the House of Lords made two attempts to regulate marriage in the same year as the 1689 Toleration Act. In 1690, the year following the Toleration Act, the House of Commons introduced a bill on clandestine marriage, and in 1691 the Lords introduced a bill regulating the marriages of minors.³¹ The MfS responded by actively lobbying Parliament to ensure that nothing prejudicial to Friends was inserted into any proposed legislation. They agreed to print the Quaker marriage certificate and distribute it to certain members of Parliament.³² Friends were active in speaking with those who they thought would influence Parliament, but a clause was nevertheless inserted in the clandestine marriage bill mandating that no one should marry without banns being called in their parish church. The MfS found this provision unacceptable, but any action it may have considered taking proved unnecessary when, according to the MfS minutes, the Commons threw out the bill.[33] However, the MfS was lobbying Parliament again in 1691 over proposed clandestine marriage legislation. Friends found some of the Lords sympathetic, but again the bill failed to pass into law.[34] The MfS briefly discussed a bill relating to marriage in 1698, but nothing appears to have come of it.[35]

Parliamentary activity on clandestine marriages in the 1690s energized the London Yearly Meeting (LYM), which recommended in its minutes that due care and attention be given to marriage procedure among Friends, noting in 1693 that there had been serious endeavors to pass legislation against clandestine marriages. The LYM stressed the need for an orderly marriage procedure that would demonstrate to all in authority that Quaker weddings were not clandestine affairs.[36] The MfS, as it had done prior to 1689, continued to seek legal opinions in cases where the validity of a marriage was challenged. In 1691, the Book of Cases recorded an opinion in the case of James Brown, who stood to inherit his grandfather's plantation on the Caribbean island of Nevis (and its slaves, though the MfS made no comment on this), but his uncle challenged the inheritance on the grounds that James's mother and his late father, being married as Quakers, were not legally married. Legal counsel's opinion was that if they had lived together as husband and wife, and had children, they were married and the children legitimate. Counsel made the further point that many persons had inherited estates without being able to prove that their parents had married according to the form of marriage used in the Church of England.[37] Two additional lawyers in this case declared Quaker marriages lawful and the children legitimate.[38]

The MfS usually sought examples from within the Society of Friends where a marriage outside the Church of England was challenged but proved lawful. Cases occurring outside the Society were not usually recorded in the collections of precedents, although one such case was written down in the first volume of cases. In October 1693, William Heath, an agent on James Island in the River Gambia on the African coast, had invited several persons to dinner and in their presence announced that he took an African woman, Speranca, to be his wife. Speranca later gave birth to a daughter, Elizabeth, in England. After Heath's death, his brother challenged the validity of

Speranca's marriage to William, but the court found the marriage valid, and Elizabeth the rightful heir of her father.[39] The position on marriages conducted in Africa continued to interest the MfS ten years after Heath's marriage, when it recorded in its minutes that the MfS would make enquiries of the Royal African Company as to its law and customs for marriage.[40]

Although Quakers refused to pay marriage fees and other dues to the Church of England, they were compliant in paying most civil taxes, including stamp duty payable on certain documents. In 1694, the MfS minutes state that Friends were to use stamped parchment for their marriage certificates.[41] In 1695, an act of Parliament levied a tax of five shillings on each marriage license and marriage certificate. It was followed by a second act the same year that levied a fee of 2s. 6d. on each marriage, with a greater fee for those of the social status of gentleman or above. To avoid evasion of the tax, the act stipulated where and how marriages were to take place, with penalties for clergy who did not comply. Certain loopholes in the act were closed up by an act of 1696, which also stiffened the penalties for clergy and introduced fines for a man marrying without banns or license, and for parish clerks and sextons who were complicit in the proceedings.[42] Additional legislation was enacted in 1698 and 1712.[43]

The 1695 acts were intended to raise revenue for the war with France, though there is no evidence in the MfS minutes that Friends had any issues with the use to which the duty was to be put.[44] The Friends' intention to comply with the law is reflected in a query of 1695 sent to the MfS: could a marriage certificate be signed if it was not stamped according to the act? The MfS replied that it could, but the certificate would have to be stamped subsequently.[45] The MfS monitored the 1696 act as it progressed through Parliament but focused on whether the terms were prejudicial to Friends; it concluded that they were not.[46] A misunderstanding of the 1696 legislation resulted in two Worcester Quakers' being summoned three years later, but the MfS wrote to advise them that this was in error.[47]

The MfS continued to receive news of lawsuits concerning the validity of Quaker marriages. In 1699–1700, the MfS advised Suffolk Friends on a lawsuit in which an heir was accused of being illegitimate, his parents having married among Friends. The jury eventually found for the heir.[48] In January 1701, the MfS received news from Hampshire concerning a Quaker widow denied her rights by Robert Knollys (or Knowles), lord of the manor of Millbrook near Southampton.[49] At no point was it suggested that Knollys was making the widow, Cordelia Cowdry, and her infant daughter homeless, but the estate was clearly of financial importance to her and her dowry appears to have been invested in it.[50] Knollys's motivation is unknown, but his justification was that because Cordelia and her husband, Thomas, had married as Quakers, they had not been legally married and so she had no widow's rights with respect to the lease.[51]

By February 1701, the MfS had employed an attorney in Cordelia Cowdry's defense. It had not been possible to resolve the case in Hampshire, and it was referred to the Court of Common Pleas, sitting in London.[52] This demanded resources far beyond those available to the young widow, who wrote to the MfS in June 1701 that she was happy to refer the management of her case to Friends, but warned that she could not bear the costs, especially if she lost the land.[53]

The case was complex. Robert Knollys was dead by July 1701, but this did not halt the case, which by November 1701 was being pursued once more.[54] At some point a new tenant, Robert Hewett, had been admitted to the copyhold estate. Cordelia Cowdry had apparently successfully ousted Hewett from the estate, and it was Hewett who appears to have pursued the case after Knollys's death.[55]

Despite the involvement of the MfS, the case dragged on without resolution. The LYM discussed the case in 1703, leaving it to the care of the MfS in order that Cowdry should not lose her dowry or her child suffer on account of her Quaker marriage.[56] By January 1704 the legal counsel acting on her behalf was hopeful of a positive outcome, telling representatives from the MfS that the Quakers were now a "considerable people" and that their marriages were regular.[57] But the case remained unresolved, and the LYM later that year urged the MfS to continue to offer its assistance.[58]

During the case, the MfS sought legal counsel and opinions on the issue of Quaker marriages. One attorney pleaded in the Cowdry case that what made a marriage was the mutual consent of the parties involved. The form of marriage in the Book of Common Prayer added to the solemnity of matrimony, but not to its essence or validity. He believed that there was no law that invalidated marriages not contracted according to the Book of Common Prayer.[59] Counsel cited the biblical precedent of Boaz, who took Ruth as his wife by stating his intent before witnesses.[60] (A similar argument had been made by Margaret Fell in 1667, who had argued that in neither the Old nor the New Testament were people married by a priest, nor did it say that they should be.)[61] The Marriage Act of 1540 was cited in the case as allowing as lawful marriages made by a declaration between the couple.[62] But this was a misunderstanding of the text of the act, which in fact made no such provision.[63]

During the Cowdry case, the MfS wrote to its correspondents in the west of England asking for examples of widows who surrendered their widow's estate upon marriage among Friends.[64] A widow who remarried would expect to lose any estate she held through being a widow. If a widow remarried among Quakers and lost her widow's estate, her Quaker marriage must, therefore, be recognized in common law, even if it was not recognized in statute or ecclesiastical law. The MfS heard from a Dorset correspondent of a woman who had lost her widow's estate for that reason, and a similar example was received from Wiltshire.[65]

The MfS may well not have realized at the outset how much of its resources it would end up committing to the Cowdry case, but it may have regarded the case as something of a test case for the validity of Quaker marriage. The outcome was not, however, decisive. Shortly before a third and final hearing before the Court of Common Pleas, the plaintiff's solicitor offered a settlement that the Friends accepted, possibly because of their uncertainty as to the outcome of the case if it were decided in court. The case against Cordelia Cowdry in the Court of Common Pleas appears to have concluded in June 1705, with her child's name on the copyhold lease alongside the names of two members of the MfS acting as trustees.[66] The terms of the lease and matters concerning the trustees continued to occupy the MfS for some time to come, but Cordelia Cowdry had, if indirectly, retained the lease on her property.[67]

Cowdry's was not the only legal case in which the MfS was directly involved, but its importance lies in its effect on campaigning by the MfS. For a year or so after the case, the MfS proactively campaigned on Quaker marriages, rather than reacting to individual cases and parliamentary bills as it had done previously.

This lobbying activity is not explicitly linked in the MfS minutes to the Cowdry case, but the timing strongly suggests that it was prompted by it. The LYM of 1704 had already asked Friends in the counties to send relevant cases concerning marriage to Benjamin Bealing, clerk of the MfS.[68] In February 1705, the MfS discussed a possible approach to Queen Anne by women Friends concerning marriage, and a few weeks later agreed to make enquiries among French Protestants in England about their marriages. In June 1705, the MfS agreed to write to Queen Anne respectfully asking her, in her instructions to judges before they set out on their circuits, to express her dislike of any precedent being made against the validity of Quaker marriages. A paper concerning marriage by Theodore Eccleston, a leading member of the MfS, was to be sent out to the quarterly meetings, and it was agreed that a collection of legal precedents concerning marriage should be published.[69] In the same year, LYM recorded that the MfS was to advise Friends when to make representations to members of Parliament concerning Friends' marriages.[70]

It is not clear whether all the proposals discussed in the minutes of the MfS in 1705 resulted in action, though the manuscript selection of marriage cases extracted from the Books of Cases may have been part of its activity.[71] But whatever action was taken, it came to nothing. By early 1707, the MfS had consulted attorneys for its arguments in favor of Friends' marriages. George Whitehead and a small committee of Friends were appointed to make representations to Parliament, but the MfS, perhaps having lost the will to engage with the issue, referred the matter to the LYM.[72]

Two years later, the anti-Quaker polemicist Francis Bugg would claim that a Quaker had said to his face, "Well thou may'st write what thou wilt, we matter it not, for we have more Interest in the House of Commons than you have."[73] But, in reality, lobbying for a change in the law was a long and frustrating process for Friends. The MfS had amended the wording of the marriage certificate in 1709, but legal challenges continued to be made.[74] In 1715, Phillip Whiting of the small town of Portchester in Hampshire wrote to the MfS concerning a case against him.[75] The case concerned the validity of his mother-in-law's Quaker marriage and the threat this posed to Whiting's inheritance. The details of the case were complex, and, as in Cordelia Cowdry's case, legal assistance was provided, but the case remained unresolved three years later.[76]

The business of paying marriage fees to the parish priest continued to concern Friends. In December 1712, Samuel Wareing wrote to the MfS that after he married Elinor Staples of Charlbury, Oxfordshire, the priest of Charlbury demanded marriage fees. The MfS advised him to attend court if the demand was pursued, and to send a copy of the demand to the MfS.[77] Only weeks later, in February 1713, the MfS heard that John Clarke of Mildenhall, Suffolk, was being excommunicated for not paying the marriage fee.[78] Cumberland Friends were reported in January 1718 as being prosecuted for nonpayment of marriage fees.[79]

In 1718, the MfS sought a legal opinion for a Quaker ordered by the justices to pay a marriage fee. The counsel, Thomas Lutwyche, maintained that Quaker marriages had never yet been determined in law to be valid, and he made the point that if Quakers contested the marriage fee, they were admitting that their marriages were not good in law.[80] This opinion, though recorded in the Book of Cases, was unlikely to have been what the MfS wished to hear, and Friends throughout the country continued to be pursued for marriage fees for several years thereafter.

The continued claims against Friends for marriage fees and the need to recognize Friends' marriages by statute law led the MfS to make considerable efforts to influence parliamentary legislation. Attempts were made by Parliament to regulate clandestine marriage in 1717 and again in 1719.[81] When the MfS learned in 1717 that a bill on clandestine marriage was likely to be brought before Parliament, it sought legal counsel and agreed on an amendment to be laid before Parliament. The proposed amendment provided that the act should not hinder marriages by Quakers, as their marriage certificates were stamped according to the law.[82] Friends spoke with Lord Parker, the Lord Chief Justice, who was supportive of Friends' marriages, and with another person of influence who was unnamed in the MfS minutes.[83] Theodore Eccleston was to draw up instances of Friends' marriages that had been proceeded against in the courts, and any special pleadings by lawyers on their behalf.[84] He managed this within three weeks, but it took longer than that for the committee appointed to read all the cases and legal opinions he collected, and, before they had done so, the MfS minuted that the business of clandestine marriages was to be discontinued.[85]

When the 1719 bill against clandestine marriage was introduced, the MfS appointed a committee to attend the meetings of the parliamentary committee discussing the bill to ensure that nothing prejudicial to Quaker interests was included. The MfS committee turned up repeatedly during February 1719, but the matter was adjourned time and again. With considerable persistence, and despite several further adjournments by the parliamentary committee, Quaker lobbying was finally successful in getting a clause inserted into the bill favorable to Quaker marriages, only to see the bill fall in the Commons.[86]

In the 1720s, the MfS continued to receive occasional reports of demands by parish priests for marriage fees. In August 1725, William Tomlinson wrote to the MfS that Henry Adams, who had married Tomlinson's sister, was being pursued by the parish priest of Warrington, Cheshire, for both marriage fees and a mortuary fee for his late father.[87] Legal opinion was given in a Durham case from 1727 that Quakers were exempt from marriage fees by the terms of the 1689 Act of Toleration.[88] The reliability of this advice is doubtful; no such exemption had been explicitly stated in the act.[89] But legal opinion was increasingly irrelevant, as demands by parish priests for marriage fees declined, though intermittent news of such cases did appear in the minutes of the MfS. In 1729, the MfS heard of a case in Staffordshire, and Westmorland Friends wrote to the MfS for advice after Friends had been summoned before the justices for not paying marriage fees. As with earlier cases, the MfS wrote to Westmorland with advice, having searched the books of precedents for relevant legal opinions.[90]

In January 1738, the MfS received a letter from Wellingborough in Northamptonshire requesting advice after a parish priest demanded a marriage fee from a Friend.[91] But by the 1730s, the minutes of the MfS show that such demands for marriage fees were uncommon, while minutes referring to challenges to the validity of a Quaker marriage by a landlord or putative heir had dwindled to nothing. The claim thirty years earlier by counsel in the Cowdry case that Quakers were respectable may have been premature at the time, but it was now increasingly a reality insofar as marriage was concerned.

The issue remained that Friends' marriages were still not recognized by statute law. But the MfS had many other items on its agenda and did not actively campaign to change the law as it stood on marriage. It did continue to monitor parliamentary activity for any proposed legislation that might affect Friends. In 1752, the MfS heard of a bill brought before Parliament to encourage, as described in its meeting minutes, the marriage of poor persons. The MfS appointed a Friend, Richard Partridge, to monitor whether this might affect Quakers.[92]

The issue of clandestine marriage remained, sporadically, on the parliamentary agenda. After the failed attempts of the 1710s, further efforts were made in 1733, 1736, and 1740, but these failed to pass into law.[93] In March 1753, the MfS noted that a bill concerning clandestine marriage had been introduced in Parliament, and, as on previous occasions, appointed some Friends to ensure that it would not prove prejudicial to Quakers. The number of Friends appointed grew with every meeting of the MfS; by the end of March, no fewer than fourteen Friends had been appointed. A clause was proposed to be offered to Parliament, providing that the terms of the act should not extend to marriages solemnized among the people called Quakers in their meetinghouses.[94] The bill passed into law later that year, to take effect from March 25, 1754, and required marriages to be celebrated in an

Anglican church, but two faith groups, Quakers and Jews, were exempt from its provisions.[95] It has commonly become known as Hardwicke's Act after Lord Hardwicke, then Lord Chancellor.[96]

The active lobbying by the MfS yielded a partially successful outcome, in that Quaker marriage ceremonies were now implicitly recognized in law, though they were still not explicitly recognized.[97] But if this worried Friends, it was not recorded in the minutes of the MfS. Probert has noted that there was still legal ambiguity around Quaker marriages after 1754, but she found no direct legal challenge to Quaker marriages in the second half of the eighteenth century.[98]

QUAKERS AND MARRIAGE LEGISLATION AFTER 1754

After passage of the 1753 Marriage Act, the Meeting for Sufferings continued to monitor bills coming before Parliament and appointed committees to take action if any proposals were likely to affect Friends.[99] Hardwicke's Marriage Act had its opponents both inside and outside Parliament, and several unsuccessful attempts were made, even as late as 1781, to amend or repeal it.[100] Though Quaker marriages were still not explicitly recognized in law, the implicit recognition of the 1753 act had been enough to ensure that Quaker weddings were now regarded as valid in law. The MfS continued to discuss matters relating to Quaker marriage discipline and, where necessary, reminded Friends to comply with any laws regarding the registration of their marriages. The MfS did not devote much of its time to marriage registration in the latter half of the long eighteenth century, though it was concerned to comply with the law. In 1777 it considered the impact of the stamp duty on Friends' marriage certificates, and in 1783 it issued an epistle to Friends on their responsibilities with respect to a new law imposing a stamp duty on registration of births, marriages, and burials.[101] The subject of stamp duty appeared briefly in the minutes again in 1800.[102] In 1832, the LYM issued a printed set of instructions regarding the correct procedure for completing registers.[103]

The Marriage Act of 1836 finally brought Quaker marriages within the sphere of explicit legal regulation, and further legislation in 1847 recognized as valid any Quaker marriage that had taken place prior to the Marriage Act of 1836.[104] The MfS's immediate reaction to the 1836 legislation was to appoint a committee, and the following year to revise the wording used when registering births, marriages, and burials. In 1838 it amended the rules in the book of discipline in light of the 1836 act.[105] The MfS's need to ensure that Quaker marriage procedure was legally watertight is shown in the minutes as late as 1855–56, when the MfS sought advice on a change in Friends' marriage procedure and how it might affect the validity of their marriages. The 1836 act had been passed according to the usage of the Society of Friends at the time, but since then there had been slight changes to the procedure. Would this invalidate Quaker marriages? The legal opinion was that it would not affect the validity of Friends' marriages, and the matter appears to have been dropped.[106]

CONCLUSION

By the time the 1836 Marriage Act was passed, the Meeting for Sufferings no longer needed to lobby Parliament as it had done so tirelessly a century or so earlier. Quakers no longer suffered for marrying among Friends, either from the threat of civil lawsuit or by being pursued for marriage fees. The MfS had ensured that the monthly and quarterly meetings knew of their obligations regarding stamp duties and any other legislation.

The struggles of the later seventeenth and early eighteenth centuries had been fought by the MfS with a considerable investment of Friends' time and financial resources. While the MfS tended to react to specific cases or parliamentary bills rather than to mount sustained and lengthy campaigns, when it did respond, it invariably committed itself, whether that meant taking action itself or giving advice to suffering Friends. It may be this dogged response by the MfS that saw a substantial decrease by the 1730s in cases of Friends suffering on account of their marriages. The Marriage Act of 1753 represented a legal watershed for Quakers, but in implicitly recognizing Quaker marriages, it was acknowledging a trend in evidence many years before. If the 1753 act had its weaknesses as far as Quakers were concerned, its provisions were sufficient for the Meeting for Sufferings. Though matters concerning the law and Quaker marriage continued to appear in its minutes after 1753, they were infrequent compared to the earlier period. For many years prior to the 1836 act, the MfS had been able to assume that the validity of Quaker marriages would remain unchallenged, and that Quakers would not suffer for having married among Friends.

NOTES

1. George Fox, *Concerning Marriage* (London, 1661), 4–5.
2. Craig W. Horle, *The Quakers and the English Legal System, 1660–1688* (Philadelphia: University of Pennsylvania Press, 1988), 234.
3. Joseph Besse, *A Collection of the Sufferings of the People Called Quakers*, 2 vols. (London: Luke Hinde, 1753), 1:53, 118, 318, 319, 542.
4. Rebecca Probert, *Marriage Law for Genealogists: The Definitive Guide* (Kenilworth, UK: Takeaway, 2012), 103–6.
5. Julian Hoppit, *A Land of Liberty? England, 1689–1727* (Oxford: Clarendon Press, 2000), 62.
6. R. B. Outhwaite, *Clandestine Marriage in England, 1500–1850* (London: Hambledon Press, 1995); Lawrence Stone, *Road to Divorce: England, 1530–1987* (Oxford: Oxford University Press, 1990).
7. Michael R. Watts, *The Dissenters: From the Reformation to the French Revolution* (Oxford: Clarendon Press, 1978), 270.
8. Rebecca Probert, *Marriage Law and Practice in the Long Eighteenth Century: A Reassessment* (Cambridge: Cambridge University Press, 2009), 152–60, 329–32.
9. Rufus M. Jones, *The Later Periods of Quakerism*, 2 vols. (London: Macmillan, 1921), 1:187–90; Edwina Newman, "Quakers and the Family," in *The Oxford Handbook of Quaker Studies*, ed. Stephen W. Angell and Pink Dandelion (Oxford: Oxford University Press, 2013), 434–44.
10. William C. Braithwaite, *The Second Period of Quakerism*, 2nd ed. (Cambridge: Cambridge University Press, 1961), 458.
11. Ibid., 254, 257–58; William C. Braithwaite, *The Beginnings of Quakerism*, 2nd ed. (Cambridge: Cambridge University Press, 1955), 146; George Fox, *The Journal of George Fox*, ed. John L. Nickalls (Cambridge: Cambridge University Press, 1952), 519.
12. Jones, *Later Periods of Quakerism*, 1:187–90.
13. Norman C. Hunt, *Two Early Political Associations: The Quakers and the Dissenting Deputies in the Age of Sir Robert Walpole* (Oxford: Clarendon Press, 1961), 18–31.
14. London Yearly Meeting (LYM), Meeting for Sufferings (MfS), Book of Cases (BoC), vol. 2 (1695–1738), LSF; the separate manuscript of ca. 1700 is titled "Councils Opinions in Cases of Marriage" and is a loose booklet inserted at the end of vol. 2.
15. A copyhold property was one where the terms of the lease and the names of the tenants were copied into the manor court records; the tenants retained their own copy of the agreement.
16. LYM, MfS, BoC, vol. 1 (1661–95), 28–29, LSF.
17. Braithwaite, *Beginnings of Quakerism*, 145; Kristianna Polder, *Matrimony in the True Church: The Seventeenth-Century Quaker Marriage Approbation Discipline* (Farnham, UK: Ashgate, 2015), 45–47; John Punshon, *Portrait in Grey: A Short History of the Quakers*, 2nd ed. (London: Quaker Books, 2006), 102.
18. Probert, *Marriage Law and Practice*, 154–55.
19. LYM, MfS, BoC, vol. 1 (1661–95), 64–65, LSF.
20. Ibid., "Councils Opinions in Cases of Marriage," loose booklet inserted at the end of vol. 2 (1695–1738), fol. 7r–v.
21. On marriage and the law in Scotland, see Eleanor Gordon, "Irregular Marriage: Myth and Reality," *Journal of Social History* 47, no. 2 (2013): 507–25; T.C. Smout,

"Scottish Marriage, Regular and Irregular, 1500–1940," in *Marriage and Society: Studies in the Social History of Marriage*, ed. R. B. Outhwaite (London: Europa, 1981), 204–36; and Edward H. Milligan, *Quaker Marriage* (Kendal, UK: Quaker Tapestry Booklets, 1994), 18–19.

22. Maria Luddy, "Marriage, Sexuality, and the Law in Ireland," in *The Cambridge Social History of Modern Ireland*, ed. Eugenio F. Biagini and Mary E. Daly (Cambridge: Cambridge University Press, 2017), 344, 346; Milligan, *Quaker Marriage*, 18.

23. George Elliott Howard, *A History of Matrimonial Institutions*, 3 vols. (Chicago: University of Chicago Press, 1904), 2:134–35, 239–56, 284–96, 308–11, 315–27.

24. Alton Monthly Meeting, Men's Meeting Minutes, 1676–1744, p. 86, 24M54/34, Hampshire Record Office, Winchester, UK.

25. Ibid., 102.

26. Milligan, *Quaker Marriage*, 13.

27. Probert, *Marriage Law and Practice*, 157.

28. Lawrence Stone, *Broken Lives: Separation and Divorce in England, 1660–1857* (Oxford: Oxford University Press, 1993), 67–68.

29. LYM, MfS, Minutes, vol. 17 (1703–5), 64, 75, LSF. For two further cases of alleged bigamy, see Arnold Lloyd, *Quaker Social History, 1669–1738* (London: Longmans, Green, 1950), 58, 61.

30. Society of Friends, Southern Monthly Meeting minute book, 1717–33, 1699/32, fols. 70v–71r, 77r–v, 146r–148r; and Wiltshire Quarterly Meeting minute book, 1708–34, 1699/40, pp. 381, 479, both at Wiltshire and Swindon History Centre, Chippenham, UK.

31. Outhwaite, *Clandestine Marriage in England*, 13–14.

32. LYM, MfS, Minutes, vol. 7 (1689–91), 186, LSF.

33. Ibid., 190, 196, 200.

34. Ibid., vol. 8 (1691–93), 1, 3, 6, 9.

35. Ibid., vol. 13 (1698–99), 59, 70–71.

36. LYM, Minutes, vol. 1 (1672–93), 266, 310, 320–21, LSF.

37. LYM, MfS, BoC, vol. 1 (1661–95), 216–17, LSF.

38. Ibid., 260–61.

39. Ibid., vol. 2 (1695–1738), 103–4.

40. LYM, MfS, Minutes, vol. 16 (1702–3), 288, LSF.

41. Ibid., vol. 9 (1693–95), 200.

42. Outhwaite, *Clandestine Marriage in England*, 14–15; Probert, *Marriage Law and Practice*, 175–76.

43. Outhwaite, *Clandestine Marriage in England*, 15.

44. Ibid., 14–15.

45. LYM, MfS, Minutes, vol. 10 (1695–96), 19, LSF.

46. Ibid., 32, 201–2, 207–8, 211.

47. Ibid., vol. 14 (1699–1701), 90–91, 95.

48. Ibid., 128, 135–36, 143, 154, 161, 174–75.

49. Ibid., vol. 15 (1700–1702), 5. The child was a daughter; see General Register Office, Society of Friends Registers, Romsey and Southampton Monthly Meeting Book, p. 206, RG 6/1273, National Archives, London.

50. LYM, Minutes, vol. 3 (1702–8), 86, LSF. I have written more extensively about Cordelia Cowdry's case in Rosalind Noreen Johnson, "Protestant Dissenters in Hampshire, c. 1640–c. 1740" (PhD diss., University of Winchester, 2013), 198–202; the summary here is a revised version of that work.

51. Hampshire Quarterly Meeting, Men's Meeting Minutes, 1697–1734, fols. 26r, 29v, 24M54/2, Hampshire Record Office, Winchester, UK. Knollys's first name is given as Robert in the minutes of LYM, MfS, vol. 15 (1700–1702), 123, LSF.

52. LYM, MfS, Minutes, vol. 15 (1700–1702), 14, LSF.

53. Ibid., 104.

54. Ibid., 234; Alton Monthly Meeting, Men's Meeting Minutes, 1676–1744, 24M54/2, fols. 24v, 29v, Hampshire Record Office, Winchester, UK.

55. LYM, MfS, BoC, vol. 2 (1695–1738), 90–95, LSF.

56. LYM, Minutes, vol. 3 (1702–8), 86, LSF.

57. LYM, MfS, Minutes, vol. 16 (1702–3), 332, LSF.

58. LYM, Minutes, vol. 3 (1702–8), 125–26, LSF.

59. LYM, MfS, BoC, vol. 2 (1695–1738), 116–26, LSF.

60. Ibid., 112–15.

61. Margaret Fell, *A Touch-Stone, Or, A Perfect Tryal by the Scriptures, of all Priests, Bishops, and Ministers* (London, 1667), 70.

62. LYM, MfS, BoC, vol. 2 (1695–1738), 112–15, LSF. The act concerned was 32 Hen. 8 E.38.

63. Danby Pickering, ed., *The Statutes at Large*, 46 vols. (Cambridge: Printed by J. Bentham, 1762–1807), 5:55–56.

64. LYM, MfS, Minutes, vol. 17 (1703–5), 35, 39–40, LSF.

65. Ibid., 50, 70, 187.

66. Ibid., 114, 117, 121, 124–25, 222–23, 225, 251, 259, 262–63. In 1707 Cordelia Cowdry married Benjamin Bealing, clerk of the MfS. See RG 6/1273, p. 207, National Archives, London.

67. LYM, MfS, Minutes, vol. 18 (1705–7), 28, LSF; ibid., vol. 19 (1707–9), 12, 15, 103, 120, 121, 122, 137.

68. LYM, Minutes, vol. 3 (1702–8), 125–26, LSF.

69. LYM, MfS, Minutes, vol. 17 (1703–5), 174, 215, 239, 240, LSF. See also Johnson, "Protestant Dissenters in Hampshire," 201–2.

70. LYM, Minutes, vol. 3 (1702–8), 206, LSF.

71. LYM, MfS, BoC, "Councils Opinions in Cases of Marriage," loose booklet inserted at the end of vol. 2 (1695–1738), LSF.

72. LYM, MfS, Minutes, vol. 18 (1705–7), 184, 194, 198, 201, 227, 268, LSF.

73. Francis Bugg, *Some Remarks on the Quakers written Paper, Presented by them to Members of Parliament* (N.p., [1709]).

74. LYM, MfS, Minutes, vol. 19 (1707–9), 265, 280–81, LSF.

75. Ibid., vol. 22 (1715–19), 3, 9, 21.

76. Ibid., 348, 362.

77. Ibid., vol. 21 (1712–15), 14–15.

78. Ibid., 33.

79. Ibid., vol. 22 (1715–19), 273.

80. LYM, MfS, BoC, vol. 2 (1695–1738), 222–23, LSF.

81. Outhwaite, *Clandestine Marriage in England*, 16, 72.

82. LYM, MfS, Minutes, vol. 22 (1715–19), 173–74, LSF.

83. Ibid., 180–81.

84. Ibid., 180–81, 184.

85. Ibid., 185, 186, 187, 188, 193, 203, 206, 209.

86. Ibid., 355–72; LYM, Minutes, vol. 5 (1714–20), 356, LSF.

87. LYM, MfS, Minutes, vol. 24 (1725–30), 21–22, LSF.
88. LYM, MfS, BoC, vol. 2 (1695–1738), 269–70, LSF.
89. Watts, *Dissenters*, 259–60; Pickering, *Statutes at Large*, 9:19–25.
90. LYM, MfS, Minutes, vol. 24 (1725–30), 282, 303, 313, LSF.
91. Ibid., vol. 26 (1735–39), 406–7.
92. Ibid., vol. 29 (1749–56), 79.
93. Outhwaite, *Clandestine Marriage in England*, 71, 72–73.
94. LYM, MfS, Minutes, vol. 29 (1749–56), 234, 241, 244–45, LSF.
95. Milligan, *Quaker Marriage*, 16–17, 29; Probert, *Marriage Law and Practice*, 220–22, 234–35.
96. Outhwaite, *Clandestine Marriage in England*, 77, 99.
97. Milligan, *Quaker Marriage*, 17.
98. Probert, *Marriage Law and Practice*, 330; Probert, *Marriage Law for Genealogists*, 104–5.
99. LYM, MfS, Minutes, vol. 30 (1756–61), 500–501, 508, LSF; ibid., vol. 31 (1761–66), 263–64.
100. Outhwaite, *Clandestine Marriage in England*, 99–121.
101. LYM, MfS, Minutes, vol. 34 (1775–77), 506, LSF; ibid., vol. 35 (1777–80), 5; LYM, MfS, *To the Monthly Meeting of Friends of* [blank] *The Legislature having laid a tax of three pence on the register of every marriage, birth and burial* [...] (London, 1783).
102. LYM, MfS, Minutes, vol. 40 (1796–1803), 376–77, LSF.
103. LYM, *Rules Respecting Registers* [...] (London, 1832).
104. Probert, *Marriage Law for Genealogists*, 104–5.
105. LYM, MfS, Minutes, vol. 44 (1831–39), 340, 375–84, 529, LSF.
106. LYM, MfS, BoC, vol. 4 (1802–1918), 186–89, LSF.

CHAPTER 7

Family, Unity, and Identity Formation
Eighteenth-Century Quaker Community Building

EMMA LAPSANSKY-WERNER

In August 1805, Philadelphian Mary Drinker Cope wrote to her eleven-year-old son, Francis, then a resident student at Westtown School some twenty-five miles away. Accompanying her letter was "a present, a mark of my love," and an admonition that generosity and selflessness were the foundations of a righteous and contented life. Mary reminded Francis of the intrinsic reward of virtue: "is there a ... pleasure in this world, equal to that of having a heart capable of enjoying the happiness of others?" Thus gently and lovingly, the mother encouraged her son to "study the paths of life and where they lead."[1]

Westtown School, opened in 1799, was among several new additions to a tradition of Quaker educational efforts dating back to the time of George Fox. Mary Cope's gentle advice was illustrative of a delicate recipe of theology, economics, politics, worldview, and pragmatism through which early nineteenth-century Atlantic-world Friends endeavored to build a cohesive religious culture and identity. Though that recipe contained many ingredients, central to it was a unique array of mandates for family and home life, and what Friends described as a "guarded education" designed to nourish the "tender plants" of the next generation of Quakers, insulating them from the corrupting influence of the "world."[2]

In the years between the 1650s and 1680s, the dynamism of the founding generation—combined with an identity borne of persecution—had fostered cohesiveness among Quakers and a sense of moral superiority.[3] But in the century following the 1689 Toleration Act, as oppression diminished in England, prosperity increased in both England and America, and Friends scattered across the globe, Quakers found themselves drawing upon other aspects of what they dubbed their "peculiar" faith and lifestyle to preserve unity among their attenuated membership.[4] Despite their dispersed communities, those who remained Friends succeeded in maintaining a unity based on religious commitment and social reform that was strong enough that even today Quakers remain shrouded in a powerful, if vague, mystique. The few modern people who have contemplated that mystique at all often imagine Quakers as having a commitment to pacifism; a lifestyle grounded in frugality, integrity, and charity; a consistent posture of nonconformity; and a tight-knit community life. This stereotype has persisted, partly as a result of the identity, imagery, and membership disciplines that the "Friends in the Truth" embraced as they solidified their communities in the long eighteenth century. This chapter explores these standards.

Though the origins of Quaker identity are multifaceted, by the early nineteenth century, British and American novelists were able to call upon stock images of Friends in their work.[5] A reader has only to peruse the writing of Sarah Stickney Ellis, Amelia Opie, George Lippard, or Herman Melville to imagine Quaker men as stalwart, altruistic, and unyielding in the face of moral dilemmas and Quaker women as patient, stoical, compassionate, pious, resolute, strong-willed, and serene. Harriet Beecher Stowe, whose 1852 *Uncle Tom's Cabin* has been translated into dozens of languages, is arguably the best-known publicist of the archetypal Quaker. A prototype of public virtue, a defender of justice and Enlightenment-infused rationality, and a high-minded protector of the underdog, the "Quaker" character had become by Stowe's time—and remains so today—a model of no-nonsense piety and morality, an archetype of practicality, tranquility, composure, kindheartedness, and the courage of one's convictions.[6] It was to this standard, solidified in Quaker culture in the long eighteenth century, that Mary Drinker Cope gently guided her son in 1805.

In addition, many Quakers were noteworthy for their commitment to intentional communities. William Penn was convinced that given the right environment, leadership, and insulation from corruption, human beings could lead divinely grounded, peaceful lives. He had sought to create such an environment in Philadelphia, calling his endeavor "an Holy Experiment."[7] The Copes shared family and friendship ties with a few hundred Friends who, in the eighteenth century, planted the foundations of Quaker networks worldwide. They were among the group who shaped their monthly, quarterly, and yearly meeting communities around the concepts of shared authority and obligation upon which William Penn had shaped his "Frame of Government" for Pennsylvania.[8] Friends have repeatedly experimented with dozens of "intentional communities" based upon similar high-minded principles.[9] What buttresses, distinguishes, and sustains those three-century-old community foundations?

Many scholars have explored eighteenth-century Quaker strategies for the broad-based "inward" journey of defining a spiritual, economic, and institutional identity in the context of the Atlantic world's emergence as a powerful marketplace of goods and ideas.[10] To be sure, Britain, especially London, remained the Quaker seat of power through the long eighteenth century. Even so, after Penn established the world's only Quaker-run government, a site of Friends' vitality shifted to Philadelphia; by 1750, it had become the second-most important urban center in the British Empire thanks to the leadership of Quaker agricultural, mining, printing, international commerce, and banking dynasties.[11]

Over the succeeding half century, Quakers throughout the Atlantic world fashioned a discipline that governed every aspect of their lives, as Andrew Fincham's chapter in this volume describes. Of special importance in this "Quaker way" of living were child-rearing practices; these guided not only family life but also the curricula of the many Quaker schools that began to spring up in 1690s England and America.

Though Quakers were not the first—or only—religion to prescribe and restrict elements of adherents' daily lives, the distinctive blend of behaviors and underlying beliefs that constitute what early Friends dubbed their "Holy Conversation"[12] gave their narrative a uniquely hopeful tinge. Optimistic to a fault, Friends were frantic and distraught when, in the 1820s, factionalism that had been percolating for a generation unsettled the formula and discipline they had crafted for fifteen decades. Even as the discipline was articulated in published form by the end of the eighteenth century, there were signs of trouble, and scholars are still investigating the implications and causes-versus-effects of the multivariate factors that led to what has been described as the "Hicksite-Orthodox Schism." Traveling across Ireland, England, New York, and trans-Appalachian America, itinerant ministers Hannah Barnard and Elias Hicks began to shift and to question the emphasis and relative importance of the tenets that earlier Friends had assigned to points of doctrine such as the Bible and Christ. What followed was an unsettling of the stable eighteenth-century communities Friends had created. The transition of American Quaker community building from the late seventeenth to the early nineteenth century might be grouped into five broad categories: some dynamics of general historical change; the influence of geographical place; the centrality of a "holy conversation" in family life and education; the pursuit of virtue in public life; and the challenge of modernity. This chapter invites discourse on the implications of these five phenomena.

DYNAMICS OF HISTORICAL CHANGE

Historians David Hackett Fischer and Richard D. Brown have posited theories of historical change that illuminate the phenomenon of eighteenth-century American Quakerism. Fischer describes historical narrative as being more about *change* than about *events*. What enlivens historical narrative, he argues, is the varying *rate* of change, and the appearance of periods of "deep change" during which many aspects of life are transformed simultaneously and rapidly. Brown suggests an array of particular variables associated with initiating and sustaining "modernity." Among the variables fueling a period of "deep change" are, first, rapid developments in "mass" transportation and navigational instruments, enabling Westerners to travel in groups with relative predictability and safety. Second was the increasing sophistication of "portable" financial tools such as banking, private investing, insurance, and "credit." The third variable was the increasing democratization of communication, such as relatively inexpensive printing, mass-produced paper, and a rising literacy rate. Finally, there was the ascendance of "individuality" and the concept of self-actualization.[13]

Though none of these variables was new in the eighteenth century, their confluence dramatically increased the pace of change. Quaker faith and culture, born in England, developed simultaneously with these variables of Western modernization, and helped to usher in industrialization and modernization. Quakers were trendsetters in the Western development of coal and lead mining and iron production (1650s); printing (1660s); Atlantic-world international trade, including agricultural products, maritime occupations, and slave trading (1670s); strategic land management (exemplified by Penn's sophisticated regional-planning schemes in the 1680s); public education and banking (1690s); and canals and railroads (early nineteenth century). They made effective and lucrative use of their penchant and reputation for high integrity, sturdy work ethic, and fair dealing.[14] Prototypes of the Protestant capitalists described by historical economist Max Weber, Quaker business owners eschewed arbitrary bartering in favor of one fair price for all.[15] William Penn's experiment, initiated at the end of the seventeenth century, epitomized these aspects of emerging capitalism and modernity.

QUAKERISM AND THE POWER OF PLACE

By the 1680s, after nearly three decades of a largely itinerant existence in war-torn, enclosure-marked England, Quakers, like Puritans, Mennonites, and other European Protestant religious dissenters who were weary of derision and persecution, sought to make a world where they and like-minded comrades would find religious shelter and economic well-being. Unlike many other dissenters, William Penn intended to have God help him make a world that would accommodate not only people like himself but also different varieties of fellow travelers. Thus the Commonwealth of Pennsylvania, established in 1681 by a royal charter to William Penn, was founded on the principle of religious freedom.

Opening his community to religious dissenters from several European cultures, Penn took some unprecedented steps toward embracing a more multicultural community than was typical in English society. Describing his new lands as "a collection of Divers Nations in Europe: as French, Dutch, Germans, Swedes, Danes, Finns, Scotch, French and English, and of the last equal to all the rest,"[16] he envisioned a community that included Indigenous Americans. Indeed, after some initial hesitation, Penn opened his community to Jews and to Catholics, reasoning that all who lived "peaceably" and agreed to follow the colony's laws should be viewed as God's children.[17] Ambivalent about the role of Africans, Penn first used slave labor on his farm near Philadelphia but later freed his slaves. Thus by 1710 a sprinkling of Africans and African Americans had joined the multivariate and enterprising populace vying for a place in Penn's land of opportunity. Within a generation, non-Quakers outnumbered Quakers, though Quakers controlled the government until the 1750s. Quakers continued to dominate economic and public life in Pennsylvania well into the twentieth century, even as they collaborated with other "Divers" people in pursuit of the public good. For example, British Quaker financier Robert Morris teamed up with Jewish refugee Haym Salomon to raise money for the American Revolution. In addition, the Quaker Robert Bridges helped African American James Forten open what became a prosperous sail-making enterprise. Forten, who had been educated in a school established for African Americans by the Quaker Anthony Benezet, had distinguished himself in the Revolutionary War.[18]

The Philadelphia Yearly Meeting (PYM), which included more than a dozen fledgling meetings—some of them across the Delaware River in what was known as "West Jersey"—was established in 1681. By the 1720s, with more than two dozen meetings within a fifty-mile radius of Philadelphia, each representing a node of family or community settlement in Pennsylvania, New Jersey, and Delaware, the PYM had established itself as the center or metropole of American Quakerism. Most of the first land purchasers in Penn's Woods were either friends or acquaintances of the proprietor or relatives of Quakers who had settled in New Jersey by the 1670s. Within a few decades, a few dozen men, including the Vaux, Morris, Shinn, Drinker, Cope, and other families, had purchased more than fifty thousand acres of land, an average of more than seven hundred acres per family. A few Delaware Valley Friends also acquired large landholdings as far away as Berks and Wayne Counties, upward of one hundred miles from Philadelphia; some four dozen fledgling monthly meetings dotted the countryside within that radius.[19] Quakers were soon outnumbered in every region they inhabited; though they constituted half of the population of Pennsylvania's Delaware Valley in 1690, by 1760 they were grossly outnumbered by more than five to one. Nevertheless, though openness to other groups allowed more than sixty thousand German and Scots-Irish Lutherans, Presbyterians, Methodists, Baptists, Jews, and others to sprinkle themselves among Pennsylvania's "Quaker places,"[20] Friends' influence in economic, political, and cultural life remained strong.

While Philadelphia remained a principal American Quaker "place," Quaker families soon began to scatter geographically beyond the city. By 1752, for example, the Quaker ironmaster John Potts had purchased a thousand acres in Montgomery County, more than forty miles from Philadelphia; he also purchased acreage in Virginia in order to expand his mining and foundry operation.²¹ Although Quakers were the minority wherever they settled, "unity," but *not* "uniformity," was maintained between communities by exchanges of visits and epistles. "Intervisitation"—frequent visits by members of meetings as close as Delaware, New York, New England, Maryland, and North Carolina, and as far afield as London and the Caribbean—regularized and stabilized Quaker theology and practice.²² Since Friends' theology required neither a consecrated building, nor scheduling, nor specially appointed leaders, Friends were free to establish a "worship place" wherever a group chose to gather.

In this way, Quaker families established dynasties of Quaker leadership that would, over the course of the eighteenth century, spread across the globe. Unlike New England's Puritan communities, where landholdings tended to be small and compact, some Pennsylvania Quakers amassed huge tracts of land. These could spread across multiple places in Pennsylvania, New Jersey, Delaware, Virginia, North Carolina, and the Caribbean (where Friends both held and trafficked in slaves).²³ With iron mills, stone quarries, gristmills, shipbuilding enterprises, and agricultural products in the mid-Atlantic and the South, frugal Quakers used the New World's seemingly limitless natural resources to create extraordinary economic wealth. Meanwhile, intending to insulate their children from the secular world, Quaker families distributed their land to their progeny, urging them to establish local monthly meetings in the new communities, to worship together regularly, to choose mates from among Friends' families, to consume frugally, and to remain connected to regional and global Quaker networks.²⁴

Harm de Blij and Jen Jack Gieseking have expanded scholars' appreciation of the "power of place" in initiating, defining, and responding to culture.²⁵ Stephanie Grauman Wolf, Barry J. Levy, Henry Cadbury, David Maxey, Larry Gragg, and David Hackett Fischer are among the scholars who have chronicled how eighteenth-century American Quakers sought to "derive profit from virtue."²⁶ These scholars agree that a constellation of unique characteristics of Quaker theology—including perspectives on childhood, education, ethnic diversity, authority, and leadership—led Quakers to define and manage space in unique ways, just as Puritanism encouraged New Englanders to define, distribute, and manage land, or "place," to meet their goals.²⁷ Across their widespread networks, Pennsylvania Quakers set down their peculiar linkages of monthly meetings (what might be described as "neighborhood" groups), quarterly meetings (regional), and yearly meetings (area-wide).²⁸

In planning his "Great Town" on the banks of the Delaware and Schuylkill Rivers, Penn had put great faith in the power of "place"—physical, cultural, emotional, and educational environments that he reasoned would promote virtue. Influenced by John Locke and Thomas More, who promoted Enlightenment ideas about the equality and perfectibility of humans, Penn envisioned that his design would be practical as well as spiritually nurturing. Wide streets, open markets, and designated community spaces, along with careful strategizing of land sales in order to keep land values high, could, he believed, help Philadelphia avoid the congestion and chaos that had devastated London in the Great Fire of 1666. With treaties, he planned to avert tensions with the Indigenous peoples who had occupied the region prior to Europeans' arrival. And he assigned each ethnic group its own neighborhood, linking these outlying areas with roads that led into Philadelphia, the marketing and political hub, where major decisions were made and economic power was seated.[29]

An environment that would "always be healthy and never be burnt"[30] was a high priority in Penn's plan for his "City of Brotherly Love." So was a ban on theaters and alehouses, gambling, swearing, and public drunkenness. These restrictions reflected his conviction that a physically and morally sound environment would lead residents to govern themselves wisely, especially since the central political power would lie firmly in the hands of those who had already demonstrated virtue (i.e., Quakers).

Despite its centrality and dominance, Philadelphia was not the first of the "places" where Quakers planted their idealistic outposts. The New England Yearly Meeting had been established by 1661, linking fledgling meetings in Newport and Providence, Rhode Island, with equally tiny groupings of Friends in the nearby areas of Sandwich and Salem, Massachusetts. The Maryland Yearly Meeting, anchored by Third Haven Monthly Meeting, in Easton, Maryland, has records that date to the 1670s, and in Barbados, a 1680 census counted five meetinghouses—a total of about five hundred Friends—among the twenty thousand Europeans. In those years, when a typical monthly meetinghouse might seat a few dozen members, most of them members of one or two extended families, the handful of monthly meetings that would constitute the New York Yearly Meeting (1695) and North Carolina Yearly Meeting (1698) also established footholds. These emergent communities, cemented by farms, mills, mines and quarries, craftspeople and printers, and a shared interdependence among households, provided opportunities for independence, economic achievement, broad-based leadership, and the critical practical support of a reliable community to assist with child-rearing, resource shortfalls, medical emergencies, and vocational training. Such support networks released men to crisscross the Atlantic world pursuing commercial enterprises. It also enabled women and men to travel in order to remain connected to Quakers' scattered religious settlements. Visitation among distant monthly and yearly meetings secured like-minded mates for young American Quakers, and reinforced spiritual beliefs and discipline.

Thus, for Quakers, "place" did not signify geographic parochialism or impermeable tribalism. As early as the 1650s, men or women, traveling alone or in groups of two or three, had left their homes in the English countryside to pursue a "leading"—a command from God to take a spiritual message abroad.[31] These missionaries established a tradition of "sojourning" (as it was called) for months or years, secure in the knowledge that family and meeting members back in their home "place" would care for their families, crops, and livestock, as had been commonplace in the British countryside before enclosure. This tradition of family and community responsibility, deeply embraced by Friends in the early years, when their faith could result in imprisonment, became, by the eighteenth century, a ritualized staple of Quaker community life. Travel was not limited to trained or "professional" ministers. (Indeed, Quakers attributed their vitality and superiority to having no such officials!) All a traveling Friend needed was the blessing of other members of the meeting, who might also make material contributions to the mission. This tradition of meeting support for "traveling Friends," amplified in each succeeding century by the increasing efficiency of travel, has remained vibrant in modern times.[32] Between 1750 and 1830, as new monthly meetings took root across the Western world, outposts scattered west to Ohio and Indiana and north to Nova Scotia and Upper Canada (Ontario). Australia also spawned "Quaker places."[33]

So began traditions that have endured for several centuries: at the local communicants' discretion, Quaker worship "places" may be indoors or out; they may be private homes or designated meetinghouses. Worshipful deportment and lifestyle, an aspect of the "Holy Conversation,"[34] and/or visitors from near or distant meetings became the only requirements for making places sacred. Visitors arrived at worship gatherings with written introductions from their meeting of origin and from other meetings in which they had "sojourned." Often, visitors brought printed materials: "books of discipline" from distant yearly meetings or publications on

Friends' theology from Quaker printers in London, Philadelphia, and New York. To ensure propriety and consistency, elected yearly meeting committees exercised oversight over Quaker publications, and both oversight committees and books of discipline were periodically reviewed and updated.[35]

Publications, including books and epistles (the PYM distributed its first *Book of Discipline* in 1704),[36] facilitated ongoing communication among yearly meetings and remote monthly meetings. This correspondence outlined the essentials of worship and spiritual behaviors that constituted the "Holy Conversation": a lifestyle humble and prayerful in both secular and religious comportment, applicable to both personal and public affairs. For example, the PYM's 1704 *Book of Discipline* included prohibitions against cursing, gambling, wagering, public drunkenness, theater, and racing and other competitive sports. A Quaker-led government translated these restrictions into laws that governed local Quakers and non-Quakers alike.[37]

Quaker travelers and publications were abundant. Historian Jordan Landes has identified dozens of British traveling ministers, and hundreds of Quaker books and pamphlets flowed out of London to colonial Friends "beyond the seas."[38] Lacking a central theological authority, Quaker unity of belief depended upon such frequent discourse among its far-flung congregants. Quakers on the frontiers were eager to welcome traveling ministers bearing epistles—dispatches from individuals or meetings designed to spark discussion about the subtleties of divine guidance. Early and resolute adopters of printing technology, Friends quickly maximized its potential, repeatedly publishing and widely distributing the words of their founders and other weighty Friends.[39] As Andrew Fincham observes in his chapter in this volume, Quaker printed materials also included queries—that is, questions designed to examine oneself and the health of any meeting. Since Quaker theology relies on the concept of the gradual unfolding of God's word, remote meetings expectantly awaited newcomers' fresh ideas and new printed works. These newcomers brought a letter of introduction from their meetings of origin; someone with a surname familiar to the receiving meeting often signed these letters. Even the occasional disruptive visitor, or a fraudulent or mendacious letter of introduction, did not permanently tarnish Friends' trust in this tradition.[40]

Thus, throughout the eighteenth century, all that was required to make a "Quaker place" was a number of like-minded families, a modest meeting space, and some printed words to stimulate self-examination. By the 1820s, swept up in the religious frenzy accompanying the Second Great Awakening and the Civilization Fund Act passed by Congress in 1819,[41] which provided generous incentives to promote Christianity among Indigenous Americans, Quakers were among the caravan of Americans who carted their religious zeal west to make "places" in the Mississippi Valley and beyond. By that time, Friends had solidified methods for regulating the "Holy Conversation" that had come forward from the seventeenth century.

FUNDAMENTALS OF THE "HOLY CONVERSATION":
QUAKER EDUCATION, EXEMPLARY LIVES, AND QUAKER "SAINTS"

Through a delicate mix of affection and coercion, example and reprimand, kindness and ostracism, Quaker meetings held adult members to high standards of morality and self-reflection; at the same time, they reminded themselves that children were "tender plants" who needed to be lovingly molded into virtuous adults.[42] Mindful that tending the "outward plantation" not overshadow concern for the "inward plantation," meeting guidelines set clear standards for choosing a mate, selecting a place to live, and acceptable ways to acquire and manage economic resources. Adults were urged to be models for their children, to apprentice teenagers to other Quakers only, and, if necessary, to call upon the meeting to help discipline unruly offspring. The stakes were high: parents whose children strayed or "married out" could expect to see their own standing in the meeting diminished.[43]

To meet their objectives, Quaker communities designed and encouraged education based on righteous Friends' modeling virtuous lives, an exemplary curriculum of "useful" manual skills, and tutelage in Quaker theology. Anxious that their children not be corrupted by exposure to worldly ways, the London Yearly Meeting had, as early as the 1690s, endorsed schools where Friends' children learned the "nurture and admonition and fear of God." Advice from London was specific about this: "so far as they are able or may be capable [Friends should] provide school-masters and mistresses, who are faithful Friends, to teach and instruct their children, and not to send them to such schools where they are taught the corrupt ways, manners, fashions and language of the World, and of the heathen in their authors, and names of the heathenish gods and goddesses, tending greatly to corrupt and alienate the minds of children into an averseness or opposition against the Truth, and the simplicity of [Truth.]" Concern was further reflected in the "advice and counsel of Friends that special care be taken to put them apprentices to honest Friends, that they may be preserved in the Way of Truth."[44] Penn, Fox, and other seventeenth-century leaders who took these guidelines seriously wrote curricula designed to be "useful" and to have both girls and boys learn to read and to cypher.

The William Penn Charter School, established in Philadelphia in 1689 (and "chartered" by Penn himself in 1701), began as a "Public Grammar School" (the fifth elementary school in British America, and the first outside New England).[45] It continues to serve Quaker and non-Quaker families into the twenty-first century. Penn Charter School's first headmaster was George Keith, a surveyor of New Jersey and Pennsylvania. Keith, who had arrived in the colony with the qualifications of having traveled in Quaker ministry with both Fox and Penn in the 1670s, was considered a model of Quaker virtue. In 1708, the New England Yearly Meeting acknowledged its goal that "Friends do their endeavors to gett Friends School-masters or Mistresses. And in the want of such to have their children taught att home. . . . and not send them to Such that are not Friends because of the Danger of being Corrupted with the Hurtfull Conversation of Other Youth."[46] In ensuing decades, networks of apprenticeship and informal boarding schools brought small groups of young people into contact with virtuous adults and teachers—many of whom had access to publications of early Quaker theologians and philosophers—both local and from "across the seas." Following the model of English abolitionist and naturalist John Fothergill's Ackworth School, established in 1779, more fledgling Quaker schools sprang up in New England and New York, with the Moses Brown School in Providence, Rhode Island, firmly situated by 1801, after several false starts beginning in the 1770s.[47] Westtown School in eastern Pennsylvania opened in 1799.

By 1805, when Francis Cope was at Westtown, one of his teachers would have been twenty-seven-year-old mathematician Enoch Lewis, who had studied at the William Penn Charter School and already had more than a decade of teaching experience.[48] There, Lewis may have been exposed to George Keith's 1693 tract "An Exhortation & Caution to Friends Concerning Buying and Keeping of Negroes," which admonished "in true Christian Love . . . to all our Friends and Brethren, Not to buy any Negroes, unless it were on purpose to set them free."[49] Whether from exposure to Keith's ideas or from familiarity with the work and writings of other well-known abolitionist Quakers, such as Benjamin Lay, John Woolman, Moses Brown, John Pemberton, Anthony Benezet, or Benezet's friend John Fothergill, Lewis was a committed abolitionist.⁵⁰ In the 1790s, Lewis had worked with Andrew Ellicott, the Maryland Quaker who had included the free African American mathematician Benjamin Banneker in the surveying team that designed Washington, DC. This too may have influenced Lewis's intellectual development. Whatever the impetus, by 1801 Enoch Lewis had bought and freed a slave, and he and his wife were en route to becoming fervent abolitionists.⁵¹ While we await a full scholarly exploration of the relationships between the friendships, libraries, and curriculum strategies of seventeenth- and eighteenth-century Quaker teachers, we may note that many early Quaker educators were themselves abolitionists who inspired abolitionist sentiments in their students. Lucretia Mott, one of the best-known nineteenth-century abolitionist leaders, encountered the ideas of abolitionist Elias Hicks in the early 1800s, first as a student and then as a teacher at the Nine Partners School, which had been established in Dutchess County, New York, in the 1790s.⁵²

By 1723, William Penn, George Fox, and all of the founding generation of Quaker thinkers and teachers had passed away. But new, more complex thinkers had appeared to replace them and to expand the founders' notions of virtue. Deeply conscious and proud of what came to be known as their "peculiar" status in the world, many students of Quaker schools and their families sought to live up to the legacy of their ancestors. They consented to have their secular and religious lives scrutinized and supervised under the monthly-quarterly-yearly meeting structure, and they attempted to align their lives with the values, disciplines, and behaviors of the seventeenth-century Religious Society of Friends. But how to accomplish this goal?

One way was to remain loyal to their departed ancestors. Throughout the eighteenth century—and in fact well into the twenty-first—living Quakers regularly republished, and widely disseminated, their forebears' writings. By 1738, the London Yearly Meeting had further solidified the importance of the parents' teachings by defining a status known as "birthright Friend," signifying a child born to Quaker parents who was to be raised in a Quaker family and community and inculcated in the tenets of the "Holy Conversation." Quaker educator John Comly was Enoch Lewis's Westtown School colleague. Comly's *English Grammar Made Easy to the Teacher and Pupil* was repeatedly reprinted and widely used to teach reading and grammar in Quaker and non-Quaker schools. In his memoir, Comly recalled his own early childhood socialization: "the incalculable advantages of taking little children to [Quaker] meetings, and of habituating them early to the discipline of stillness, can never be fully appreciated. It may be the means of laying the foundation, very early in life, for the most exalted virtues.... May parents, who have the important charge of leading on the rising generation, seriously and rightly consider their duty toward their tender children." Remembering how he was taught to avoid prejudice, Comly "believe[d] the first book put into my hands was Woolman's or Benezet's *Primer*."[53] Noting his own learning about injustice toward Indigenous Americans, Comly took care that his school texts, which were regularly reprinted over a period of five decades, always included biographies of abolitionists and/or Native American advocates, or excerpts of their writings.[54]

Indeed, in the absence of official liturgy and published doctrines, printing, reprinting, and recirculating the words of early Quaker writers quickly became a mainstay of Friends' strategy for managing unity among their many meetings that were scattered both geographically and theologically. Republished in the early nineteenth century as a collection of volumes known as *Friends Library*, the "must-have" reading for nineteenth-century Friends included several dozen seventeenth-century men and women, as well as the esteemed eighteenth-century abolitionist writings of John Woolman, James Pemberton, and others. Young Friends encountered these readings at their monthly, quarterly, or yearly meetings. Middle-class Friends often included these materials in their home libraries. A representative library of a twentieth-century Quaker family often included the same books, passed down over generations, with gift plates from parents to children and marginal notes attesting to the fact that the children had indeed perused the volumes.[55]

VIRTUE IN PUBLIC LIFE: ETHICS AND NONVIOLENCE IN
GOVERNMENT, COMMERCE, AND COMMUNITY LIFE

As Quakers struggled to find and make their "places" in the eighteenth-century world, they were challenged on every side by the turmoil that surrounded them. The Great Awakening presented a shifting notion of God's role in the cosmos. The War of the Austrian Succession, or King George's War (1740–48), and the global Seven Years' War (1756–63) reminded Friends of the insanity of wars and violence, and inspired them to expand and defend their posture of frugality and nonviolence. Pennsylvania, the only colony where Friends controlled the government, was a seat of tension between Quaker ideals and the reality of living out those ideals. As the burgeoning economy had allowed Philadelphia Friends to become increasingly wealthy, it became more difficult to maintain the ban on extravagance. Historian Jack Marietta has illuminated some of those tensions: how would Friends balance the demands of government, especially defense, and still maintain their religious principles against violence and war? Marietta quotes John Woolman, a New Jersey Friend best remembered for decrying injustice against Indigenous Americans and African Americans: "And does not protecting wealth inevitably lead to war?" Woolman cautioned Friends to be "particularly careful to have our minds redeemed from the love of wealth ... so no temporal concerns may ... hinder us from diligently following the dictates of Truth." His pamphlet *Plea for the Poor: A Word of Remembrance and Caution to the Rich* reminded Friends that "the desire to riches ... and selfishness hath been the original cause of [wars]."[56]

Similar concerns led Philadelphian James Pemberton to resign from the Pennsylvania Assembly and to compose a treatise "containing some reasons for [Quakers] not complying with human injunctions and institutions in matters relative to the worship of God." Explaining that he and his family were among the "number of pious, sober, and substantial people ... sincere followers and disciples of Christ" who had established Pennsylvania, he felt called to take up the cause of Indigenous Americans who had been wronged both by the infamous 1737 "Walking Purchase" (which cheated them out of thousands of acres of land) and by the governor's 1756 declaration of war on them.[57] Educated in Philadelphia's Quaker school with Friends' ideals of justice, James, a young man in his thirties, joined his father, Israel Pemberton, and a group of New Jersey Friends to spearhead the "Friendly Association for Regaining and Preserving Peace with the Indians by Pacific Measures." By 1795, the PYM had institutionalized the "Friendly Association," renaming it the Philadelphia Yearly Meeting Indian Committee, which worked closely with the New York Yearly Meeting Indian Affairs Committee, established at approximately the same time. Though these groups aimed to befriend and assist the region's Native Americans, some modern historians note that Quakers' involvement in Indian affairs, during and after the Seven Years' War, was complex and multifaceted, and awaits deeper research by scholars.[58]

In the 1790s, under the auspices of the Indian committees, a group of five Quaker men—Henry Simmons, Halliday Jackson, Joel Swayne, John

Pierce, and Joshua Sharpless—visited the Seneca Nation, aiming to introduce English Quaker culture into native communities. Over succeeding decades, more missionaries followed. The resulting diaries, reports, and correspondence chronicle their hopes and their struggles to understand Indigenous languages, and offer glimpses of both the successes and the challenges of their efforts. Thus by 1819, when Congress passed the Civilization Fund Act, which awarded grants to establish schools to convert Indigenous Americans to Christianity and to English-language culture, Quaker organizations had already established a track record with many of the regions' Native Americans.

The tensions leading to the American Revolution also caused Friends anguish. As with the Seven Years' War, some refused to pay taxes to support the war, while others, who opted to join the fray, withdrew from the main body of Friends and established the Free Quakers, building a separate meetinghouse, where their families worshipped until the 1830s.[59] Others equivocated, providing economic or material support but refusing to take up arms. A few accepted exile to British lands in Nova Scotia. Many more remained in their homes, sacrificing their wealth and status in support of their faith. A few agreed with Anthony Benezet, the abolitionist schoolmaster, who hailed the war as a lesson from God to show Friends that "our wants being made less, the perplexing, dangerous snares & engagements which attend the amassing of wealth would be much lessened." Many individuals and yearly meetings made their peace with the idea that if wealth were amassed honestly and used for philanthropy, the "dangerous snares" could be minimized.[60]

Quaker men were not alone in their struggles to make sense of the war. Elizabeth Drinker, whose husband was one of seventeen war-resisting Friends stripped of their wealth and exiled to Virginia in 1777, had started keeping a journal in the wake of the Seven Years' War when she was twenty-three years old. Though her journal's first years mostly record her private life, the political energy of the 1780s transformed her into a fervent Federalist. Drinker was among a coterie of Quaker women in Pennsylvania, New York, and New England who envisioned their own freedom in the freedom of the new nation. Poet Hannah Griffitts, who gave voice to Friends who supported the Revolution even as they denounced the violence of war, chose not to marry. Taking the unusual position that "everyone is not fitted for the single Life, nor was I ever moulded for the wed[d]ed one," Griffitts's sentiments echoed a trend not uncommon among Friends.[61] Whether because of the paucity of appropriate mates, or the availability of sufficient economic resources so that marriage could be superfluous, or because women were able to achieve the status and dignity of adulthood by assuming authority in meeting affairs, a "sizeable percentage" of Quaker women (and men) remained unmarried.[62] Whatever the causes, some scholars have argued that in Britain—and even more so in America—Quaker women increasingly exercised "considerable power and authority" in their households and in their communities as the eighteenth century drew to a close.[63]

These women's thinking, often recorded in "commonplace books," informal notebooks that chronicled personal and intellectual life paths, is emblematic of American Quakers' routes through the tumultuous Enlightenment era, which caused political, social, economic, and philosophical tremors in America and around the world. Technology, imperialism, and global trade, catalyzed by the advent of the worldwide Seven Years' War, heralded major transformations in power and authority.

For Quakers, especially those in America, the upheaval accelerated the sort of self-examination they were already prone to: what does this upheaval tell us about God's directives? Different Friends answered the challenge in different ways. However, by century's end, the issue of slavery dominated Friends' spiritual agenda, in what one scholar has described as "a complex pattern of engaging with issues of racial equity . . . [grappling] with both theory and practice."[64] Though raised in seventeenth-century English society, which was based upon servitude and apprenticeship, George Fox expressed concerns, albeit tentative and indirect, about a system of permanent bondage based on race. In the 1670s, he suggested that masters teach their slaves religion. Over succeeding generations, Quakers' objections to the system of slavery became more focused: racial slavery violated the Golden Rule; slaves could be controlled only with violence, or the threat of violence. A group of Quakers in Germantown had noted in 1688 that since slaves had *reason* to be angry, slavery also invited slaves' violence against their masters. Over the long eighteenth century, under the weight of revolutions that touted the "rights of men," British and American Friends became leaders in the international antislavery movement.

By the 1720s, Philadelphia nonconformist Benjamin Lay was excoriating Quakers and non-Quakers alike with his antislavery publications in what one historian has called "guerrilla street-theater."[65] Other Philadelphia voices, with echoes as far afield as England, New England, North Carolina, and the Caribbean, soon joined the chorus. John Woolman's treatise *Some*

Considerations on the Keeping of Negroes (1754), and his international travel on behalf of abolition, placed Woolman in the forefront of the antislavery campaign. His *Journal*, regularly reprinted and continually quoted in Quaker school curricula, is widely remembered for its focus on Woolman's lifelong discovery and expansion of his social conscience. Though Woolman was not the first Quaker to agonize over the brutality of racial slavery, he was critical to the centrality of abolitionism in Quaker thought and to the belief that Quakers who kept slaves risked damaging their own souls.

By 1780, all of the American yearly meetings had, at least in theory, banned slaveholding among their membership, though it was not until 1840 that the last Quaker-held slave was freed.[66] Home from exile in Virginia, Henry Drinker bought land and developed a scheme to undercut slave-grown sugar by manufacturing maple syrup. Though Drinker's plan was doomed to failure, abolitionist Quakers repeatedly experimented with "free produce" projects.[67] Thus an antislavery initiative slowly made its way onto Quakers' social, economic, political, and theological agenda, which also included resistance to war, championing Indigenous rights, and humanitarian relief. Over the course of the long eighteenth century, Quakers came to be viewed—and to view themselves—as a manifestation of the "conscience" of America, and indeed of the world, as they developed an ever more strident diatribe that greed and self-indulgence fed slaveholding and led to violence and war.[68]

Both fiction and reality reflected the conundrum of conscience versus economics, even as Quakers themselves recognized that human perfection was a "journey, not a destination," and that sometimes their most intractable impediment was their own flawed selves. By the end of the eighteenth century, two pious Quakers, Hannah Barnard and Elias Hicks, would raise troubling questions about doctrine, community life, and slavery that would rend Friends' communities asunder.[69]

THE CHALLENGE OF MODERNITY: "IN THE WORLD BUT NOT OF IT"

By the end of the eighteenth century, Quakers had codified their founders' theology into a lifestyle shaped by conscience, introspection, and a quest for human perfection. Individuals and families who could not, or chose not to, meet the requirements of piety, frugality, nonviolence, commitment to social justice, and limited engagement with the "world's people" trickled away to less restrictive communities.⁷⁰ Those who remained were dedicated to William Penn's challenge that "true religion don't turn men out of the world, but enables them to live better in it, and excites their endeavors to mend it."⁷¹ Friends challenged themselves to walk the fine line of insulating themselves and their children from the violence, judgment, gossip, and time wasting associated with the "world's people," while refusing to isolate themselves completely from that world. Often describing their lofty goals as being "in the world but not of it," and pursuing the "pleasure in ... having a heart capable of enjoying the happiness of others" (as opposed to "worldly" pleasures), Friends embraced empathy and advocacy for those "low in the world."⁷²

In his treatise *Primitive Christianity Revived* (1699), William Penn had distilled Quaker theology and practice into twelve guidelines. Friends, he asserted, should be *against* swearing, tithing, making war against any Christians, marriage to non-Friends, pagan holidays, reverential titles, and any harm toward *anyone* in *or* outside the Religious Society of Friends. Friends should stand *for* "plainness" in speech, apparel, and prayer, *for* charity (i.e., gathering and distributing resources to help those in need), *for* remaining in touch with the words of founding Friends, and *for* requiring the meeting's approval for marriage. Friends should also be *for* regularly held worship and business meetings, and should care for Friends' community life and support humanitarian efforts for members and nonmembers. Finally, as he had outlined in *No Cross, No Crown*, Penn asserted that Friends should be willing—perhaps even *eager*—to sacrifice or suffer in the service of their faith. These guidelines, first articulated at the beginning of the long eighteenth century, continue to set the template for monthly meetings' organization and agendas and for the curricula of Quaker schools.⁷³ Though the specifics for executing that template have been contested at various times and places, the goals have remained intact for more than three centuries.

From worship groups to public schools, mines, mills, shops, hospitals, banks, and housing cooperatives, all conceived on the basis of participatory nonhierarchy, Friends have aspired (with mixed success) to live within the template of their eighteenth-century organizational structure. Supported by the memories and writings of Quaker exemplars, they have aimed to teach their children "Truth," righteousness, charity, justice, nonviolence, social conscience, self-abnegation, and the equality of all creatures before God. Neither individuals nor Friends' communities have always succeeded in meeting those goals, which have, in modern times, been reduced to the acronym SPICES (simplicity, peace, integrity, community, equality, and stewardship). This trivializes the gravity of those goals. Even so, the aspiration endures. Several of the early schools have survived into the twenty-first century. Dozens of seventeenth- and eighteenth-century worship houses, peppering the globe, remain hallowed "places" where modern-day Friends worship and organize their forays into the "corrupt" world to "mend it." The printed words of early Quaker visionaries are still reprinted, reread, and revered. Most of the communal living systems in which Quakers have sought self-government apart from the main society have been flawed and/or transitory, but that has not deterred Friends from repeating such experiments at many times and in many places around the world. In these and other ways, modern Quakers continue the tradition set by early Friends of aiming to be the world's "conscience."

NOTES

1. Mary Drinker Cope to Francis Cope, August 9, 1805, Cope-Evans Family Papers, HCLQSC.

2. A number of scholars have ruminated on various aspects of this phenomenon. See, for example, Barry J. Levy, "'Tender Plants': Quaker Farmers and Children in the Delaware Valley, 1681–1735," *Journal of Family History* 3, no. 2 (1978): 116–35; J. William Frost, *The Quaker Family in Colonial America: A Portrait of the Society of Friends* (New York: St. Martin's Press, 1973).

3. Estimates of mid-seventeenth-century England's population put Quaker numbers at about sixty thousand, or roughly 1 percent of the population. This minority status is indicative of Friends' desire—and need—to reinforce that cohesiveness. Stephen Broadberry, Bruce M. S. Campbell, Alexander Klein, Mark Overton, and Bas van Leeuwen, *British Economic Growth, 1270–1870* (Cambridge: Cambridge University Press, 2015), chap. 1 and table 5.06.

4. Some aspects of that attenuation are summarized in Emma Lapsansky-Werner, "Quaker Life and Communities at the Turn of the Century," in *The Quakers, 1656–1723: The Evolution of an Alternative Community*, ed. Richard C. Allen and Rosemary Moore (University Park: Penn State University Press, 2018), 216–37.

5. James Emmet Ryan, *Imaginary Friends: Representing Quakers in American Culture, 1650–1950* (Madison: University of Wisconsin Press, 2009). See also Erin Bell, "Stock Characters with Stiff-Brimmed Bonnets: Depictions of Quaker Women by Outsiders, c. 1650–1800," in *New Critical Studies on Early Quaker Women, 1650–1800*, ed. Michele Lise Tarter and Catie Gill (Oxford: Oxford University Press, 2018), 91–109.

6. Modern examples of such tropes include the American films *Angel and the Badman* (1947) and *High Noon* (1952); the "Limitations" episode of the American television series *Law and Order: Special Victims Unit* (season 1, episode 14), which featured a Quaker character (https://www.imdb.com/title/tt0629677); and the HBO TV series *Six Feet Under* (https://www.imdb.com/title/tt0248654).

7. William Penn, *A Collection of the Works of William Penn, in Two Volumes, to Which Is Prefixed a Journal of his Life* (London: J. Sowle, 1726).

8. J. William Frost, "William Penn's Experiment in the Wilderness: Promise and Legend," *Pennsylvania Magazine of History and Biography* 107, no. 4 (1983): 577–605.

9. In *God's Government Begun: The Society for Universal Inquiry and Reform, 1842–1846* (Bloomington: Indiana University Press, 1995), Thomas D. Hamm describes several "intentional communities" in various sections of the midwestern United States. See also Emma J. Lapsansky-Werner, "A Revolution in Her Own Time: Philadelphia's Friendship Cooperative Housing, Inc. (1946–1962)," in *Keeping Us Honest, Stirring the Pot: A Festschrift in Honor of H. Larry Ingle*, ed. Chuck Fager (Fayetteville, NC: Kimo Press, 2011), 77–90.

10. See, for example, Neva Specht, "Removing to a Remote Place: Quaker Certificates of Removal," *Quaker History* 91, no. 1 (2002): 45–69; Margaret Hope Bacon, ed., *Wilt Thou Go on My Errand? Three Eighteenth-Century Journals of Quaker Women Ministers: Susanna Morris, 1682–1755; Elizabeth Hudson, 1722–1783; Ann Moore, 1710–1783* (Wallingford, PA: Pendle Hill, 1994); Nathaniel Philbrick, *Away off Shore: Nantucket Island and Its People, 1602–1890* (New York: Penguin Books, 1994).

11. Anthony N. B. Garvan, "Proprietary Philadelphia as an Artifact," in *The Historian and the City*, ed. Oscar Handlin and John Burchard (Cambridge: MIT Press, 1963), 177–201.

12. Barry J. Levy, "The Birth of the 'Modern Family' in Early America: Quaker and Anglican Families in the Delaware Valley, Pennsylvania, 1681–1750," in *Friends and Neighbors: Group Life in America's First Plural Society*, ed. Michael W. Zuckerman (Philadelphia: Temple University Press, 1982), 29.

13. David Hackett Fischer, *Historians' Fallacies: Toward a Logic of Historical Thought* (New York: Harper and Row, 1970); Richard D. Brown, *Modernization: The Transformation of American Life, 1600–1865* (New York: Hill and Wang, 1976).

14. Richard C. Allen and Rosemary Moore, "The Friends and Business in the Second Period," in Allen and Moore, *Quakers, 1656–1723*, 260–61; Garvan, "Proprietary Philadelphia as an Artifact."

15. In his landmark study *The Protestant Ethic and the Spirit of Capitalism* (1905; translated into English by Talcott Parsons [London: Routledge, 1930]), Max Weber argued that the Protestant values of abstemiousness and ethical behavior provided firm underpinnings for capitalist economic systems, which are largely based on faith rather than on concrete economic exchanges.

16. William Penn, "A Further Account of the Province of Pennsylvania," quoted in David Hackett Fischer, *Albion's Seed: Four British Folkways in America* (New York: Oxford University Press, 1989), 429.

17. Russell Weigley, *Philadelphia: A Three-Hundred-Year History* (New York: W. W. Norton, 1982), 50.

18. Julie Winch, *A Gentleman of Color: The Life of James Forten* (Oxford: Oxford University Press, 2002), chap. 2.

19. Historic American Buildings Survey, *Silent Witness: Quaker Meeting Houses in the Delaware Valley, 1695 to the Present* (Philadelphia: Philadelphia Yearly Meeting of the Religious Society of Friends, 2002), 50; Arthur J. Mekeel, "The Founding Years, 1681–1789," in *Friends in the Delaware Valley: Philadelphia Yearly Meeting, 1681–1981*, ed. John M. Moore (Haverford, PA: Friends Historical Association, 1981), 14–53.

20. Fischer, *Albion's Seed*, 424–30; Weigley, *Philadelphia*, 47.

21. Craig W. Horle, Joseph S. Foster, and Laurie M. Wolfe, eds., *Lawmaking and Legislators in Pennsylvania: A Biographical Dictionary*, vol. 3, *1757–1775* (Harrisburg: Commonwealth of Pennsylvania House of Representatives, 2005).

22. Gary B. Nash's *Warner Mifflin: Unflinching Quaker Abolitionist* (Philadelphia: University of Pennsylvania Press, 2017) contains dramatic evidence of interrelationships based on marriage, landholdings, religion, and reform along the East Coast between New York and Virginia.

23. Richard Dunn, *Sugar and Slaves: The Rise of the Planter Class in the English West Indies, 1624–1713* (Chapel Hill: University of North Carolina Press, 1972), chap. 3.

24. Levy, "'Tender Plants.'"

25. Harm de Blij, *The Power of Place: Geography, Destiny, and Globalization's Rough Landscape* (New York: Oxford University Press, 2009); Jen Jack Gieseking, William Mangold, and Cindi Katz, *The People, Place, and Space Reader* (New York: Routledge, 2014).

26. David W. Maxey, "The Union Farm: Henry Drinker's Experiment in Deriving Profit from Virtue," *Pennsylvania Magazine of History and Biography* 107, no. 4 (1983), 607; Larry Gragg, *Englishmen Transplanted: The English Colonization of Barbados, 1627–1660* (Oxford: Oxford University Press, 2003); Levy, "'Tender Plants,'" 132–34; Fischer, *Albion's Seed*, 429–35. Levy and Maxey, in particular, have explored colonial Quakers' penchant for purchasing large parcels of land in order to create protected "places" in which to pursue their community mission.

27. See, for example, Sumner Chilton Powell, *Puritan Village: The Formation of a New England Town* (Middletown: Wesleyan University Press, 1963); Linda Auwers Bissell, "From One Generation to Another: Mobility in Seventeenth-Century Windsor, Connecticut," *William and Mary Quarterly* 31, no. 1 (1974): 79–110.

28. A must-read for understanding the complexity and authority of Quaker hierarchical structure—and its power over its adherents—is Susan Forbes, "Quaker Tribalism," in Zuckerman, *Friends and Neighbors*, 145–73.

29. Seventeenth- and eighteenth-century maps show that roads from areas on the periphery of downtown Philadelphia were laid out to carry market goods from the hinterlands into the city. Until well into the twentieth century, there were few—and poor—arteries linking peripheral areas with one another. See Garvan, "Proprietary Philadelphia as an Artifact," 199–200.

30. Quoted in William E. Lingelbach, "William Penn and City Planning," *Pennsylvania Magazine of History and Biography* 68, no. 4 (1944): 400.

31. See Bacon, *Wilt Thou Go on My Errand?*

32. Forbes, "Quaker Tribalism," 149. In the twenty-first century, many yearly meetings continue to budget funds to support Friends' travel on behalf of various kinds of Quaker "witness." For example, the Philadelphia Yearly Meeting has continued the work of the bequest of John Pemberton through a committee known as the "Traveling Witness Granting Group"; see https://www.pym.org/grants/travel-witness.

33. Friends World Committee for Consultation, *Quakers Around the World: Handbook of the Religious Society of Friends* (London: Friends World Committee for Consultation, 1994).

34. Moore, *Friends in the Delaware Valley*, appendices prepared by Barbara L. Curtis, 249–51.

35. Frost, *Quaker Family in Colonial America*, 5.

36. Weigley, *Philadelphia*, 249–50.

37. Ibid., 46.

38. Jordan Landes, *London Quakers in the Trans-Atlantic World: The Creation of an Early Modern Community* (London: Palgrave Macmillan, 2015), 107, 171–75; Henry J. Cadbury, *The Church in the Wilderness: North Carolina Quakerism as Seen by Visitors; The Historical Lecture Delivered at the 251st Session of North Carolina Yearly Meeting* (Greensboro: North Carolina Friends Historical Society, 1948).

39. David D. Hall, *Cultures of Print: Essays in the History of the Book* (Amherst: University of Massachusetts Press, 1996), 133–50.

40. Specht, "Removing to a Remote Place."

41. "Civilization Fund Act, 15th United States Congress, Statutes at Large: 3 Stat. 516b, Effective: March 3, 1819," in Donald A. Grinde Jr. ed., *Native Americans* (Washington, DC: CQ Press, 2002), 57.

42. Levy, "'Tender Plants,'" 128.

43. Frost, *Quaker Family in Colonial America*, 133–47.

44. LYM, *Advices*, 1690, quoted in ibid., 93; *Christian and Brotherly Advices of London Yearly Meeting*, quoted in Rayner Wickersham Kelsey, *Centennial History of Moses Brown School* (Providence: Moses Brown School, 1919), 6–7.

45. William Penn Charter School, "*. . . Better Than Riches*": *A Tricentennial History of William Penn Charter School, 1689–1981* (Philadelphia: William Penn Charter School, 1988).

46. Kelsey, *Centennial History of Moses Brown*, 9.

47. Ibid., 8.

48. On Lewis, see Paul W. Graseck, "Quaker, Teacher, Abolitionist: The Life of Educator-Reformer Enoch Lewis, 1776–1856" (PhD diss., University of Connecticut, 1996).

49. George Keith, "An Exhortation & Caution to Friends Concerning Buying or Keeping of Negroes" (1693), *Pennsylvania Magazine of History and Biography* 13 (1889), http://www.qhpress.org/quakerpages/qwhp/gk-as1693.htm.

50. There is extensive scholarship on Quakers and their involvement in the eighteenth-century abolitionist movement. A small selection of recent work is found in the introduction to this volume, n. 6.

51. Graseck, "Quaker, Teacher, Abolitionist," 18–20.

52. Esther L. S. McGonegal, "Nine Partners Boarding School (1796–1863)," *Bulletin of Friends Historical Society of Philadelphia* 10, no. 1 (1920): 11–15.

53. John Comly, *Journal of the Life and Religious Labors of John Comly, Late of Byberry Pennsylvania, Published by His Children* (Philadelphia: T. E. Chapman, 1854), 7–8.

54. John Comly, *Comly's Primer, or the First Book for Children* (Philadelphia: Kimber and Sharpless, 1826). Comly also wrote a spelling book and several other schoolbooks for children over the next several decades.

55. Joseph Rakestraw (printer), *Catalog of Books in Friends Library, Cherry Street Below Fifth, Philadelphia* (Philadelphia: Joseph Rakestraw 1853); Joseph Smith, *A Descriptive Catalogue of Friends' Books, or Books Written by Members of the Society of Friends, Commonly Called Quakers, from Their First Rise to the Present Time* (London: E. Hicks, 1893). Some volumes from the Maier family library are available in the Morris-Shinn-Maier archives at HCLQSC, http://archives.tricolib.brynmawr.edu/repositories/5/resources/544/collection_organization.

56. Quoted in Jack D. Marietta, "War, Wealth, and Religion: The Perfecting of Quaker Asceticism, 1740–1783," *Church History* 43, no. 2 (1974): 234.

57. James Pemberton, *An apology for the people called Quakers, containing some reasons for their not complying with human injunctions and institutions in matters relative to the worship of God* [...] (Philadelphia: James Chattin, 1757), 2.

58. See, for example, Michael Goode, "A Failed Peace: The Friendly Association and the Pennsylvania Back Country During the Seven Years' War," *Pennsylvania Magazine of History and Biography* 136, no. 4 (2012): 472–74; Jean R. Soderlund, *Lenape Country: Delaware Valley Society Before William Penn* (Philadelphia: University of Pennsylvania Press, 2015).

59. Charles Wetherill, *History of the Religious Society of Friends Called by Some the Free Quakers in the City of Philadelphia* (Philadelphia: Centennial Press, 1894). It should be noted that this volume, published by a descendant of one of the leaders of the Free Quakers, has a hagiographic tone.

60. Quoted in Marietta, "War, Wealth, and Religion," 239, 240.

61. Catherine La Courreye Blecki and Karin A. Wulf, eds., *Milcah Martha Moore's Book: A Commonplace Book from Revolutionary America* (University Park: Penn State University Press, 1997), 97.

62. Frost, *Quaker Family in Colonial America*, 150; Levy, "'Tender Plants,'" 129.

63. Naomi Pullin, *Female Friends and the Making of Transatlantic Quakerism, 1650–1750* (Cambridge: Cambridge University Press, 2018), 99–105.

64. Elizabeth Cazden, "Quakers, Slavery, Anti-Slavery, and Race," in *The Oxford Handbook of Quaker Studies*, ed. Stephen W. Angell and Pink Dandelion (Oxford: Oxford University Press, 2013), 347–62.

65. Marcus Rediker, *The Fearless Benjamin Lay: The Quaker Dwarf Who Became the First Revolutionary Abolitionist* (Boston: Beacon Press, 2017), 16, 102.

66. Cazden, "Quakers, Slavery, Anti-Slavery, and Race," 362.

67. Maxey, "Union Farm," 612.

68. Rediker, *Fearless Benjamin Lay*, 1–6, 191–205. Rediker's narrative chronicles Lay's ability to garner the attention of many others at home and abroad in bringing this issue to the forefront. See also Nash, *Warner Mifflin*, 96–97.

69. Chuck Fager, *Without Apology: The Heroes, the Heritage, and the Hope of Liberal Quakerism* (Media, PA: Kimo Press, 1996).

70. Frederick B. Tolles, *Meeting House and Counting House: The Quaker Merchants of Colonial Philadelphia, 1682–1763* (New York: W. W. Norton, 1948), 142–43; Pullin, *Female Friends*, 126–32.

71. William Penn, *No Cross, No Crown* (1669; repr., Richmond, IN: Friends United Press, 1981), 36.

72. William Henry Williams, *America's First Hospital: The Pennsylvania Hospital, 1751–1841* (Philadelphia: Haverford House, 1976); see also Charles Cherry, *A Quiet Haven: Quakers, Moral Treatment, and Asylum Reform* (Madison: Fairleigh Dickinson University Press, 1989).

73. Tolles, *Meeting House*, 71; Pullin, *Female Friends*, 120–21; Jean R. Soderlund, "Women's Authority in Pennsylvania and New Jersey Quaker Meetings, 1680–1760," *William and Mary Quarterly* 44, no. 4 (1987): 722–49.

PART 3

Expressions of Quakerism Around the Atlantic World

CHAPTER 8

Quakers, Indigenous Americans, and the Landscape of Peace

GEOFFREY PLANK

In 1761, a group of Quakers in Britain published an account of the religious experiences of an Indigenous American man living in the foothills of the Appalachian Mountains. The man's life changed after he went alone into the woods "in great bitterness of spirit." After five days, "it pleased God to appear to him to his comfort, to give him a sight of his inward state, and also an acquaintance with the works of nature. For he apprehended a sense was given him of the virtues and natures of several herbs, roots, plants and trees, and the different relations they had to one another, and he was made sensible that man stood in the nearest relation to God, of any part of the creation."[1] The man described in this pamphlet was the Munsee religious leader Papunhank, who had come to Philadelphia in wartime in 1760 to plead for peace. Though he had never met a Quaker before his visit to the city, he seemed to have already discovered many of the core tenets of Quaker belief, alone in the woods in direct communion with God.[2]

Papunhank's experience seemed to confirm the Quakers' conviction that God could speak to anyone directly, outside the context of any formal religious ritual. He also affirmed some common Quaker assumptions about God's relationship with the natural world.[3] Quakers frequently sought divine lessons from nature. Since the earliest days of their religious society, some Quakers had emulated Adam, who stood in Paradise and "gave names to all cattle, and to the fowl of the air, and to every beast of the field" (Gen. 2:20, KJV). Some believed that they could learn even more than he did and come closer to God.[4] With his inspired understanding of the "virtues and natures" of the plant life around him, Papunhank seemed to have acquired that kind of knowledge. He had the sort of wisdom Quakers had long sought. His insight was especially exciting, new, and different for the Quakers because it was embedded within an Indigenous North American landscape.

The Quakers had first learned to worship outdoors in pastoral England, where fields were comprehensively tended and grazed. Quakers on both sides of the Atlantic had a particular love of pastures, because these were the kinds of fields that the first Quakers crossed, and sheep, pastures, flocks, and shepherds were celebrated in the Bible. Many early Quakers had formative religious experiences outdoors. Quakers preached in fields and on hillsides to distance themselves from churchly artifice and clerical regulation. In quieter, more solitary moments, they often went alone into the countryside for solace and inspiration. This impulse to pray outdoors had egalitarian implications for them. It seemed to prove that anyone entering a field might receive wisdom. But there were discriminatory implications as well. As a community, Quakers associated English-style agriculture and husbandry with virtue, and when they first encountered the landscape of North America in the seventeenth century, they often responded with horror.

The Quakers' love of pastures caused trouble when they moved to North America. Like other English colonists, they brought domestic animals with them as part of a comprehensive effort to re-create a familiar landscape and way of life. William Cronon, Virginia DeJohn Anderson, Jon T. Coleman, and others have described how the introduction of livestock, and European agriculture generally, transformed the landscape of North America and challenged Indigenous Americans both ideologically and in their mode of subsistence.[5] The transformation of the landscape generated conflict in every part of North America the English and Welsh colonized, but the resulting controversies had a particular, troubling resonance for Quakers, not just because they were pacifists but also because they laid bare in concrete terms a dilemma at the heart of their beliefs. The Quakers' egalitarianism was usually biblically informed, and therefore exalted one way of life over others. Quakers debated among themselves whether

Indigenous Americans could receive salvation without instruction from missionaries, without knowledge of Christianity or the adoption of a European way of living. They never came to consensus on these questions, and their debates had national significance because Quakers would assume prominent roles in the formulation of US policy toward Indigenous Americans from the 1790s onward. The Quakers' love of pastures and flocks informed their plans for Indigenous Americans, especially on Indian reservations.

Any effort to explain Quakers' religious understanding of the countryside should start in the 1630s, with the earliest religious experiences of the men and women who eventually became the first Quakers. Mary Penington, for example, grew up an orphan in that decade, and she struggled against the instructions she received from her adoptive families. The decade was a time of intense religious controversy, and she sought refuge outside: "When alone in the fields, and possessed with fears, I accounted prayers my help and safety." By the time she was twenty-one, she had married, given birth to a son and daughter, and lost her husband in the English Civil War. She remained as skeptical and agitated as she had been as a child, and she looked for "remote places to pray in, such as the fields, gardens, or out-houses, when I could not be private in the house. I was so vehement in prayer, that I thought no place too private to pray in, for I could not but be loud in the earnest pouring out of my soul." Years later, she was still in a "restless, distressed state," and she continued to seek comfort outdoors, remembering, "I often retired into the country, without any company but my daughter and her maid; and there I spent many hours each day in bemoaning myself and desiring the knowledge of the truth." Fittingly, her first encounter with a Quaker occurred outside. She was walking in a park with her second husband, Isaac Penington, when they met him. The man "saw us as he rode by, in our gay, vain apparel. He cried out to us against our pride, etc., at which I scoffed, and said he was a public preacher indeed, who preached in the highways."[6]

Though men and women like Penington may initially have scoffed, Quakers often preached outdoors and on highways in the 1650s and 1660s. On several occasions between 1676 and 1720, the London Yearly Meeting asked monthly and quarterly meetings to provide "an exact account among themselves of those that first brought the message of glad tidings among them."[7] Dozens of meetings across England responded with their origin stories, and many recalled early moments of inspiration outdoors. In many parts of the country, traveling ministers preached in markets and along the streets because that was where they could reach the largest audience. For this reason, as recounted in Norman Penney's edition of *The First Publishers of Truth*, residents of Carlisle, Falmouth, Kendall, Oxford, Selby, Settle, Stafford, and Wensleydale, and villages like Portinscale in the Lake District, Elloughton in Yorkshire, and Coggeshall in Essex, first encountered Quakerism along the roadside.[8] In 1658, a traveling Quaker minister in Henley-on-Thames stood on a stool in a gateway facing the market and preached. Recounting the event nearly fifty years later, the Quakers in Henley reported that "many people gathered" to listen and "two or three" were convinced (218). In other places, Quakers gathered outdoors because they were driven from the buildings where they had planned to assemble. In Holme Abbey in Cumbria, William Dewsbury began preaching in the church, but after he had "sounded the day of the Lord that would overtake the workers of iniquity," the people "were so alarmed that they haled him out of the graveyard and violently drove him out of the town." Dewsbury retreated to a "little hill" where he resumed his teaching (72). Traveling ministers in Canterbury met in the local Baptist meetinghouse until they were locked out and forced to preach in the churchyard (146). In Malpas, Cheshire, and in Stoke Climsland, Cornwall, ministers similarly preached in churchyards, though in those instances it is not clear whether they were forced out of the churches or simply chose not to enter them (17, 21). There was no ambiguity as to why James Lancaster preached from the water under a bridge in St. Bees. He had been chased there by the Quakers' opponents and thrown off the bridge (36–37). Traveling ministers did not always speak outdoors. They also held meetings in private houses, but sometimes the crowds they drew were too large to fit inside private homes. In Colchester, Quaker ministers worshiped in a yard "where it's thought there were about a thousand people." The Quaker weaver and minister Thomas Shorthand spoke to this crowd "out of a hay chamber window" (96).

These early Quaker ministers preached outside for several pragmatic reasons. Streets, markets, yards, and hillsides were less closely guarded than churches and other public buildings. They were accessible and could accommodate large audiences. Even after Quaker meetings had established themselves, similar considerations sometimes drove them outside. In Pardshaw in Cumberland, for example, so "many were convinced of the truth that the houses could not contain them, but they met out of doors for many years at a place called Pardshaw Cragg" (37). But it is also clear from the meetings' reports that some early Quakers simply preferred to gather outdoors. In Dent, the Quakers worshipped "time after time and year after year, one meeting on top of Helms Knot Hill, another on the Riggs [common land] near Sedburgh, another in James Capstock's low field below Gawthorpe" (334; see also 330). In Bolton, Quakers gathered with George Fox "on the side of a mountain," and "shortly after" with James Nayler "upon a hillside." Bolton meetings continued "sometimes upon the hills without and sometimes in houses and barns, as it pleased the Lord to make way for his Truth in the hearts of his people" (56–58). The Quakers in York, Winterbourne, and Reading reported early meetings in orchards, and Felton in Gloucestershire hosted its first meeting "in an open field" (3, 104, 318).

As Mary Penington suggested in her account of her experiences, worshipping outdoors could provide an escape from pretense and religious formality. The open air gave space to those who sought to ignore, violate, or even defy social conventions. In the privacy of open spaces, Penington avoided scrutiny and the tedious disputations of "loose Protestants" and "canonical priests."[9] She was also able to pray at the top of her lungs. For the Quakers in general, gathering outside was leveling. William Spurry Sr. reported that the early Quakers in London called themselves "plain north country ploughmen." He first encountered them worshipping in the garden of a private house (163). But worshipping outdoors was more than an egalitarian statement. For some Quakers it was a transcendent experience.

Of all the early outdoor Quaker worshippers, the most celebrated and influential was George Fox (242–43, 333). Fox's journal contains an intriguing passage that helps explain what being outdoors meant to him. Describing a religious experience in 1648, he wrote, "I was come up in spirit through the flaming sword, into the paradise of God. All things were new; and all the creation gave unto me another smell than before, beyond what words can utter. I knew nothing but pureness, and innocency, and righteousness; being renewed into the image of God by Christ Jesus, to the state of Adam, which he was in before he fell. The creation was opened to me; and it was showed me how all things had their names given them according to their nature and virtue." Fox believed he saw creation even more clearly than Adam had seen it in paradise.[10]

William Dewsbury had a similar experience.[11] Dewsbury was originally a shepherd from Yorkshire, and he connected the Kingdom of God to the pastoral scenery of his youth.[12] In an essay published in 1655, Dewsbury proclaimed that "the Lord will make the Earth as the Garden of Eden, and hath begun his great and strange work in this nation." He declared that God was "now gathering his elect together, his scattered sheep, that have been scattered in the cloudy and dark day, and will bring them from the people, and will gather them from the countries, and will bring them to their own land, and I will feed them upon a good pasture, and upon the high mountains of Israel shall their fold be, and there shall they lie in a good fold, and in a fat pasture shall they feed upon the mountains of Israel."[13]

Dewsbury used agricultural metaphors that appeared to refer to contemporary British practices as well as to the world and the teachings of the Bible. Drawing on extensive biblical reading, he and other seventeenth-century Quakers meditated and gave lessons on topics like seeds, hedges, husbandry, and sheep.[14] Sheep provided the early Quakers some of their most powerful metaphors. The Bible led them to believe that sheep had Christlike properties, and they frequently compared God's people to sheep.[15] For Quakers, sheep were emblems of humility, community, obedience, sacrifice, and almighty power. In the New Testament, sheep were also pitted against adversaries and villains. Some of these bad characters, like errant shepherds, could still be found in Britain, while others, like wolves, had been banished from the island. The sheep's ultimate confrontation comes in the Book of Revelation when the Lamb contends with beasts. These images from the Bible affected the early Quakers' response to physical landscapes, and not just in the pastoral parts of Scotland, Ireland, England, and Wales but also in North America. As the Quakers initially saw it, America was barren and inhospitable. It was a harsh environment for sheep.

In 1658, Josiah Cole and Thomas Thurston became the first Quakers to enter the territory that eventually became Pennsylvania. English Quakers published several reports of their journey, celebrating the two men and expressing astonishment that they had survived. The men had entered a "large uncultivated tract of land very hard," and had "not only hunger and cold to encounter with, in the winter season, but were often in danger of being devoured by wild beasts, or of perishing in unknown waters, marshes and bogs." They survived only with God's assistance.[16]

Decades later, in 1696, Quakers Jonathan Dickenson and Robert Barrow were shipwrecked with some others on the coast of Florida, and again English Quakers celebrated their survival. According to Dickenson's account of their ordeal, "The wilderness country looked very dismal, having no trees but only sand-hills covered with shrubby palmetto, the stalks of which were prickly." Like Cole and Thurston, they thought they would have died if they had been on their own, but God was with them. They prayed, and he delivered them out of those barren lands. Though separated by forty years, these Quaker travelers described the American wilderness very similarly. There was an important contrast, however. The region that frightened Cole and Thurston became Dickenson and Barrow's refuge. The shipwrecked Quakers traveled north and found comfort "amongst faithful Friends" in Philadelphia.[17]

When William Penn gave Philadelphia its name in 1681, Quakers had been visiting the Delaware Valley and its environs for many years, and some already believed that the region was blessed. The Lenape, Munsee, and other Indigenous peoples who lived there managed local diplomacy carefully, and so they treated Quaker visitors kindly.[18] When Thurston fell ill on his travels, an Indigenous American man carried him on his back for miles. Early Quaker commentators on Cole and Thurston's travels assumed that Indigenous Americans were cannibals, and they marveled that the Quakers had survived this encounter with "men-eaters."[19] Some Quaker writers insisted that only the intervention of "a more than human power" could explain the Indigenous peoples' good behavior.[20]

In 1672, when Fox visited the Delaware Valley, he also enjoyed friendly encounters with Indigenous Americans. After returning from his travels, he advised other Quakers to "have meetings" with the Indigenous people, and "answer the light, truth, and spirit of God" in them.[21] Quaker immigrants soon began coming to the region, and in eastern New Jersey, near the mouth of the Delaware River on Cape May, and further upstream on both banks of the Delaware, they negotiated with Indigenous peoples to purchase land. They also sometimes made elaborate promises intended to secure good relations in the future and guarantee lasting peace. Like all other newcomers to North America, Quakers had many motivations for coming, and some Quakers doubted that their arrival would benefit the Indigenous people. They voiced skepticism about the value of the Quakers' promises, and chastised one another for exploiting Indigenous Americans and occupying too much land.[22] One of the sharpest and most revealing criticisms was directed at William Penn.

In 1682, Penn proposed purchasing land near the future site of Perth Amboy, New Jersey. Quaker Samuel Groom, the surveyor of East Jersey, described Penn's proposal as "madness," explaining that the Indigenous people "must have land (and choice too) to plant on, they will not part with all presently, neither will they sell land within 4, 6, or 8 miles of their settled plantations." Groom quoted them: "We (say they) plant 7 or 14 years in one place, and when the ground grows waste, we remove to another place. Neither (say they) will we sell land near us, because cattle, horses, hogs will destroy our fruits, for we neither keep such things nor fence." Groom had observed that in Indigenous settlements far from colonial towns, "their plantations are as neat dressed as most of our garden ground about London, full of Indian corn, pease, beans . . . water and muskmelons, potatoes squashes and other fine things, and they generally live together like country villages, every family apart, and every man and woman hath their pieces of land, and things upon it, and work as we do, in such work as pleaseth them best, and indeed, if one have but a bit of victuals, and others want, they will divide it amongst them all, though never so little."[23] Groom argued that the Quakers should leave such villages alone.

Groom believed that Indigenous Americans were good custodians of the local landscape, and his description of their villages suggests that they were equal to the rural English in maintaining a healthy and righteous environment. At the same time that Groom was writing, others were making similar assertions about Indigenous American spiritual life, suggesting that Indigenous Americans were fully capable of caring for their own souls. In 1682, Quakers in London published the purported dying words of a man they described as an "Indian King" named Ockanickon, who had been buried among the Quakers in accordance with his own request, in Burlington, New Jersey. Ockanickon did not describe himself as a Christian, nor did he invoke specifically Christian teaching in his parting words of advice. But he exhibited exemplary humility and seemed animated by divine love.[24] That same year, the Scottish Quaker theologian George Keith asserted that Indigenous Americans had "a divine law in their hearts." Keith believed that it followed logically that "all men," regardless of their exposure to the written Gospel, could be inspired directly by God.[25] But as Dickenson's story suggests, other Quakers thought that the Delaware Valley was special. They were wary of Indigenous Americans who lived elsewhere, in apparently unwholesome environments.

Beginning in 1699, Quakers in Philadelphia and London circulated and promoted Dickenson's shipwreck story. Eventually, at least sixteen editions would appear in print. In 1707 the Quaker historian William Sewel translated it into Dutch.[26] Like the authors of previous Quaker commentaries on Cole and Thurston's travels, Dickenson assumed that the Indigenous peoples he encountered were cannibals. More emphatically, he asserted that the people he met in Florida had killed and devoured the entire crew of a Dutch vessel that had run aground on that coast a year earlier. Extrapolating even more speculatively, he declared that the Quakers were "the first company that are known to have escaped."²⁷

When the Quaker printer Tace Sowle published Dickenson's account of his ordeal in 1700, she placed this quotation from the Psalms on the title page: "The dark places of the Earth are full of the habitations of cruelty" (Ps. 74:20, KJV). Ten years later, the Quaker political economist John Bellers used similar language when he described America as one of the "dark corners of the world" that lacked the "light of the Gospel of peace." Bellers believed that America needed "light." He also thought the continent needed "inhabitants" and "tillage."²⁸ Quakers who expressed such views exhibited a moral understanding of geography, associating vast, wild landscapes with wickedness and more settled and cultivated places with sanctuary and salvation. Bellers was concerned with economic differences, but other Quakers analyzed the problem more cosmically and invoked the apocalypse. According to Dickenson, the shipwrecked Quakers in Florida read to each other from Revelation as they slogged northward.²⁹ Perhaps coincidentally, the place where they found refuge had been named after a city described in that book. According to Revelation, Philadelphia was a place that God had always loved, and he promised to spare its inhabitants on the Day of Judgment.³⁰

Dickenson's narrative recounts several episodes in which the Quakers and their shipmates narrowly escaped execution. In one dramatic episode, warriors snatched the clothes off the Quakers and charged at them, "foaming at the mouth like wild boars, and taking their bows and arrows and other weapons," but the attack mysteriously ended. "Suddenly we perceived them to look about and listen, and then desisted to prosecute their design." Sensing an opportunity, the Quakers gave the warriors an English Bible and a "large book" by Robert Barclay, almost certainly his four-hundred-page *Apology for the True Christian Divinity*. The warriors could not read, but some at least seemed to recognize the charitable gesture. They began to tear pages out of the Bible and Barclay's book, and gave them back to the Quakers to serve as paper clothing.³¹ As presented by Dickenson, this incident is a parody of a debate that had preoccupied Fox, Keith, and others in the 1670s, 1680s, and 1690s. What was the role of book learning, and the Bible in particular, in salvation? Was it possible for Indigenous Americans to receive God's light without knowing who Christ was?³² The answer to these questions had implications for any Quaker interested in converting

Indigenous peoples to Christianity. Dickenson hinted at his own position when he described his reception at a Spanish mission in Florida. He was impressed by the effectiveness of Spanish missionary work.

The leaders of Spain's Franciscan and Jesuit missions had their own ways of associating horticulture with righteousness.[33] In Florida, Spanish missionaries supervised farming communities with hundreds of workers. The Indigenous people who came to the missions received instruction on the cultivation of crops and keeping livestock, and many were forced to labor. Their diet changed and their health deteriorated as they adopted intensive maize agriculture, not only to feed themselves but to help supply St. Augustine and other Spanish colonial markets.[34] Dickenson noted that the Indigenous people at the mission were "very industrious," but he failed to recognize that their work was exploited. He declared that the Indigenous people at the mission had "plenty of hogs and fowls, and large crops of corn." He also observed that some were receiving education. In addition to overseeing the laborers, the Spanish missionaries taught them Christian doctrines. Dickenson watched one of them instructing the next male generation: "The Indian boys, we saw, were kept at school in the church, the friar being their school-master."[35]

Dickenson's naiveté regarding the Spanish is surprising. A sixteenth-century treatise by the Dominican friar Bartolomé de Las Casas had appeared in English in the 1650s and contained a stinging indictment of Spain's exploitation of Indigenous Americans.[36] There is little direct evidence that seventeenth-century Quakers discussed Las Casas specifically, but other English colonists did, and his stories of Spanish atrocity spread widely.[37] In general, Quakers opposed coercive, exploitive missionary efforts, and it is likely that the more they learned about Spanish relations with Indigenous Americans, the more hesitant they became about following Spain's example. At the time of the founding of Pennsylvania, Penn referred vaguely to the "unkindness and injustice" toward Indigenous Americans that had been displayed by previous colonial groups.[38] He vowed to do better, and for the next several decades, Pennsylvanian Quakers were wholly unlike the Spanish in their approach to the conversion of Indigenous peoples. Despite their theological interest in the salvation of Indigenous Americans, from the 1680s through the 1750s Quaker colonists made few efforts to bring the local Algonkian peoples into their fold. During the early years of colonization, they expended more energy on another project: acquiring and transforming land.

In 1684, the Welsh Quaker Thomas Ellis arrived to establish Haverford, Pennsylvania. He came with his own family and fourteen others. They distributed the land among themselves, thirty acres each, reserving plots for eight more families that were already on their way. The Quaker settlers arrived with livestock, and they set aside common land for grazing.[39] Even before they had cut down any trees or erected any fences, they gloried in the landscape they were creating. Upon his arrival on the site, Ellis wrote this poem:

> Pennsylvania an habitation,
> With certain, sure and clear foundation
> Where the dawning of the day,
> Expels the thick, dark night away.
> Lord, give us here a place to feed,
> And pass my life among thy seed,
> That in our bounds, true love and peace,
> From age to age may never cease.
> Then shall the trees and fields increase,
> Heaven and Earth proclaim thy peace,
> That we and they—forever Lord,
> Shew forth thy praise, with one accord.[40]

Ellis seems to have been happy with his original thirty acres, but by the 1690s Quaker families in the vicinity of Haverford typically held more than three hundred acres. Their livestock also proliferated.[41]

Haverford was typical of southeastern Pennsylvania. After 1683, when Penn invited non-Quakers to join in the mass migration, the colonial population began to spread and expanded exponentially, exceeding ten thousand by the 1690s and one hundred thousand by the 1730s.[42] European immigrants, Quaker and non-Quaker alike, occupied hundreds of acres per family. Rural Quaker families cleared new farms for each of their male children.[43] By 1754, the transformation of the landscape seemed complete. In his first published essay, the Quaker reformer John Woolman marveled at the change: "The wilderness and solitary deserts in which our fathers passed the days of their pilgrimage are now turned into pleasant fields. The natives are gone from before us, and we establish peaceably in the possession of the land, enjoying our civil and religious liberties; and, while many parts of the world have groaned under the calamities of war, our habitations remain quiet, and our land fruitful."[44]

Woolman exaggerated, of course, when he claimed that the "natives" were "gone." After European immigrants began to arrive in large numbers, some Indigenous communities suffered contagious disease. Some left the Delaware Valley for the north and west, settling with other displaced people in the upper reaches of the Susquehanna River and the foothills of the Appalachian Mountains. Other Munsee and Lenape people chose to stay close to their original homes. Some became servants or did piecework for the colonists. Some maintained intact communities, farming and minding their own affairs despite the presence of large numbers of immigrants around them.[45] Some continued to pursue old ways of subsistence. In 1797, Hannah Freeman, wrongly identified as the last "woman of the Delaware Tribe" in Chester County, Pennsylvania, recalled that during her childhood in the 1730s she and her parents spent their winters in a cabin with her grandmother and two aunts. They moved each summer to plant corn elsewhere. Eventually, however, "the country becoming more settled, the Indians were not allowed to plant corn any longer." Her father moved to the upper Susquehanna, but the women remained where they were, surrounded by colonists.[46]

Woolman's suggestion that there were no "natives" in the vicinity reflected a general Quaker outlook in the early 1750s. Before the outbreak of the Seven Years' War, women like Hannah Freeman barely registered in Quaker consciousness. Those Quakers who concerned themselves with Indigenous Americans concentrated on those who lived apart from them, to the north, south, or west of the principal zone of Quaker settlement. The outbreak of war in 1754 altered their perspective. After the Delaware took up arms against Pennsylvania, the militaristic policies of the colonial governor brought the horrors of warfare close to home. In 1755, Pennsylvania's governor issued a proclamation offering bounties for the scalps of Delaware men, women, and children. This led directly to the killing of a woman and child in New Jersey, and those killings were a crisis for Quakers in the colony. Woolman joined others in making plans for the colony's first Indian reservation.[47]

The Quakers' plans were eventually superseded by those of the Presbyterians, who established the Brotherton Indian Reservation. Nonetheless, the Quakers' scheme is worth examining as a clue to their thinking at a critical moment. The principal aim of their project was to provide a refuge for Indigenous people, "a proper place of residence where they might live comfortably together." The land would be owned by Quakers who would make every effort to keep the residents safe, not only from other colonists but also from the Indigenous American warriors fighting in the west. The Quakers expected that the residents would support themselves "by hunting and fishing and what they could raise out of the earth," but if money was available, the Quakers intended to assist them by "fencing their ground, furnishing them with stock, or utensils of husbandry." Quakers would also help by "providing a school or schools among them" if sufficient funds were available.[48]

Papunhank's arrival in Philadelphia complicated the Quakers' understanding of their mission. Quakers traveled great distances to see him. Over several days in August 1761, "upwards of four score" Quakers gathered to worship with Papunhank at a treaty gathering in Easton, Pennsylvania. They worshipped with Papunhank outdoors and in tents, sitting beside other Indigenous Americans. Prominent Quaker ministers, including Isaac Child, Susannah Hatton, and Mordecai Yarnell, spoke at the meetings. At the largest gathering, according to the Quakers' reports, the "doctrine of the Gospel was preached" and "the testimony of truth was exalted."[49] But on other occasions, Quakers simply listened to Papunhank. Israel Pemberton joined Papunhank and other Indigenous Americans in worship at dawn. He sat quietly and may have been the only Quaker in attendance.[50]

Responding to Papunhank's visit to Philadelphia, the London Yearly Meeting celebrated the "present visitation of divine love and light extended to the Indians," but the English Quakers counseled their North American cousins not to approach him too quickly or interfere rashly in Indigenous American spiritual development. "May heavenly council be waited for, that therein you may be instructed how to go in and out before that people, as the work is the Lord's and he is able to perfect it by or without visible means to his own praise."[51] God could guide Papunhank without the help of the Quakers. Perhaps Indigenous Americans would find their own way to salvation. Similar thoughts contributed to Woolman's reticence during his visit to Papunhank's village in 1763. When Papunhank told him that he wanted to join the Moravians, Woolman replied that "there were people among all religions who sought and loved God."[52] Woolman left the next day, and his departure from Papunhank's village marked a turning point. Remarkably, given the enthusiasm shown by the Quakers at Easton only two years earlier, after 1763 Quaker religious outreach to Indigenous Americans paused for twenty years. In 1771, some Philadelphia Quakers tried to find schoolteachers willing to work and live with Indigenous Americans, but no one applied.⁵³ Eventually, the Revolutionary War intervened.

The notion that the Quakers withdrew from politics around the time of the American Revolution is a myth, but with regard to Indigenous Americans, at least during the war, Quakers had little opportunity to engage politically or influence events. Most American patriots despised their pacifism, and the Quakers' professed kindness toward Indigenous Americans ran against the temper of the times.⁵⁴

In 1784, after Pennsylvania militiamen killed ninety-six Indigenous Americans at a Moravian mission in Ohio, Quaker reformer Anthony Benezet published a passionate lament invoking the wisdom of Papunhank and reminding his readers of the welcome the Indigenous peoples had given their first Quaker visitors to the Delaware Valley. In contrast to Quaker commentators in the seventeenth century, Benezet did not consider those acts of kindness miraculous. Instead, he argued that Indigenous Americans were naturally kind. But Benezet also warned his readers that the Indigenous people were capable of violence if they were deprived of their livelihoods and mistreated. "The peace and safety of our wide extended frontiers," he wrote, "the lives and welfare of so many innocent helpless people, depends on the maintenance of a friendly intercourse with our Indian neighbours." "What greater instances of patriotism," Benezet asked, "of love to God and mankind, can be shown [than] to promote to the utmost of our power not only the civilization of these uncultivated people, who Providence has, as it were, cast under our care, but also their establishment in a pious and virtuous life."⁵⁵

Benezet did not speak for all Quakers. In 1785, Friends in London published another captivity narrative, this one recounting the suffering of a family of Quakers who had been taken from their farm in Pennsylvania in 1780 by Iroquois warriors. Along with the story they included a poem that reiterated the old argument that the natural landscape of North America, its forests and deserts, made the Indigenous people cruel. The poem began,

> As the forest issues the fell boar,
> So human ravagers, in deserts bred,
> On the defenceless, peaceful hamlet pour
> Wild waste o'er all, and sudden ruin spread!⁵⁶

Unlike the author of this poem, Benezet insisted that the uncolonized forests and fields of North America produced good people. Despite this disagreement, the logic of Benezet's argument led to a conclusion that might have been endorsed by the poet. To protect Indigenous people from dispossession and violence, to prevent them from seeking retribution, and, overall, to promote righteousness and peace across the continent, Quakers would have to change the material circumstances of Indigenous Americans, "civilize" them, and direct them toward piety and virtue.

Following the inauguration of George Washington, Quakers began to play an influential role in US policy toward Indigenous Americans. In the summer of 1790, Washington's secretary of war, Henry Knox, asked a group of Philadelphia Quakers to board and educate two boys, ages twelve and sixteen, who had been sent to him as part of a diplomatic overture from the leaders of the Creeks. The Quakers agreed, and over the next decade, when Seneca, Stockbridge, and Tuscarora delegates sent children to be cared for by the US government, Knox and his successors repeatedly turned to Quakers to foster them. Partly as a result, Quakers became prominent in American diplomacy, sending and relaying messages and gifts between the federal government and members of various tribes. They sent seeds and farming equipment to the Creeks, and in general their communications with the leaders of Indigenous groups emphasized the importance of European-style agriculture.[57] In the 1790s, Quakers undertook other efforts, independent of the federal government, to reach out to the Indigenous peoples of New York State and the Northwest Territories. In these efforts the Quakers again emphasized European farming methods, but they were much less insistent than other religious groups about instructing Indigenous Americans in specific Christian doctrines.

When Halliday Jackson arrived among the Seneca in 1798, he reported that his heart was "filled with compassion for the distressed situation of the inhabitants of the wilderness." "In days of old," he wrote, "they were in possession of the goodly parts of the land, and did eat of the goodly fruits thereof, and the wild deer of the forest were then in abundance." Those days were over because the Seneca had been displaced by "wars and fightings" and now lived in "desert places." In his first speech among them, he asked them to remember happier times, when Indigenous peoples welcomed the arrival of Quakers. He hoped they could reestablish that kind of good will. He told them that the Quakers would "minister to their necessities, and supply them with implements of husbandry to till the land, that they might cease to pursue the wild beasts of the forest, and look for sustenance to their fields, their fruit trees, and their vineyards and have flocks and herds and swine in abundance, and corn in their houses, and bread without scarcity, and themselves become clothed with garments which their own fingers have made."[58]

Six years later, a Quaker missionary to the Miami named Gerald T. Hopkins told a gathering of Indigenous people near Fort Wayne that they were like the ancient Britons before the Romans arrived. After the Roman conquest, the Britons had abandoned the ways of their ancestors. Instead, they "cultivated the earth and we are sure the change was a happy one."[59] Hopkins's inaccurate summary of British history echoed arguments that had been advanced by Thomas Jefferson. In general terms, Hopkins endorsed the Enlightenment theory of human development, which suggested that hunters should evolve into pastoralists before becoming farmers, eventually adopting all the attributes of civilized life. The theory had implications for gender.[60] Quaker missionaries had expectations for Indigenous women and were even more emphatic about the conduct of men. They wanted to get Indigenous American men into cornfields.[61] Daniel K. Richter has emphasized the multiple ironies embedded in their plans. The Quakers' proposals reflected their own values and agenda and did not quite track the common Enlightenment vision of progress. By asking Indigenous men to give up hunting, the Quakers were suggesting that they abandon their most profitable economic activity. Furthermore, while they gave them tools, seeds, and domestic animals to assist them in finding an alternative way of life, they imagined that Indigenous Americans would become subsistence farmers and did little to help them develop the infrastructure or markets they would need to sell agricultural produce. Jefferson praised Quaker missionaries for promoting among Indigenous Americans "habits of industry, comfortable subsistence, and civilized urges."[62] But in practical terms, the Quaker program was a recipe for poverty.

To understand the Quakers' intentions in this period, it is useful to reconsider the Quakers' origin stories—the mythical landscapes the early Quakers glimpsed in visions, and the role Friends believed their ancestors had played in transforming the geography of eastern North America. After Halliday Jackson reported to Quakers in Philadelphia about his missionary efforts among the Seneca and the friendly welcome they initially gave him, the Philadelphia Quakers thought Jackson's activities might signal the start of a momentous change. They wrote effusively, "May thy labours be crowned with the increase of plenty, that it may create a new spirit in the hearts of thousands to lay their shoulders to the work, and may tens of thousands follow them as they have followed thee and thy brethren that sojourn with thee.... Then it will be said before the days of many generations, that the desert aboundeth with every good thing, and the wilderness appeareth beautiful as the Garden of Eden."[63]

Two noteworthy features of nineteenth-century Quaker missionary work among Indigenous Americans—their meek approach to formal religious instruction and their stern emphasis on the adoption of European-style agriculture—reflected concerns and predilections dating back to the Quakers' origins. Many early Quakers believed that God spoke to them in pastures and gardens. They revered such places because they seemed accessible and provided an escape from artifice, pride, antagonism, and deceit. They imagined rural scenes as peaceful, and from the vantage point of the English countryside some thought that they could see Eden. In their enthusiasm, they contrasted the rural landscapes of seventeenth-century England and Wales with the godforsaken wilderness.

The Quakers' encounter with Indigenous Americans complicated their assumptions about landscape. Were uncolonized regions of North America really "wilderness," or did they contain gardens? Was it possible that God had already spoken to the people who inhabited those places? There were always some Quakers who recognized the gardens in America and answered "yes" to the second question. Papunhank's arrival in Philadelphia in 1760 changed the thinking of several important Quaker leaders, including Woolman and Benezet. Nonetheless, the Quakers' reverence for their ideal rural landscape persisted. A patchwork of pastures, orchards, cropland, and gardens continued to remind them of Eden. Additionally, and more significantly for Indigenous Americans, at the start of the nineteenth century, many Quakers believed that the spread of that landscape across vast regions of eastern North America had given them a glimpse of God's promised future.

NOTES

1. *An Account of a Visit Lately Made to the People Called Quakers in Philadelphia, by Papoonahoal, an Indian Chief* (London: S. Clark, 1761), 19–20.

2. For more on Papunhank, see Michel Goode, "Dangerous Spirits: How the Indian Critique of Alcohol Shaped Eighteenth-Century Quaker Revivalism," *Early American Studies* 14, no. 2 (2016): 258–83; Richard W. Pointer, "An Almost Friend: Papunhank, Quakers, and the Search for Security amid Pennsylvania's Wars, 1754–65," *Pennsylvania Magazine of History and Biography* 138, no. 3 (2014): 237–68; and Geoffrey Plank, *John Woolman's Path to the Peaceable Kingdom: A Quaker in the British Empire* (Philadelphia: University of Pennsylvania Press, 2012), chaps. 6 and 7. For more on Quakers and Indigenous Americans generally, see Ignacio Gallup-Diaz and Geoffrey Plank, eds., *Quakers and Native Americans* (Leiden: Brill, 2019); and Carla Gerona, "Imagining Peace in Quaker and Native American Dream Stories," in *Friends and Enemies in Penn's Woods: Indians, Colonists, and the Racial Construction of Pennsylvania*, ed. William A. Pencak and Daniel K. Richter (University Park: Penn State University Press, 2004), 42–62. This chapter does not directly address the pattern of Quaker relations with Indigenous Americans on Long Island or in New England. For those regions, see Marie Balsley Taylor, "Apostates in the Woods: Quakers, Praying Indians, and Circuits of Communication in Humphrey Norton's *New England's Ensigne*," in Gallup-Diaz and Plank, *Quakers and Native Americans*, 30–53; Stephen Angell, "'Learn of the Heathen': Quakers and Indians in Southern New England," *Quaker History* 92, no. 1 (2003): 1–21; Christopher Densmore, ed., "Indian Religious Beliefs on Long Island: A Quaker Account," *New York History* 73, no. 4 (1992): 431–41; and Meredith Baldwin Weddle, *Walking in the Way of Peace: Quaker Pacifism in the Seventeenth Century* (Oxford: Oxford University Press, 2001).

3. On early modern Quakers and nature, see Geoffrey Peter Morries, "From Revelation to Resource: The Natural World in the Thought and Experience of Quakers in Britain and Ireland, 1647–1830" (PhD diss., University of Birmingham, 2009); Donald Brooks Kelley, "'A Tender Regard to the Whole Creation': Anthony Benezet and the Emergence of an Eighteenth-Century Quaker Ecology," *Pennsylvania Magazine of History and Biography* 106, no. 1 (1982): 69–88; and Geoffrey Plank, "'The Flame of Life Was Kindled in All Animal and Sensitive Creatures': One Quaker Colonist's View of Animal Life," *Church History* 76, no. 3 (2007): 569–90.

4. Douglas Gwyn, *Apocalypse of the Word: The Life and Message of George Fox* (Richmond, IN: Friends United Press, 1986), 63; Morries, "From Revelation to Resource," 62–69.

5. William Cronon, *Changes in the Land: Indians, Colonists, and the Ecology of New England* (New York: Hill and Wang, 1983); Virginia DeJohn Anderson, *Creatures of Empire: How Domestic Animals Transformed Early America* (New York: Oxford University Press, 2004); Jon T. Coleman, *Vicious: Wolves and Men in America* (New Haven: Yale University Press, 2006).

6. Mary Penington, *Experiences in the Life of Mary Penington* (Philadelphia: Biddle Press, n.d.), 17–18, 29, 31–32, 40.

7. Norman Penney, ed., *The First Publishers of Truth* (London: Society of Friends, 1907), 1.

8. Ibid., 27, 44, 69, 71, 96, 209, 213, 229, 246, 290, 297, 302, 308, hereafter cited parenthetically in the text.

9. Penington, *Experiences in the Life*, 17.

10. For discussions of this vision, see Gwyn, *Apocalypse of the Word*, 63; Morries, "From Revelation to Resource," 62–69.

11. William Dewsbury, *The Faithful Testimony of That Antient Servant of the Lord and Minister of the Everlasting Gospel William Dewsbury* [...] (London: Andrew Sowle, 1689), 272, 282.

12. On Dewsbury's life, see Catie Gill, "Dewsbury, William," in *Oxford Dictionary of National Biography* (Oxford: Oxford University Press, 2004).

13. William Dewsbury, "A True Prophecie of the Mighty Day of the Lord," in *Faithful Testimony of That Antient Servant*, 111.

14. Erin A. Bell, "From Ploughing the Wilderness to Edging the Vineyard: Meanings and Uses of Husbandry Among Quakers, c. 1650–c. 1860," *Quaker Studies* 10, no. 2 (2006): 135–59.

15. For other examples, see Martha Simmons, *A Lamentation for the Lost Sheep of the House of Israel* (London, 1655); James Naylor, *The Lambs Warre Against the Man of Sinne* (London, 1657).

16. Joseph Besse, *A Collection of the Sufferings of the People Called Quakers*, 2 vols. (London: Luke Hinde, 1753), 2:189.

17. Jonathan Dickenson, *God's Protecting Providence, Man's Surest Help and Defence* (London: T. Sowle, 1700), 4, 14, 89.

18. See, generally, Jean R. Soderlund, *Lenape Country: Delaware Valley Society Before William Penn* (Philadelphia: University of Pennsylvania Press, 2015).

19. Josiah Coale, *The Books and Divers Epistles of the Faithful Servant of the Lord Josiah Coale* (London, 1671), 21–22; Henry J. Cadbury, ed., *Narrative Papers of George Fox, Unpublished or Uncorrected* (Richmond, IN: Friends United Press, 1972), 174.

20. Besse, *Collection of the Sufferings*, 2:196. See also Francis Howgill, *The Deceiver of the Nations Discovered* (London: Thomas Simmons, 1660), 15.

21. George Fox, *An Epistle to all Planters, and such who are Transporting themselves into Foreign Plantations in America* (London: Ben Clark, 1682).

22. Geoffrey Plank, "Discipline and Divinity: Colonial Quakerism, Christianity, and 'Heathenism' in the Seventeenth Century," *Church History* 85, no. 3 (2016): 519–21.

23. Minute Book of the Lords Proprietors of New Jersey, 1664–1683, Penn MSS, vol. 2, 31, LSF.

24. *A True Account of the Dying Words of Ockanickon, an Indian King* (London: B. Clark, 1682).

25. George Keith, *Truth's Defense* (London, 1682), 85.

26. Jonathan Dickenson, "God's Protecting Providence: A Journal by Jonathan Dickenson," ed. Charles M. Andrews, *Florida Historical Quarterly* 21, no. 2 (1942): 113–14.

27. Dickenson, *God's Protecting Providence*, preface.

28. John Bellers, *Some Reasons for an European State* (London, 1710), 3.

29. Dickenson, *God's Protecting Providence*, 14.

30. Rev. 3:7–10. For an analysis of the millenarian expectations surrounding Philadelphia and Pennsylvania generally, see Patrick M. Erben, *A Harmony of the Spirits: Translation and the Language of Community in Early Pennsylvania* (Chapel Hill: University of North Carolina Press, 2012). For a vivid sense of how the book of Revelation inspired and informed the perspective of one Quaker colonist in Pennsylvania, see Rachel Cope and Zachary McLeod, eds., *The Writings of Elizabeth Webb: A Quaker Missionary in America* (University Park: Penn State University Press, 2019), 49–178.

31. Dickenson, *God's Protecting Providence*, 23.

32. Plank, "Discipline and Divinity." See also Justin J. Meggitt, *Early Quakers and Islam: Slavery, Apocalyptic, and Christian-Muslim Encounters in the Seventeenth Century* (Uppsala: Swedish Science Press, 2013).

33. See Jorge Cañizares-Esguerra, *Puritan Conquistadors: Iberianizing the Atlantic, 1550–1700* (Stanford: Stanford University Press, 2006), 178–214.

34. Clark Spencer Larsen, Mark C. Griffin, Dale L. Hutchinson, Vivian E. Noble, Lynette Norr, Robert F. Pastor, Christopher B. Ruff, et al., "Frontiers of Contact: Bioarchaeology of Spanish Florida," *Journal of World Prehistory* 15, no. 1 (2001): 69–123; David J. Weber, *The Spanish Frontier in North America* (New Haven: Yale University Press, 1992), 100–105.

35. Dickenson, *God's Protecting Providence*, 75–76.

36. [Bartolomé de Las Casas], *The Tears of the Indians: Being an Historical and True Account of the Cruel Massacres and Slaughters of above Twenty Millions of Innocent People* (London: Nath. Brook, 1656).

37. Margaret Newell, *Brethren by Nature: New England Indians, Colonists, and the Origins of American Slavery* (Ithaca: Cornell University Press, 2015), 242–43. For speculation on Quakers and Las Casas, see Angell, "'Learn of the Heathen,'" 9.

38. "William Penn to the Kings of the Indians, October 18, 1681," in *The Papers of William Penn*, ed. Richard S. Dunn and Mary Maples Dunn, 5 vols. (Philadelphia: University of Pennsylvania Press, 1981–87), 2:128–29. See Daniel K. Richter, "Land and Words," in Richter, *Trade, Land, Power: The Struggle for Eastern North America* (Philadelphia: University of Pennsylvania Press, 2013), 135–54.

39. Barry J. Levy, "'Tender Plants': Quaker Farmers and Children in the Delaware Valley, 1681–1735," *Journal of Family History* 3, no. 2 (1978): 117–18.

40. Quoted in George Smith, *History of Delaware County* (Philadelphia: Henry B. Ashmead, 1862), 458.

41. Levy, "'Tender Plants,'" 121–22.

42. James T. Lemon, *The Best Poor Man's Country: A Geographical Study of Southeastern Pennsylvania* (Baltimore: Johns Hopkins University Press, 1972), 48.

43. Levy, "'Tender Plants.'"

44. John Woolman, *Some Considerations on the Keeping of Negroes Recommended to the Professors of Christianity of Every Denomination* (Philadelphia: James Chattin, 1754), 19.

45. Soderlund, *Lenape Country*, 167–84.

46. Dawn G. Marsh, *A Lenape Among the Quakers: The Life of Hannah Freeman* (Lincoln: University of Nebraska Press, 2014), 189–91.

47. Peter Silver, *Our Savage Neighbors: How Indian War Transformed Early America* (New York: W. W. Norton, 2008), 161–63; Plank, *John Woolman's Path*, 127–29.

48. Articles of the New Jersey Association for Helping the Indians, 975B, HCLQSC.

49. "Report of the trustees of the Friendly Association who attended the Indian treaty at Easton in the 8th month 1761," Papers Relating to the Friendly Association, 4:143, HCLQSC.

50. Israel Pemberton to Mary Pemberton, August 5, 1761, ibid., 4:153.

51. Epistle from London Yearly Meeting to Philadelphia Yearly Meeting, May 31 to June 7, 1762, Miscellaneous Papers from the Philadelphia Yearly Meeting, 8a, FHLSC.

52. Ralph H. Pickett, "A Religious Encounter: John Woolman and David Zeisberger," *Quaker History* 79, no. 2 (1990): 86. This conversation is recorded in David Zeisberger's journal, and Zeisberger attributes these words to "the Quakers" without specifying whether it was Woolman or his traveling companion who spoke.

53. "Message from the Friendly Association to Netalwalem and the rest of the Delaware Indians at Kaikailammapakung," May 18, 1771, Papers Relating to the Friendly Association, 4:423, HCLQSC.

54. See Silver, *Our Savage Neighbors*.

55. Anthony Benezet, *Some Observations on the Situation, Disposition, and Character of the Indian Natives of This Continent* (Philadelphia: Printed and sold by Joseph Crukshank, 1784), 51, 52. On the massacre, see Rob Harper, "Looking the Other Way: The Gnadenhutten Massacre and the Contextual Interpretation of Violence," *William and Mary Quarterly* 64, no. 3 (2007): 621–44.

56. *A Narrative of the Captivity and Sufferings of Benjamin Gilbert and His Family* (London: James Phillips, 1785), 117.

57. Stephanie Gamble, "'Strong Expressions of Regard': Native Diplomats and Quakers in Early National Philadelphia," in Gallup-Diaz and Plank, *Quakers and Native Americans*, 93–114.

58. Anthony F. C. Wallace, ed., *Halliday Jackson's Journal to the Seneca Indians, 1798–1800* (Harrisburg: Pennsylvania Historical and Museum Commission, 1952), 5–6.

59. Quoted in Daniel K. Richter, "'Believing That Many of the Red People Suffer Much for the Want of Food': Hunting, Agriculture, and a Quaker Construction of Indianness in the Early Republic," *Journal of the Early Republic* 19, no. 4 (1999): 607.

60. Rosemarie Zagarri, "Morals, Manners, and the Republican Mother," *American Quarterly* 44, no. 4 (1992): 192–215.

61. Karim M. Tiro, "'We Wish to Do You Good': The Quaker Mission to the Oneida Nation, 1790–1840," *Journal of the Early Republic* 26, no. 3 (2006): 367–68.

62. Richter, "'Believing That Many of the Red People Suffer,'" 610–11.

63. Wallace, *Halliday Jackson's Journal*, 21.

CHAPTER 9

A Complex Faith
Strategies of Marriage, Family, and Community Among Upper Canadian Quakers, 1784–1830

SYDNEY HARKER AND ROBYNNE ROGERS HEALEY

Located north of Lake Ontario in the British North American colony of Upper Canada,[1] the West Lake[2] and Yonge Street Quaker communities existed on the margins of both the British Atlantic and the Quaker Atlantic worlds. They were situated about 170 miles apart, a considerable distance. West Lake lay at the eastern end of the lake on the Bay of Quinte at the mouth of the Saint Lawrence River, and the Yonge Street community was toward the northern end of Yonge Street, the military artery connecting Lake Ontario and Lake Simcoe (map 9.1). Friends established these communities at different times and under different circumstances. West Lake (near Adolphustown) was established in 1784 when migrant Dutch American Quakers, political refugees of the American Revolution, settled alongside, and identified with, United Empire Loyalists predominantly from Dutchess County, New York. Yonge Street (at Newmarket) was settled in 1801 by two groups of Friends, from Vermont and Pennsylvania, respectively, drawn by the prospect of free land and the desire to live out their unique testimonies freely.

This comparative community study of West Lake and Yonge Street, two of the three Quaker communities established in Upper Canada after the American Revolution, reveals how both communities used similar strategies to strengthen their meetings on the Upper Canadian frontier.³ An examination of Quaker conflict and accommodation within the two communities themselves, as well as in mainstream Upper Canadian society, demonstrates Friends' evolving definitions of faith through the latter part of the long eighteenth century. Though geographically distant from each other, the West Lake and Yonge Street Meetings formed intercommunity bonds. They also formed strong connections to the broader Quaker Atlantic network and participated in the correspondence and ministerial visits that bound this transatlantic faith community together. Both played an important part in uniting the Upper Canadian meetings in 1810 into the Canada Half-Year's Meeting under the authority of the New York Yearly Meeting (NYYM).⁴ Migration from the United States and Britain increased the size of both meetings. The two communities suffered through epidemics, the trials of the War of 1812, and schisms that ultimately led to their fragmentation. The specifics of these challenges differed in each community, as they did in meetings throughout the Quaker Atlantic world.

Despite its transatlantic character, Quakerism was lived in its local contexts, and its local expressions shaped transatlantic Quakerism as much as the Quakerism of the center(s) influenced the margins. Local circumstances also shaped the ways that Quakers formed and maintained their religious

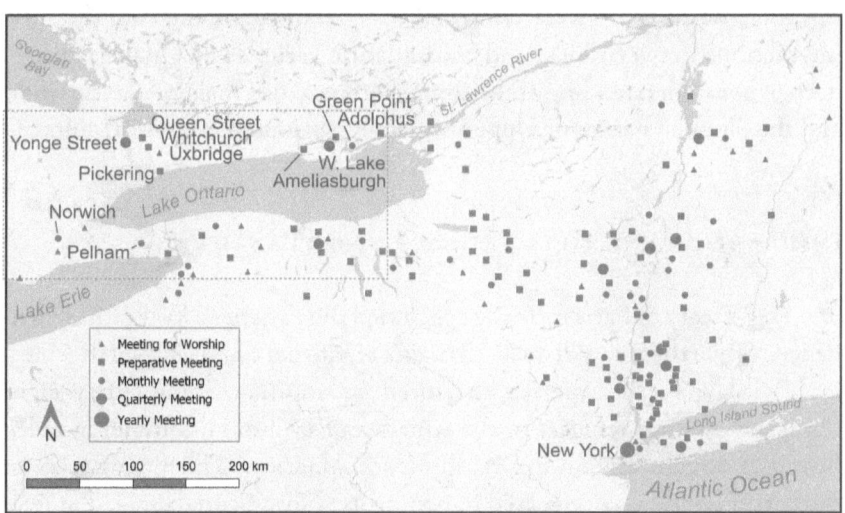

MAP 9.1 Meetings of the New York Yearly Meeting of Friends, after S. Ricketson, Map of the Meetings Constituting the New York Yearly Meeting of Friends, 1822. CYMA. Map by John Grotenhuis.

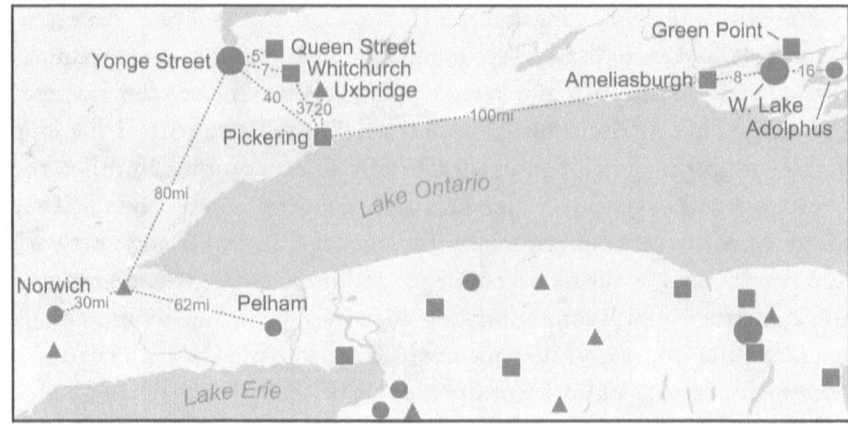

MAP 9.2 Inset detail of meetings of the New York Yearly Meeting of Friends, after S. Ricketson, Map of the Meetings Constituting the New York Yearly Meeting of Friends, 1822. CYMA. Map by John Grotenhuis.

communities.[5] This included the manner in which meetings dealt with the requirement for endogamy, the ways in which young Quakers on the frontier sought appropriate spouses, the role of intermarriage among weighty families (both within and outside the community), and the influence of strong individuals whose personalities or connections could sway entire meetings when there were doctrinal disagreements. Understanding the interactions between local and transatlantic varieties of Quakerism will deepen our understanding of the complexities of the Quaker Atlantic world and the pluralist nature of Upper Canada's religious and political culture.

IMMIGRATION AND THE MAKING OF UPPER CANADA

The 1783 Treaty of Paris formally concluded the American War of Independence. While the treaty reduced Britain's territorial claims in North America, British North America remained substantial. Some thirty-eight thousand political refugees of the American Revolution, commonly called Loyalists, sought asylum in British North America.[6] The majority, about thirty thousand, were relocated to peninsular Nova Scotia, divided in 1784 into Nova Scotia, New Brunswick, and Cape Breton. Six thousand overwintered in camps in the Eastern Townships and in June 1784 sailed up the Saint Lawrence River to the nine newly surveyed Royal Townships and five

Cataraqui Townships in the western reaches of the colony of Quebec. West of those townships, the Grand River Reserve was set aside for Iroquois Loyalists, members of the Six Nations Confederacy. In a lottery system of sorts, United Empire Loyalists were granted allotments of varying sizes, with expectations that the land would be developed.[7] Once settlers proved they had fulfilled their settlement duties, the Crown granted them a patent.

In 1791, the Constitution Act divided the province, still governed by the 1774 Quebec Act, into Upper and Lower Canada and designated a governing structure for the two colonies. Drafted in the shadow of the French Revolution and the wake of the American Revolution, the 1791 Constitution Act set out to establish British parliamentary institutions and to create an explicitly British society, including an established church and a social order that included a landed aristocracy. To that end, one-seventh of future land grants were set aside as Crown reserves and one-seventh were set aside as Clergy reserves. The Crown was represented in Lower Canada by a governor and in Upper Canada by a lieutenant governor.

The first lieutenant governor, John Graves Simcoe, believing that thousands of Loyalists still lived in the young United States of America, offered free two-hundred-acre land grants to entice settlers to help tame the frontier. These immigrants are often called "late Loyalists," although their commitment to the prospect of free land almost certainly outweighed their loyalty to British political ideals. With waterways as the only border between the United States and Upper Canada, Simcoe imposed plans for settlement and defense that saw settlers moved into the forests north and west of the new capital at York (now Toronto).[8] A significant wave of immigrants arrived in Upper Canada between 1791 and 1812, when relations between the United States and Britain soured to the point that President Madison declared war on Britain. American immigration was largely responsible for the growth of the population from roughly ten thousand in 1791 to roughly eighty thousand in 1812, and had created a province with a very North American or colonial culture.[9]

During the war with Britain, the British territories closest for American invasion were the Canadas. The war waged for two years, testing relations between "Loyalist" and "American" Upper Canadians. After 1815, distrust of American settlers and the end of the Napoleonic Wars combined to make Britain the most important source of immigrants to British North America. In what has been termed the Great Migration, between 1815 and 1850, between eight hundred thousand and one million British migrants came to Britain's North American colonies.[10] Upper Canada received a large portion of these immigrants, changing the nature of its colonial society. By 1815, the population was largely American born; in 1841, when the Act of Union united Upper and Lower Canada, almost 70 percent of those not born in the Canadian colonies were British immigrants.[11] The three distinct stages of settler migration to colonial Upper Canada provide a unique opportunity to examine the creation and development of the colony and the Quaker communities Friends established there.

WEST LAKE

Situated on the narrow and winding Bay of Quinte (see map 9.2, inset detail), the community of Quakers who congregated initially in Adolphustown and later in West Lake formed the first Quaker society in Upper Canada. The meeting grew out of a disparate group of relocated political refugees who made the area their home in 1784 after the American Revolution. A few of these settlers had originally belonged to the Nine Partners Monthly Meeting (NPMM) in Dutchess County, New York; they brought their Quaker faith background with them to the fledgling colony of Upper Canada. The arrival of late Loyalists and further immigration ensured the community's growth. From this group, the first preparative meeting was established in 1798 in Adolphustown under the authority of the NPMM. Owing to its remoteness, the Adolphustown Preparative Meeting had special privileges, such as approving marriages, a responsibility normally reserved for monthly meetings.[12]

The early meetings were held in the home of Philip Dorland. Dorland and his brothers had supported the British during the American Revolution. Philip had served as a lieutenant in Abraham Cuyler's corps; his brother Thomas had served as a sergeant with the Associated Loyalists.[13] Though Philip Dorland was disowned in 1779 for a number of transgressions, including betting on horse races, committing fornication, and carrying a pistol, he retained ties to his Quaker community and by the 1790s was again expressing a faith position consistent with Quakerism.[14] This was evident in 1792, when Dorland was elected to the first Legislative Assembly of Upper Canada as the member for the riding of Prince Edward County and Adolphustown. He appeared at the assembly but refused to take the oath of office. He outlined his reasons to the assembly: "whereas from the religious principles I profess (being one of the persons commonly called Quakers) I do not feel myself at liberty nor can I consciously take an oath in the form and manner usually prescribed although I would readily affirm and subscribe a declaration to the purpose and effect therein set forth."[15] The assembly rejected Dorland's offer to affirm, and his neighbor, Major Peter van Alstine, was elected in his place. This incident reveals that, despite being formally disconnected from Quakerism for more than a decade, Dorland still identified himself as a Friend. This experience may have spurred him to seek readmission to the Society, as later the same year he sent an acknowledgment for his behavior to the NPMM.[16] The monthly meeting welcomed him back into membership and soon thereafter Dorland started a meeting for worship in his home. Out of this small meeting a vibrant Quaker community grew; the Adolphustown Preparative Meeting was granted monthly meeting status in 1801. As the Quaker population in the area expanded, new preparative meetings sprang up under its authority.

The growth of the Adolphustown Meeting created its own set of challenges related to the community's location on the Bay of Quinte. First, the physical location of the meetinghouse was problematic. It was situated on a peninsula with extremely limited land; this was worsened by the fact that the Canadian Shield reaches into the area, diminishing the quality of farmland.[17] In order to find adequate farming land, members and their children had to settle farther and farther away from the meetinghouse, predominantly west of Adolphustown in Prince Edward County and beyond. The shortage of good arable land was exacerbated by the steady influx of immigrants to the area. Small meetings for worship emerged, most very distant from the monthly meeting itself. Travel to and from the meeting posed an issue for many Friends. In addition, Friends who served on committees found it difficult to visit Friends who lived at great distances. This was the case for John Latta, whose request for membership was put off month after month, as no Friend was able to visit him owing to the "difficulty of the way at this season of the year." He requested membership in November 1801, and Friends were unable to visit him until April of the following year.[18] Although Adolphustown Township was the smallest township in the province, roughly 11,500 acres, as Friends continued to settle farther away, transportation to meetings, like religious visits, became increasingly difficult. Frontier roads were not ideal for quick visits or easy travel.

By 1821, membership in the community had shifted geographically. Adolphustown Monthly Meeting membership dwindled while membership at West Lake, fifteen miles west, grew. Given the population shift, the meeting decided to make West Lake the monthly meeting; Adolphustown, now much smaller, was reduced to a preparative meeting. This was not the first time the monthly meeting relocated out of necessity. During the War of 1812, though the West Lake Quakers abstained from fighting, the Adolphustown meetinghouse was co-opted as a temporary military barracks. This forced the meeting to be held exclusively at West Lake for the duration of the war.[19] Despite this disruption, West Lake Quakers had virtually no involvement with the war.

Given the challenges of travel between preparative meetings, community-building strategies were important to developing and maintaining this Quaker community. Intermarriage was a common means of tightening community connections, just as it was in Quaker centers such as London and Philadelphia, where wealthy Quakers used it to create or cement business connections and combine dynastic families.[20] West Lake Quakers on the edges of Upper Canada engaged in intermarriage for different reasons. In the early stages of settlement, it was a way to construct community among a group of refugees and late Loyalists who found themselves in a wholly unfamiliar place. Intermarriage enabled families to create new connections or reinforce family ties that had existed in their former communities in New York; some of these relationships are outlined in figure 9.1. John Dorland is a case in point. Two of his daughters married into the Haight family. Both the Dorland and Haight families were from Dutchess County, New York, and had been a part of the NPMM.

John Dorland arrived in Adolphustown with his family around 1796, following his brothers Thomas and Philip to Upper Canada.[21] His daughter Mary Dorland married Daniel Haight in 1789, a few years before the family relocated. Mary's younger sister Bathsheba Dorland married Daniel Haight's nephew in 1797 in Adolphustown.[22] To complicate family relations, the only child from Daniel Haight's first marriage, Philip D. Haight, married the daughter of Philip Dorland. Philip Dorland was the uncle of Daniel Haight's second wife, so when Philip D. Haight and Anna Dorland married, Philip was marrying his stepmother's cousin. One of Daniel Haight's younger sons, John, also married a daughter of Philip Dorland, Betsey Dorland. Betsey and John were first cousins once removed, this time through blood.

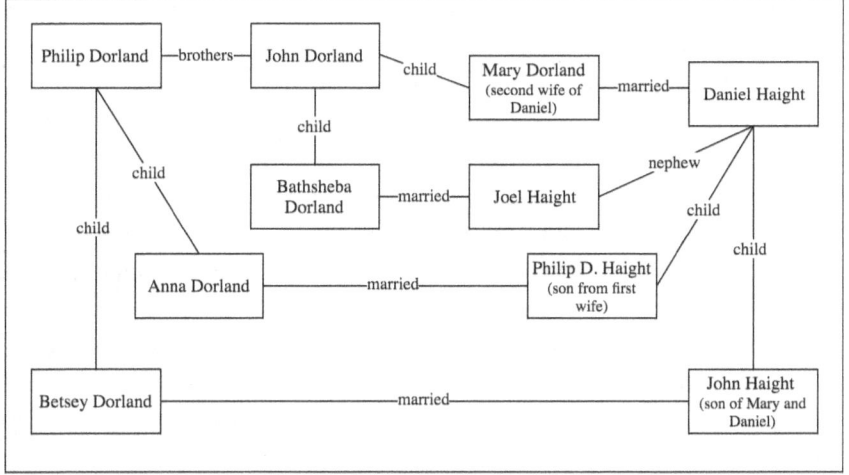

FIG. 9.1 John Dorland family relationships

These few examples from just two families show how closely knit many families became in this meeting. While this created stability, the extent of intermarriage posed distinct problems for young unmarried Quakers. In a community where most young Friends expected to marry, finding a suitable spouse—a member in good standing not too closely related—became increasingly difficult. As Friends sought potential spouses in the surrounding Quaker communities, West Lake Quakers created ties between their families and community and other, more distant Quaker meetings. A number of young male Friends traveled outside their immediate area seeking an appropriate spouse. There is evidence that some returned to New York in search of a wife. Once the Yonge Street Monthly Meeting (YSMM) was established, it became a source of marriage partners.

Traveling outside their community for a spouse allowed Quaker men to maintain familial connections and friendships. Philip Dorland, often regarded as the progenitor of the Adolphustown Meeting, sought his second wife outside Upper Canada. After the death of his first wife, the Adolphustown minutes record that Dorland paid a visit in 1807 to "his friends in New York State," taking with him a certificate of membership and a note ensuring his clearness of marriage engagements.[23] Given Dorland's own close connections with the NPMM, it is likely that he already knew of Lydia Shotwell, a weighty member there and his soon-to-be second wife. Shortly after Dorland's visit, Lydia moved to New Jersey, where she and Dorland married in 1808.²⁴ Like her husband, she quickly became an important member in the Adolphustown Meeting.

West Lake Quakers repeatedly demonstrate the pattern of seeking suitable wives outside the geographical community. Two Bowerman brothers, part of a prominent Quaker family in both the NPMM and Adolphustown Meeting, married women from the YSMM. Judah and Stephen Bowerman married sisters Abigail and Amy Hughes in 1809 and 1811, respectively. The Hughes sisters were from a weighty Yonge Street family, the daughters of a minister and elder. Their mother, Eleanor Hughes, was an ardent supporter of the Children of Peace when that schism rocked the YSMM.²⁵ According to her grandson's record, it was Amy Hughes Bowerman who ensured that the Children of Peace schism did not spread to West Lake: "It was entirely due to Amy's uncompromising attitude . . . that a division of the Society at West Lake was frustrated in 1813."²⁶ Intermarriage, then, was a significant factor in connecting individual Quaker communities, and families within communities, to the broader Quaker world.

Searching for a spouse beyond the local community was not always easy. Some men required more than one reconnaissance mission outside the West Lake community to find a wife. Consider Samuel Howe, who became a member of the Adolphustown Monthly Meeting in 1801.²⁷ He quickly became a weighty member, finding himself on important committees just a year after becoming a member. In 1802, the meeting minutes note: "Samuel How[e] a member of this meeting being desirous to go on a visit to Nine Partners and make some little stay there he *being a single man* this meeting thought well to certify on his behalf that we believe him clear of marriage or other engagements that way" (emphasis added).²⁸ The minutes suggest that the meeting understood Howe's motivation to visit Nine Partners; he was traveling to find a spouse. Unfortunately for Howe, the trip was unsuccessful, and he returned to West Lake unwed. In 1804, he tried again.²⁹ Instead of Nine Partners, Howe declared his desire to visit Yonge Street. Unsuccessful a second time, and apparently having exhausted his options of visiting nearby meetings where he might find a Quaker wife, Howe risked his membership and married a non-Friend in 1808. Because this was a disownable offense, Howe was subject to meeting discipline. The meeting minutes of September 1808 record a complaint that Howe married outside the faith; ultimately, he was disowned in July 1809.³⁰

Howe's decision to marry a local woman who was not a Quaker speaks to the difficulties that all unmarried Quakers faced in the budding colonial settlements along the Bay of Quinte. Although Howe was able to travel outside the meeting in the hope of finding an appropriate spouse, his failure led him to abandon the strictures of his faith's discipline in order to find a partner. Not only did the Quaker insistence on endogamy narrow Howe's chances of finding a suitable partner, but Howe lived in Adolphustown, where the 1807 census showed that there were 128 adult women in the community to 149 adult men.[31] With his options limited, Howe chose to marry a local woman who, like him, was also the child of a United Empire Loyalist.[32] Despite Howe's disownment, he rejoined the Adolphustown Monthly Meeting years later. In 1817, his wife, Jane, was accepted into membership; five years later, his children also became members.[33] Howe's experience reflects the challenges that West Lake Quakers experienced when they sought spouses outside their community. Sometimes, as in Howe's case, this meant crossing geographical, political, and even religious borders.

Despite evidence that male Friends traveled outside their meetings in search of spouses, Quaker women had no such opportunity. We know that Quaker women from the Hughes family of Yonge Street sometimes married and resettled outside their own meetings. It appears, however, that unmarried Quaker women faced different limitations when seeking husbands in a frontier community. This is not to say that unmarried males were sparse on the edges of colonial settlements, but unmarried Quaker males—within appropriate lines of consanguinity—were in short supply. Women could and did travel extensively in ministry. That there is no evidence of their traveling explicitly in search of a spouse indicates that restrictive gender norms dictated the movement of women, regardless of their status as the spiritual equals of male Friends.

Evidently, gendered expectations shaped Quaker women's lives.[34] Certainly, many West Lake women acted within these restrictions. Others did not. Some married eligible bachelors who were members of their geographical community but not of their faith community. Although the number of men and women marrying out of unity in the West Lake community fluctuates, early records show that women married non-Quakers at a higher rate than men did. Between 1798 and 1812, both Adolphustown and Nine Partners recorded twenty out-of-order marriages for Quaker men but twenty-five for women.[35] Although this number seems small, it is significant when we factor in the higher number of men in the community. Of the twenty-five women, nineteen acknowledged their error and requested readmission into membership. Only ten men submitted acknowledgments. The high number of Quaker women who acknowledged their transgression reveals the importance of religious community to women. Choosing marriage over singleness, they married non-Quakers. These men almost always belonged to their geographical community. These women's desire to remain members of the Quaker meeting—not just part of the geographical community—is evident in their decision to acknowledge their error and request readmission to membership even when their husbands did not become members.

A number of factors may have affected women's willingness to acknowledge their wrongdoing. In small settler communities, far from bustling cities, these women might have felt cut off from having a voice in their community if they were not members. Although they were not shunned or forbidden to attend meetings for worship, they would have lost influence, being unable to participate in meetings for business. This was a uniquely gendered problem. Their male counterparts could serve in local government offices, in patronage positions such as overseers, pound masters, fence viewers, constables, and path masters. Indeed, many Quaker men did hold these offices, and were important members in their community and influential voices in town affairs.[36] For Quaker women, shut out of these positions, participation in Quaker business meetings allowed them some influence in their community. Frontier life also lacked opportunities for social gatherings. This highlighted the importance of one's faith community, especially for young women who might otherwise have felt isolated.

Although West Lake Quakers avoided the Children of Peace schism that divided Yonge Street in 1812, discussed below, they were not immune to the tensions plaguing North American Friends in the early 1820s. West Lake Friends were not on the periphery of the Orthodox and Hicksite debates. They actively participated in the theological disagreements that visiting ministers brought with them into the community. Despite the transatlantic nature of the division, the schism itself became deeply personal in West Lake. The meeting was more than three decades old at the time of the split in 1828, but in many ways it was still a new meeting. A number of its members were newly convinced Friends who had joined the meeting as adults; they put immense trust in their local leaders. These were people who had lived their entire lives alongside Friends. They were neighbors who relied on one another for both practical assistance and spiritual support. West Lake's isolation and small size, compared to other Upper Canadian Quaker meetings, meant that it received few outside visitors. It should not be surprising that local circumstances played such a significant role in the outcome of the 1828 schism in this community. Instead of preparative meetings dividing, as happened throughout the YSMM, entire preparative meetings sided with the ministers or elders within their local meeting. The Green Point Preparative Meeting attached itself wholly to the Hicksites, following the leadership of the Hicksite-supporting minister James Noxon and his wife, Elizabeth, an elder.[37] Similarly, Ameliasburgh and Cold Creek Preparative Meeting members, including prominent members of the Dorland and Haight families, identified almost exclusively as Orthodox.[38]

The fallout from the schism devastated the West Lake community. In the immediate aftermath, fights occurred over retention of meetinghouses, meeting records, and funds. These disputes lasted for years, in some cases becoming violent. As the community crumbled and factions were divided, meetings on both sides of the schism were laid down. The Haldimand Preparative Meeting, which not only split between factions but divided an entire family, dwindled in size until it was ultimately discontinued in 1842.[39] The Leeds and Adolphus Monthly Meeting, which formed from the Leeds and Adolphus Preparative Meetings in 1825, was laid down in full by the Hicksites, while the Orthodox laid down Adolphus Preparative, attaching its members to Leeds and West Lake Preparatives.[40] As meetings were closed on both sides, members were left to travel even farther to attend meetings. Neighbors and friends were suddenly on opposing sides of the division. Large families that had been tightly linked by intermarriage were fractured between meetings, separating cousins, siblings, parents, and children. The wounds left on the West Lake community by the divide lasted for decades, as West Lake Quakers did not recover from the schism. The same community that fractured in 1828 found itself in the Supreme Court of Canada a generation later fighting over a meetinghouse when the Orthodox underwent another schism.[41]

YONGE STREET

The Yonge Street community was settled in 1801, when Timothy Rogers led a group of twenty-seven families from Vermont to the lands he had scouted the previous summer. While Rogers had originally hoped to settle forty families, his list of settlers promised "possibly about 20 good families next winter."[42] Immediately afterward, Samuel Lundy and Isaac Phillips brought a similar number of families overland from Pennsylvania to join the Vermont Quakers in building a community on the frontier. Rogers's group settled close together, many of them on contiguous lots fronting Yonge Street. Lundy's settlers took land east of Yonge Street at Queen Street and Whitchurch, also settling close to one another (see map 9.2, inset detail).[43] Unlike Adolphustown when it was settled, this community was, above all else, Quaker. It was removed from other Quaker settlements and was insulated from Upper Canadian society by three factors. First, it was on the frontier, where Friends could settle in close proximity to one another and quickly implement central organization around the structures of a Quaker meeting. Second, family and kinship ties reinforced the bonds of faith that brought this group to Yonge Street in the first place. As in West Lake, multiple sibling marriages between families were common. Third, Quaker testimonies that marked Friends as a "peculiar" people were designed as a protective barrier around the community to keep the world out and Friends in.

Chain migration, especially from western Pennsylvania, began as soon as those in Upper Canada wrote of "a land as it were flowing with milk and honey" and the government's concession that "the oath is left out and the word affirmation put in lieu thereof, and a great many deeds printed on purpose for Friends."[44] These migrations continued, enlarging the meeting and bringing weighty Friends to the community.[45] A peak in migration in 1805 suggests Yonge Street's appeal, despite its remoteness. That year, the Pelham Monthly Meeting accepted ninety-one certificates of membership for Friends at Yonge Street. This does not reflect the precise number of migrants to the community. The meeting did not accept some certificates, as was the case for John Widdifield and his family. Even so, the family remained in the community. Moreover, some individuals and families moved to the community but did not deposit their certificates that year. There were also disowned Quakers who migrated with family and friends who did not have certificates; some were later readmitted to membership after appropriate process. Nonetheless, the figure suggests the swell of migration that year.[46]

The result of this migration, especially in the case of Pennsylvania Friends, was a large, highly interrelated, and extended kinship group, which provided significant geographical stability for the community's members, unlike the situation at Adolphustown. Elizabeth Hovinen's examination of this meeting notes that "of 373 nuclear families who appear at some point in Quaker records for Yonge Street, there is evidence that 201 (almost two-thirds) remained in the area until they died or until 1837."⁴⁷ The Philadelphia Yearly Meeting (PYM) took notice of the growth in membership and the distance between Yonge Street and Pelham, both of which reported directly to the PYM. In 1804, concerned about the distance of Yonge Street from other Quaker meetings in either Upper Canada or the United States, the PYM granted Yonge Street preparative meeting status with the authority to approve marriages. Two years later, in 1806, the PYM granted Yonge Street monthly meeting status.⁴⁸

Yonge Street Friends felt confident about the future of their settlement. A school also opened in 1806 when Timothy Rogers Jr. arrived from Friends' School at Westtown.⁴⁹ Beyond formal schooling, women played an important role in informal education and the socialization of children into the community, as they did in other Quaker communities, supporting the growing community and its families.⁵⁰ The meeting was strong enough that ministers from Yonge Street began making ministerial visits to other meetings. Job Hughes visited Adolphustown in October 1806 and Jacob Winn and Rufus Rogers traveled to Black Creek, near Pelham, in the summer of 1807.⁵¹ In 1807, Asa and Mary Rogers deeded two acres of land on Yonge Street as a site for the new meetinghouse; work began on the structure in 1808. Also in 1807, Yonge Street, now the largest meeting in the colony, led the effort for unification of the three Upper Canadian meetings into the Canada Half-Year's Meeting under the authority of the NYYM (see map 9.1).⁵² This meeting would have the powers of a quarterly meeting but would meet only twice each year, a concession to distance and the difficulties of travel in the colony. The meeting alternated between Yonge Street and West Lake; its first session met in January 1810 at West Lake. It seemed to Yonge Street Friends that their community was divinely ordained for success.

As in the West Lake community, Yonge Street Friends relied heavily on intermarriage to build a strong community.⁵³ Marriage joined Friends who had originated in different American meetings. Marriage between Pennsylvania, Vermont, and New York families knit the community together, making it more stable. Settlement patterns could affect courtship, as Friends who lived in proximity to one another would have had opportunities for interaction outside meetings for worship or business. Yet the evidence suggests that distance was a minor consideration in the formation of marriages if families wanted to maintain ties with old neighbors and friends. Hovinen's analysis of intermarriage among Yonge Street's preparative meetings (Yonge Street, Queen Street, Whitchurch, Uxbridge, and

Pickering) concludes that "every group experienced more marriages with other groups than within its own."[54]

Sometimes, as noted above, finding a suitable spouse who fit the rules of consanguinity was not easy. As with West Lake Friends, Yonge Street men occasionally sought a spouse in other Upper Canadian or American meetings. Between 1803 and 1828, eleven Yonge Street men sought certificates for travel with the express purpose of finding a wife. Seven of those were for marriages to women in Upper Canadian meetings, five at West Lake and two at Pelham. Only four were for marriages outside Upper Canada: two to women from Ferrisburg Monthly Meeting in Vermont, one to Alexandria Monthly Meeting in New York, and one to Rahway Monthly Meeting in New Jersey. In the same period, eight women left the YSMM as a result of marriage. Five married members of the Adolphustown Monthly Meeting and three married men from the Pelham Monthly Meeting. None married men from American meetings. The evidence for both Yonge Street and West Lake suggests that "although women journeyed freely in ministry, social mores obviously dictated that they could not travel freely in search of a spouse."[55] Those who could not find a suitable spouse among Friends found themselves marrying contrary to the discipline. Often, these marriages were in the geographical community between a member and a disowned Friend who remained part of the community. Many Friends who married "out of order" acknowledged their error and were accepted back into membership. The number of marriages between members and former members suggests that, except for the most devout in the Society, disowned Friends living in the community were considered community members, even if they were not officially Quakers. Geographical realities made them suitable mates.

Even while things looked positive, the community began to face trials. Two ministers, Henry Widdifield (1805) and Job Hughes (1807), passed away, Hughes while he was at Yearly Meeting in Philadelphia. In 1808, Timothy Rogers started another settlement at Pickering, forty miles south of Yonge Street. Why Rogers decided to move away from the settlement he was so instrumental in establishing is difficult to determine. The decision may have been economic. Rogers recorded in his journal that he "had a great gift from the Lord to settle new country," and he did become very prosperous in Pickering. Still, about the time he decided to establish yet another settlement, his journal also noted the arrival of ministers Job Hughes and Jacob Winn and his own exclusion from the select meeting.[56] Was he jealous, or did he feel his authority diminished with their arrival? It is impossible to know with certainty. We do know that the move expanded the geographical reach of the YSMM, but the distance from the monthly meeting complicated meeting business.

More damaging to the community were the devastating epidemics that swept through the area, almost wiping out some families. The first unknown epidemic (Phebe Winn called it "the Fever") struck the community in 1809.[57] So many died that the meeting decided to decrease the size of the meetinghouse then under construction by ten feet in length and five in width.[58] Before the community had recovered from the impact of the epidemic, Friends discovered that exemption from military activities required a fine in lieu of service. They could not, and did not, support this. Monthly meeting records document £244 (roughly $25,000) distraints between February 1808 and January 1810, and eight Quakers were jailed for a month for refusing to serve or pay a fine in lieu of military service.[59]

A second destructive epidemic, possibly typhus or measles or a combination of both, swept through the community in 1812–13 at the same time that the United States declared war on Britain and invaded Upper Canada.[60] Yonge Street Quakers remained neutral in the conflict but they could not remain entirely detached from the situation that surrounded them. Their farms were situated on a major military road, their horses were impressed, and they were reminded daily of the conflict. Even so, the minutes identify only six men associated with the war effort, and only two of those joined the armed forces.[61] Their extremely low level of involvement in the war demonstrates that, despite occasional tensions with mainstream society, Yonge Street Quakers in 1812 identified themselves in sectarian terms.

As noted above, two destructive schisms, the first in 1812, challenged this cohesiveness and insularity. During the war, Yonge Street Friends were drawn into internal meeting disputes. These quarrels resulted in approximately eighteen families' leaving the monthly meeting and following David Willson to form the breakaway sect the Children of Peace, or Davidites. The majority of these Quakers came from East Gwillimbury Township, where Willson lived. They set up a meeting near the Queen Street meetinghouse, forming the community of Hope. Personal disputes and kinship connections among its leaders dominated this schism, which did not spread beyond the YSMM. As Albert Schrauwers has shown, those who joined the breakaway sect came largely from the same settlement area and shared family connections and friendships that largely originated in Bucks County, Pennsylvania.[62] As important as kinship was in this schism, it was a doctrinal dispute. This is especially evident when it is viewed from the perspective of women on both sides of the conflict.[63] Because it was a small, localized schism on the margins of the Quaker Atlantic, the separation of the Children of Peace has largely been ignored in broader Quaker historiography. It should be considered within the broader context of doctrinal controversies at the end of the long eighteenth century.

Yonge Street Friends were familiar with the doctrinal dispute that had resulted in the disownment of Hudson Monthly Meeting (New York) minister Hannah Barnard and her New Lights. In recalling the separation, Willson recorded that his "testimony" (the denial of the divinity of Christ and the value of scripture) "met with considerable opposition or obstruction in spirit." Willson's prime combatant was Mary Ray Pearson, the clerk of the women's meeting. She contested Willson's theology, asking of his wife, Phebe, "if she had discovered anything of her husband being out of his right mind," something Pearson attributed to a "fit of sickness" Willson had experienced in 1810.[64] Willson's main supporter was Rachel Hughes Lundy. Her support of David Willson and his prophecies was a turning point in the conflict. Lundy's mother, Eleanor Hughes, an elder in the YSMM, supported her daughter and, by extension, Willson. This put Hughes in direct conflict with fellow elders Mary Pearson, Isaac Phillips, and Isaac Wiggins, all of whom spoke out vehemently against Willson.[65] Pearson was also supported by elders Esther Winn Bostwick and Bostwick's mother, Phebe Winn. Interestingly, two of Eleanor Hughes's daughters married Bowermans, significant Friends in the Adolphustown Monthly Meeting, but the quarrel did not spread to that meeting. At Yonge Street, the damage was considerable. Willson claimed that his detractors "Roard like Bulls ... and Barked like Dogs," creating a commotion that extended beyond the meeting to "neighbors that did not belong to it." On the other side of the conflict, Isaac Wiggins noted that "he had never met with such a subject in all his life, nor one that had such a tendency to divide and separate Friends from one another."[66]

This schism foreshadowed the painful divisions of the 1828 Hicksite-Orthodox separation and brought discussions about doctrine to the forefront. Ministerial activity in the meeting increased, no doubt a response to David Willson's, Rachel Lundy's, and William Reid's appealing their disownments to both the Canada Half-Year's Meeting and the NYYM. Both meetings refused the appeals. Nonetheless, Quakers and non-Quakers alike became interested in the case and its doctrinal challenges. This was especially so when Willson incorporated music into his meetings and hired Richard Coates, a retired military officer, to build the colony's first barrel organ and conduct a musical ensemble that marched down Yonge Street on occasion. Furthermore, after the Children of Peace constructed their temple at Sharon, it became a tourist attraction. Jacob Albertson, a minister who visited Yonge Street in 1820, was disdainful of Willson and the Children of Peace: "the dissenting quakers go farther and farther from friends.... They have got so far as to get organs in their meeting and I am told he has taken in 12 or more young women in his house for what purpose I don't know their parents say they have sent them there because he can bring them up better than they can."[67] The schism itself remained local, but knowledge of the dispute and its implications did not. Quakers from outside the YSMM visited the community to assess the meeting and contain doctrinal disputes. Between 1815 and 1819, twenty-two ministers visited the YSMM, and between 1820 and 1828, fifteen ministerial visits were recorded. These numbers do not include visits to the Canada Half-Year's Meeting.

Despite epidemics and separations, the YSMM remained the largest meeting in Upper Canada. In 1824, Isaac Stephenson recorded a membership of 643, including four recognized ministers and eight elders, making it an attractive location to British immigrants after the Napoleonic Wars.[68] The influx of British Friends produced a more pluralistic community; out of the sixty-eight certificates of transfer deposited at the YSMM between 1814 and 1828, the largest number (eighteen) came from British Friends, fourteen Irish families and four English families.[69] The influx of these Friends, with their commitment to evangelicalism (or to orthodoxy as defined by the London Yearly Meeting), had significant consequences for the community's theological composition.

As in West Lake, local circumstances shaped the Hicksite-Orthodox separation. Beyond the addition of British Friends to the community, Yonge Street Friends who had tried to keep themselves apart from mainstream society could not withstand the encroachment of non-Quaker settlers in the area or the evangelical rival that "burned over" the northern United States and Upper Canada in the late eighteenth and early nineteenth centuries.[70] As the community began to divide theologically into Orthodox (evangelical) and Hicksite (quietist) factions, original community divisions emerged. Most Pennsylvanians joined Hicksites while most Vermonters and all of the English and Irish Friends aligned with the Orthodox faction. There were noteworthy exceptions like Nicholas Brown, the minister who had immigrated to the Pickering area from Vermont. Brown was an ardent Hicksite who traveled throughout the United States in the years preceding the schism, visiting the yearly meetings of New York, Philadelphia, and Baltimore. He was well acquainted with the politics and theology of this religious fight. When his first wife died in 1826, he married Margaret Judge, the daughter of Hugh Judge, one of the most outspoken supporters of the Hicksite cause in the NYYM. The Browns and Hugh Judge played a pivotal role in the yearly meeting separation; this was bound to have repercussions on the local community.

This schism devastated the YSMM. We know from the letters and diaries of visiting ministers that relationships in the community were strained at least four years before the actual separation in 1828.[71] This is reflected in meeting minutes where clerks recorded consensus-based decisions. Minute books, which had customarily been filled with business, changed noticeably. This was especially the case in preparative meetings, where for consecutive months clerks recorded nothing but the meeting date. The actual separation happened in the summer of 1828 following the split in the NYYM. Both factions considered themselves the true Religious Society of Friends; they began to disown those who had attached themselves to the opposite group. The Orthodox, who were the majority, retained ownership of meetinghouses, although not without disputes. Friends enlisted the help of their neighbors to occupy and claim meetinghouses. For instance, at the end of one particularly fractious meeting, local Hicksites complained, "Many people, not members, were present, some of whom were taken in at the windows; their minds were much excited, in consequence of the publications which had been circulated. Violence was anticipated from the ruder part, as many, both orthodox young men and strangers, were prepared with clubs, expressing their intention of turning out the Hicksites, and kicking them when out."[72] The Orthodox also developed closer ties with their Methodist and Presbyterian neighbors, who shared their theological principles. The Hicksites, who eventually gathered under the Genesee Yearly Meeting, took this as further evidence of the depravity that had crept into the Society. Fighting over meetinghouses, heckled in meetings, and consumed with trying to figure out which Friends belonged to what group, both groups saw their business activity grind to a halt. Some meetings were so badly divided they were closed, or "laid down." Others lingered on, but without the enthusiasm and momentum of earlier years. Like salt rubbed in a wound, the schism happened just as the Children of Peace were pouring resources into the construction of their temple in the village of Hope. Whereas other North American Quaker communities split in two at this time, the YSMM fragmented into three distinct groups.

CONCLUSION

At the end of the long eighteenth century, Upper Canadian Quakers were divided. Among North American Friends, including those in Upper Canada, class differences, urban-rural divisions, and power struggles in the yearly meetings all complicated theological arguments. The conflicts percolated down to the local meetings. Overcoming differences in doctrine had become impossible, although each faction employed every tool of persuasion at its disposal in vain. In addition to enlisting the help of traveling ministers, local Quaker meetings instructed their neighbors on the finer points of their quarrels with the aid of pamphlets published by the Meeting for Sufferings that Friends who attended yearly meeting brought back to Upper Canada.[73] Yonge Street Friends, especially, took their differences into the customary haven for colonial political disputes—the tavern—distributing pamphlets there to stir up support. With their own community broken apart, and aware of their doctrinal similarity with other religious groups, Quakers were more prepared to look outside their faith community to create links with members of the larger society. The widespread realization that they could reform their own faith community, even if it meant ripping it apart, translated to shaping the larger society in which they lived. The activism of looking inward and reshaping the Society of Friends was refocused outward into an activism that sought to reform Upper Canada's religious and political culture.

NOTES

1. Upper Canada was created in 1791 when the Constitution Act divided the province of Quebec into Upper and Lower Canada. Between 1783, after the American Revolution, and 1791, the area known later as Upper Canada was western Quebec. In 1841, Upper and Lower Canada were reunited and Upper Canada became Canada West until Confederation in 1867, when it became known as Ontario. While we use the term Upper Canada

throughout this chapter, we recognize that the area was properly western Quebec when the first Loyalists arrived.

2. The West Lake community began at Adolphustown. Beginning in 1811, as members settled more densely in Prince Edward County, west of Adolphustown, the monthly meeting alternated its meeting for business between the two meetinghouses. By 1821, the monthly meeting had moved to West Lake permanently.

3. Pelham Monthly Meeting, the third Quaker community, was located near Niagara. Like Adolphustown, the Pelham Meeting was peripherally related to the Loyalist migration to Upper Canada.

4. This meeting had the authority of a quarterly meeting but, owing to distances, met only twice a year.

5. This was not unique to Quakers. Migration studies in the Upper Canadian context have shown the importance of local conditions in shaping community experiences and expressions. Local particularities do not negate common structures and processes from which we can draw general conclusions about early communities, as Darrett B. Rutman argues in "Assessing the Little Communities of Early America," *William and Mary Quarterly* 43, no. 2 (1986): 163–78.

6. The numbers are difficult to state with accuracy. Maya Jasanoff does a careful analysis of the extant records and estimates that sixty thousand Loyalists left the new United States. See Jasanoff, *Liberty's Exiles: American Loyalists in the Revolutionary World* (New York: Knopf, 2011), 357.

7. The British government allotted land according to status and rank. Heads of families received 100 acres plus 50 acres for each additional family member. Single men were entitled to 50 acres. Noncommissioned officers received 200 acres and privates 100 acres, with 50 acres for each additional family member in each case. The land allotment to officers was more generous: 1,000 acres for field officers, 700 acres for captains, and 500 acres for subalterns, staff officers, and warrant officers. Gerald M. Craig, *Upper Canada: The Formative Years, 1784–1841* (1963; repr., Toronto: McClelland and Stewart, 1991), 5–6.

8. York, established in 1793, was supposed to be a temporary capital until a capital could be established near today's London, Ontario. Between 1791 and 1793, the capital was located in Kingston.

9. The exact population in 1812 is difficult to determine. Joseph Bouchette lists the 1811 population of Upper Canada as seventy-seven thousand and the 1814 population as ninety-five thousand. See Bouchette, *The British Dominions in North America*, 2 vols. (London: H. Colburn and R. Bentley, 1831), 1:108; Bouchette, *A Topographical Description of the Province of Lower Canada: With Remarks upon Upper Canada* (London: W. Faden, 1815), 596. On the colonial culture of the province, see Jane Errington, *The Lion, the Eagle, and Upper Canada: A Developing Colonial Identity* (Montreal: McGill-Queen's University Press, 1987), 35–54.

10. As Donald Harman Akenson has contended, there is wide variation in figures because it is difficult to estimate the precise number of immigrants to Upper Canada during this period. See Akenson, *The Irish in Ontario: A Study in Rural History*, 2nd ed. (Montreal: McGill-Queen's University Press, 1999), 14–15. The figures here are from J. M. S. Careless, *Canada: A Celebration of Our Heritage*, 2nd ed. (Mississauga: Heritage, 1997). Certainly, the census indicates the tremendous growth of Upper Canada: in 1842 the recorded population was 487,053; by 1851 it was 952,004. Statistics

Canada, *Census of Upper Canada (1842)* (Ottawa, 1842), https://library.queensu.ca/data/census-1665–1871-uc.

11. Statistics Canada, *Census of Upper Canada (1842)*.

12. The NPMM allowed the Adolphustown Preparative Meeting to conduct marriages, deal with discipline, and accept acknowledgments.

13. United Empire Loyalists Centennial Committee, *The Centennial of the Settlement of Upper Canada, 1784–1884* (Toronto: Rose, 1885), 167.

14. "Nine Partners Digest: A Book of Testimonies, Marriages, Births, Deaths, Removals, and Manumission of Slaves, 1769–1798," May 21, 1779, FHLSC.

15. Alexander Fraser, ed., *Sixth Report of the Bureau of Archives for the Province of Ontario, 1909* (Toronto: L. K. Cameron, 1911), 4.

16. NPMM, 1790–1797, December 19, 1792, FHLSC.

17. Also called the Laurentian Plateau, the Canadian Shield is the exposed portion of the North American continental crust. It is one of the world's largest continental shields and covers eight million square kilometers.

18. Adolphustown Monthly Meeting, 1798–1813, December 17, 1801, and April 15, 1802, CYMA.

19. Albert C. Bowerman, *The "Bowerman" Family of Canada, Descendants of Ichabod Bowerman of Dutchess Co., N.Y., 1683–1796* (Bloomfield, ON: Canadian Quaker Archives, 1904), 35.

20. Edwina Newman, "Quakers and the Family," in *The Oxford Handbook of Quaker Studies*, ed. Stephen W. Angell and Pink Dandelion (Oxford: Oxford University Press, 2013), 435.

21. John Dorland's family first appears in the "Annual Return of the Inhabitants of Adolphustown, April 6, 1796," in *Appendix to the Report of the Ontario Bureau of Industries, 1896* (Toronto: Warwick Bros. and Rutter, 1898), 29.

22. Nine Partners Women's Monthly Meeting, 1794–1811, December 20, 1797, FHLSC.

23. Adolphustown Monthly Meeting, 1798–1813, November 19, 1807, CYMA. Dorland's first wife was also from Dutchess County.

24. Hugh D. Vail, "Records of Rahway and Plainfield [NJ] Monthly Meeting of Friends (Formerly Held at Amboy and Woodbridge) from 1687 to 1825," *New York Genealogical and Biographical Record* 9, no. 1 (1878): 35.

25. Robynne Rogers Healey, *From Quaker to Upper Canadian: Faith and Community Among Yonge Street Friends, 1801–1850* (Montreal: McGill-Queen's University Press, 2006), 71.

26. Bowerman, *"Bowerman" Family of Canada*, 50.

27. Adolphustown Monthly Meeting, 1798–1813, October 22, 1800, CYMA.

28. Ibid., December 17, 1801.

29. Ibid., December 20, 1804.

30. Ibid., September 15, 1808, and July 20, 1809.

31. "Annual Return of the Inhabitants of Adolphustown, taken the 2nd and 3rd days of 3rd month, 1807," in *Appendix to the Report of the Ontario Bureau of Industries*, 39.

32. Richard A. Preston, ed., *Kingston Before the War of 1812: A Collection of Documents* (Toronto: Champlain Society and University of Toronto Press, 1959), 349. Samuel Howe, son of United Empire Loyalist William Howe, married Jane Denyck, daughter of United Empire Loyalist Andrew Denyck.

33. Adolphustown Women's Monthly Meeting, 1808–1824, March 20, 1817, and July 17, 1822, CYMA.

34. See Sarah Crabtree, "In the Light and on the Road: Patience Brayton and the Quaker Itinerant Ministry," in *New Critical Studies on Early Quaker Women, 1650–1800*, ed. Michele Lise Tarter and Catie Gill (Oxford: Oxford University Press, 2018), 128–45.

35. Records used for this calculation include Adolphustown Monthly Meeting, 1798–1813, Adolphustown Women's Monthly Meeting, 1808–1824, CYMA; Nine Partners Monthly Meeting, 1790–1797, and Nine Partners Women's Monthly Meeting, 1794–1811, FHLSC.

36. For weighty Quaker men in such positions, see "Record of Town Meetings Held in Adolphustown, 1792–1849," in *Appendix to the Report of the Ontario Bureau of Industries*, 1–26.

37. West Lake Monthly Meeting (Orthodox), 1828–1849, October 16, 1828, CYMA. The Orthodox faction of the West Lake Monthly Meeting laid down the Green Point Preparative Meeting after it sided entirely with the Hicksite faction.

38. West Lake Monthly Meeting Book C, 1824–1837, February 19, 1829, CYMA. Just as the Orthodox faction did with Green Point, the Hicksite faction of the West Lake Monthly Meeting laid down both the Cold Creek and the Ameliasburgh Preparative Meetings when both meetings refused to acknowledge the Hicksite faction.

39. Haldimand Preparative Meeting, 1827–1842, May 11, 1842, CYMA.

40. West Lake Monthly Meeting Book C, 1824–1837, September 18, 1829, and West Lake Monthly Meeting (Orthodox), 1828–1849, October 21, 1830, CYMA.

41. *Jones v. Dorland*, 14 S.C.R. 39 (1887). The split was between the Progressives and the Conservatives, both claiming ownership of the West Lake Monthly Meeting meetinghouse.

42. "Mr. Rogers's List of Settlers," CYMA.

43. For further background on Rogers's efforts to establish the Yonge Street settlement, see Healey, *From Quaker to Upper Canadian*, 31–38.

44. Amos Armitage to Charles Chapman, quoted in *Genealogies of the Builders of the Sharon Temple*, transcribed by Albert Schrauwers, 3rd rev. and enl. ed., Sharon Temple Study Series no. 1 (East Gwillimbury, ON: Sharon Temple Museum, 1994), 9.

45. In the earliest years of settlement, before 1805, Yonge Street became home to Henry and Martha Widdifield from Muncy, Pennsylvania, both recognized ministers; Jacob and Phebe Winn from Danby, Vermont, he a recognized minister; and Job and Eleanor Hughes from Catawissa, Pennsylvania, he a recognized minister, she an elder.

46. For comparison, Yonge Street Friends deposited fifty-one certificates at Pelham in 1804 and thirty-two in 1806. Pelham Monthly Meeting of Friends, 1799–1806, CYMA.

47. Elizabeth Hovinen, *The Quakers of Yonge Street* (Toronto: York University, Department of Geography, 1978), 26.

48. YSMM, 1806–1818, August 18, 1806, CYMA.

49. Christopher Densmore and Albert Schrauwers, eds., *"The Best Man for Settling New Country . . .": Journal of Timothy Rogers* (Toronto: Canadian Friends Historical Association, 2000), 109.

50. Healey, *From Quaker to Upper Canadian*, 74–92; Elizabeth Bouldin, "'The Days of Thy Youth': Eighteenth-Century Quaker Women and the Socialization of Children," in Tarter and Gill, *New Critical Studies*, 202–20.

51. YSMM, 1806–1818, October 16, 1806, November 13, 1806, June 12, 1807, CYMA.

52. Ibid., January 13, 1807.

53. For an extensive discussion of the impact of marriage and family connections in the Yonge Street community, see Healey, *From Quaker to Upper Canadian*, 51–73.

54. Hovinen, *Quakers of Yonge Street*, 17.
55. Healey, *From Quaker to Upper Canadian*, 67.
56. Densmore and Schrauwers, "Best Man for Settling New Country," 109.
57. Phebe Winn, Diary, CYMA.
58. YSMM, 1806–1818, January 18, 1810, CYMA.
59. Ibid.
60. Of the mysterious epidemic, Timothy Rogers noted in his journal that while both typhus and measles had been identified, "mostly it has been such an uncommon Disorder that it seems to baffle the skill of the wisest and best physicians." Densmore and Schrauwers, "Best Man for Settling New Country," 117–18.
61. Healey, *From Quaker to Upper Canadian*, 46.
62. Schrauwers (transcriber), *Genealogies of the Builders of the Sharon Temple*, 47.
63. Albert Schrauwers argues that class was at the center of this schism and that doctrine was only a "nominal cause." See Schrauwers, *Awaiting the Millennium: The Children of Peace and the Village of Hope, 1812–1889* (Toronto: University of Toronto Press, 2016), 35. For another assessment of the schism as doctrinally based, see Healey, *From Quaker to Upper Canadian*, 113–29.
64. David Willson, *The Separation of the Children of Peace*, transcribed by Albert Schrauwers, vol. 1 of *The Ark Papers*, Sharon Temple Study Series no. 8 (East Gwillimbury, ON: Sharon Temple Museum, 1994), 9, 10, 31–32.
65. Pearson was no stranger to doctrinal disputes. Before arriving in Upper Canada, the Ray family had been members of the Hudson Monthly Meeting, thirty miles from Creek Monthly Meeting, the home of Hannah Barnard, with whose theology she was familiar. For more on Barnard, see David W. Maxey, "New Light on Hannah Barnard, a Quaker 'Heretic,'" *Quaker History* 78, no. 2 (1989): 61–86.
66. Willson, *Children of Peace*, 11, 14.
67. Jacob Albertson to Mary Albertson, October 20, 1820, Albertson File, CYMA.
68. Isaac Stephenson [Jr.] to Isaac Stephenson, Stockton on Tees, Durham, England, Stephenson letters, 1824, D-2-10, CYMA.
69. The rest of the certificates of transfer came from Pennsylvania (12), Vermont (13), New Jersey (2), New York (10), and other Upper Canadian Quaker meetings (13).
70. Whitney R. Cross, *The Burned Over District: The Social and Intellectual History of Enthusiastic Religion in Western New York, 1800–1850* (Ithaca: Cornell University Press, 1950); George A. Rawlyk, *The Canada Fire: Radical Evangelicalism in British North America, 1775–1812* (Montreal: McGill-Queen's University Press, 1994).
71. Letters of Elizabeth Robson, December 29, 1824, MS vol. 121, LSF.
72. "Extract from Letter Written by Amos Armitage and John Watson," *Friend; or Advocate of Truth, for the Year 1829* 2 (1829): 28.

CHAPTER 10

Industrial Development and Community Responsibility
The Harford Family and South Wales, ca. 1768–1842

RICHARD C. ALLEN

When the Ebbw Vale ironworks were sold in 1844, it ended nearly a hundred years of the Harford family's involvement in Welsh industry.[1] Yet surveys of the industrial development of Wales have rarely focused on these important Quaker entrepreneurs; thus some of the more distinctive features of their businesses and impact on the landscape and community relations have been ignored. Given the evidence available, this chapter focuses primarily on the Harford family and their tinplate business and ironworks at Melingriffith, Glamorganshire, and Ebbw Vale and Sirhowy, Monmouthshire, from the middle of the eighteenth century onward.[2] This study explores how the Harfords developed their various businesses and reviews their management decisions and practices. The argument here is that the cooperative relationships put in place between the Harfords as industrialists and their workforce were a key feature of their success. In a period of industrial expansion and unrest, when conflict defined many of the relationships in the coalfields and ironworks, the suggestion that the Harfords applied themselves to ethical business transactions, fair-minded labor relations, and philanthropy can be tested.

Quakers have had a long association with Wales and were among its industrial pioneers.[3] In the mid-seventeenth century, Richard Hanbury Sr.

(1610–1696) of Monmouthshire developed ironworking in Pontypool that produced excellent Osmund iron;[4] he also managed the Tintern wireworks. Hanbury expanded his business interests after receiving advice concerning tinplate manufacturing from Andrew Yarranton (1619–1684), the Worcestershire engineer and religious radical. Yarranton was imprisoned during the Restoration, but after his release he was commissioned in the mid-1660s by several unspecified "English gentlemen" to visit Saxony to learn about the tinplate industry. It is unclear whether Hanbury might have been involved, but he was certainly influenced by Yarranton's claim that the "way and manner of their Working" of tinplate was perfect for the British market. The secret process was nevertheless appropriated by others who secured a patent, and "the Richest of our Partners being not willing, or at least afraid, to offend Great men then in Power, who had their eye upon it," as Yarranton put it, "caused the thing to cool."[5] Although it is unknown what impact this had on his own immediate industrial concerns, Hanbury's progeny, especially his son Richard Hanbury Jr. (1647–1714), continued the family's business interests, while future generations of the family would diversify into mercantilism. Thus Capel Hanbury (1678–1740) became a successful merchant in Bristol, and his nephew John Hanbury (1700–1758) established himself in London and became enormously wealthy from investments in Virginia.[6] Furthermore, at an indeterminate point in the 1660s, Richard Hanbury Sr. employed Thomas Allgood of Northamptonshire as manager of the Pontypool ironworks. The Allgoods were successful Quaker entrepreneurs, particularly after Thomas's discovery of a process for lacquering plates with a decorative finish, known as "Pontypool Japanware." His two sons, Edward and Thomas, continued the business into the eighteenth century as the demand for luxury goods increased.[7]

While the Hanburys were expanding their ironworks, the Lloyd family, principally under the leadership of Charles Lloyd III (1662–1747), founded several ironworks from their Dolobran estate in Montgomeryshire.[8] Between 1709 and 1717, Lloyd received financial support from Abraham Darby of Coalbrookdale, Shropshire, for the Mathrafal forge, which remained functional until 1719. After this date, a new forge was established on the Dolobran estate and the Lloyds invested in the Bersham furnace, near Wrexham, in partnership with others.[9] The Lloyds sought new markets for the finished product, but these forges proved to be too costly for such a small operation. Indeed, they began operating when the demand for iron was high but suffered great losses when the industry contracted.[10]

Increasingly, the Lloyds fell into debt, especially when Charles Lloyd IV (1697–1767) took over the management of the estate, and by 1720 the Dolobran forge had temporarily ceased production.[11] The Bersham furnace was kept working until 1727, when Charles Lloyd III and Charles Lloyd IV were declared bankrupt.[12] Some further financial support was provided by Charles Lloyd IV's aunt, but when the Dolobran works were forced to close in 1729, he briefly absconded to France before returning to face his creditors. He refused to recognize his role in the collapse of the business until the creditors produced "several letters . . . of his hand writing owning himself a partner."[13] Although Quaker interests petered out with the collapse of the Dolobran estate, Sampson Lloyd (1664–1724), the brother of Charles Lloyd III, had established an iron industry near Birmingham.[14]

During the eighteenth century, there was a marked decline in membership of the Society of Friends, particularly when young Friends were unable to comply with the strictness of the code of conduct.[15] In essence, it was hard for Welsh Quakers "to offer anything to the middle classes which they were not already disposed to find in other forms of nonconformist worship."[16] Nevertheless, some families clung tenaciously to Quakerism, and this led to a small revival in membership toward the end of the century. The industrial development of Glamorganshire and Monmouthshire, and particularly the arrival of English Quaker entrepreneurs who were prepared to help improve the living and working conditions of their employees, facilitated this revival.

The Melingriffith Tinplate Works, four miles north of Cardiff, was successfully transformed by Quaker iron merchants in the 1760s and 1770s (see map 10.1). Richard Reynolds (1735–1816) of Bristol and later Coalbrookdale and his partners, along with John Partridge and his son from Ross-on-Wye, had already established three forges in Gloucestershire and an additional forge at Monmouth. Reynolds sought to turn Melingriffith into "a sophisticated industrial complex" that was "locked into the web of commodity exchanges that girded Britain's Atlantic empire."[17] Beginning in 1768, Reynolds, in partnership with other Quakers, including the Harford family and the Partridges of Breconshire, extended the Melingriffith site to include two rolling mills, a tin house, workmen's cottages, and outlying buildings.[18] James Harford (1734–1817) and his younger brother John (1736–1816), the sons of Truman Harford, a successful Bristol merchant, continued to advance the family's interests.[19] From the mid-1770s, Richard Reynolds relinquished his position in the business and the Melingriffith works came

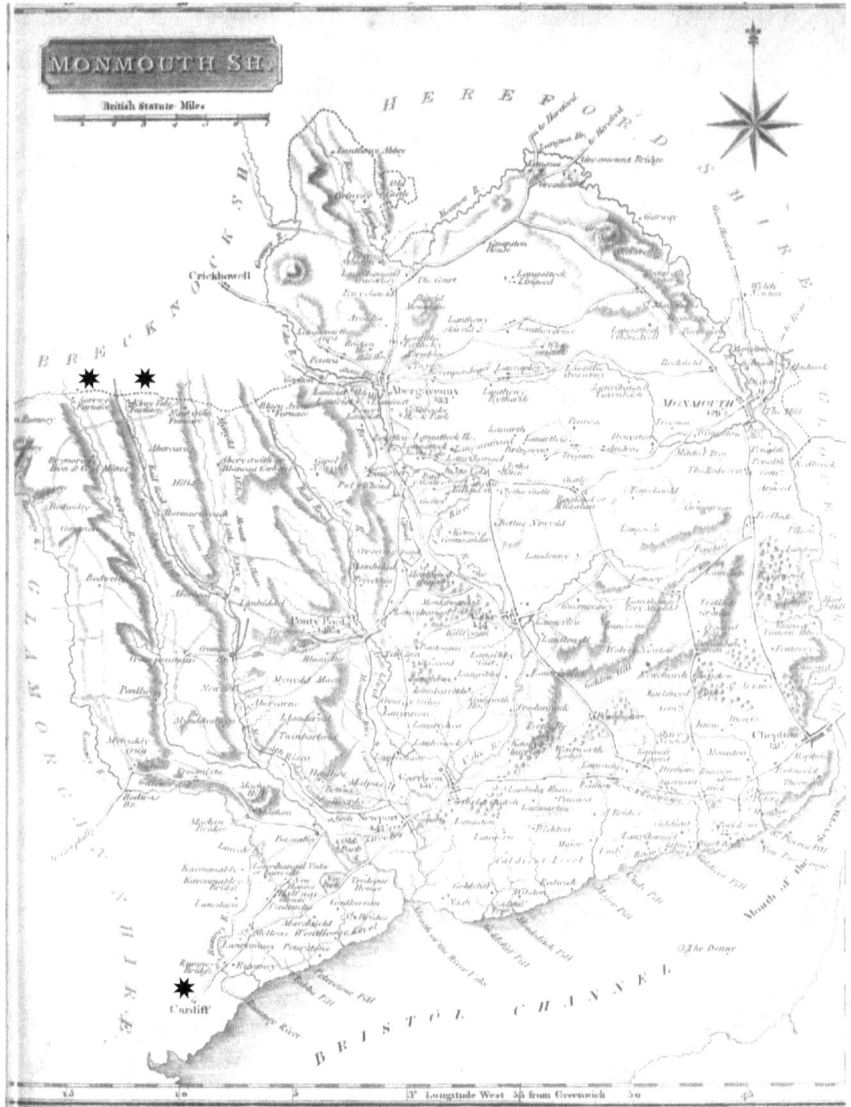

MAP 10.1 Location of the Melingriffith Tinplate Works, Glamorgan, and the Ebbw Vale and Sirhowy Ironworks, Monmouthshire, ca. 1812. From Samuel J. Neele, *Monmouthshire* (London: James Cundee, 1812), reproduced in James Dugdale, *The New British Traveller; or, Modern Panorama of England and Wales* [. . .], vol. 3 (London: J. Robins & Co., 1819), plate after p. 560, https://archive.org/details/newbritishtravelo3dugduoft/page/n10/mode/2up.

under the control of Harford, Partridge and Company. With other partners they acquired the status of innovative and efficient producers of tinplate, and at Melingriffith and the Pentyrch works (purchased in 1805), they provided excellent opportunities for skilled workers.

By October 1785, there were at least seventy-four workmen and managers, but the list notably excludes women and juveniles. As such, there were more than one hundred people working at Melingriffith, including migrants from various parts of South Wales, outside specialists from Bristol and Shropshire who worked in the adjacent coalfield, and Walloon finers and hammer men.[20] The Melingriffith works prospered under the control of the Harfords and their associates,[21] and other family members were involved in promoting legislation for the construction of the Glamorgan Canal between Merthyr and Cardiff. It is suggested that by the turn of the nineteenth century, it was the largest tinplate works in the world, with approximately thirteen thousand boxes of "the very best tin plates" shipped from Bristol annually.[22] By January 1810, however, the partnership had been dissolved, and in 1812 the tinplate and ironworks at Melingriffith, Pentyrch, and Monmouth were controlled by Richard Blakemore and Company.[23]

In the final decades of the eighteenth century, the Harfords turned their attention to Monmouthshire (see map 10.1).[24] In 1791 a deal had been struck with Jeremiah Homfray (1759–1833),[25] who had invested more than £2,000 in the business,[26] and the following year Harford, Partridge and Company, and Thomas Hill (and associates), of Staffordshire, agreed to develop Nant-y-glo as a new ironworks.[27] Initially, there were some disputes that curtailed production in 1793. The Harfords and their partners wrote to Hill explaining that they were "fearfull" that the development of Nant-y-glo over the proposed Varteg site would "fall very short when bro[ugh]t to a trial." Indeed, there were greater mineral resources at the latter and easier carriage to Newport for shipping. They felt that the extraction of coal at Varteg would enhance the business just as much as the output of the iron furnaces. Moreover, they believed that instead of erecting four to eight furnaces on the Nant-y-glo site, there would only be enough land for four. They had expended an additional £2,600 and sought Hill's approval.[28] Together they assembled two furnaces, various forges, a steam engine, and a casting shop,[29] but it was clear by December 1794 that there was insufficient capital to fully develop the Nant-y-glo works.[30] Hill was aggrieved that an additional £483 had been spent alongside his initial investment of £10,000, and the bitter disagreement resulted in the ironworks' lying dormant until 1796. Hill withdrew from the partnership in April 1796, as did Homfray, who sold his share for £500 to the Harfords.[31] The company continued to develop the site thereafter and it became profitable.[32] By 1811 the Harfords had a balance of £56,508, which represented an increase of £9,000 from 1808 and as much as £48,000 from the earlier partnership with Homfray. Specifically, the Harfords had improved their capital investment by 50 percent between 1805 and 1815.[33]

In other ways the Harfords attempted to improve the economic infrastructure of the area by adopting new methods of iron production.[34] This was nowhere more apparent than in their support for Samuel "Iron Bottom" Rogers's improvement of the puddling process, which had been largely ignored by many ironmasters. Although it allowed them to manufacture wrought iron of superior quality, the use of the process was not fully adopted and ceased to be used after the death of Richard Summers Harford (1763–1837).[35] The Harfords were also thwarted in their efforts to fully develop the economic potential of the region. In September 1799, Richard Summers Harford complained to his solicitors that his application for a tramway had been denied. This would damage his trade, he stated, as "my coal will be entirely shut out from the market." He observed that the upper ford at Glangrwyney, near Crickhowell, Breconshire, was "so very bad as to be impassable." This action, Harford felt, would effectively throw him "out of the market" and compel him to cease production at the Llwyd Coed colliery.[36] The situation only gradually improved, while the communication routes between the two works at Ebbw Vale and Sirhowy required the Harfords to invest heavily in the construction of a mountain tunnel in 1832 to connect the two worksites, tram roads, and locomotives.[37]

In their business transactions, the Harfords recognized that there ought to be fair dealing, but still they could be shrewd businessmen. Occasionally, they drew on their Quaker connections. In the case of a potential contract with John White of Bishopwearmouth, Solomon Chapman of Sunderland was asked to provide an opinion concerning White's "respectability & responsibility supposing we should send him Iron—and also to what extent it would be safe to trust him we are entire strangers to each other of course we do not like to go to any unlimited extent without some information."[38] Clearly, such cautious behavior could lead to tension. In his dealings with Richard Crawshay over the development of the Glamorgan Canal Company between 1788 and 1793, James Harford was a demonstrably capable businessman and a foil to Crawshay's trademark stubbornness. Indeed,

Crawshay referred to him as "a rude, selfish, Jew, Quaker" who had "the manners of a bear," while in February 1791 he confided to a business associate that James Harford was "a mercenary Fellow & must be treated as Circumstances require."[39]

Throughout the 1790s and early 1800s, various lawsuits were entered in the Court of the Exchequer on behalf of and against the Harfords.[40] On May 23, 1795, a letter was sent to John Powell, John Harford's solicitor, concerning the irregular business activities of Moses David. Harford inferred that at the root of the problem was Walter Watkins of Dan-y-Graig, Breconshire, who had bought coal from David and his associates against the wishes of the Harfords and David's better judgment—"if he has any," Harford noted![41] In January 1818 another lawsuit was pursued against Richard Fothergill (1758–1821), "an unworthy neighbor," who was accused of the "unwarrantable detention of our property at Sirhowy." In 1778, a forty-year lease had been signed by Fothergill and the Harfords, and on its termination the Harfords sought £2,500 for renewal or £40,000 for full purchase. Consequently, Fothergill rejected the terms and removed all his machinery at Sirhowy.[42] A further case in 1837 alleging breach of contract held at the Court of Common Pleas, London, was defeated by Harford, Davies and Company.[43] Quakers had long used the law to protect themselves, especially during their persecution in the seventeenth century, but they subsequently became adept at using the law for their own ends or acting as a lobbying group for social, religious, and economic change, and arguing that certain procedures were unlawful.[44] In this context, the Harfords were no different from their forbears as they initiated lawsuits to defend their individual and property rights. In a period of fierce industrial rivalry, the Harfords ensured that their businesses were free from impropriety, and they presented themselves to the wider community as respectable and economically responsible. Despite these lawsuits, there were occasions when the ironmasters cooperated to ensure commercial success. Between 1809 and the 1820s, meetings were held in Newport to fix the price of iron tram plates.[45]

Rapid industrialization meant speculating in potentially risky businesses, and Quakers were cautious about securing their long-term investments without compromising their ethical position.[46] The Harfords' initial profitability encouraged them to borrow funds to offset the costs of expansion.[47] And yet they did not always avoid the financial pitfalls associated with the rising cost of the extraction of minerals and the production of high-quality iron.⁴⁸ Unfortunately, economic growth in 1824 was swiftly followed by a deep economic recession, and their precarious financial situation became apparent between 1825 and 1826 during the banking crisis. The Harfords asked their customers for prompt payment and offered discounts if they paid quickly, and in 1827, to keep their business afloat, Summers Harford informed William Crawshay that they could pay him £10,000 of their short-term £40,000 loan. The economic downturn continued, and further periods of uncertainty during the 1830s led two furnaces at Ebbw Vale to be closed in 1836.⁴⁹

Throughout this period, the Harfords worked closely with their suppliers to ensure that they received quality goods, whatever they were selling. Thus, upon settling a bill with Richard Rogers, a cheese merchant of Newport, in May 1824, they commented, "We have rec[eive]d the cheese & as far as we have yet tried, it has given us good satisfaction. Quality is of the first consequence, in this as in every other article of consumption, & where particular attention is paid, success is almost sure to follow & persons will feel more confidence in dealing, where they know the party to be conscientiously careful."⁵⁰ Where the quality was inferior, Richard Summers Harford requested that the merchant send a better sample.⁵¹ Similarly, when merchants were trying to force down their prices, the Harfords responded in no uncertain terms. Thomas Powell of Newport was informed in 1824 that although they were prepared to "sacrifice" 2s. 6d. per ton of tram plate, they were content to do so "to please a customer who is very hard in making his bargains."⁵² In contrast, in 1827, Pierce and Shannon of Limerick were told, "we are not disposed to vary from the prices quoted in our circular and beg respectfully to remark that we do not view thy constant endeavours to beat down our prices to be meeting us in a mercantile manner."⁵³

The Harfords' business acumen is shown in their decision to buy £7,500 in shares in the Monmouth Canal Company in 1792.⁵⁴ Not only did this venture improve their transport of goods but they profited from shares in the canal and later in the railways.⁵⁵ Their involvement was not, however, without risk. In June 1798, Richard Summers Harford wrote to John Powell of the Brecon and Abergavenny Canal Company about a writ that had been served on his sisters for their nonpayment of canal "calls." Harford suggested that they had not been given notice of the "call" and considered it unfair that "they should be subjected to expences undeservedly."⁵⁶ More worrying for the Harfords and their partners, the Partridges, was a bill brought before Parliament in 1802 to change the provisions outlined in the act that created the Monmouthshire Canal Company. The Harfords disliked the spirit of "speculation" that had taken over the enterprise and the clauses in the bill, which would force them to use specified roads. They argued that, apart from cutting into their profits, it would produce a monopoly for "a Company of Adventurers, through a large Tract of Country," and would destroy that "Spirit of Competition in the Adoption of Improvements, which has always been found of the greatest advantage to a manufacturing Country."[57] The following year, the Harfords issued a writ against Glamorgan Canal Navigation for diverting water from the Melingriffith works and issued a further writ for trespass.[58] The issues took many years to resolve, but by June 1817 the Committee of the Brecon and Abergavenny Canal Company adopted the principle of protecting the rights of traders to restrict further speculation and exorbitant rises in the use of other canals.[59]

As with many other aspects of the business, the Harfords managed their workforce carefully. The supervision of labor was strict and could even involve a close examination of workers' personal relationships. Thus on April 6, 1785, John Vaughan, who was based at the Machen forge, wrote to his brother at Melingriffith about "the love affair" that was being conducted by a fellow employee, Walter Davies. Vaughan insisted that if Davies did not end the affair, he would be dismissed. Moreover, Vaughan wrote, "if Davies deserves to go to Bridwell you'd do well to send him there for an example to others of his sort."[60] At the Ebbw Vale works, where the Harfords initially employed forty men, the contracts show the relationship between the Quaker employers and workers, skilled and unskilled.[61] On March 10, 1796, Jenkin Griffith was contracted to site the new boiler, for which he was to be paid £11 on condition that he "compleats the job in a workmanlike manner." The following day he was approached to do some work on the furnace walls for twelve guineas, but a clause was added specifying that if this was insufficient to meet his or the workmen's needs, then he was to be paid an additional sum for work undertaken on the chimney.[62] For many other contractors, the arrangements were equally favorable. That same month, John Miles accepted John Harford's offer to provide coke for the Ebbw Vale furnace for the year at 12s. per week, "before the Furnace is blown," plus accommodations, and then 1s. per week after the furnace was in full operation. The work involved unloading the wagons after they had been brought to the coal mines. He was then to set about producing coke for the ironworks, but, significantly, the onus was on him to "carry all his own water, take up the rails from the pits that are fill'd & lay them to other empty pits—as often as its necessary." This was to ensure that the miners were not kept waiting. Furthermore, he was to "work by any instructions, & to obey any orders respecting his work, or the management of the yards, which may from time to time, be given him."[63]

Far more stringent terms of engagement were applied to other workers, especially regarding regular attendance at work, with fines for absenteeism.[64] The memorandum book indicates that the company provided many laborers with housing, but this privilege was conditional upon their being hospitable to the lodgers they took into their homes, and they were to charge no more than "Sixpence a week from any one such Lodger for his Bed or more than one shilling for a man and wife, lodging, for their Bed."[65] This applied to Thomas Williams, a carpenter, who in 1796 was not to charge any person more than 9d. per week for lodging "on a feather or flock bed or more than 6d. a week for lodging on any other kind of bed."[66] Clearly, in these cases the Harfords sought to provide adequate accommodation for any worker, temporary or otherwise, while also ensuring that such provision was not exorbitant. The selling of alcohol was expressly forbidden, as Quakers pointed out that immorality was related to excessive consumption of alcohol and they often issued strong warnings because of the way it contaminated mind and soul.[67] If this measure was disobeyed, a penalty of five guineas was imposed. The discovery of such activity was predicated on the statements of witnesses before a magistrate.[68]

The employment practices of the Harford family constituted a balance between the pressures of capitalist enterprise and their paternalistic ethos. The memorandum book shows that the Harfords relied upon the "faithfulness" of prospective workers. In May 1796, George Jones of Merthyr was employed as a blacksmith on condition that he would "engage to be allways just and faithful to the interest of the said company and will not on any pretence whatever absent himself for one day during this agreement from his work without leave from the company under a penalty of one Guinea for each day he so quits or leaves his work."[69] Conditional contracts applied to many employees, including Thomas Phillips, a laborer.[70] "Faithfulness" extended as far as the selling of any surplus coal by employees. Thus, in 1796, John Morgan, a collier, could sell "the small and other coal that the Company may not call for," while honoring the agreement not to sell the "large or such as will do for coaking." Failure to comply resulted in a surcharge of five guineas for every sack sold.[71] The Monmouthshire quarter sessions reveal that the Harfords were prepared to prosecute anyone who stole from them.

Among several others, John Thomas and Timothy O'Bryan, laborers, were indicted for stealing fifty-six pounds of coal between 1828 and 1829, while in September 1839, John Harris, John Viner, and Robert Williams, laborers, were prosecuted for housebreaking and theft.[72]

The Harfords' role in industrial expansion was a form of benign paternalism that placed the welfare of the workforce at the heart of business profitability. While a fit and healthy workforce would ensure efficiency, the Harfords' management ethos was unusually enlightened. At the Melingriffith ironworks, the Men's Friendly Society was founded on New Year's Day 1786 and organized around "Articles of a Society of Tradesmen, Manufacturers, and others . . . for the purpose of relieving each other in times of affliction and distress." The benefit club was organized in the same manner as Quaker monthly and quarterly meetings. Money was raised by subscription from members, who had to be over thirty-five years of age, earn at least 8s. per week, and be in excellent health. They paid 1s. every four weeks, and "fines" were levied on those who did not attend meetings without good cause. By 1798 there were at least sixty-three members, though membership was not solely the preserve of Melingriffith employees, as membership lists included schoolmasters, farmers, skilled artisans, and a butler, while John Harford was among those who received payments. As with many similar friendly societies, discipline was enforced. Apart from fines, members could be expelled if they broke the rules or brought the club into disrepute, especially those who "curse, swear, game, offered to lay wagers, or use any indecent language." It is an interesting feature of the club that Quaker employers agreed that "every member shall go to Church or some other place of worship on Sundays at least between each meeting of the society," and attend the parish church on Easter Monday before they were allowed to enjoy themselves at the annual feast. Clearly, the Harfords did not impose their own religious beliefs on their employees.[73]

Payments were made to sick members and a salaried doctor looked after their health. This was an enormous benefit to the Harfords' workers and their families. Dr. Morgan was paid £20 in 1775 "for attending the Manufactory for one year," while even more generous provision was later in place at Ebbw Vale, where a surgeon was paid £500 per annum and another £400 at Sirhowy.[74] In order to qualify, Melingriffith members had to have been affiliated for two years, while the nature and duration of the illness, and the state of the clubs' finances at that particular time, determined relief payments. Members could receive a pension once they were sixty-five, while funeral costs of deceased members and their families were paid if the club's reserves allowed.[75] At Ebbw Vale, there were benefit clubs and a doctor's club. Between 1805 and 1832, the contributions to this organization increased significantly, from £104 to £501, and financial assistance was provided for other charitable organizations, such as the Women's Benefit Society at Rhyd-y-Blew.[76] In addition, workers and their families were provided with a school, library, and reading room. In 1786–87, measures were taken at Melingriffith to refit the school, and a new school, based on the Joseph Lancaster model, was founded in the early nineteenth century. In October 1807, the Harfords invited Lancaster to address the workers about establishing a school and collecting a subscription, including provision for girls, that reflected the egalitarian ethos of Quakerism.[77] The inhabitants (125 subscribers) gave generously and more than £19 was raised, including ten guineas donated by John Harford and his nephew Samuel (1766–1838). Lancaster commented, "I am glad there are such a number of Benevolent characters among you.... The youth will hold them in veneration ... [and bear] witness that the labour of virtue bringeth forth pleasure." Additional sums were raised, including £53 that enabled the school to operate during the final year that the Harfords were involved in the Melingriffith works.[78]

Little is known about any educational provision at Ebbw Vale and Sirhowy except that it was based on individual philanthropy or religious denominations or was centered on the industrial works. Clearly, by 1814 the Harfords had provided for the basic education of the children at their ironworks. The school accounts show expenditures amounting to £9 1s. between 1814 and 1815, which steadily increased annually and amounted to £28 2s. 9d. between 1817 and 1818. By then, the school was administered by the Lancastrian Society.[79] In a much later report conducted for the Children's Employment Commission in 1842, Rhys William Jones, the inspector, offered a statistical report concerning the reading and writing habits of children and young adults at the Sirhowy and Ebbw Vale ironworks (table 10.1).

Of the 533 children and young persons employed in the ironworks, there was an attempt to offer rudimentary reading skills to more than 50 percent (294), but a considerable proportion of those who had attended either day or Sunday schools were unable to write; only forty-six possessed that specific skill. Significantly, the statistics provide no details on female literacy rates; instead, a composite picture emerges of such attributes. Individual examinations provide some interesting, if somewhat dispiriting,

TABLE 10.1   Reading and writing habits of children and young adults at the Sirhowy and Ebbw Vale Ironworks, Monmouthshire, ca. 1842

Total number		Nature of employment	Number under 13 years		Number between 13 and 18 years		Number who can read	Number who can write	Number maimed or crippled	Number who have been to day-school	Number attending Sunday School	Remarks
M	F		M	F	M	F						
		Sirhowy										
13	14	At the blast furnaces	4	5	9	9	19	3	—	—	25	
90	90	At the colliery and mine works	27	7	63	83	71	5	—	2	115	
		Ebbw Vale							—			
27	22	At the blast furnaces	13	6	14	16	25	3	—	17	32	
136	12	At the rolling mill	66	4	70	8	100	20	—	70	115	
92	34	At the colliery and mine works	50	9	42	25	76	13	—	16	124	
3	—	At the engines, machines, &c.	—	—	3	—	3	2	—	3	1	
361	172		160	31	201	141	294	46	—	108	412	

Source: Reproduced from House of Commons, *Royal Commission on Children's Employment in Mines and Manufactories: First Report* [. . .] Part Two (London: House of Commons, 1842), 624.

assessments of their lives and abilities. Mary Ann Williams, age thirteen, had been at school "a little while and now go every Sunday, but cannot read." Her limited attendance can be explained by her long working day keeping a ventilation door open in the colliery for twelve hours for 4s. per week. This was essential work, as her father had been killed in a mining accident, and she had three younger siblings who were not employed. David Davies and Jacob Morgan, both age ten, Ann Morris, age twelve, and Hannah Hughes, age twenty-two, had not attended school and were unable to read. Jacob Morgan, who swept up the cinders at the Sirhowy works, had been working underground for two years. Clearly, for Jacob there was financial pressure to assist his father, as there were seven children in the household. Evan Evans, a young forge worker, was not sure of his age but was approximately eight years old. He had attended Sunday school and could "say the spelling of two letters," while John Williams, age fifteen, fared a little better in that he could read. John's examination provides a graphic illustration of the dangers associated with the employment of young children. He had been employed from the age of six at the forge, but when he was twelve years old, he lost his right arm. He explained to the inspector that it was "taken off near the socket. I was hooking up behind the rolls and [it] fell down and my arm was drawn in. I was a long time ill but am well now."[80] In the late 1840s, a few years after the Harfords had sold the business, commissioners reporting on the state of education in Wales offered a stark, if prejudicial, account of the educational provision in the area. In the 1848 report, the inspector stated that the day school was held "in a long, low, narrow room." The children read without any superintendence and the teacher had no assistant. Clearly, there was a rudimentary appreciation of how to read and write, while there was a limited knowledge of the Bible and the wider world. Indeed, it was recorded that "two thought the people in Scotland black, and two white, England was part of Wales, Ireland a town, the weeks in the year were 40, 60, 50 ... March had 21 days."[81]

Despite the limited educational provision and the arduous working conditions, the good relations between the Harfords and the wider community helped these Quaker industrialists avoid the mass demonstrations by workers during periods of depressed trade. Unlike the workforces at the Cyfarthfa and Nant-y-glo ironworks, where the workers were embittered by the harsh economic conditions imposed by their employers, the Harford workforce enjoyed much better conditions.[82] In the Commission on Children's Employment report of 1842, Frank Jowin, a surgeon, observed that although children were employed from an early age, they were "not overworked relative to the physical strength." He noted that they were generally "well formed, healthy and robust, and during the raging of fevers or epidemic diseases the mortality amongst them is small." He attributed this to their constitutions, the environmental conditions, and the use of ventilation in the ironworks. Significantly, he commended the quality of food and accommodation provided, stating: "I know of no class of labourers better housed than those attached to these and some of the neighbouring works."[83] As a result of the influx of migrant workers, there was a need for housing. At Nant-y-glo between 1793 and 1795, houses were "built into a bank and had three levels on the lower side but only two on the upper side. There were two houses in each unit, the lower house having just two rooms and a larder whilst the upper house was of two floors and had four rooms plus a larder."⁸⁴ More cottages with small gardens, communal washhouses, and bakehouses were built by the Harford family between 1810 and 1830 to accommodate their expanding workforce.⁸⁵ By 1824 they had built 103 cottages in Bedwellty parish, and by 1842 there were 407 cottages. A year later, the Harford accounts indicate that they owned 604 workmen's cottages and another six agent's houses in the Sirhowy valley.⁸⁶ The rents in 1824 were between 1s. 6d. and 2s. per week, which has been assessed at between 10 and 13 percent of a miner's income.⁸⁷

Alive to the need to improve food supplies for the burgeoning industrial community, the Harfords offered smallholdings near the ironworks in the understanding that the company received some of the produce.⁸⁸ In January 1800, a lease between Richard Summers Harford and John Davies of Trevethin (Pontypool) for Dyffryn farm at a yearly rental of twenty-five guineas stipulated that Davies was to offer "all Straw, Hay & Corn of every kind that he may wish to dispose of at a fair market price."⁸⁹ In February 1810, the company leased the Gwaun Helig, Llwynau, and Sychffoes farms in Bedwellty parish to Thomas Watkins, as long as he provided six horses to pull limestone trucks, did not sell any of his hay or straw, and left the farm in good repair at the end of his tenure. The following year, the tenancy was extended for seven years, during which time he was "to manage the land in a proper husbandlike manner—to improve the farms as much as lies in his power."⁹⁰ These reciprocal arrangements, especially the Harfords' "honest, if limited, concern for the security and well-being of the men they employed," helped forge harmonious relations in the community. Moreover, the works and the small holdings "ensured, even under the prevailing truck system an ample, fresh and healthy supply of food."⁹¹

As demonstrated at Melingriffith, the beneficence of the Harford family extended beyond their own workforce. In June 1817, Richard Summers Harford, together with other entrepreneurs (Joseph Bailey of Nant-y-glo and Benjamin Price of Abergavenny), agreed to "take upon themselves separately all expenses of paupers that are not parishioners and may actually become chargeable through or owing to the iron and coal works."⁹² Philanthropy, quite apart from donations for poor relief, can also be detected. Joseph Wood, in his account of his travels in Monmouthshire in 1813, described a visit to Monmouth gaol with Richard Summers Harford, Harford's wife, and Imm Trusted of Ross-on-Wye. They spoke to William Glover, who had "in a most cruel and barbarous manner murdered his father and mother." Glover had formerly been an employee of the Harfords' and had lived near their home. Yet although Glover had committed such a heinous crime, Harford spoke of his former good character, sobriety, and industry, especially his previous kindness to his mother. The four Friends then had "a religious opportunity" with him in the gaoler's house, where Glover fully acknowledged and regretted his action.[93]

Rapid industrialization after 1750 inevitably increased tensions in the Welsh valleys. Strikes were a commonplace means of expressing discontent at reductions in wages or potential unemployment, while the use of "tommy/truck" or company shops where laborers were forced to purchase poor-quality goods at inflated prices caused resentment. Riots were frequent, especially when the price of grain was artificially high or when grain was transported to other works despite local need. Moreover, the growing demand for democratic rights was given expression in violent outbursts against the unrepresentative and oppressive parliamentary system. The owners of these industrial centers forcibly challenged the growing solidarity of the working class.[94] And yet did the philanthropy of Quaker ironmasters, which benefited their workforce, the local community, and efforts to improve working and living conditions, mollify the rioters? The economic recession at the end of the Napoleonic Wars led to a fall in wages and considerable tension between the workers and the industrialists. In 1816 the blast furnaces at Ebbw Vale were forcibly stopped, but the agitators left peacefully after accepting the Harfords' terms.[95] After this date, however, even Harford property was not immune to attack. In the strike of May 1822, soldiers were deployed to ensure that coal reached the ironworks, and the Riot Act was read to stop any escalation of violence,[96] while in 1826 the Harfords were "obliged to put out our Furnaces at this place [Ebbw Vale] for 3 or 4 months."[97]

On other occasions, workers and Quaker industrialists reached amicable agreements, but in the summer of 1831, at the height of political unionism and the Great Reform Act campaign, the ironmasters and coal owners requested that troops be deployed to suppress riotous behavior. In contrast, the Quaker Joseph Tregelles Price and his cousins Edwin and Nathaniel Tregelles, at the Neath Abbey ironworks, sought to pacify their workforce and emphasized that joining unions and engaging in strikes would undermine cordial relations.[98] After all, Price had refused to employ child labor (or at least refused to employ children under the age of thirteen) in his works and outlawed the use of pernicious truck shops, demonstrating that he had the workers' "moral and social welfare at heart."[99] Heightened unrest in Merthyr (May–June 1831), which came hard on the heels of the French Revolution of 1830 and the reform campaign in Britain,[100] scared the authorities, especially when the red flag was raised in the town. In the ensuing days, the Argyll and Sutherland Highlanders sought to disperse the crowds and defend the property and lives of the industrialists. Violence erupted, and for more than a week Merthyr was in the hands of between seven thousand and ten thousand rioters.[101] A further wave of political protest and rioting threatened to engulf the whole of South Wales. In a letter to the vicar of Abergavenny on June 5, Charles Lloyd Harford (1799–1882) explained that the Merthyr workers were attempting to persuade the Ebbw Vale men to work only at the furnaces. He noted that "many of the Rioters are now armed" and expressed his view that "means should be provided for protection if required."[102]

By June 7 the Merthyr authorities had reasserted control and arrested twenty-six rioters identified as leaders of the armed insurrection. In the ensuing trial, they were sentenced to transportation, while two others, Lewis Lewis and Richard Lewis (Dic Penderyn), age twenty-three, received the death penalty. Price questioned the allegations of seditious violence leveled at the ringleaders and, although he did not condone their actions, he visited Penderyn in prison. Persuaded of his innocence, he solicited several witness statements and helped petition for clemency. Price's efforts were rewarded with an initial reprieve, but ultimately the sentence was carried out and Penderyn was hanged. This principled stand, although limited and by no means indicative of any deeper democratic impulse, was nonetheless based on an absolute commitment to the rights and liberties of the individual. In Penderyn's case, Price was determined to bring the matter to light. In so doing, he was following a tradition established by his coreligionists two hundred years earlier.[103] In the aftermath of the Merthyr rising and the failure of the Great Reform Act of 1832 to assuage working-class demands for democratic rights, greater emphasis was placed on asserting collective action. The Chartist movement emerged out of this disillusionment and gained considerable traction from the mid-1830s onward, as the Chartists articulated the opinions of the workforce in public gatherings and in the short-lived but influential newspaper the *Western Vindicator*.[104] These radical reformers' meetings were attended by the Harfords and other industrialists, but their motives were mixed.[105] At several meetings, Summers Harford (1795–1873) was cheered, but prior to the planned uprising in Newport in November 1839, there allegedly were plots to kill him.[106] In response to heightened tensions in the region, Summers had a police officer positioned at Ebbw Vale, but the failure to provide adequate surveillance prompted him to call for a countywide police force.[107] Significantly, as the Harfords became aware of rumors about planned attacks on ironmasters, various members of the family took remedial action, and on November 3, 1839, Charles Lloyd Harford and his wife, children, and servants, left Sirhowy for the safety of Cheltenham. As they left, Charles recalled that the furnaces had been extinguished and that there were "already assembled large masses of miners ... armed, ammunitioned, and ready for action."[108]

By 1842 the Ebbw Vale and Sirhowy Ironworks had 2,579 employees: 1,930 male adults (age eighteen and older), 116 female adults (age eighteen and older), 201 male and 141 female workers between the ages of thirteen and eighteen, and 160 male children and 31 female children under age thirteen.[109] Yet financing the Harford family business had been a constant battle since the mid-1820s. Overreliance on unsecured loans proved to be the catalyst for the collapse of the company; its debts amounted to nearly £450,000, while its liquid assets totaled only £93,000. The works were valued at this time at just £270,000.[110] It is difficult to ascertain how, given the Quaker business ethos concerning probity, they were able to trade at such high risk. Moreover, how did Quaker meetings, locally and nationally, sanction such uncertain activities?

The collapse of the Harford enterprise at Ebbw Vale largely reflected the lack of accessible capital during a severe economic depression. Like other industrial entrepreneurs, the Harfords had invested heavily in their businesses over several decades and had borrowed large sums. They were increasingly unable to pay off the principal sum and the annual interest and consequently became insolvent. In the light of Quaker business ethics, how should the Harfords be assessed? The sale catalogue suggests that there was plenty of coal and ironstone still available, a good transport system was in operation above and below ground, and a good level of bar iron was being produced (twenty-six tons annually). But given that the Harfords were carrying considerable debts on top of high wage bills, any downturn in the economy had a twofold effect. It squeezed profit margins and forced the Harfords either to reduce workers' wages or to lay workers off, which could result in rioting.[111] Moreover, the business had two mortgages totaling £95,000, with high interest rates on both; additional loans had been taken out to cover existing debts. This situation was exacerbated by the fierce competitiveness of other British ironmasters, while the Harfords suffered substantial financial losses in the early 1840s from their other business connections with Baltimore and Philadelphia. The *Monmouthshire Merlin* blamed the government for its "unwise" protectionist policies and the loss of free trade in the supply of iron to the American government. For the Harfords, this protectionist policy was truly catastrophic, and the company was forced into liquidation.[112] Eventually, in 1844, the Harfords' ironworks and collieries were sold for £216,000 to the Darbys of Coalbrookdale, who occupied the site until the mid-1860s. This was a bargain for the Darbys, as the site and all its associated properties had previously been estimated at £700,000.[113]

Finally, as this study has demonstrated, the Harfords invested heavily in the moral and social welfare of their workers and, crucially, in wider philanthropic activity. It could thus be argued that their investment in these policies came at a high cost. Once implemented, they could not be abandoned, which certainly added financial pressures. The reality was that their paternalistic business model was not sustainable in the long term given the highly competitive capitalist practices of the industry. It is a testament to their steadfast commitment to improving the quality of their workers' living and work conditions, including the provision of education, that the Harfords managed to provide such benefits for several decades. Yet the stark reality of the company's collapse in 1842 was laid bare in the *Monmouthshire Merlin*. On August 19, 1843, it reported that the company's weekly wage bill had been reduced from £2,090 to £1,787 for a four-day week, and that the overall workforce had been reduced by 340 positions, while more workers would soon lose their jobs as well. Indeed, a week later, the editor commented that in the harsh economic conditions of the 1840s, many former workers now faced "starvation, crime, disease and death." He observed that there was a "bond that exists between the master and his men . . . [which was] something more than employment."[114] Although the Harfords' businesses had failed by the time this editorial appeared, this was a sentiment that successive generations of the family had attempted to uphold through their initiatives in South Wales.

NOTES

1. Harrill's Sale Catalogue of the Ebbw Vale and Sirhowy Ironworks, April 18, 1844, MS PXM280.672.EBB, Newport Central Library, Wales.

2. For details, see Edgar L. Chappell, *Historic Melingriffith: An Account of Pentyrch Iron Works and Melingriffith Tinplate Works* (Cardiff: Priory Press, 1940). For the Harfords' business interests, see Maybery Collection, MSS I and II, NLW; Ebbw Vale Memorandum Book, 1796–1819, D2472.1, GWA; Ebbw Vale Letter Book, 1824–27, D2472.2, GWA; Ebbw Vale Steel, Iron and Coal Company Journal, 1791–96, 1814–15, D2472.3–4, GWA; Unknown Chancery Master's Exhibits, *Davies v. Harford*, Ebbw Vale and Sirhowy Ironworks, Monmouthshire, ledgers, 1809–13, 1817–20, 1824, 1827–30, C 114/124–27, NA.

3. Richard C. Allen, *Quaker Communities in Early Modern Wales: From Resistance to Respectability* (Cardiff: University of Wales Press, 2007). See also Thomas Mardy Rees, *A History of the Quakers in Wales and Their Emigration to North America* (Carmarthen, UK: W. Spurrell and Son, 1925); Arthur Raistrick, *Quakers in Science and Industry: Being an Account of the Quaker Contributions to Science and Industry During the Seventeenth and Eighteenth Centuries* (Newton Abbot: David and Charles, 1968), chap. 4.

4. Raistrick, *Quakers in Science and Industry*, 146–48; Amy Audrey Locke, *The Hanbury Family*, 2 vols. (London: Arthur L. Humphreys, 1916), 2:238–43.

5. Andrew Yarranton, *England's Improvement by Sea and Land* [...], 2 parts (London: T. Parkhurst and N. Simmons, 1681), part 2, 150–52.

6. Locke, *Hanbury Family*, 2:243–46, 249–53, 289. For further details of the Hanbury family, see Richard Hanbury Tenison, *The Hanburys of Monmouthshire* (Aberystwyth: National Library of Wales, 1995).

7. Reginald Nichols, *Pontypool and Usk Japanware* (Pontypool: Privately printed, 1981). For luxury goods, see Maxine Berg, *Luxury and Pleasure in Georgian Britain* (Oxford: Oxford University Press, 2005).

8. Lloyd family business interests are discussed in E. Ronald Morris, "The Dolobran Family in Religion and Industry in Montgomeryshire," *Montgomeryshire Collections* 56 (1959–60): 124–47; Humphrey Lloyd, *The Quaker Lloyds in the Industrial Revolution* (London: Hutchinson, 1975), 33, 39–40.

9. John Kelsall's diaries (1716–22, 1722–25, 1725–27), S186–88, LSF; Lloyd, *Quaker Lloyds*, 47–49, 52–53.

10. Thomas Southcliffe Ashton, *Iron and Steel in the Industrial Revolution* (Manchester: Manchester University Press, 1951), 13–16.

11. John Kelsall, "A Journal and Historical Account of the Chief Passages, Concerns and Exercises of My Life, 1700–1736," 194/1, 204, LSF.

12. Kelsall's diaries (1727–30), August 3, September 4, and November 17, 1727, January 6, 1728, S189, LSF; Lloyd, *Quaker Lloyds*, 55–56.

13. The letters are dated February 11, 1728, and October 23, 1728, S189, LSF; Kelsall, "Journal and Historical Account," 194/1, 234, LSF; Lloyd, *Quaker Lloyds*, 57–59.

14. Lloyd, *Quaker Lloyds*, 159–215.

15. Allen, *Quaker Communities*, chaps. 5 and 7.

16. Margaret Fay Williams, "Glamorgan Quakers, 1654–1900," *Morgannwg* 5 (1961): 73–74.

17. Chris Evans, "Global Commerce and Industrial Organisation in an Eighteenth-Century Enterprise: The Melingriffith Company," *Welsh History Review* 20, no. 3 (2001): 432–33.

18. For these developments, see Chappell, *Historic Melingriffith*, 30–37. For details of the Melingriffith works, see DMG Melingriffith Iron and Tinplate Works Records, 1770–1970, Glamorgan Archives (GA); Account Book, 1779–80, DX809, GA; Correspondence,

Accounts, Cash and Stock Books, c. 1769–Nineteenth Century, Trostre Collection, 19–49, Carmarthenshire Archive Service; Accounts and Production Records, 1779–1934, 1991/25, Welsh Industrial and Maritime Museum; Account Books, Correspondence, Historical Research Material, 1772–1948, Edgar Chappell Papers F1–9, NLW.

19. The family's business interests were located at Bassaleg, Machen, Tredegar, and Monmouth, and on the Welsh borders (Newent and New Weir). See Chappell, *Historic Melingriffith*, 37–38. The Harfords were initially Bristol merchants and soap makers. See Russell Mortimer, "Quakerism in Seventeenth Century Bristol" (master's thesis, University of Bristol, 1946); Peter Wakelin, "Harford, James (1734–1817)," *Oxford Dictionary of National Biography* (Oxford: Oxford University Press, 2004), http://www.oxforddnb.com/view/article/49071.

20. Evans, "Global Commerce," 428–32.

21. The associates included John, James, Samuel, and Richard Summers Harford, John Partridge of Monmouth, William Green of Bristol, Philip Crocker of Westbury-on-Trym, and several female shareholders, notably Alicia Calder, Sarah Davies, and Elizabeth Weaver. See Chappell, *Historic Melingriffith*, 43.

22. Ibid., 41–42.

23. Ibid., chap. 6; Raistrick, *Quakers in Science and Industry*, 149. Other Quakers were involved in this later partnership, including Richard Blakemore (Staffordshire), Thomas Pritchard (Ross-on-Wye), and Richard Jones Tomlinson (Bristol).

24. See Oliver Jones, *The Early Days of Sirhowy and Tredegar* (Risca: Starling Press, 1969), 47–49, 56–57; Arthur Gray-Jones, *A History of Ebbw Vale* (Risca: Starling Press, 1971); John Gwyn Davies, "Industrial Society in North-West Monmouthshire, 1750–1851" (PhD diss., Aberystwyth University, 1980), 2–28; Thomas E. Davies, "The Ironmasters, Ironworks, and People of the North West Monmouthshire Area, 1780–1850," (MPhil diss., Swansea University, 2008).

25. Jeremiah Homfray was the brother of Samuel (1762–1822), the owner of the Penydarren ironworks in Merthyr Tydfil.

26. The agreement with Homfray was ratified on July 6, 1792, in a deed of partnership. See John Lloyd, *Early History of the Old South Wales Ironworks, 1760–1840* (London: Bedford Press, 1906), 151–52.

27. Deed of Partnership, February 2, 1792, Maybery Collection, MS I, 254, NLW.

28. Harford, Partridge & Co. to Thomas Hill, April 12, 1793, Maybery Collection, MS II, 2793, NLW.

29. Assessment of two furnaces and mines at Nant-y-glo (£200), ibid., 2797.

30. Harford, Partridge & Co. to Thomas Hill, December 25, 1794, ibid., 2795; Chappell, *Historic Melingriffith*, 43; Lloyd, *Early History*, 166–67.

31. Dissolution of partnership with Jeremiah Homfray, April 30, 1796 (affidavit, May 12, 1796), Maybery Collection, MS I, 1908, NLW; "Observations of Jeremiah Homfray [. . .]," ca. 1791–94, ibid., 1910.

32. When the company purchased the Sirhowy ironworks outright in 1818, it increased the number of furnaces at the works to seven. See Frederick J. Ball, "The Development of the Iron Industry, 1780–1845," in Ball's unpublished and undated edited collection of essays (in author's possession) titled "Ebbw Vale," 43.

33. Ledgers, 1809–13, C 114/124, NA. See also Ball, "Development of the Iron Industry," 42, 50n30.

34. The use and development of tram roads by the Harfords and other ironmasters is discussed in Clifford Davies, "The Evolution of Industries and Settlements Between Merthyr Tydfil and Abergavenny from 1740–1840" (master's thesis, Aberystwyth University, 1949), 50–53.

35. See Thomas G. Grey-Davies, "Iron Bottom Rogers," *British Steelmaker* (April 1961): 124–25. A reference to this process may have been inferred in a letter written to the proprietors of the Wicker Ironworks, Sheffield, in July 1825 that stated, "We are using cast iron bottoms in our puddling Furnaces (upon our patent principle) to good effect." See Ebbw Vale Ironworks Co. to William and Edward Smith of Wicker Ironworks, Sheffield, July 21, 1825, Ebbw Vale Letter Book, 1824–27, D2472.2, 162, GWA.

36. Richard Summers Harford to Walter and John Powell, September 14, 1799, October 31, 1799, Maybery Collection, MS II, 3816, 3924, NLW.

37. "Sale Particulars and Plan of the Ebbw Vale and Sirhowy Iron Works, with a wharf at the shipping port of Newport," April 18, 1844, D.749.508, GWA; Oliver Jones, "The Sirhowy-Ebbw Vale Tunnel," *Presenting Monmouthshire* 31 (Spring 1971): 21–25.

38. Ebbw Vale Ironworks Co. to Solomon Chapman, Sunderland, June 1, 1824, Ebbw Vale Letter Book, 1824–27, D2472.2, 6, GWA.

39. See Richard Crawshay to Thomas Dadford, January 4, 1791, and Richard Crawshay to James Cockshutt, February 10, 1791, in *The Letterbook of Richard Crawshay, 1788–1797*, ed. Chris Evans (Cardiff: University of Wales Press, 1990), xix–xx, 90, no. 309, and 92, no. 319.

40. "Writ to Summon James Harford, John Partridge, Richard Summers Hartford, John Harford, Thomas Phillips and Robert Guest to answer Evan Harry," May 12, 1795, Maybery Collection, MS I, 1905, NLW; "Writ to Summon John Harford and Richard Rose to Answer Moses Davies in a Plea of Trespass at the Exchequer," May 12, 1795, ibid., 1906.

41. John Harford to John Powell, May 23, 1795, Maybery Collection, MS II, 2796, NLW. For other writs and settlements, see June 10 and July 8, 1795, ibid., 2798–99.

42. Richard Summers Harford to Walter Powell, January 15, 1818, February 9, 1818, July 31, 1819, ibid., 2800–2801, 3821; "Monmouth Assizes, Important Case: Harfords, Crocker, and Others v. Richard Fothergill," *Cambrian* (Swansea), August 29, 1818, 4.

43. *Barnard Versus Harford [...] 23 October 1837* (London: William Snell, 1838), M280, 672, Newport Central Library, Wales.

44. Craig W. Horle, *The Quakers and the English Legal System, 1660–1688* (Philadelphia: University of Pennsylvania Press, 1988); Erin Bell, "The Quakers and the Law," in *The Quakers, 1656–1723: The Evolution of an Alternative Community*, ed. Richard C. Allen and Rosemary Moore (University Park: Penn State University Press, 2018), 263–86.

45. January 13, 1809, January 2, 1811, Ebbw Vale Memorandum Book, 1796–1819, D2472.1, GWA. In 1824 these meetings were increasingly abandoned as the demand for iron increased. See Richard S. Harford to John Vaughan, Kidwelly, June 17, 1824 ("We have no metal to dispose of at this place or Sirhowy or should be happy to quote our price"); Richard S. Harford to Tarratt and Timmins, Lea Brook Iron Works, near Wednesbury, June 28, 1824 ("We have abandoned Quarterly Meetings of the Trade generally in this county and ... the probability of prices continuing as they are at present. The demand appears steady, but whether such as to warrant an advance the writer is not able to judge");

Richard S. Harford to Gilbert Cowan and Co., Glasgow, July 12, 1824 ("I am just returned from Merthyr where I attended a meeting of the Iron Masters adjourned from Newport"). See Ebbw Vale Letter Book, 1824–27, D2472.2, 29, 35 and 76, GWA. See also Davies, "Ironmasters, Ironworks, and People," 52–54.

46. See Karen Tibbals, "Early Quakers and 'Just Debt,'" in *Quakers and the Disciplines*, vol. 4, *Quakers, Business, and Industry*, ed. Stephen W. Angell and Pink Dandelion (Philadelphia: Friends Association for Higher Education, 2017), 133–68.

47. See ledgers, 1817–20, C 114/125, NA; "Draft agreement and bond between the Harfords and their partners and Jones, Jones, and Davies of Abergavenny Bankers for £30,000 and £40,000 to secure £17,366, etc.," November 14, 1822, D749/450-1, GWA.

48. Ball, "Development of the Iron Industry," 42. Between 1805 and 1815 there was a significant increase in the use of coal (66 percent), coke (49 percent), limestone (43 percent), and ore (13 percent).

49. Ball, "Development of the Iron Industry," 44–45, 51n, 53–59; "Meeting of the Ironmasters, Newport, December 3, 1836," in Madeleine Elsas, ed., *Iron in the Making: Dowlais Iron Company Letters, 1782–1860* (Cardiff: University of Wales Press, 1960), 12.

50. Ebbw Vale Ironworks Co. to Richard Rogers, Newport, May 20, 1824, Ebbw Vale Letter Book, 1824–27, D2472.2, 15, GWA; Arthur Gray-Jones, "Quaker Ironmasters in Monmouthshire (1796–1842)," *Welsh Outlook* 12 (February 1925): 42.

51. This concerned the purchase of oats. Ebbw Vale Ironworks Co. to Thomas Emery, Newport, November 3, 1827, Ebbw Vale Letter Book, 1824–27, D2472.2, 401, GWA.

52. Ebbw Vale Ironworks Co. to Thomas Powell, Newport, June 1, 1824, ibid., 19. Nevertheless, the deal was still in the balance, as the Harfords refused to pay the exorbitant prices for pit wood.

53. Ebbw Vale Ironworks Co. to Pierce and Shannon, Esq., Limerick, December 31, 1827, ibid., 416.

54. Ivor Wilks, *South Wales and the Rising of 1839: Class Struggle as Armed Struggle* (London: Croom Helm, 1984), 45.

55. For canal construction and development, see Robin Dean, "The Growth and Development of Monmouthshire Waterways," *Presenting Monmouthshire* 14 (Autumn 1962): 17–21.

56. Richard Summers Harford to John Powell, Brecon, June 25, 1798, Maybery Collection, MS I, 629, NLW.

57. "Reasons of Messrs. Harford, Partridge, and Company opposing certain Clauses of a Bill brought in by the Monmouthshire Canal Company" (ca. 1802), ibid., 803.

58. Richard Blackmore, on behalf of Harford, Partridge & Co. and himself, to W. and J. Powell, January 19, 1803, and "Writ to summon the proprietors of the Glamorganshire Canal Navigation to appear at the Exchequer to answer James Harford [. . .]," April 27, 1803, Maybery Collection, MS II, 2705, and MS I, 1917, respectively, NLW.

59. Brecknock and Abergavenny Canal Company, "Resolution of Committee as to Protecting Iron Matters," June 26, 1817, Maybery Collection, MS I, 984, NLW.

60. Quoted in Chappell, *Historic Melingriffith*, 41.

61. See list of laborers at Ebbw Vale, March 1796, Ebbw Vale Memorandum Book, 1796–1819, D2472.1, 8, GWA. For how working practices and workloads changed during British industrialization, see Chris Evans, "Work and Workloads During Industrialization: The Experience of Forgemen in the British Iron Industry, 1750–1850," *International Review of Social History* 44, no. 2 (1999): 197–215.

62. Ebbw Vale Ironworks Co. agreement with Jenkin Griffith, March 10–11, 1796, Ebbw Vale Memorandum Book, 1796–1819, D2472.1, 1, GWA.
63. John Harford (Ebbw Vale Ironworks Co.) agreement with John Miles, March 28, 1796, ibid., 2–3.
64. Ebbw Vale Memorandum Book, 1796–1819, passim.
65. Agreement between John Harford (Ebbw Vale Ironworks Co.) and Richard Walters, a mason, March 28, 1796, ibid., 3.
66. Agreement between Thomas Phillips, John Harford, and Thomas Williams, a carpenter, July 20, 1796, ibid., 38–39; Gray-Jones, "Quaker Ironmasters," 42–43.
67. In 1775, in a testimony against Owen Edwards of Pontypool, the Monmouthshire Friends noted that Edwards's heavy drinking had caused his business to collapse, leaving his wife destitute. See March 22, 1775, April 9, 1786, Monmouthshire Monthly Meeting minutes of the Religious Society of Friends (Quakers), 1745–91, D/DSF/354, GWA. See also Davies, "Industrial Society in North-West Monmouthshire," 288–90.
68. Agreement between John Harford (Ebbw Vale Ironworks Co.) and Richard Walters, a mason, March 28, 1796, Ebbw Vale Memorandum Book, 1796–1819, D2472.1, 3, GWA.
69. Agreement between John Harford (Ebbw Vale Ironworks Co.) and George Jones of Merthyr, May 19, 1796, ibid., 17–18.
70. Agreement between John Harford (Ebbw Vale Ironworks Co.) and Thomas Phillips, a laborer, 23 July 1796, ibid., 39–40.
71. Agreement between John Harford (Ebbw Vale Ironworks Co.) and John Morgan, a collier, March 28, 1796, ibid., 3–4.
72. "Parish of Bedwellty, Epiphany 1829, 1830, and 1839, Q. I[ndictments] & P[resentments]/ 208.0017," and "Q. I&P/217.0014; Q. I&P/258.0032," GWA. In the latter case, the men stole three pairs of Cossack boots (£1), six shawls (£2), twenty yards of calico (5s.), two half crowns (5s.), one hat (5s.), one cloth cap (2s.), monies (2s.), and other goods belonging to Richard Summers Harford.
73. Chappell, *Historic Melingriffith*, 45–48.
74. "Charles Lloyd Harford, Sirhowy, January 27, 1840," in Elsas, *Iron in the Making*, 73. See also individual accounts in Ebbw Vale Steel, Iron and Coal Company Journal, 1814–15, D2472.4, GWA. On July 1, 1814, William Steel, surgeon, was paid £23.2.0 (p. 2).
75. Chappell, *Historic Melingriffith*, 45–48.
76. Frederick J. Ball, "Wages and Labour Conditions," in Ball, "Ebbw Vale," 72. For the Women's Benefit Society, see Ebbw Vale Steel, Iron and Coal Company Journal, 1814–15, D2472.4, 2, GWA, where £31.7.9 was collected on July 1, 1814.
77. For examples, see Gillian Mason, "Quaker Women and Education, 1642–1840" (master's thesis, Lancaster University, 1987).
78. Chappell, *Historic Melingriffith*, 48–50 (Lancaster's letter quoted on 49).
79. Ledgers, 1817–20, C 114/125, NA.
80. House of Commons, *Royal Commission on Children's Employment in Mines and Manufactories: First Report* [. . .] *Part Two* (London: House of Commons, 1842), 625–26 (examination nos. 62–68).
81. House of Commons, *Reports of the Commissioners of Inquiry into the State of Education in Wales* [. . .] (London: House of Commons, 1848), 387–88.
82. Working conditions were also allegedly good for the workers at the Quaker-owned Neath Abbey ironworks. For details, see Richard C. Allen, "'An Indefatigable

Philanthropist': Joseph Tregelles Price (1784–1854) of Neath, Wales," *Quaker Studies* 23, no. 2 (2018): 219–37.

83. House of Commons, *Royal Commission on Children's Employment*, 624–25.

84. Davies, "Ironmasters, Ironworks, and People," 182, citing Jeremy B. Lowe, *Welsh Industrial Workers Housing, 1775–1875* (Cardiff: National Museum of Wales, 1985), 16–17.

85. See, for example, Ebbw Vale Steel, Iron and Coal Company Journal, 1814–15, D2472.4, 4, GWA. On July 1, 1814, the accounts recorded that the sums of £1484.19.10 and £1373.0.8 were spent for the "Row of Houses" at Hendre and Sychffoes.

86. For housing, social conditions, and Harford initiatives, see Davies, "Evolution of Industries and Settlements," 88–90; Frederick J. Ball, "Housing and the Industrial Revolution in Ebbw Vale," *Presenting Monmouthshire* 10 (Autumn 1960): 10–14.

87. Ball, "Housing and the Industrial Revolution," 11.

88. Lease for Dyffryn farm agreed between John Harford (Ebbw Vale Ironworks Co.) and Edmund Edmonds of Torcrug, June 28, 1796, Ebbw Vale Memorandum Book, 1796–1819, D2472.1, 28, GWA; Gray-Jones, "Quaker Ironmasters," 44. For details of Harford-owned farmlands, see Ebbw Vale Steel, Iron and Coal Company Journal, 1791–96, D2472.3, and 1814–15, D2472.4, GWA.

89. Lease for Dyffryn farm agreed between Richard Summers Harford (Ebbw Vale Ironworks Co.) and John Davies of Trevethin, January 23, 1800, Ebbw Vale Memorandum Book, 1796–1819, D2472.1 (unpaginated), GWA.

90. Lease for Gwaun Helig, Llwynau, and Sychffoes farms agreed between Richard Summers Harford and Thomas Watkins, February 15, 1810, August 24, 1811, ibid.

91. Gwaldus M. Tuckett, "Quaker Ironmasters in Monmouthshire (1793–1864)," *Wayfarer* 3, no. 11 (December 1928): 167.

92. Agreement dated June 11, 1817, and cited in Gray-Jones, *History of Ebbw Vale*, 65. Richard Summers Harford objected to a further obligation to pay the militia tax "on account of my religious principles."

93. Owen Parry, ed., "Welsh Quakers in the Light of the Joseph Wood Papers," *Bulletin Board of Celtic Studies* 25, no. 2 (1972–74): 179. Regrettably, Glover committed suicide in prison in November 1813. See *Cambrian* (Swansea), November 20, 1813, 3.

94. David J. V. Jones, *Before Rebecca: Popular Protests in Wales, 1793–1835* (London: Allen Lane, 1973); Chris Evans, *The Labyrinth of Flames: Work and Social Conflict in Early Industrial Merthyr Tydfil* (Cardiff: University of Wales Press, 1993).

95. "Monmouthshire, Newport, Oct. 22," *Times* (London), October 26, 1816, 3. Details of the riot are provided in "To the Editor of the Cambrian [. . . from] a Friend to Justice, Abergavenny, 23 October 1816," *Cambrian* (Swansea), November 2, 1816, 3.

96. "Riots in Monmouthshire," *Cambrian* (Swansea), May 11, 1822, 3. The following week, however, half a mile of tram road was damaged. See "Riots in Monmouthshire," *Cambrian* (Swansea), May 18, 1822, 3.

97. Ebbw Vale Ironworks Co. to William Yalden and Company, Llanelli, August 31, 1826, Ebbw Vale Letter Book, 1824–27, D2472.2, 279, GWA.

98. "Another Account," *Cambrian* (Swansea), June 11, 1831, 3; "Union Clubs: Advantages of Open and Friendly Discussion Between Masters and Men," October 1, 1831, ibid., 3. Charles Lloyd Harford followed Price's example, as he and other industrialists in South Wales would dismiss any worker affiliated with a union.

99. George Eaton, *Joseph Tregelles Price, 1784–1854: Quaker Industrialist and Moral Crusader* (Neath: Glamorgan Press, 1987), 19.

100. See Nancy D. LoPatin, *Political Unions, Popular Politics, and the Great Reform Act of 1832* (Basingstoke: Macmillan 1999); John E. Archer, *Social Unrest and Popular Protest in England, 1780–1840* (Cambridge: Cambridge University Press, 2000); Katrina Navickas, *Protest and the Politics of Space and Place, 1789–1848* (Manchester: Manchester University Press, 2015).

101. Gwyn A. Williams, *The Merthyr Rising* (London: Croom Helm, 1978; repr., Cardiff: University of Wales Press, 1988).

102. Charles Lloyd Harford to the vicar of Abergavenny, June 5, 1831, Home Office, 52/16 (426), NA.

103. See Allen, "'Indefatigable Philanthropist,'" 230–33. I am grateful to the editors of *Quaker Studies* for allowing this discussion to be reproduced here.

104. See David Williams, *John Frost: A Study in Chartism* (Cardiff: University of Wales Press, 1939), 100, 104, 107, and wider assessments in David J. V. Jones, *The Last Rising: The Newport Insurrection of 1839* (Oxford: Clarendon Press, 1984); Wilks, *South Wales and the Rising*; and Malcolm Chase, *Chartism: A New History* (Manchester: Manchester University Press, 2007).

105. On April 23, 1839, for example, "Crozier" (presumably Crawshay) Bailey, ironmaster of Nant-y-glo, wanted Henry Vincent, the Chartist spokesman and editor of the *Western Vindicator*, thrown in a pond after Vincent had held a meeting at Blaenau, Monmouthshire. See "The Life and Rambles of Henry Vincent," *Western Vindicator* (Monmouth), May 4, 1839, 3.

106. "Chartist Meeting at Tredegar," *Monmouthshire Merlin*, May 4, 1839, 3; "Chartist Meeting at Coalbrook Vale," ibid., May 25, 1839, 3; "Chartist Meeting at Blackwood," ibid., July 13, 1839, 4; "The Queen v. John Owen; The Evidence of John Thomas and David Jones, December 31, 1839," Chartists "Special Commission" Trials, vol. 13, doc. 105, 3–4, Newport Central Library, Wales.

107. "Tredegar Police," *Glamorgan, Monmouth and Brecon Gazette and Merthyr Guardian*, August 25, 1838, 3; "Constabulary Act," *Monmouthshire Merlin*, January 4, 1840, 3.

108. See Wilks, *South Wales and the Rising*, 192–93, citing Mayor (Thomas) Dyke to the home secretary, Monmouth, November 4, 1839, Treasury Solicitor and Her Majesty's Procurator General, Papers, 11/500, NA; for an account of the proceedings, see *Monmouthshire Beacon*, November 9, 1839, 3, col. 3.

109. House of Commons, *Royal Commission on Children's Employment*, 46. Additionally, nearly six thousand people were dependent on the works—1,847 at Sirhowy and 3,931 at Ebbw Vale.

110. Davies, "Ironmasters, Ironworks, and People," 144–45; and, all in the *Monmouthshire Merlin*, "The Bankruptcy of the Ebbw Vale and Sirhowy Iron Company," June 30, 1843, 4; "Advertising," July 8, 1843, 1; and "Harford, Davis, and Co.'s Bankruptcy," August 19, 1843, 3.

111. Harrill's Sale Catalogue of the Ebbw Vale and Sirhowy Ironworks; Ball, "Development of the Iron Industry," 52n87, citing correspondence from Edwin Chadwick, July 11, 1843, 45/454, NA.

112. "Failure of Messrs. Harfords and Davies," *Monmouthshire Merlin*, June 17, 1843, 3; "The State of South Wales," ibid., July 1, 1843, 3; Davies, "Ironmasters, Ironworks, and People," 65.

113. "Advertisement: The Ebbw Vale & Sirhowy Iron Works, Monmouthshire," and "Harford's Bankruptcy," both in *Monmouthshire Merlin*, March 30, 1844, 1 and 3,

respectively; Harrill's Sale Catalogue of the Ebbw Vale and Sirhowy Ironworks. In July 1841, the Harfords had attempted to sell the two ironworks for £500,000 to the Guests of Dowlais, Merthyr Tydfil. See Ball, "Development of the Iron Industry," 47, citing *Lady Charlotte Guest: Extracts from Her Journal, 1833–1852*, ed. Vere Brabazon Ponsonby, Earl of Bessborough (London: John Murray, 1950), 124.

114. "Harford, Davis, and Co.'s Bankruptcy," *Monmouthshire Merlin*, August 19, 1843, 3; "Landlords, Tenants, Master-Miners, and Workmen," editorial, ibid., August 26, 1843, 3.

Conclusion

ROBYNNE ROGERS HEALEY

The essays in this volume provide us with a number of insights into Quakerism in the transatlantic world in the long eighteenth century. First, this Quaker world was a diverse place. Certainly, many factors unified the Quaker Atlantic. Friends and non-Quakers could expect to move from one Quaker community to another and find familiar aspects of Quakerism. Many of the testimonies outlined in each yearly meeting's book of discipline were similar. And the structure of Quaker church government was analogous. The hierarchical organization of meetings created by George Fox's "Gospel Order" provided a well-ordered structure replicated around the Atlantic world. The smallest units, or local congregations (particular meetings in Britain and preparative meetings in North America), were organized under the authority of local monthly meetings. Monthly meetings were gathered into regional quarterly meetings, and the quarterly meetings came under the authority of a yearly meeting. In all cases, business flowed up or down from one level to another through representatives and documents such as responses to the queries or epistolary correspondence. The yearly meetings also had administrative meetings, such as meetings for sufferings, that managed their affairs when the yearly meeting itself was not in session.

This structure provided stability and a measure of uniformity to the Atlantic Quaker world.

Quakers could move, as travelers or settlers, through this Quaker world and expect to find consistency in the expression of their faith. Eighteenth-century Quaker worship was generally silent. While meetings for worship were punctuated by spoken ministry, the nature of ministerial exhortation and the delivery of those messages had changed significantly from the Quakerism of the first and second periods. Quaker communities shared a number of common ideals: the practice of simplicity or plainness; a commitment to endogamy, or marriage within the faith; arrangements to facilitate child-rearing and education to produce faithful, gainfully employed Friends; refusal to pay tithes or swear oaths; care for the poor and persecuted; and a shared obligation to Quaker discipline. Local communities were connected to the larger Quaker network through the traveling ministry, epistolary correspondence, and Quaker publications. Through means such as yearly meetings, beginning with the London Yearly Meeting (LYM), Friends worked to create and sustain unity among Quakers in an ever-enlarging space. Erica Canela and Robynne Rogers Healey's chapter demonstrates how yearly meetings used one kind of Quaker writing to enforce uniform behavior and piety among Friends, particularly the young. The evolution of memorial testimonies over the century demonstrates their development as a form of Quaker literature that connected Friends to their spiritual ancestors. At the same time, the memorials' focus on discipline reveals that eighteenth-century Quakers increasingly found assurance of their redemption in conformity to the discipline, or in how they behaved, rather than in what they believed. The Quaker family became the site for socialization into this disciplined world of Quaker faith and practice, as is evident in Emma Lapsansky-Werner's chapter.

Belief and behavior are also at the center of Elizabeth Cazden's exploration of the testimony of inequality. Although Quakers today consider equality one of the core tenets of their faith, Cazden's case study of New England Friends reveals that most eighteenth-century Quakers neither endorsed nor practiced social, economic, or political equality, accepting the hierarchically structured world of their contemporaries. At the same time, Lapsansky-Werner's chapter points to the long eighteenth century as the period during which the aspirations of early Friends and the quest for human perfection were codified. Through this process, Quakers formed an identity based on a shared set of ideals that endures to this day.

Despite the similarities across the Atlantic world, there were differences. Jon Mitchell's examination of three methods of Quaker worship in this period reveals that the practice of silence in Quaker meetings was not always the same, both within and between meetings. As eighteenth-century Quakers sought a relationship with the divine that echoed the confident experience of early Friends, they adopted and adapted contemplative practices used by other Christians. These practices were themselves shaped by the theological context in which they were formed, giving rise to theological and doctrinal diversity in the transatlantic Quaker world. In the same way, the diverse needs and experiences of local Quaker communities made it impossible for Quakerism to be identical from meeting to meeting. We have seen, for instance, in Andrew Fincham's comparison of the books of discipline for the LYM and the Philadelphia Yearly Meeting (PYM) that disciplines developed in response to local situations within meetings. Fincham's work also points to the decision of yearly meetings to impose more uniformity of behavior in the last part of the long eighteenth century in an effort to "purify" the Religious Society of Friends.

The impact of local circumstances on expressions of Quakerism is presented in many of these essays, but especially in the three chapters that make up the final section of this book. Geoff Plank's work highlights some of the paradoxes evident in eighteenth-century Quakerism. Quaker reverence for English pastoral spaces, where early Friends had encountered God in a powerful way, complicated their relationship with the North American wilderness and the Indigenous people who inhabited it. Plank indicates the ways in which Quakers participated in the British and American colonizing enterprises, showing that Quaker reformers like Anthony Benezet insisted that the North American wilderness "produced good people," a position at odds with Quakers in London, who contended that the North American wilderness "made the Indigenous people cruel." His conclusions, like Cazden's, complicate the way we understand the Quaker testimony of equality. The chapters by Sydney Harker, Robynne Rogers Healey, and Richard Allen give us insights into the lived experiences of Quakerism in communities on the margins of the Quaker world. These communities were similar to Quaker communities elsewhere, as is evident in the template of Quaker organization that forged frontier Upper Canadian Quaker meetings and the Harfords' investment in the moral and social welfare of their workers. Even so, immediate contexts had an impact. Quakers in Upper Canada adapted their community-building strategies within the context of the discipline to accommodate the political, economic, and social circumstances in which they lived and worshipped. Similarly, the Quaker business practices that had created a large group of wealthy merchants and entrepreneurs were powerless in the face of the severe economic depression experienced by Welsh Friends at the end of the long eighteenth century.

The effect of local expressions of Quakerism relates to the second insight provided by these essays. Influence between Quaker metropoles and peripheries flowed both ways; influence also flowed between metropoles and, increasingly, between meetings on overlapping peripheries. The template of Quaker community organization provided a model for community development and fostered the physical expansion of the Religious Society of Friends. As Quakers spread throughout the Atlantic world, superior meetings imposed a structure that promoted the growth of strong faith communities. Even so, as has been shown, each meeting interpreted the frameworks within which it formed its communities. A diverse set of factors, including location, individual personalities, and events, played significant roles in individual meetings and in how those meetings navigated the growing Quaker network. While the LYM remained the recognized center of Atlantic Quakerism, North American yearly meetings became metropoles themselves. What emerged in the long eighteenth century was a complex constellation of centers and peripheries, each influencing the other in an attempt to maintain Quaker unity. At the start of the period, correspondence between the colonial meetings all moved through the LYM. For instance, when the PYM wanted to know the practice of Friends in other British colonies, it asked the LYM to gather this information: "we take ye Freedom to acquaint you that our request unto you was that you would be pleased to consult or advise with Friends in other plantations where they are more numerous than with us, because they hold a correspondence wth you & not with us, and your meeting may better prevail wth ym and your advice prove more effectual."[1] After the American Revolution, the American yearly meetings maintained their correspondence with the LYM, but they also began an annual epistolary correspondence with one another.

Complex layers of marginalization and authority operated both within the Quaker network itself and in relationships between Quakers and mainstream society. This is evident in examinations of Quakers who lived in Quaker centers, as shown by Erin Bell's and Rosalind Johnson's analyses of London records. Bell's comparison of representations of Quakers and Jews (both religious minorities) in Old Bailey records indicates that fear of religious nonconformity affected depictions of Quakers. Stock representations of Quakers in legal proceedings, whether criminal or civil (as in the case of marriage), placed Friends outside the social or political center. This continued despite Quakers' own efforts, supported by a persistent and at times effective lobby, to present themselves as respectable citizens who were also a "peculiar people." The tension that Bell and Johnson identify between these conflicting representations highlights the importance of understanding the consequences of perceptions of identity that shifted over time and place and from different perspectives, both Quaker and non-Quaker.

Those who lived on geographic peripheries could navigate their relationship with mainstream society according to a different set of regulations, or the same set of regulations that functioned differently in an altered environment. The collection of tithes, for instance, was not as pressing an issue for Quakers living on the edge of empire as it was for those at its centers. On the other hand, the testimony against war took primacy of place for those who lived in the direct line of armed conflict. Similarly, concerns over legal recognition of Quaker weddings and the legitimacy of the children born of a Quaker marriage functioned differently around the Quaker Atlantic. Marriage was fundamentally important to all Quakers; the commitment to the principle of endogamy did not vary from meeting to meeting. Even so, the capacity to work within the parameters established by the discipline depended on several factors. Distance from a meeting that had the authority to approve marriages and the means to fulfill traditional committee obligations meant that superior meetings had to choose between applying the organizational model unchanged and revising the template to accommodate particular needs. To this end, superior meetings were willing to relinquish their authority to approve marriages for some very small meetings so as to create optimal conditions for following the discipline.

Circumstances at the periphery shaped both the structure of Quaker organization and important testimonies. Consider women's meetings. Women had played a critical role in George Fox's religious experiences and in the foundation and survival of the Society of Friends. Early in the history of Quakers, women's meetings such as the Two Weeks' Meeting and the Box Meeting were established, although both meetings were restricted to charitable work. Fox had urged Friends to establish parallel women's and men's meetings at every level, a position not embraced by all Quakers. The Wilkinson-Story controversy of the 1670s, which resulted in a minor schism, was a response to both the decision to allow women's meetings and to Foxian centralization. The LYM Women's Meeting was not established until 1784. North American yearly meetings, by contrast, established parallel women's meetings at every level from the start. Similarly, where English meetinghouses originally allotted a small gallery, loft, or shed for women's meetings, colonial meetinghouses were constructed with roughly equal space for women.[2] The allocation of equal space for men's and women's meetings, which resulted in what is now accepted as the standard rectangular design of Quaker meetinghouses, originated in mid-eighteenth-century urban Philadelphia.[3] In some cases, English customs affected the size and shape of the meetinghouse; in others, necessity was the governing factor. Significantly, the influences that governed meeting practices were not unidirectional.

The impact of Quaker peripheries on Quaker metropoles is especially evident in the testimonies on slaveholding and war. We have established that Quakers in the long eighteenth century profited from the institution of slavery. Quakers owned slaves and participated in the sale of slaves and the products of their labor. But it was Quakers on the periphery—those who worked and lived in the British colonies, and witnessed the impact of slavery and the slave trade—not those at the center, who first questioned Quakers' position on slavery and the slave trade. This is borne out in the different number of advices with this focus contained in the LYM Discipline (one) and the PYM Discipline (twenty-one), as itemized in table 3.1 in Fincham's chapter in this volume. Clearly, members of the PYM, which included Friends in New Jersey, were more exercised about slavery and the slave trade than were members of the LYM. This is notable given that in 1732, when Benjamin Lay arrived in Philadelphia, "more than half the members of the Philadelphia Monthly Meeting owned slaves."[4] Lay's attacks on powerful slaveholding Philadelphia Quakers between 1732 and his death in 1759 have earned him the title of "the first revolutionary abolitionist." Certainly, Lay challenged power dynamics within the PYM and played a significant role in shifting Philadelphia Quakers' attitudes about the trade. By 1754, the PYM had formally endorsed a position against the holding of slaves, publishing John Woolman's abolitionist pamphlet *Some Considerations on the Keeping of Negroes*. The LYM followed suit and in 1758 issued a printed epistle condemning "the iniquitous practice of dealing in negroes, or other slaves" and any Quaker participation in "this unrighteous gain of oppression."[5]

Quakers did not move quickly or easily to their position against slaveholding. Meeting records show that the PYM was seeking guidance on the question of slavery and slaveholding from the beginning of the period under study. Consider the following excerpt from the 1712 PYM epistle to the LYM:

> And now dear Friends we impart unto you a concern yt hath rested upon the mind of some of our Brethren for many years. Touching ye importing and having of negro slaves and detaining them and their posterity as such without any limitation or time of redemption from that condition—this matter was laid before this meeting many years ago and the thing in some degree discouraged, as may appear by a minute of our yearly meeting 1696, desireing all merchants & traders professing Truth Truth [sic] amongst us to write to their correspondents that they send no more negroes to be disposed of as above yet notwithstanding as our settlements increased so other traders flocked in amongst us over whom we had no Gospel authority and such love increased and multiplied negroes amongst us to ye grief of divers Friends whom we are willing to ease if ye way might appear clear to ye satisfaction of ye general and it being again last yearly meeting again moved and friends in divers other provinces being more concerned in it than those we thought it rather too weighty to come to a full conclusion therein[.] This meeting desires therefore your assistance by way of advice and council, yt which if you will be pleased to take into your weighty consideration after having advised wth ye Friends of ye other American provinces we hope we shall have a due regard unto your advice and council.[6]

Two years later, in 1714, the PYM again requested guidance from the LYM about the owning and selling of slaves, and reminded their London brethren that they had asked the LYM to consult with other meetings with which PYM did not traditionally correspond.[7]

In 1727, the PYM asked the LYM whether the slave trade was consistent with Quaker principles. The LYM responded, "the importing of negroes from their native country and relations by friends, is not a commendable nor allowed practice, and is therefore censured by this meeting."[8] This advice was sent to the PYM but was not circulated to other meetings until the 1750s, when it appeared in the *Book of Extracts*. Until the middle of the century, when yearly meetings took clear positions on slavery and disownment for participation in the practice, "moral discomfort about slavery coexisted with a reluctance to challenge it."[9] Midcentury reformation of Quakerism in both North America and the United Kingdom was a significant factor in pushing yearly meetings to articulate stronger opposition to slavery. Even so, as Elizabeth Cazden has argued, "slavery was treated as an American problem." British meetings rarely disciplined slave traders, and even though the LYM praised American abolition efforts, it refused to campaign for abolition of the trade, despite the PYM's appeals for British involvement.[10] American Quaker involvement in abolition continued to expand. After the American Revolution, the presence of younger Friends in leadership positions in the LYM, and the presence of American abolitionist ministers at yearly meeting sessions, created an opportunity for action. The 1783 LYM decided to petition the House of Commons to end the slave trade. Thereafter, Quakers in the LYM did take an active role in abolition. While the Quaker metropole of London became an important center of antislavery activism in the British Empire, the momentum to clarify this testimony, so central to Quaker identity and witness, emerged not in the center but on the periphery.

The Quaker position on war took shape from a similar dialectic between the peripheries and centers. Decisions to wage the eighteenth-century wars of empire were made at the center. The wars themselves were often waged outside imperial metropoles, where Quaker positions on war were neither clear nor consistently interpreted. Friends actively involved in Atlantic commerce stood to profit from the sale of military wares and privateering. Sharpening the line between martial and nonmartial activities resulted in ongoing revision of the testimony against war. By the French Revolutionary Wars of the 1790s, the LYM was insisting that all Friends stay out of war and war-related activities. The accomplishment of a strict pacifist position, another defining testimony for Quakers, was the result of pressure from the periphery on the center.

Finally, the third conclusion highlighted by the preceding chapters is that the transatlantic world changed significantly over the course of the long eighteenth century. Doctrinal controversies bracket this era. Following the Keithian controversy, the bounds of Quaker orthodoxy were generous. Eighteenth-century Quakerism allowed for considerable theological flexibility, reinforced by the focus on behavioral uniformity. This changed as the century progressed. As yearly meetings underwent reformation, they focused more on enforcing behavioral uniformity. This in turn produced an emphasis on the primacy of theological uniformity. Reform "purified" the Society, but the retreat into sectarianism made Quakerism less tolerant of difference. The Hicksite-Orthodox Schism that concluded the long eighteenth century was both acrimonious and extensive. It divided much of North American Quakerism and unsettled that which it did not divide. The depth of disagreement between the factions and the geographic magnitude of the schism had a critical impact on the Religious Society of Friends. Separation became a way of addressing conflict, as is evident in the ongoing religious schisms in nineteenth-century Quakerism. Moreover, the meddling of the LYM and English Quakers in the North American conflict marked the end of the close relationship between the meetings on opposite sides of the Atlantic. The LYM refused to acknowledge the Hicksite yearly meetings, breaking the connection between North American Hicksites and Britain. And while the Orthodox meetings maintained correspondence with the LYM, the relationship was weakened.

The Religious Society of Friends emerged from the long eighteenth century reduced in numbers but not in its commitment to the battle against evil in oneself and in the world. The essays in this volume have examined the diverse, paradoxical, and transformed world of transatlantic eighteenth-century Quakers. It has not been possible to capture the entirety of this long period of Quakerism spread across a vast geographical space. We have asked new questions. We have both challenged and endorsed traditional interpretations. Most important, we hope we have opened space for further research and dialogue.

NOTES

1. LYM, Epistles Received, 1–2 (1683–1738), Pennsylvania Epistle, 1714, LSF.
2. Margaret Hope Bacon, *Mothers of Feminism: The Story of Quaker Women in America* (San Francisco: Harper and Row, 1986), 46.
3. Catherine C. Lavoie, "Quaker Beliefs and Practices and the Eighteenth-Century Development of the Friends Meeting House in the Delaware Valley," in *Quaker Aesthetics: Reflections on a Quaker Ethic in American Design and Consumption, 1720–1920*, ed. Emma Lapsansky-Werner and Anne A. Verplanck (Philadelphia: University of Pennsylvania Press, 2003), 161–63.
4. Marcus Rediker, *The Fearless Benjamin Lay: The Quaker Dwarf Who Became the First Revolutionary Abolitionist* (Boston: Beacon Press, 2017), 56.
5. LYM, *Extracts from the Minutes and Advices of the Yearly Meeting of Friends Held in London* (London: J. Phillips, 1783), 227.

6. LYM, Epistles Received, 1–2 (1683–1738), Pennsylvania Epistle, 1712, LSF.
7. Pennsylvania Epistle, 1714, ibid.
8. LYM, *Extracts from the Minutes and Advices*, 227.
9. Elizabeth Cazden, "Quakers, Slavery, Anti-Slavery, and Race," in *The Oxford Handbook of Quaker Studies*, ed. Stephen W. Angell and Pink Dandelion (Oxford: Oxford University Press, 2013), 350.
10. Ibid., 352–53.

SELECTED BIBLIOGRAPHY

Allen, Richard C. *Quaker Communities in Early Modern Wales: From Resistance to Respectability*. Cardiff: University of Wales Press, 2007.

Allen, Richard C., and Rosemary Moore, eds. *The Quakers, 1656–1723: The Evolution of an Alternative Community*. University Park: Penn State University Press, 2018.

Angell, Stephen W., and Pink Dandelion, eds. *Early Quakers and Their Theological Thought, 1647–1723*. Cambridge: Cambridge University Press, 2015.

———, eds. *The Oxford Handbook of Quaker Studies*. Oxford: Oxford University Press, 2013.

Barbour, Hugh. *The Quakers in Puritan England*. New Haven: Yale University Press, 1964.

Barbour, Hugh, and J. William Frost. *The Quakers*. New York: Greenwood Press, 1988.

Barclay, Robert. *An Apology for the True Christian Divinity: Being an Explanation and Vindication of the Doctrines of the People Called the Quakers*. 1678. Reprint, Glenside, PA: Quaker Heritage Press, 2002.

Beck, William, and T. Frederick Ball. *The London Friends' Meetings*. London: F. Bowyer Kitto, 1869. Reprinted with a new introduction by Simon Dixon and Peter Daniels. London: Pronoun Press, 2009.

Bell, Erin. "Eighteenth-Century Quakerism and the Rehabilitation of James Nayler, Seventeenth-Century Radical." *Journal of Ecclesiastical History* 59, no. 3 (2008): 426–46.

Bellers, John. *Watch unto Prayer, or Considerations for All Who Profess They Believe in the Light*. London, 1760.

Benezet, Anthony. *Some Observations on the Situation, Disposition, and Character of the Indian Natives of This Continent*. Philadelphia: Printed and sold by Joseph Crukshank, 1784.

Besse, Joseph. *A Collection of the Sufferings of the People Called Quakers*. 2 vols. London: Luke Hinde, 1753.

Birkel, Michael. *Silence and Witness: The Quaker Tradition*. New York: Orbis Books, 2004.

Braithwaite, William C. *The Beginnings of Quakerism*. London: Macmillan, 1912. 2nd ed., Cambridge: Cambridge University Press, 1955.

———. *The Second Period of Quakerism.* London: Macmillan, 1919. 2nd ed., Cambridge: Cambridge University Press, 1961.

Brock, Peter. *Pacifism in the United States: From the Colonial Era to the First World War.* Princeton: Princeton University Press, 1968.

———. *The Quaker Peace Testimony, 1660 to 1914.* York, UK: Sessions Book Trust, 1990.

Brook, Mary. *Reasons for the Necessity of Silent Waiting, in Order to the Solemn Worship of God: To Which Are Added, Several Quotations from Robert Barclay's Apology.* London: Mary Hinde, 1775.

Brown, Christopher Leslie. *Moral Capital: Foundations of British Abolitionism.* Chapel Hill: University of North Carolina Press, 2006.

Carey, Brycchan. *From Peace to Freedom: Quaker Rhetoric and the Birth of American Antislavery, 1657–1761.* New Haven: Yale University Press, 2012.

Carey, Brycchan, and Geoffrey Plank, eds. *Quakers and Abolition.* Urbana: University of Illinois Press, 2014.

Comly, John. *Journal of the Life and Religious Labors of John Comly, Late of Byberry, Published by His Children.* Philadelphia: T. E. Chapman, 1854.

Crabtree, Sarah. *Holy Nation: The Transatlantic Quaker Ministry in an Age of Revolution.* Chicago: University of Chicago Press, 2015.

Dandelion, Pink. "Guarded Domesticity and Engagement with 'the World': The Separate Spheres of Quaker Quietism." *Common Knowledge* 16, no. 1 (2010): 95–109.

Densmore, Christopher, ed. "Indian Religious Beliefs on Long Island: A Quaker Account." *New York History* 73, no. 4 (1992): 431–41.

Densmore, Christopher, and Albert Schrauwers, eds. "*The Best Man for Settling New Country . . .*": *The Journal of Timothy Rogers.* Toronto: Canadian Friends Historical Association, 2000.

Dixon, Simon. "Quakers and the London Parish, 1670–1720." *London Journal* 32, no. 3 (2007): 229–49.

Dunn, Richard S., and Mary Maples Dunn, eds. *The Papers of William Penn.* 5 vols. Philadelphia: University of Pennsylvania Press, 1981–87.

———, eds. *The World of William Penn.* Philadelphia: University of Pennsylvania Press, 1986.

Eiler, Ross E. Martinie. "Luxury, Capitalism, and the Quaker Reformation, 1737–1798." *Quaker History* 97, no. 1 (2008): 11–31.

Forbes, Susan S. "Quaker Tribalism." In *Friends and Neighbors: Group Life in America's First Plural Society*, edited by Michael W. Zuckerman, 145–73. Philadelphia: Temple University Press, 1982.

Fox, George. *The Journal of George Fox.* Edited by John L. Nickalls. Cambridge: Cambridge University Press, 1952.

Frost, J. William. "Quaker Antislavery: From Dissidence to Sense of the Meeting." *Quaker History* 101, no. 1 (2012): 12–33.

———. *The Quaker Family in Colonial America: A Portrait of the Society of Friends.* New York: St. Martin's Press, 1973.

———, ed. *The Quaker Origins of Antislavery.* Norwood, PA: Norwood Editions, 1980.

Gallup-Diaz, Ignacio, and Geoffrey Plank, eds. *Quakers and Native Americans.* Leiden: Brill, 2019.

Gragg, Larry. *The Quaker Community on Barbados: Challenging the Culture* of the Planter Class. Columbia: University of Missouri Press, 2009.

Greene, Jack P., ed. *Creating the British Atlantic: Essays on Transplantation, Adaptation, and Continuity*. Charlottesville: University of Virginia Press, 2013.

———. *Peripheries and Center: Constitutional Development in the Extended Polities of the British Empire and the United States, 1607–1788*. New York: W. W. Norton, 1990.

Healey, Robynne Rogers. *From Quaker to Upper Canadian: Faith and Community Among Yonge Street Friends, 1801–1850*. Montreal: McGill-Queen's University Press, 2006.

Holcomb, Julie. *Moral Commerce: Quakers and the Transatlantic Boycott of the Slave Labor Economy*. Ithaca: Cornell University Press, 2016.

Jones, Rufus M. *The Later Periods of Quakerism*. 2 vols. London: Macmillan, 1921.

Kershner, Jon R. *John Woolman and the Government of Christ: A Colonial Quaker's Vision for the British Atlantic World*. Oxford: Oxford University Press, 2018.

Landes, Jordan. *London Quakers in the Trans-Atlantic World: The Creation of an Early Modern Community*. London: Palgrave Macmillan, 2015.

Lapsansky, Emma Jones, and Anne A. Verplanck, eds. *Quaker Aesthetics: Reflections on a Quaker Ethic in American Design and Consumption, 1720–1920*. Philadelphia: University of Pennsylvania Press, 2003.

Larson, Rebecca. *Daughters of Light: Quaker Women Preaching and Prophesying in the Colonies and Abroad, 1700–1775*. New York: Knopf, 1999.

Leach, Robert J., and Peter Gow. *Quaker Nantucket: The Religious Community Behind the Whaling Empire*. Nantucket: Mill Hill Press, 1997.

Levy, Barry J. *Quakers and the American Family*. Oxford: Oxford University Press, 1988.

———. "'Tender Plants': Quaker Farmers and Children in the Delaware Valley, 1681–1735." *Journal of Family History* 3, no. 2 (1978): 116–35.

Marietta, Jack D. *The Reformation of American Quakerism, 1748–1783*. 1984. Reprint, Philadelphia: University of Philadelphia Press, 2007.

Marsh, Dawn G. *A Lenape Among the Quakers: The Life of Hannah Freeman*. Lincoln: University of Nebraska Press, 2014.

Maxey, David W. "New Light on Hannah Barnard, a Quaker 'Heretic.'" *Quaker History* 78, no. 2 (1989): 61–86.

McDaniel, Donna, and Vanessa Julye. *Fit for Freedom, Not for Friendship: Quakers, African Americans, and the Myth of Racial Justice*. Philadelphia: Quaker Press of Friends General Conference, 2009.

Mekeel, Arthur J. *The Quakers and the American Revolution*. 1979. Reprint, York: Sessions Book Trust, 1996.

Milligan, Edward H. *Quaker Marriage*. Kendal, UK: Quaker Tapestry Booklets, 1994.

Moore, John M., ed. *Friends in the Delaware Valley: Philadelphia Yearly Meeting, 1681–1981*. Haverford, PA: Friends Historical Association, 1981.

Morgan, Nicholas J. *Lancashire Quakers and the Establishment, 1660–1730*. Halifax, UK: Ryburn, 1993.

Murphy, Andrew R. *William Penn: A Life.* New York: Oxford University Press, 2019.

Nash, Gary B. *Forging Freedom: The Formation of Philadelphia's Black Community, 1720–1840.* Cambridge: Harvard University Press, 1988.

Nash, Gary B., and Jean R. Soderlund. *Freedom by Degrees: Emancipation in Pennsylvania and Its Aftermath.* New York: Oxford University Press, 1991.

Plank, Geoffrey. *John Woolman's Path to the Peaceable Kingdom: A Quaker in the British Empire.* Philadelphia: University of Pennsylvania Press, 2012.

Plant, Helen. "Subjective Testimonies: Women Quaker Ministers and Spiritual Biography in England, c. 1750–1825." *Gender and History* 15, no. 2 (2003): 296–318.

Pointer, Richard W. "An Almost Friend: Papunhank, Quakers, and the Search for Security amid Pennsylvania's Wars, 1754–65." *Pennsylvania Magazine of History and Biography* 138, no. 3 (2014): 237–68.

Polder, Kristianna. *Matrimony in the True Church: The Seventeenth-Century Quaker Marriage Approbation Discipline.* Farnham, UK: Ashgate, 2015.

Probert, Rebecca. *Marriage Law and Practice in the Long Eighteenth Century: A Reassessment.* Cambridge: Cambridge University Press, 2009.

Pullin, Naomi. *Female Friends and the Making of Transatlantic Quakerism, 1650–1750.* Cambridge: Cambridge University Press, 2018.

Punshon, John. *Portrait in Grey: A Short History of the Quakers.* London: Quaker Home Service, 1984. 2nd ed., London: Quaker Books, 2006.

Raistrick, Arthur. *Quakers in Science and Industry: Being an Account of the Quaker Contributions to Science and Industry During the Seventeenth and Eighteenth Centuries.* Newton Abbot: David and Charles, 1968.

Rediker, Marcus. *The Fearless Benjamin Lay: The Quaker Dwarf Who Became the First Revolutionary Abolitionist.* Boston: Beacon Press, 2017.

Roberts, Helen. "Friends in Business: Researching the History of Quaker Involvement in Industry and Commerce." *Quaker Studies* 8, no. 2 (2003): 172–93.

Ryan, James Emmett. *Imaginary Friends: Representing Quakers in American Culture, 1650–1950.* Madison: University of Wisconsin Press, 2009.

Soderlund, Jean R. *Lenape Country: Delaware Valley Society Before William Penn.* Philadelphia: University of Pennsylvania Press, 2015.

———. *Quakers and Slavery: A Divided Spirit.* Princeton: Princeton University Press, 1985.

Spencer, Carole Dale. *Holiness: The Soul of Quakerism; An Historical Analysis of the Theology of Holiness in the Quaker Tradition.* Milton Keynes: Paternoster, 2007.

Tarter, Michele Lise, and Catie Gill, eds. *New Critical Studies on Early Quaker Women, 1650–1800.* Oxford: Oxford University Press, 2018.

Temple, Brian. *Philadelphia Quakers and the Antislavery Movement.* Jefferson, NC: McFarland, 2014.

Tolles, Frederick B. *Meeting House and Counting House: The Quaker Merchants of Colonial Philadelphia, 1682–1763.* New York: W. W.

Norton, 1948. 2nd ed., Chapel Hill: University of North Carolina Press, 2012.

———. *Quakers and the Atlantic Culture.* New York: Macmillan, 1960.

Tousley, Nikki Coffey. "The Experience of Regeneration and Erosion of Certainty in the Theology of Second-Generation Quakers: No Place for Doubt?" *Quaker Studies* 13, no. 1 (2008): 6–88.

Walvin, James. *The Quakers: Money and Morals.* London: John Murray, 1997.

Waring, Mary. *A Diary of the Religious Experience of Mary Waring, Daughter of Elijah and Sarah Waring, Late of Godalming.* London: William Phillips, 1809.

Weddle, Meredith Baldwin. *Walking in the Way of Peace: Quaker Pacifism in the Seventeenth Century.* Oxford: Oxford University Press, 2001.

Woolman, John. *Some Considerations on the Keeping of Negroes Recommended to the Professors of Christianity of Every Denomination.* Philadelphia: James Chattin, 1754. Reprint, New York: Grossman, 1976.

Worrall, Arthur J. *Quakers in the Colonial Northeast.* Hanover: University Press of New England, 1980.

CONTRIBUTORS

RICHARD C. ALLEN, Fellow of the Royal Historical Society, holds visiting fellowships at the Australian National University, Canberra, and Newcastle University. He is also a former reader in early modern cultural history at the University of South Wales. He has published extensively on Quakerism, migration, and identity. His most recent works are *Quaker Communities in Early Modern Wales: From Resistance to Respectability* (2007), and the co-edited *Irelands of the Mind* (2008), *Faith of Our Fathers: Popular Culture and Belief in Post-Reformation England, Ireland, and Wales* (2009), *The Religious History of Wales: A Survey of Religious Life and Practice from the Seventeenth Century to the Present Day* (2013), and, with Rosemary Moore and others, *The Quakers, 1656–1723: The Evolution of an Alternative Community* (2018). He is currently writing *Welsh Quaker Emigrants and Colonial Pennsylvania*, and co-authoring, with Erin Bell, *Quaker Networks and Moral Reform in the North East of England*.

ERIN BELL is senior lecturer in the Department of History, College of Arts, at the University of Lincoln, UK. She has a particular interest in the different experiences of male and female Friends, and in considering how mainstream attitudes toward other religious communities related to and informed attitudes toward and depictions of Quakers. She also works on the representation of the past in factual television programming and is a member of the Lincolnshire Area Meeting. In addition to her book *History on Television*, co-authored with Ann Gray (2013), she has published widely on representations of Quakers in popular culture and the law in the early modern period. She is currently working, with Richard Allen, on *Quaker Networks and Moral Reform in the North East of England.*

ERICA CANELA is a final-year part-time PhD candidate in religion and theology at the University of Birmingham, UK. Her thesis is titled "Quakers and Religious Identity in Herefordshire and Worcestershire, c. 1640–1725." She is the recipient of several awards for her work in Quaker history, including the 2014 David Adshead Award and the 2015 Gerald Hodgett Award. Her article "The Commendable Life and Noble Death of Humphrey Smith" was recently published in *Quaker Studies*, and she is writing two volumes for the Brill Research Perspectives in Quaker Studies series on early Quakerism.

ELIZABETH CAZDEN, an independent scholar based in Providence, Rhode Island, holds degrees from Oberlin College, Harvard Law School, and Andover Newton Theological School. Her publications include a biography of nineteenth-century feminist minister Antoinette Brown Blackwell; articles in both scholarly and general publications; and the chapter "Quakers, Slavery, Anti-Slavery, and Race" in *The Oxford Handbook of Quaker Studies* (2013). She has presented her work at the American Society of Church History, the Quaker Studies Research Association, and the Conference of Quaker Historians and Archivists, among others. Her current project focuses on Rhode Island Quakers and slavery.

ANDREW FINCHAM received his doctorate from the School of Philosophy, Theology and Religion at the University of Birmingham, UK where his research sought evidence and explanations for the causal relationship between business success and ethics. His doctoral dissertation, "Causes of Quaker Commercial Success, 1689–1813," used social network theory to account for the importance of Quaker discipline. Other subjects on which he has published include Quaker occupations, George Cadbury and corporate social responsibility, and a Quaker refutation of Max Weber's Protestant ethic. His pioneering perspective on the relationship between Quakers and commerce was nominated for the 2017 Michael K. O'Rourke Best Publication Award, and his statistical model of eighteenth-century Quaker populations was shortlisted for the 2019 Michael K. O'Rourke Research Publication Award.

SYDNEY HARKER is a doctoral candidate in history at Queen's University in Kingston, Ontario. She completed her master of arts in interdisciplinary humanities with a specialization in history at Trinity Western University in 2018. She is the recipient of a Joseph-Armand Bombardier CGS Master's Scholarship from the Social Sciences and Humanities Research Council of Canada (2017–18), the Canadian Friends Historical Association Scholarship (2016–18), and the John Webster Grant–John Moir Graduate Essay Prize from the Canadian Society of Church History (2017). In 2018, she received a Social Sciences and Humanities Research Council of Canada Doctoral Fellowship (2018–22). Her research interests include gender and religion in nineteenth-century Ontario.

ROBYNNE ROGERS HEALEY is a professor of history and the co-director of the Gender Studies Institute at Trinity Western University in British Columbia, Canada. She is associate editor (history) of the Brill series Research Perspectives in Quaker Studies, convenes the Conference of Quaker Historians and Archivists, and serves as publications chair for the Canadian Friends Historical Association. Her publications include *From Quaker to Upper Canadian: Faith and Community Among Yonge Street Friends, 1801–1850* (2006), *Quaker Studies: An Overview; The Current State of the Field* (2018, with C. Wess Daniels and Jon Kershner), and many articles and chapters in the field of Quaker history, especially related to eighteenth-century topics and the evolution of the peace testimony. She is currently working on two projects: a small monograph on Quaker quietism and a collaborative project on nineteenth-century Quaker women.

ROSALIND JOHNSON is a visiting fellow at the University of Winchester, UK. She works as a researcher for a county history project in Wiltshire and previously taught at the universities of Winchester and Chichester. Her principal research interests lie in the field of religious history in the long eighteenth century, particularly the history of Quakers. She is currently working on the history of Quakers and marriage, and on the history of Quakers in the city of Salisbury, UK, and is particularly interested in the position of women in religious groups, in expressions of popular piety, and in examining how nonconformists interacted with their conformist neighbors. Her publications include "The Case of the Distracted Maid: Healing and Cursing in Early Quaker History," *Quaker Studies* (June

2016) and "The Lives of Ejected Hampshire Ministers After 1662," *Southern History* (September 2014). She is currently researching the extent of Quaker faithfulness to the tithe testimony.

EMMA LAPSANSKY-WERNER is professor emerita of history and curator emerita of the Quaker Collection at Haverford College, where she continues to teach and to consult with students and with scholars, and to lecture and publish on various Quaker and African American history topics. Some of her recent publications include *Quaker Aesthetics* (2003, with Anne Verplanck); *Back to Africa: Benjamin Coates and the American Colonization Movement* (2005, with Margaret Hope Bacon), and many articles and chapters on Quaker history. With Gary Nash and Clayborne Carson, Lapsansky wrote *The Struggle for Freedom*, a college text on African American history, the third edition of which appeared in 2018. She is also a coauthor of the Pearson Education American history high school textbook. Lapsansky frequently consults with museums and precollegiate curriculum developers on enriching and enlivening public history and classroom history presentations, and with authors seeking editorial or research advice. She is currently at work on a history of a Bryn Mawr Quaker family and a study of a mid-twentieth-century Philadelphia multicultural intentional community.

JON MITCHELL was awarded a PhD in 2018 in theology and religious studies from the School of Philosophy, Religion and History of Science, University of Leeds, UK. His dissertation was titled "Religious Melancholia and the York Retreat, 1730–1830." He was the recipient of a 2016 Arts and Humanities Research Council grant, which enabled him to expand his PhD research to include Friends Hospital in Philadelphia. He is currently exploring Buddhist contemplative practice while supporting the work of his mentor, Dr. B. Alan Wallace, to create a Center for Contemplative Research in Italy. This retreat center will cater to contemplatives seeking long-term solitary retreats dedicated to practices of internal stillness, clarity, and insight.

GEOFFREY PLANK is a professor of early modern history at the University of East Anglia, UK. His research examines early modern debates over conquest, settlement, warfare, and slavery in the context of transatlantic imperialism. He is interested in the ways in which the European colonization of the Americas affected ordinary lives, and has studied a variety of groups, including French- and English-speaking colonists, Scottish Highlanders, Quakers, and Native Americans. His books include *John Woolman's Path to the Peaceable Kingdom: A Quaker in the British Empire* (2012); *Quakers and Abolition* (2014, with Brycchan Carey); and *Quakers and Native Americans* (2019, with Ignacio Gallup-Diaz). He is also the author of many chapters and articles on eighteenth-century Quakerism.

INDEX

Act of Toleration (1689), 2, 136, 138, 153
    attitudes towards, 51, 114, 117
    rights included, 7, 118, 133–34, 145
Act of Union (1840), 204
Adolphustown Meeting, 200, 204–9, 212–14, 216
    See also West Lake Meeting
Affirmation Acts, 2, 118
African Americans, 156–57, 164, 166
Africa, Western, 139–40
agriculture, 154, 158, 180, 184, 188, 193–95
American Friends Service Committee, 44
Alton Monthly Meeting, 137
    See also Hampshire Friends
American Revolutionary War, 39, 52, 116–17, 192, 200, 202–4, 254, 258
    Quaker positions on, 14, 167–68
Anglicans/Anglicanism, 6, 56, 113–15, 117–20, 128, 137
    See also Church of England
Anne, Queen of Great Britain, 118, 142
Antisemitism, 115, 120, 129n21
apophasis, Quaker, 100–101, 106
apophatic movement, medieval, 90, 91, 95
Ashbridge, Elizabeth, 36–37

Backhouse, William, 91
    Guide to True Peace, A, 92, 101–2
Balby Monthly Meeting, 67
Baptists, 6, 47, 157
Barbados, 48, 58, 159

Barclay, Robert, 7, 8, 44, 94, 96, 98–100, 104
    Apology for the True Christian Divinity, 7, 92, 102, 187
Barnard, Hannah, 2, 13–14, 155, 169, 216, 223n65
Barrow, Robert, 184–85
Bellers, John, 92, 104, 187
Benezet, Anthony, 82, 100, 157, 163, 165, 167
    on Indigenous relations, 192–93, 195, 253
    on war, 167
Besse, Joseph, 119
Bible, interpretation of, 104, 184
    doctrine of, 155
Birkel, Michael, 90, 91, 95, 101–102
Bland, Mary, 124–25
Blasphemy Act, 117
Book of Cases, 135–36, 139, 143–44
Book of Common Prayer, 141
Book of Extracts, 11, 77, 80, 258
Bowerman, family, 208, 216
Bugg, Francis, 9, 143
business, 11–12, 40n5, 158, 224
    and commerce, 12, 224, 226, 241, 254
    and industry, 224–26, 228–34, 238–42
    Board of Trade, 46, 50
    merchants, 48, 53
Braithwaite, William, 67, 71, 114, 134
Bridges, Robert, 157
British Empire, expansion of, 45–46
    Charles I, 48
    attitudes towards, 51–52

Bronner, Edwin, 72, 73, 83
Brook, Mary, 92, 98–99, 101
    Reasons for the Necessity of Silent Waiting, 92, 98, 102–3
Brown, James, 139
Brown, Nicholas, 218
Brown, Richard D., 155

Cadbury, Henry, 158
Canada, 160, 167, 203
    Upper Canada, 200–201, 203–5, 220n9
Canada Half-Year's Meeting, 201, 213, 216
capitalism, Quakers and, 156, 233, 242
Caribbean, 139, 158
Catholicism, 93, 95, 116, 118, 156, 188
    See also mysticism, Catholic
Canons and institutions, 68
Chartist movement, 240
children, 55, 58, 71, 96, 134, 139, 170, 193, 213, 255
    and development, 30, 50, 56, 78, 154, 158, 252
    and education, 162–65, 193, 213, 235 (*see also* education)
    and physical labor, 235–37, 239, 241
    and membership, 11, 209
Children of Peace, 208, 210, 215–17, 219
    See also Willson, David
Christ, 6, 8, 45, 57, 97, 104, 117, 155, 184, 187
    divinity of, 14, 216
Church of England, 7, 118, 133–34, 137, 139, 140
City of London, 116–17, 119, 121, 124
Civil War, English, 56, 165, 181
Civilization Fund Act (1819), 162, 167
Clandestine Marriage Act (1753), 134, 139, 147
Cole, Josiah, 184–86
Collection of Testimonies, A, 26, 30, 41n21
colonial meetings, early traits of, 49–51, 73, 152–62, 203, 210
colonization, of North America, 5, 180, 188
Comly, John, 164–65
community, 58, 73, 201, 206, 212, 220n5, 252
    foundations of, 153–55, 158, 201
Constitution Act (1791), 203
convincement, 97, 109n50
Cookworthy, William, 71, 82, 87n70

Cope, Francis, 163
Cope, John, 34–35
Cope, Mary Drinker, 152–54
Corporation Act (1661), 117
Corbett, Thomas, 136
Cornwall, 182
Court of Common Pleas, 141–42, 230
Cowdry, Cordelia, 140–43, 145, 149
Crabtree, Sarah, 76
crime, 113–28, 255
    See also larceny; murder; violence
Crisp, Stephen, 7, 8

de Molinos, Miguel, 93–95, 98, 105
    Spiritual Guide, 94
death, 28, 31–33, 35
Delaware Friends, 73, 157
Delaware Valley, 157, 185–86, 190, 192
devil, the, 35, 99
Dewsbury, William, 182–84
Dickenson, Jonathan, 184–88
Diggers, 53
diplomacy, 185, 193
discipline, 9, 11, 30, 36, 56, 65–66, 154, 252
    advices, 66, 70–76
    books of, 66, 73, 77, 79–80, 160–61
    differences in, 76, 81–82
    origins of, 68–69, 72
disownment, 14, 49–50, 68, 81–82, 212, 214
dissenters, 6, 53, 115, 118, 123–24, 156
    See also Test Act (1673)
Dorland, John, 206
Dorland, Philip, 204–5, 207
Drinker, Elizabeth, 167
Drinker, Henry, 168
Durham Monthly Meeting, 78
Dutchess County, New York, 164, 200, 204, 206
Dyer, Mary, 57

Ebbw Vale, Wales, 224, 229, 231, 239, 241
Eccleston, Theodore, 143–44
education, 152, 162–63, 188
    See also children: and education
Ellis, Sarah Stickney, 153
Ellis, Thomas, 189
Endelman, Todd, 120, 127
endogamy, 9, 202, 209, 252, 255

See also marriage
Enlightenment, 56, 153, 159, 168, 194
epidemics, 215, 223n60
epistles, 12, 37, 46, 47, 49, 52, 58, 67–68, 77, 146, 256–57
equality, belief in, 3, 12, 28, 31–32, 44–45, 59, 159, 252
evangelicalism, 13, 14–15, 25, 217

factionalism, 66, 154
faithfulness, concept of, 30–31, 39
family, 136, 152, 154, 160, 206–7, 212
　structures of, 28, 55–56, 58–59
Fell, Margaret, 2, 141
Fénelon, François, 90, 103–4, 105
First Great Awakening, 45, 165
Fischer, David Hackett, 155, 158
Five Mile Act (1665), 119
Florida, 184, 187–88
Fothergill, John, 163
Fox, George, 6–7, 47, 67, 135, 163, 183, 255
　Gospel Family Order, 7, 8, 47, 56, 81, 84n6, 251
　interactions with Indigenous Americans, 185
　life of, 2, 8
　on slavery, 58–59, 168
　theology of, 52, 56–59, 71, 168, 183
France, war with, 118, 140
Free Produce Movement, 168
Free Quakers, 167
Freeman, Hannah, 190
French Revolution, 203, 240, 258
Friends, stereotypes of, 116, 119–24, 127–28, 153
Friends Library, 165
Fry, John, 78
funerals, 77, 82, 235

gambling, 159, 161
gender equality, 31, 38, 55–56, 194
　differences in 126, 128, 153, 209–10, 256
Genesee Yearly Meeting, 9, 218
George I, king of Great Britain, 52
Gill, Catie, 3
Glamorgan Canal Company, 228–29, 232
Glamorganshire, 224, 226
Gloucestershire Friends, 183, 226

Glover, William, 238–39
Gragg, Larry, 158
Great Book of Suffering, 7
Great Fire of London (1666), 159
Great Reform Act (1832), 239–40
Griffitts, Hannah, 167
Groom, Samuel, 185–86
Guyon, Madame, 90, 93, 95, 98, 105
　Short and Easy Method of Prayer, 94, 101–2
Griffin, Mary, 34

Haight, family, 206
Hall, David, 70
Hampshire Friends, 137, 140–41, 143
Hardwicke Marriage Act (1754), 146
Harford, family, 224, 226, 228–42
hats, wearing of, 53, 66, 68
Haverford, Pennsylvania, 189
Heath, William, 139–40
Henley Friends, 182
Hicks, Elias, 14, 155, 164
　on slavery, 164, 168
Hicksite-Orthodox Schism (1827–28), 2–3, 15–16, 210–11, 216–18, 259
Hicksites, 14–15, 211
　origins of, 154–55
holy conversation, 154, 155, 160–65
Holy Spirit, 14, 89, 97–99, 102
Hopkins, Gerald T., 194
Hovinen, Elizabeth, 212–14
Howe, Samuel, 208–9
Hughes, family, 208–9, 213–14, 216

Independents, 6
Indigenous Americans, 156, 159, 162, 179–81, 253
　attitudes towards, 31, 58, 165, 179, 181, 186
　injustices against, 73–74, 165–67, 190
　Quaker interactions with, 167, 185, 187, 191, 193–95, 196n2
Inward Light, 6, 15, 90, 91, 97, 104
Ireland, 6, 37, 136, 154, 184
Iroquois, 192, 203

Jackson, Halliday, 193–95
Jacobite Uprising, 52
Jamaica, 9

James II (duke of York), 8
James, Thomas, 121–22
Jefferson, Thomas, 194
Jerusalem, 6, 117
Jews, 113–16, 120–24, 126–27
Jones, Rufus, 71, 90, 95

Kaiserman, Aaron, 114, 127
Keith, George, 8, 66, 163, 186
   See also Keithian controversy
Keithian controversy, 2, 8, 73, 258
King George's War, 165
Kingdom of God, 183
kinship, 15, 212, 215–16
   See also family
Knollys/Knowles, Robert, 140–41
Knox, Henry, 193

Lamb, Charles, 114
Lamb's War, 6
Lancaster, Joseph, 235
Landes, Jordan, 161
larceny, 122–23
Las Casas, Bartolomé de, 188
Lay, Benjamin, 163, 168, 256
Lenape, the, 179, 185, 190
Levelers, 53
Levens, Roger, 120–21
Levy, Barry J., 158
Lewis, Enoch, 163–64
liberal Quakerism, 44
Lippard, George, 153
literacy, 155, 235
Lloyd, family, 225–26, 240–41
lobbying, 7, 12, 13, 50, 230, 255
   See also London Meeting for Sufferings: lobbying activities
Locke, John, 159
London Yearly Meeting, 9, 24, 50, 58, 252, 254
   advice from, 11, 65, 100, 139, 141–43, 162–64, 181, 257
   and counsel on Indigenous Americans, 191
   early governance of, 45, 47–52, 65, 68–83, 256
   on education, 30
   on the Hicksite-Orthodox Schism, 14–16, 259
   on slavery, 12–13, 24, 258
London Meeting for Sufferings, 47–49, 71
   advice from, 51–54, 71, 79–83
   establishment of, 114, 135–36
   lobbying activities, 48, 138–47 (see also lobbying)
   origins of, 114, 135
long coda, 2
Loyalists, 13, 200, 202–4, 206, 220n6
   See also American Revolutionary War
Lundy, Rachel, 216
Lundy, Samuel, 211–12

Marietta, Jack, 166
marriage, 54, 68, 71, 134, 202, 255
   advices on, 77
   discipline, 134, 170
   legislation on, 134–50
   practices of, 133, 135, 206, 208–10, 212–14
Marriage Act (1540), 141–42
Marriage Act (1836), 146–47
Maryland Yearly Meeting, 158–59
Massachusetts Friends, 48, 51, 159
Maxey, David, 158
meetinghouses, 58–59, 78, 159, 211, 218, 256
Melingriffith Tinplate Works, 226–28, 232, 234–35
Melville, Herman, 153
membership, 11, 31, 47, 67, 83, 153, 210, 214, 226, 234
   birthright, 11, 164
   certificates of, 11
Methodism/Methodists, 35, 93, 97, 157
Middlesex, 119
migration, 9–11, 115, 202–4, 212, 217, 220n10
   transatlantic, 189, 201
Militia Acts, 117–18
militia service, 51, 53, 76, 192
ministry, 46, 50, 181
   travelling, 161, 173n32, 182
missionaries, 160, 167, 188, 194–95
Mississippi Valley, 162
Monmouth Canal Company, 231–32
Monmouthshire, 224–28, 238, 242
Moravians, 94, 191–92

More, Thomas, 159
Moses Brown School, 163
Mott, Lucretia, 164
Munsee, the. *See* Lenape
murder, 120–21, 125–26, 238
  See also crime
music, 217
mysticism, Catholic, 90–92, 93–96, 106
  See also de Fénelon, François; Guyon, Madame; Molinos, Miguel

Napoleonic Wars, 203, 217, 239
Nayler, James, 6, 114, 117, 183
New England Yearly Meeting, 49, 52–53, 55, 158–59, 164
New Jersey, 157–58, 185, 190
New Jersey Friends, 157, 166, 214, 256
New York Yearly Meeting, 9, 15, 159, 201
New York Yearly Meeting Indian Affairs Committee, 166
Newgate Prison, 115, 119
Newport Friends, 159
Nine Partners Monthly Meeting, 204–6, 208–9
Nine Partners School, 164
nonconformists. *See* dissenters
nonviolence, 76, 165–66
  See also peace testimony
North Carolina Yearly Meeting, 158–59
Nova Scotia, 160, 167, 202

oaths, 2, 71, 77, 116, 118, 124–27, 205
Ockanickon, 186
Ohio, 160, 192, 202
Old Bailey, 114, 115, 118–19, 127
  Proceedings of the Old Bailey, The, 113, 116, 119
  See also crime
Opie, Amelia, 153
Ordinary's Accounts, 115–17, 127
  See also crime
otherness, concept of, 115–16, 124

pacifism, 15, 23, 120, 128, 153, 180, 258
  See also peace testimony
pamphlets, 15, 161, 219
Papunhank, 179–80, 191–92, 195, 196n2
  See also Lenape

Parliament, British, 2, 46, 48, 135, 138–47
peace testimony, 13, 120, 122, 255
Pearson, Mary Ray, 216, 223n65
Pelham Monthly Meeting, 212–14, 220n3
Pemberton, James, 166
Penington, Mary, 181, 183
Penn, William, 8, 46–47, 105, 153, 164
  Old Bailey Trial (1670), 118
  Pennsylvania Charter, 156, 159, 185
  theology of, 153–54
  writings of, 170
Penney, Norman, 182
Pennsylvania, 37, 157, 158–59, 167, 190, 196n30, 213, 218
  and Indigenous Americans, 159, 185–88, 190–92
  emigration to, 10, 157, 184, 189–90
  governance of, 53, 73, 154, 165–66
  migration from, 200, 212, 216
Pennsylvania Provincial Assembly, 13, 166
periphery, concept of, 9, 12, 47, 50, 210, 254–56, 258
Perfect, Hannah, 124–25
perfection, concept of, 6, 169, 252
persecution, of Quakers, 2, 6, 48, 117–18, 128, 133, 153, 215, 230
  See also suffering
Philadelphia, 46, 154, 157–59, 187, 213
Philadelphia Monthly Meeting, 31, 256
Philadelphia Yearly Meeting, 8, 24, 51, 54, 161, 193, 213, 256
  early governance of, 11, 74–77, 157, 253–54
  Hicksite-Orthodox Schism, 15
  reformation efforts, 30–31
  on slavery, 12, 14, 257
Philadelphia Yearly Meeting Indian Committee, 166
philanthropy, 12, 24, 167, 224, 235, 238–39, 242
Phillips, Isaac, 211–12, 216
Phillips, Richard, 92, 103–4
  Concise Remarks on Watchfulness and Silence, 103–4
Phipps, Joseph, 92, 105
Pickering, Ontario, 214
Pietism, 93, 94

plainness, testimony of, 12, 69, 122
　　See also simplicity
Plymouth Colony, 45
Poll Act (1691), 118
Poor Jewry Lane (London), 124
poor relief, 11, 54–55, 71
Presbyterians/Presbyterianism, 47, 61n15, 190, 218
print culture, 50, 66, 154–55, 160, 165
　　print technology, 161
Probert, Rebecca, 134, 136, 146
property rights, 56, 133, 135, 230
Protestantism, 90, 92–93, 156
Providence Friends, 159
Publishers of Truth, 6, 57
Pullin, Naomi, 3
Puritanism, 53, 56, 92–93, 97, 100–101

Quaker governance, 47–49, 57, 73, 251
　　and meeting structures, 7, 74–79, 154, 158, 182
Quaker Street (London), 124, 127, 128
Quebec, 203, 219n1
Quietism, 1, 12–13, 24, 31, 84, 90–96, 102, 106
queries, 45, 50, 54, 58, 78, 161

rationalism, 13
Recusancy Law (1581), 117
reformation, Quaker, 12, 30, 31, 37, 258–59
Restoration, 2, 6–7, 113, 117, 133, 138
Revelation, Book of, 184, 187, 197n30
Reynolds, Richard, 226
Rhode Island Friends, 53, 55, 56
Richter, Daniel K., 194
Rigbie, James, 32, 35–36
riots, 239–41
Rogers, Timothy, 211–12, 214
Rome, 114
Royal African Company, 140
Rule and Exercises of Holy Dying, The (1651), 24
Rutty, John, 89

Salem, Massachusetts, 73, 159
salvation, 25, 31, 41n13, 98, 106, 181, 187–88
Schism Act (1714), 118
schools, 154, 162–71, 191–92, 213, 235
　　See also education

Scotland, 6, 136, 184
scripture, 2, 14, 30, 56, 216
Second Day's Morning Meeting, 7, 47
Second Great Awakening, 161
Seneca Nation, 167, 193–94
Seven Years War, 52, 54, 128, 165–66, 168, 190
Simcoe, John Graves, 203
simplicity, 79, 171, 252
　　See also plainness
sin, 6, 96–97, 102
Sirhowy, 223, 229–30, 234–36, 238, 241
Shackleton, Abraham, 13–14
Shoemaker, Robert, 116
slavery, 4, 81, 168–69, 256–58
　　abolition of, 12–14, 32–33, 40n6, 57, 163
　　attitudes towards, 24, 58–59, 73, 156
　　Transatlantic, 4, 11, 12, 48
Smith, Nigel, 101
social reform, 153
Sowle, Tace, 40n2, 187
Spencer, Carole Dale, 89, 90, 91, 100
Staffordshire, 145, 228
Stephan, Scott, 25
Story, John, 66
Stowe, Harriet Beecher, 153
suffering, 7, 38, 83, 113, 192
　　See also persecution
Suffolk Friends, 140, 143
Swarthmoor Hall, 50

Tarter, Michele Lise, 3
tax, 53, 76, 140
　　refusal to pay, 13, 39, 49, 51, 118–19, 167
Test Act (1673), 118
testimony writing, memorial, 23–26, 33, 39–40
　　characteristics of, 26–40
Thomas, Evan, 36, 38–39
Thurston, Thomas, 184–86
Tithe Commutation Act (1836), 119
tithe testimony, 77, 79, 82, 84n5, 114, 115, 119, 128, 255
Tolles, Frederick B., 49
truth, use of term, 49, 55, 67–68, 77–78, 81, 162, 166, 170

Vermont Friends, 200–201, 213–14, 217–18
violence, 121–22
    See also murder; crime
Virginia, 9, 158, 167, 169

Wales, 6, 133, 184, 224, 228, 237, 240
Wales Yearly Meeting, 9
War of 1812, 201, 203, 206, 215
Waring, Mary, 99
Washington, George, 193
wealth, attitudes towards, 54–55, 158, 166–67
Weber, Max, 156
Welsh Friends, 226, 254
Western development, 155–56
West Lake Meeting, 200, 206, 208–9, 211, 214
    See also Adolphustown Meeting
Westtown School, 152, 163, 213
Whitehead, George, 2, 70, 143
Wiggins, Isaac, 216
wilderness, concepts of, 184–85, 187, 189, 195, 253
William Penn Charter School, 163
Willson, David, 215–17
    See also Children of Peace
Wiltshire Quakers, 138, 142
Winn, Jacob, 213–14

Wolf, Stephanie Grauman, 158
women, 3, 28, 32, 67, 126, 168, 213, 255
    and gender roles, 55–58, 153, 213
    and meetings, 255–56
    and ministry, 32, 43n42, 60, 160, 209, 214
    and political action, 167–68
Wood, Mary, 33
Woolman, John, 54, 105, 163, 165–66, 168–69, 189–90
worship, 1, 7, 81, 89–91, 99, 138, 160, 180, 252–53
    and connections to nature, 180–83, 191, 196n3
    instances of, 182–83, 191
    methods of, 92, 100, 104, 161
    quietist waiting/prayer, 92–94, 96–99, 101–2
    watchfulness, 103–6

Yarranton, Andrew, 225
Yonge Street Monthly Meeting, 200, 207, 211–18
York Friends, 183
York Quarterly Meeting, 69
youth, 30, 32, 37, 42n34

zealousness, 26–28

www.ingramcontent.com/pod-product-compliance
Lightning Source LLC
Chambersburg PA
CBHW022041290426
44109CB00014B/930